About Island Press

Island Press is the only nonprofit organization in the United States whose principal purpose is the publication of books on environmental issues and natural resource management. We provide solutions-oriented information to professionals, public officials, business and community leaders, and concerned citizens who are shaping responses to environmental problems.

In 2000, Island Press celebrates its sixteenth anniversary as the leading provider of timely and practical books that take a multidisciplinary approach to critical environmental concerns. Our growing list of titles reflects our commitment to bringing the best of an expanding body of literature to the environmental community throughout North America and the world.

Support for Island Press is provided by The Jenifer Altman Foundation, The Bullitt Foundation, The Mary Flagler Cary Charitable Trust, The Nathan Cummings Foundation, The Geraldine R. Dodge Foundation, The Charles Engelhard Foundation, The Ford Foundation, The Vira I. Heinz Endowment, The William and Flora Hewlett Foundation, The W. Alton Jones Foundation, The John D. and Catherine T. MacArthur Foundation, The Andrew W. Mellon Foundation, The Charles Stewart Mott Foundation, The Curtis and Edith Munson Foundation, The National Fish and Wildlife Foundation, The National Science Foundation, The New-Land Foundation, The David and Lucile Packard Foundation, The Pew Charitable Trusts, The Rockefeller Brothers Fund, Rockefeller Financial Services, The Surdna Foundation, The Winslow Foundation, and individual donors.

COMPETITIVE ENVIRONMENTAL STRATEGY

Also by Andrew J. Hoffman

From Heresy to Dogma: An Institutional History of Corporate Environmentalism (1997)

Global Climate Change: A Senior-Level Debate at the Intersection of Economics, Strategy, Science, Politics, and International Negotiation, editor (1998)

COMPETITIVE
ENVIRONMENTAL
STRATEGY

A Guide to the Changing Business Landscape

ANDREW J. HOFFMAN

ISLAND PRESS
Washington, D.C. • Covelo, California

Library of Congress Cataloging-in-Publication Data

Hoffman, Andrew J., 1961–
    Competitive environmental strategy : a guide to the changing business
landscape / Andrew J. Hoffman.
        p.   cm.
    Includes bibliographical references and index.
    ISBN 1–55963–771–4 (acid-free paper) — ISBN 1–55963–772–2 (pbk. :
acid-free paper)
    1. Industrial management—Environmental aspects—United
States. 2. Strategic planning—Environmental aspects—United States.
3. Environmental policy—United States. I. Title.
    HD30.255 .H638 2000
    658.4'08—dc21   00–008012
                                                                              CIP

Printed on recycled, acid-free paper ✳

Manufactured in the United States of America
10 9 8 7 6 5 4 3 2 1

Dedicated to the reader—
Part of a new generation of business leaders with a vision that blends
economic, environmental, and social objectives. You will
translate that vision into corporate reality.

Contents

List of Tables, Figures, and Boxes

Tables

Figures

Boxes

Preface

Environmental issues remain a tough sell in today's business schools. Most schools are able to justify only one offering on the topic, and attendance remains low. In a 1998 survey, the World Resources Institute found that "only 16 percent of [business] schools have incorporated business–environment subjects into their core curricula, . . . most students are not trained to consider environment as a key factor in business decision making."[1] One major impediment to gaining student interest is faculty members' and students' perception of environmental protection as an issue of "socially responsible business." In this context, it lies on the periphery of "real" business decision making and therefore outside the realm of standard business education. In the core business curriculum, students are taught to increase shareholder return, net present value (NPV), operational efficiency, return on investment (ROI), and return on equity (ROE). But in the pursuit of "socially responsible" environmental management, they are taught to pursue moral objectives aimed at improving general social welfare. Environmental management thus becomes disconnected from the core curriculum. It becomes, as John Ehrenfeld describes it, education at the "end-of-the-pipe." Or as a flyer for Students for Responsible Business proclaims, "This is stuff we'll never see in class." This disconnection is neither an effective way to entice management students into the classroom nor an accurate representation of what is now happening in the business world.[2]

This book was written to break down the disconnection between environmental issues and business management, not only for the business student but also for the business manager. Companies today are not wrestling with a social responsibility agenda. They are searching for tools to integrate environmental objectives into business strategy and metrics to translate progress into language that shareholders and business managers appreciate (such as ROI and NPV). As corporations face emerging environmental issues, they also face new types of business pressures. Environmental issues appear on the corporate screen not through the imposition of some subjective sense of social values but through specific business constituents with specific business interests, such as insurers, suppliers, and banks. As a result, environmentalism alters market environments. This can yield new types of business opportunities—electric and hybrid automobiles, biotechnology, and alternative energy sources are examples of ways in which companies are capitalizing on these market shifts. The impetus is not an appeal to "socially responsible" management but the need to develop a competitive strategy in a changing business environment. In the end, this book is about a shift in mind-set from environmental *management* to environmental *strategy*.

The simple fact is that environmental strategy and economic strategy are now inextricably intertwined. For example, Interface, Inc., a manufacturer of commercial carpets, is pursuing an innovative strategy for reducing the use of virgin materials by leasing instead of selling carpets to its customers. In this way, the company retains the carpet materials and continually recycles them into new product. From 1995 to 1996, sales at the publicly traded company grew from $800 million to $1 billion while the company's use of raw material dropped by almost 20 percent per dollar of sales.[3] The British Petroleum Company enjoyed a public relations bonanza with governments, the environmental community, and the general public following chief executive officer John Browne's May 1997 speech acknowledging the reality of climate change and announcing the company's plans to take steps to reduce carbon emissions.[4] The Minnesota Mining and Manufacturing Company (3M), through its Pollution Prevention Pays (3P) program, claims to have reduced pollution production and energy use by 50 percent from 1975 to 1990, yielding a savings of $530 million.[5] Are these environmental actions driven by a social responsibility agenda? Although management decision making is not totally devoid of social responsibility, these are fundamentally strategic actions driven by fundamental business concerns for product development, corporate strategy, and operations management. They are examples of environmental strategy.

This book was written for those who are interested in understanding the interconnections between business management and environmental protection both in education and in practice. Paying attention to environmental issues has become an integral part of the way business practitioners do their jobs. But unfortunately, the management profession remains the last among professional fields to acknowledge this fact. Consider the fact that environmental issues are not perceived as a separate or disconnected area within the fields of engineering, law, public policy, and public health. Work on environmental issues within these fields provides opportunities to apply learned skills in solving environmental problems. The disciplinary basis of each field is not compromised; rather, it is channeled, focused, and strengthened. Within universities, students are responding. Between 1989 and 1992, enrollment in environmental engineering programs in the United States jumped by more than 25 percent, and it continues to climb.[6] As these students move on to professional careers, they have little difficulty finding jobs.

This book takes a lesson from these other professional fields and connects management and environmental issues in a constructive way, reflecting the needs and realities of the business world. It removes environmental issues from under the social responsibility umbrella and presents them in terms that complement the field of management.

For both economic and ecological reasons, environmental and business issues cannot remain separate and disconnected. First, such segregation leaves the business manager at a strategic disadvantage, unable to efficiently recognize the reality of a changing society, one that will demand ever greater corporate responsibility in protecting the environment. Second, environmental problems cannot be resolved unless business becomes a constructive force in resolving them. These two considerations must become synergistic, and individuals who manage and operate within the world of business today are making that synergy happen. In the United States today, almost three-quarters of the population describe themselves as either "active environmentalists" (21 percent) or "sympathetic toward environmental concerns" (51 percent).[7] Many of these same people also work within a business of some kind. Is there a tension here? Are these people forced to choose between their personal values regarding environmental protection and their professional values in the workplace? Increasingly, the answer to this question is no. To accurately reflect this emerging business reality, this book delivers the message that one can be a good manager *and* a good environmentalist. The two are consistent. The combination is not inconsistent. Strategic environmental management is synonymous with good business management.

To understand the business implications of environmental issues (or the environmental implications of business issues), one must consider questions such as the following: Who is exerting environmental pressures on the firm? What form do these pressures take? What do they mean for competitive strategy and organizational design? What limitations and opportunities do these pressures create? With questions such as these as a guide, this book presents environmental issues in the language of core business interests.

However, this book is not meant to be a complete analysis of competitive environmental strategy. Completeness, I believe, is not possible at the present time. The interconnection of these two issues is changing too rapidly for any clear consensus to be articulated; there exist too many competing notions about what form that intersection takes. I offer this book as both a baseline source of information, to help you develop an appreciation for the fundamentals of today's business reality, and a challenge, to inspire you to connect environmental initiatives to core business objectives.

To make your study of environmental strategy complete, I recommend that you supplement this book with readings on environmental marketing, environmental accounting, industrial ecology, life-cycle analysis, total quality environmental management, sustainable development, and other issues by authors more qualified than me. To help you find these authors, move beyond the basics in this book, and probe more deeply into your own core beliefs about the environment, I have recommended additional readings at the close of each chapter and have included several boxes that introduce underlying issues in environmental strategy. I hope that you find this book both satisfying in its explanation of the core concepts of corporate environmentalism and challenging in its ability to provoke you to think more deeply about what they mean and where they may be going.

Acknowledgments

The content of this book evolved over a period of four years. During that time, I developed and fine-tuned a course on corporate environmental strategy, first at Northwestern University's Kellogg Graduate School of Management and then at Boston University's School of Management, and developed my academic research and writing. In fact, many of the chapters in this book began as personal teaching notes for this class. I want to thank the Northwestern University Environmental Council, which granted me a post-doctoral fellowship from 1995 to 1997, and the Kellogg Environmental Research Center, which supported much of my work during these formative years. I also want to thank Max Bazerman, Don Jacobs, and Jim O'Connor, whose encouragement and support made my experiences and productivity at Northwestern possible; my academic co-writers, Max Bazerman, John Ehrenfeld, James Gillespie, Don Moore, Willie Ocasio, Leigh Thompson, Marc Ventresca, and Kim Wade-Benzoni, who helped me formulate some of my ideas; Julie Smith and Edith Jenkins Callaghan for editing earlier drafts of this manuscript; Todd Baldwin for valuable guidance in putting this book together; and my many other friends and colleagues who have generously given their time, support, and feedback: Dave Brown, Candy Brush, Chris Cook, Dan and Lauren Crews, Kevin Fachetti, Janice Hersey, Jim Post, Gwen Ruta, and Susan Svoboda. Finally, I would like to thank my students at both Kellogg and Boston University, who helped me form my ideas as the classes evolved. This book is truly the product of an interactive educational process, for which I am grateful.

ANDREW J. HOFFMAN
Boston, Massachusetts

Part I

A NEW FRAMEWORK FOR BUSINESS STRATEGY

Chapter 1

FROM ENVIRONMENTAL MANAGEMENT TO ENVIRONMENTAL STRATEGY

Annual costs for pollution control in the United States rose from $27 billion in 1972 to more than $90 billion in 1990 and are projected to reach $155 billion by the year 2000.[1] No small sum, this will amount to roughly 2 percent of U.S. gross domestic product. The effect of such expenditures on economic competitiveness is clear. Or is it?

There is little disagreement that environmentalism affects corporate management, altering profit and loss statements and influencing both domestic and international strategy. Yet, although many within industry and government vilify environmentalism as a threat to economic growth, others take advantage of the economic opportunities it offers. For example, the Carrier Corporation, a division of the United Technologies Corporation, invested $500,000 to eliminate its use of toxic solvents to clean copper and aluminum parts in the manufacture of air conditioners. By the end of one year, the company recouped $1.2 million in reduced manufacturing costs.[2] E. I. du Pont de Nemours and Company implemented a $500 million capital improvement plan at three chemical plants in North Carolina and South Carolina, which, reduced emissions of airborne toxins by 60 percent and increased production by 20 percent.[3] Electrolux has developed environmental products, including a solar-powered lawn mower, chain saws lubricated by vegetable oil, and water-saving washing machines, that generated 3.8 percent higher profits in 1997 than did its conventional products.[4]

What is going on here? What allows these companies to see an opportunity where others see only a threat? Are these examples unique in the business world? Or do they represent business managers thinking about environmental issues in a strategic way? The answer to this last question is yes. Dissecting the support for this answer is the focus of this book.

At the core is a simple and straightforward question—what is the relationship between environmental protection and corporate competitiveness? There are presently two schools of thought: *(a)* the win–win perspective and *(b)* the win–lose perspective.

Pollution reductions either *(a)* boost or *(b)* inhibit corporate productivity and success in the marketplace; environmental affairs are either *(a)* a source of competitive advantage or *(b)* a drag on the firm's resources and opportunities. Which argument is right? Clearly, there are costs to environmental protection. But with increasing frequency, there is also evidence of companies gaining competitive advantage through opportunities revealed by environmentalism. The truth is that both the win–win and the win–lose perspectives are right. And they are both wrong. Simply put, they are unrealistically simple and unnecessarily polarized views of a complex issue. As is often the case, the answer lies somewhere in between. In this middle space lies a need for trade-offs and strategic decision making. In the next section, we will consider each perspective in turn and then discuss a third one, the strategic perspective.

Building a Framework for Corporate Environmental Strategy

The dichotomous framing of the environment–economics debate shares parallels with the dispute resolution field of the mid-1980s, in which writers argued whether to follow a win–lose[5] or a win–win[6] framework. Or, in the terminology of the negotiations literature, they argued over whether to follow a distributive or an integrative framework. We can understand our focus of study more clearly if we learn from this debate and the way it was resolved.

The Win–Lose Perspective

The first framework, the win–lose (distributive) framework, is the traditional formula for developing environmental regulation. It is based on a comparison of the beneficial outcomes of pollution control policy and the costs necessary for industry to secure them. By the very nature of this "cost–benefit" framing, environmental and business interests are set up in a state of opposition—environmental benefits can be gained only by imposing an economic cost. By definition, the balance between economic costs and environmental benefits becomes a zero-sum game. It can be seen in the rhetoric of articles and papers on the topic. For example, an article in the *Journal of Economic Perspectives* states that increasing stringency of environmental regulation "must," by its very nature, result in reduced profits for the firm.[7] Similarly, an often cited article in the *Harvard Business Review* argues that the trade-off is a "necessity" for achieving environmental improvements.[8]

Aggregate empirical data support much of this thinking. Environmental health and safety regulations increased from ten modest statutes in the late 1960s to more than forty-five very complex regulations in 1990.[9] As a result, firms in the United States devote significant resources each year, *net of cost savings*, to environmental protection. This led Brad Whitehead and Noah Walley of McKinsey & Company to a sober approach to corporate environmental strategy. "Ambitious environmental goals," he wrote, "have real economic costs. As a society, we may rightly choose those goals despite their costs, but we must do so knowingly. And we must not kid ourselves. Talk is cheap; environmental efforts are not."[10] Thus, regulation forces companies to do what they

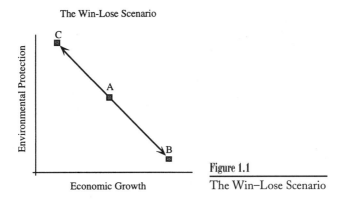

Figure 1.1
The Win–Lose Scenario

would rather not. Viewing environmental issues through this perspective leads corporate managers to see them strictly as matters of regulatory compliance or corporate social responsibility and not related to competitive strategy.

But in the negotiations literature, win–lose models are seen as incomplete because they ignore the possibility of outcomes that can be better for both parties. As shown in figure 1.1, distributive bargaining allows environmental gains to be achieved only at the expense of economic growth. That is, the pool of resources is considered fixed, and parties negotiate over their allocation. As environmental protection is weakened, we move to the southeast (point *B*), satisfying economic interests. As environmental protection is strengthened, we move to the northwest (point *C*), at the expense of economic interests. Mutual gain solutions are outside the realm of possibility.

The win–lose perspective reinforces confrontational rather than cooperative approaches toward resolving opposing interests in real-world conflicts (such as the escalated tension accompanying logging practices in the face of endangered species protection or power generation under increasingly stringent clean air requirements). On the basis of win–lose positions, economic and environmental interests fight a battle over concessionary agreements, with each side pursuing its own goals. Moreover, the two parties often demonize each other. Environmentalists are perceived as insensitively seeking environmental protection at all costs and willing to sacrifice economic development and human economies toward that end. Corporate decision makers are perceived as pursuing economic growth at all costs and willing to forfeit environmental considerations to increase profit. Joint solutions through cooperative decision making become impossible. Yet clearly, this is not always true.

The Win–Win Perspective

The second framework, the win–win (integrative) framework, proposes that the needs for environmental protection and economic growth can be mutually satisfied. The argument of the win–win proponents is that the economics–environment relationship is a false dichotomy when framed within the cost–benefit model. They see no trade-off between the two. Instead of defining environmental gains in opposition to economic costs, this school of thought holds that "the costs of addressing environmental regulations can be minimized, if not eliminated, through innovation that delivers other competitive benefits" to the firm.[11] The cost–benefit equation is reconstructed to include economic gains that offset economic costs. In essence, the term *economics* in the economics-versus-environment debate is redefined in cooperative rather than competitive terms, with environmental benefits.

Some argue that economic benefits can be gained through "innovation offsets," which can lead to absolute advantages for firms seeking creative responses to environmental regulation that are consistent with the firms' competitive objectives. For example, Harvard Business School professor Michael Porter and his co-author Claus van der Linde argued that "emissions are a sign of inefficiency and force a firm to perform non-value creating activities such as handling, storage and disposal . . . reducing pollution is often coincident with improving the productivity with which resources are used."[12] Another supporter of this argument, Al Gore, argued that "some companies have found that in the process of addressing their environmental problems they have been able to improve productivity and profitability at the same time . . . an emphasis on environmental responsibility makes good business sense."[13] In the end, win–win proponents argue that the key to realizing such benefits lies in "a new frame of reference for thinking about environmental improvement,"[14] one that steps out of the traditional cost–benefit model.

Anecdotal evidence supports this argument. For example, Balzers Process Systems, a manufacturer of equipment used in the production of optical components, semiconductors, and compact discs, faced an environmental compliance problem in 1991. Balzers used Freon to clean parts before shipment, but the Environmental Protection Agency (EPA) had fined the small company $17,000 for leaks in its system. As a term of the settlement, the company sought a new cleaning process. It switched to a water-based solution in 1993, eliminating the use of Freon entirely. The company found that with no change in customer satisfaction, the new system cost half of what the old system had cost to run, about $100,000 per year. Furthermore, the new cleaning system posed no threat to employee safety, as had the Freon system. In the words of Paul Keough, deputy regional administrator for the EPA, "Here's a situation where we had a problem with a company and they used it as an opportunity."[15] Only after the EPA forced the company out of its old mind-set was it able to find the economic opportunity that was exposed by environmental improvement.

But is this framework too simple? In the negotiations literature, win–win models are seen as shortsighted in their failure to address the inevitable distributive aspect of most negotiations. As depicted in figure 1.2, integrative bargaining allows for a steady satisfaction of both environmental and business interests. In reality, however, the win–win formulation is possible only in certain circumstances. It is not always possible to achieve all of one's interests and have the other party do so as well. The costs of environmental protection are at times real and have to be acknowledged. For example, federal efforts in 1991 to protect the northern spotted owl in the Pacific Northwest excluded large tracts of federal land from logging. The supply of raw timber decreased, mill capacity was eliminated, logging jobs were lost, and lumber prices increased. The distributive aspect of the relationship between economics and the environment cannot be denied.

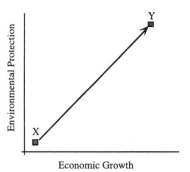

Figure 1.2
The Win–Win Scenario

A Strategic Perspective

A more balanced and accurate approach to handling corporate environmental issues is to recognize that the relationship between environmental and economic interests is neither purely cooperative nor purely competitive. Even the case of the northern spotted owl has both integrative and distributive components.[16] Although some logging companies were hurt by restrictions on the timber supply from federal lands, windfall profits accrued to others that relied on timber from private lands and smaller, more efficient timber mills. Today, Oregon remains one of the largest producers of timber products in the United States, but instead of relying on 300-year-old trees from public lands, the industry obtains smaller timber from privately held, sustainable tree farms. Despite a cutback in timber-related employment, most timber-dependent counties in Oregon report rising property values, increasing timber-related wages, and an overall increase in jobs. This is due to newer and leaner operations that have risen up to replace the aging mills and retraining of the workforce for the region's growing high-tech industry.[17] Thomas M. Power, chairman of the Department of Economics at the University of Montana, reported that from 1988 to 1994, jobs in the region grew by 18 percent, contrary to dire predictions; his report was endorsed by thirty-four economists from the Pacific Northwest.[18]

The disagreement between the win–lose and win–win arguments centers on the extent to which real opportunities exist for improving production processes through environmental protection. Win–lose proponents argue that although some mutual gain in economic and environmental interests may once have been possible, those opportunities have long since passed. The "low-hanging fruit" of environmental opportunity was found when the pollution control emphasis was on early (and simple) reductions in pollution. Now, they argue, as we move toward ever stricter controls, those opportunities are more difficult to find, if they exist at all. Win–win proponents counter with the oft-told story of the economist walking with his son. The son tugs on his father's coat and says, "Daddy, there's a twenty-dollar bill on the ground." The father replies, "It couldn't be, Son. If there was, someone would have already picked it up by now."

Amory Lovins, director of research for the Rocky Mountain Institute, has challenged this kind of thinking in terms of the problem of climate change, arguing that "we do not need to worry about how the climate science turns out or whether this is a real problem or not." Instead, he believes that "protecting the climate will be highly profitable rather

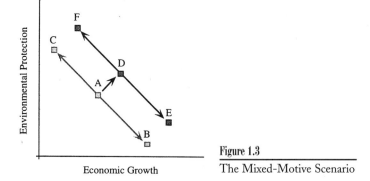

Figure 1.3

The Mixed-Motive Scenario

than costly." He sees "$10,000 bills lying all over the floor" of factories "of every imaginable variety"[19] and believes that climate change can be controlled with positive consequences for the bottom line. His point is that companies are not always on the innovation frontier and often do not recognize opportunities that lie before them. Most business executives concede that there are opportunities in energy conservation but are convinced that climate change will impose serious costs on industry and that hidden opportunities are not as abundant as Lovins suggests. The middle ground between these views highlights two facets of the issue. First, markets and companies are not always efficient, and therefore, environmental improvements may offer strategic benefits (integrative opportunities exist). Second, business managers are not stupid, and it would be naive not to acknowledge that environmental initiatives often cost companies significant amounts of resources (distributive aspects cannot be denied).

In the negotiations literature, a balance between integrative and distributive thinking is referred to as a mixed-motive model.[20] The mixed-motive perspective acknowledges the possibility of mutual gain solutions while simultaneously acknowledging their distributive aspects. As shown in figure 1.3, opportunities often exist to merge the win–win and win–lose perspectives. Negotiators can expand the realm of possible outcomes through more creative responses to environmental pressures (from point A to point D) and then allow each party to argue over whether to move toward point E or point F. For example, to gain a rancher's endorsement of a plan to reintroduce endangered wolves into Yellowstone National Park, environmental groups created a special fund to compensate the rancher for any loss of livestock due to wolf predation.[21] The introduction of a new variable reduced the rancher's downside and enabled the parties to reach a compromise.

Another way to think about the mixed-motive framework is in terms of trade-offs. To capture the mixed-motive framing of the relationship between environmental protection and corporate competitiveness, the business manager is required to think opportunistically about environmental protection. Although compliance costs are a factor in the corporate equation, trade-offs are possible in considering how best to meet—or exceed—demands for environmental performance and economic growth simultaneously. Interestingly, the American public has grown to expect a merge of these two objectives. Roughly 70 percent of Americans think that there is no tension between environmental protection and economic development and that the two can work together. When compromise is impossible, the public comes down solidly on the side of the environment: 63 percent believe that environmental protection should be favored over economic development when a reasonable compromise between the two cannot be found.[22] How can this mind-set be applied within a business context? It requires the business manager to move from focusing on *environmental management* to focusing on *environmental strategy*.

Moving from Environmental Management to Environmental Strategy

It bears repeating: This book is not about environmental management. It is about environmental *strategy*. The distinction is more than semantic. It represents a fundamental difference in the way one views both environmental problems and the role of the corporation in responding to them. Viewed through the traditional lens of environmental management, discussions of the relationship between economic and environmental objectives become stuck in the win–lose mind-set. This mind-set can take two forms within the corporation—regulatory compliance or social responsibility.

In the first case, one might consider the relationship between corporate activities and the environment in terms of how environmentalism acts as a constraint, as depicted by the arrow moving from right to left in figure 1.4. Viewed through this lens, environmentalism is lamented as a useful social endeavor but a decidedly unproductive intrusion into corporate affairs. It is a restriction on or a deviation from the central corporate activities. Environmental problems are treated as an economic externality or market failure. Pollution results only because firms are not required to pay a price for certain scarce environmental resources, such as clean air and water,[23] and solutions must be artificially introduced through regulation. This perspective leads one to focus on what companies *must* do to remain legal members of the community. For the manager, the issue boils down to *regulatory compliance*.

Alternatively, one might consider the relationship in terms of the effects of business activities on the environment, as depicted by the arrow moving from left to right in the figure. In this format, one focuses on the environmental damage caused by industrial activity. One might point out that industry in the United States releases into the air and water and onto the land as much as 4 billion pounds of hazardous or toxic chemicals each year[24] and contributes to increasing problems of greenhouse gas buildup, ozone depletion, air and water pollution, and decreasing landfill space. One might also point out that resource extraction is increasing, leading to worldwide collapse of fisheries and destruc-

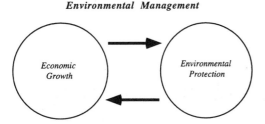

Environmental Management

Economic Growth

Environmental Protection

Figure 1.4

The Relationship between Business and the Environment: *Environmental Management*

tion of habitat. Faced with such facts, one might focus on what corporations *should* do to offset these transgressions. Environmental management becomes an issue of *social responsibility.*

In both cases, corporations are expected to do little to protect the environment unless the government forces them or society shames them. Corporate management is driven by either legal sanctions (civil, administrative, and criminal penalties) or social sanctions (protests, negative press, diminished reputation and image), both of which are perceived fundamentally as external to business interests. Environmental issues become a threat or an unwanted constraint on corporate affairs from sources external to the market system. Corporate environmental management is then predicated on buffering the operating core from these constraints and managing them through external interaction and end-of-the-pipe solutions.

But the reality of environmentalism in the business context is becoming more complex than regulatory compliance or social responsibility reveal. We now live in an age when environmental concerns originate from a broader system of pressures than merely government and activist forces. Insurance companies, investors, local communities, labor unions, international regimes, the media, financial institutions, consumers, and suppliers all apply pressure on corporations to handle environmental affairs. Through so complex a web of constituents, environmentalism becomes transformed from something external to the market environment to something central to the core objectives of the firm. As such, corporations must trigger a more complex set of organizational and strategic responses than merely the management of these external pressures. The reality is that environmental protection and economic competitiveness are becoming increasingly intertwined, as depicted in figure 1.5. The intersection of the two issues is occupied by external constituents that demand both economic and environmental performance from the corporation.

Environmental concerns are growing within the external corporate environment such that they are beginning to permeate many arenas of corporate affairs. The extent of that overlap can be debated, but its increasing size cannot. This is where the strategic aspect finally emerges. Companies must now consider how to devote resources to environmental initiatives in a way that satisfies their economic objectives. A shift from environmental management to environmental strategy moves the issue from the outside to the inside of the corporate mind-set. Rather than denying or lamenting environmental pressures, managers must now consider how environmentalism and business strategy overlap. Although this mind-set does not guarantee competitive success, the important point is

Environmental Strategy

Economic Growth

Environmental Protection

Figure 1.5

The Relationship between Business and the Environment: *Environmental Strategy* that it links environmental protection and economic competitiveness in such a way that strategic managers must find ways to satisfy both simultaneously. This linkage has three components, which form the structure of this book:

1. *What are the sources of environmental pressures?* Managers must consider the full scope of the resource, market, and social constituency demanding environmental performance, moving beyond a strict focus on regulatory compliance or social responsibility.

2. *What are the corporate implications of environmental issues?* As business and environmental concerns overlap, managers must understand how concepts such as competitive strategy, technological development, organizational management, and the business system are redefined. To capture the opportunities this redefinition creates, one must leave behind taken-for-granted notions of corporate objectives and protocols and begin to reconsider basic conceptions of the business system.

3. *What is the trajectory of these changes?* The constituencies driving environmental strategy are growing in number, and their demands are becoming more complex. To develop effective long-term strategy, managers must project into the future to determine the implications of this trajectory and consider the possibility of influencing its final form.

Why Environmental Strategy Is Distinct

By now, a question may have arisen in your mind: Why this book? If environmental issues have now entered the realm of corporate strategy, so what? Why dedicate an entire book to the study of the business implications of this one strategic issue? Are the many other books on strategic management not sufficient? The answer lies in what makes environmentalism different. It comprises a blend of characteristics that make it distinct from other pressures familiar to the firm. On the one hand, it has many characteristics similar to those of other social issues such as gender equity, affirmative action, and labor relations, but it is also distinct from these issues in several ways. On the other hand, it has technical and economic components that make it similar to other strategic issues such as consumer demand, materials processing, and competitive strategy, but again it has differences that require special attention. For the organization and the manager, it is the issue's ability to *merge the social and the technical* in its effects on corporate practice that makes environmentalism unique.

The Social Dimensions of Corporate Environmentalism

On its most fundamental level, environmentalism is a social movement much like those associated with gender equity, civil rights, and labor relations. It has constituent groups that lobby for social change at all levels of society. However, the makeup of this constituency is more troublesome for the corporation than is that of other social movements. Membership in the environmental movement is indeterminate. In settling issues of labor relations, managers negotiate with workers and union officials. In settling issues of civil rights and gender equity, managers might interact with the organizations set up to represent women and minority workers. However, with the environment, there is no natural constituency or standard bearer. A high-quality environment tends to be a public good, which when achieved cannot be denied to others, even those who resist environmental reform. With many environmental issues, those who act to protect the environment can expect to receive no personal material benefits.[25] Therefore, the firm is left to decide who are legitimate representatives for environmental concerns.

Often, those representatives are organized nonprofit environmental groups. But the indeterminism of environmentalism also means that it attracts a wide range of supporters across social, economic, and demographic lines. Those representing environmental interests to the firm or to society at large go beyond the community of nongovernmental organizations (NGOs). Others, such as employee groups, labor unions, community groups, consumers, environmental activists, investors, insurers, government agencies, and industry competitors, have become active environmental advocates. Even internal managers can become advocates for the environment. A 1991 report by The Conference Board noted that "younger managers and their families [have begun] making [environmental] demands on top management that previous generations would never have dared to do."[26] Interacting with such a wide range of interests creates new challenges in dealing with and understanding the full social pressures for environmental protection. In particular, those pressures transcend the social realm and now enter the market, resource, and political realms.

Further, the social aspect of environmentalism has a decidedly nonsocial constituent. Beyond a constituency of social advocates, there is also the environment itself to contend with. The prominence and power of environmental change (and in the most extreme case, environmental catastrophe) act as another form of social pressure, placing demands on our social, political, economic, and technological structures that are distinct from any other demands the corporation faces. They focus attention on environmental issues without warning, imposing demands for action and change. Although they are open to social interpretation and enactment,[27] environmental events nonetheless force corporations, government agencies, and activists to devote resources and attention to the issue.

The Technological Dimensions of Corporate Environmentalism

Whereas issues such as affirmative action and gender equity have little direct effect on production processes or product development, environmentalism has a distinct technological component, directly challenging the way corporations handle material resources and produce goods and services. Since the 1960s, the technological demands for corporate environmental responsibility have shifted from removing only visible levels of contaminants from effluent streams to removing concentrations in the range of parts per billion and, at times, parts per trillion. Beyond process emissions, environmentalism also mandates changes in the content of product development. New laws mandating public disclosure of emission levels and product contents as well as the potential health effects of those chemicals create daunting technological challenges for the firm.[28] The effects of these demands are not universal. Some industries, such as the oil and chemical industries, face greater challenges in both measurement and control of hazardous emissions. Even within industries, different companies face different challenges in developing new products, processes, and raw materials in the face of environmental demands. Whereas most social issues transcend industries, the technological challenges of environmentalism add a new dimension to the strategic landscape, one that often decides which firms will succeed and which will fail.[29]

Often, firms are required to collect data, initiate change, and develop an understanding of their processes and products at levels not considered necessary for traditionally accepted strategic reasons. Strategy and technology are being redefined by constituents outside the firm. Engineers can no longer focus simply on the ends-based results of engineering calculations. They must now understand the social, political, economic, and cultural context of their task. Environmentalism signifies a redefinition of both technology and the corporation's role in developing it. New concepts such as waste minimization, pollution prevention, and product stewardship are finding their way into all aspects of operations, from process design to product development.

Beyond conceptions of technology, environmentalism challenges economic conceptions of the firm. Unlike other social issues that deal with equity and the fair distribution of opportunity and wealth, environmentalism increasingly affects basic business economics, effectively redefining the conceptions of production in industry. Issues such as gender equity and affirmative action involve some gain or loss to specific individuals within the firm, but the economic output of industrial activity usually remains fundamentally unchanged.[30] Social issues do not generally bear on the aggregate output of the economy. They bear on issues of sharing what we have, issues of social equity.

But environmentalism produces a different outcome. Environmentalism interferes with fundamental economic models of consumption and production, resulting in a net change in efficiency. For example, a debate has recently emerged over the economic effects of climate change controls. Some observers predict a drain on gross national product (GNP) of as much as 3.5 percent if aggressive emission reduction targets are set. Others estimate that modest controls on greenhouse gas emissions will not damage the economy and maintain that the world has significant opportunities to control emissions by making its energy systems and automobiles more efficient. This more efficient use of energy is projected to increase GNP by 1 or 2 percent.[31] Such a debate would not accompany new laws regarding racial or gender equity.

For the individual firm, the effects are no less direct. Environmental concerns can cause the elimination of entire product markets, such as those for chlorofluorocarbons (CFCs), DDT, and dioxin. They can also cause the formation of new markets, as they did for Freon substitutes, termed hydrochlorofluorocarbons (HCFCs), in the wake of the 1987 worldwide ban on CFC production. Finally, environmental liability has risen to levels that have shaken the basic precepts of corporate risk management. Most notably, the $5 billion in fines and penalties levied against the Exxon Corporation for the 1989 *Exxon Valdez* oil spill in Prince William Sound, Alaska, would have bankrupted many smaller corporations. Regardless, the threat of such large fines has caused most firms to alter their oil transport strategies.

In essence, what has evolved is an alteration of the core objectives of the firm and the

basic conceptions of production. Shareholder equity may remain the single most important criterion for corporate survival, but environmental responsibilities are infiltrating the
taken-for-granted beliefs that have previously guided that pursuit. Today, executives
from corporations such as the Dow Chemical Company,[32] the Monsanto Company,[33]
DuPont,[34] and the Union Carbide Corporation[35] are actively espousing the benefits of
proactive environmental management while instituting programs for community relations, product stewardship, pollution prevention, and environmental leadership, all in the
name of increasing corporate competitiveness and shareholder equity. Environmental
strategy incorporates a merger of these social considerations with the technological and
economic goals of corporate operations.

How Did We Get Here?

In a 1974 survey, The Conference Board found that the majority of companies treated
environmental management as a threat, noting "a widespread tendency in most of industry to treat pollution control expenditures as non-recoverable investments."[36] Some
twenty years later, a follow-up survey revealed that 77 percent of U.S. companies had a
formal system in place for proactively identifying key environmental issues as part of
their overall corporate strategy.[37] Finding strategic opportunity in environmental protection is a rather recent possibility. Before we examine the concept of competitive environmental strategy in depth, it is important to place it in historical context.

Within the span of four short decades, the concept of corporate environmentalism
was born and redefined through successive stages, each differing in terms of the external
pressures driving corporate activities and the internal structures and responsibilities by
which corporations responded. It is helpful to think about this evolution in four stages:
(1) industrial environmentalism (1960–1970); (2) regulatory environmentalism
(1971–1981); (3) environmentalism as social responsibility (1982–1988); and (4) strategic environmentalism (1989–1999).[38]

Industrial Environmentalism (1960–1970)

Corporate environmentalism emerged in the early 1960s in relation to issues regarding
pesticides, automobile emissions, and oil spills. Publication of Rachel Carson's book
Silent Spring, the first appearance of urban smog, the Cuyahoga River fire of 1969 in
Cleveland, Ohio, that was caused by an extreme amount of oily waste floating on the
river's surface, and the Santa Barbara oil spill of 1969 in which an oil rig off the coast of
the affluent community spilled 3.25 million gallons of oil along its pristine coastline
fueled rising public concern that something was wrong with how we were treating the
environment. Yet despite growing external criticism, industry remained firm in its beliefs
that the problem could be solved independently and through technological development.
Government intervention was viewed as unnecessary, and environmentalists' concerns
were viewed as unrealistic and unscientific. As such, environmental management within
the firm was handled primarily as an operating line function. Treated as internally
directed problem solving, it was considered an ancillary aspect of conducting business.
Firms treated environmental management merely as a technological problem to be han-

dled on a part-time basis by operations engineers in the general area of what was some-
times called "pollution control management." Management efforts focused primarily on
wastewater and air pollution control. In particular, attention was focused only on visible
forms of pollution. Often, expenditures for such efforts were so minor that firms did not
even break them out as separate items in cost statements.[39]

Regulatory Environmentalism (1971–1981)

In 1970, corporate environmentalism was radically altered with the formation of the
Environmental Protection Agency (EPA). The agency quickly became the arbiter of environmental rules and norms, negotiating on the one side with industry and on the other
with environmental activists, two groups that did not interact directly. Through this stage,
much of the present U.S. regulatory structure was conceptualized, developed, and institutionalized. Within the corporate structure, environmental management was treated as
externally directed technical compliance. In most cases, environmental management was
elevated to a corporate-level function. Environmental health and safety (EH&S) departments were established with the principal responsibility of maintaining relations with
government agencies.[40] Separated from the operating core of the company, these departments were regarded as a necessary evil and a cost of doing business. Rather than environmental protection, their function was regulatory compliance. In general, with the
exception of adding these small, specialized staffs of pollution control specialists, companies generally made no major organizational or technological changes in their efforts to
manage environmental problems.[41] Although industry looked to the EPA to define its
environmental responsibilities, it also became increasingly defensive as it perceived government regulation as disproportionately driven by environmental concerns.

Environmentalism as Social Responsibility (1982–1988)

In 1981, the administration of President Ronald Reagan attempted to roll back environmental standards in an effort to liberate industry from the burdens of government regulation. However, a public backlash quickly forced a retreat. In the aftermath, the EPA
had lost its credibility, and environmental activists began to impose on industry directly.
This increase in influence was fueled by a growth in the membership and budgets of
major environmental organizations. Consequently, industry began to take a more prominent role in establishing environmental rules and norms as a signal of its social responsibility. Throughout this period, industry adopted an increasingly cooperative stance
toward government as it once again saw itself as part of the solution, not part of the problem. Within most companies, environmental management evolved into internally
directed managerial compliance. Environmental management was elevated in importance, and environmental managers carried increasing clout. Often, centralized departments merged the many environmental responsibilities throughout the company. Their
objectives shifted from regulatory compliance at the end of the pipe to waste minimization in the process design. With this shift, the tie between environmental protection and
economic efficiency was beginning to be forged. In a departure from previous motivations, the dominant factors driving these initiatives were now "cost factors, liability concerns, public scrutiny and the indirect impact of regulations."[42]

Strategic Environmentalism (1989–1999)

Beginning around 1989, new forms of environmental pressure began to emerge. No longer merely the realm of social or government activities, environmental concerns were integrated into the expectations of economic interests such as investors, insurers, and competitors. Industry began to take a proactive stance on environmental protection as it once again perceived the problem as one it could handle itself. However, unlike the situation in the period from 1960 to 1970, autonomy was not part of the corporate perception of the solution. Instead, solutions were seen as emerging from a broad range of external constituents such as environmental groups, investors, and the government. For some firms, organizational boundaries began to blur, allowing direct influence by these external constituents. For these early adopters, environmental management became redefined as proactive management. The environmental department reached new levels of organizational power, and firms began pushing environmental considerations back down into the line operations, integrating them into both process and product decisions.

From the 1960s through the 1990s, the concept of corporate environmentalism was successively redefined. Corporate environmental pressures were government centered in the 1970s but evolved into being driven by activists, investors, insurance companies, competitors, and others within two decades. In response, the industrial organization has shifted from reactively resisting environmental concerns in the 1960s to strategically managing them. Its organizational structure for dealing with environmental concerns has grown from a small subsection of the engineering department to a large, centralized department diffusing responsibilities throughout the company. The focus of this department has expanded from air and water pollution to hazardous waste, remediation, toxic emissions, right-to-know issues, ozone, global warming, acid rain, solid waste, chlorine phase-out, and environmental justice. The department's early focus on technological solutions made room for important managerial considerations regarding community relations, NGO alliances, scientific research, and policy development. The technological component that persisted evolved from handling pollution at the end of the pipe to considering changes in product and process design. Fundamentally, corporate environmentalism evolved from an ancillary aspect of corporate operations driven by regulatory considerations to a central aspect of corporate strategy driven by a core business constituency, illustrated in figure 1.6.

Contemporary corporate decision makers who remain fixed on public opinion trends or shifts in the political agenda will find such measures an inaccurate reflection of the future form of environmental practice. Although it is true that public support for environmentalism has declined slightly since a peak that occurred around 1992,[43] a comparable decline in environmental pressures on the corporation is not to be found. Public opinion regarding the environment is driven by saliency and therefore can be easily distracted.[44] Corporate pressures on the environment, however, are driven by a complex system of institutions that are more resilient and resistant to change and redefine basic business objectives. For example, firms are not free to develop their own property in a fashion they deem consistent with their economic objectives. Communities decide on the validity of development projects through zoning requirements and political protests. Public protests are often manifestations of the NIMBY (not in my backyard) syndrome,

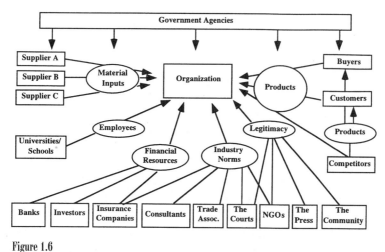

Figure 1.6

Sources of Pressure for Corporate Environmental Action

which is rapidly being replaced by the NOPE (not on Planet Earth) syndrome. In one dramatic example, Clean Harbors Environmental Services, Inc. watched its stock price drop from 25 to 4 ⁷/₈ in the face of powerful community opposition to its $13 million effort to site a hazardous waste incinerator in Braintree, Massachusetts, in the late 1980s.[45]

Firms are not free to define environmental risk management practices alone; they are bound by the norms and values of the insurance industry. Firms are not free to obtain capital on the basis of their own interpretations of the validity of a proposed project; financial institutions establish the standard evaluation procedures and norms. Firms are not even free to decide whether legal compliance is socially acceptable. In 1986, for example, the Polaroid Corporation faced an attack from Greenpeace for being the number one discharger into Boston Harbor. Despite the fact that Polaroid was in full compliance with permits issued by the Massachusetts Department of Environmental Protection, Greenpeace published a report titled "Polaroid—Instant Pollution: #1 in Toxic Waste" and hung a banner outside the company's Waltham facility, on a bridge over well-traveled Route 128, proclaiming the company the biggest polluter in Massachusetts. This provoked Polaroid's chief executive officer to establish a toxic waste reduction program more stringent than that required by law.[46]

Business professionals today find the challenge of environmentalism far greater than could have been previously imagined. And the challenge continues to grow. A 1998 survey of U.S. companies conducted by *Industry Week* found that despite declining public attention to environmentalism, 97.4 percent of those surveyed ranked environmental performance as one of their top ten priorities.[47] To make this priority an asset rather than a liability to corporate strategy requires a careful assessment of ways in which increasing environmental pressures can be integrated into efforts to achieve the corporation's objectives, in effect reducing the tension between environmental interests and business interests. With its unique blend of social and technical pressures, environmentalism can no longer be thought of as a necessary evil or a cost of doing business as defined by government regulation. It is now part of the rules of the game. For better or for worse, environmentalism has become a part of the business environment.

Competitive Environmental Strategy in Practice

At its core, competitive environmental strategy can be thought of as a change in perspective, a challenge to taken-for-granted notions of objects and actions. Consider this simple example. After dinner at my favorite restaurant, I remove a cigarette from its package and a match from its matchbox. I light the cigarette and throw the burnt match into the ashtray. I smoke the cigarette and then throw the charred butt into the ashtray as well. *What did I just do?* The answer to this question will differ, depending on when I performed this action and who was watching me. If I had performed this action in the 1950s, it is likely that people would have seen a simple technological and utilitarian act: creating a source of combustion with the match and enjoying a personal pleasure. Had I done it in the 1970s, people might have said that I was violating several codes of the Clean Air Act of 1970. Had I done it in the 1980s, people might have said I was endangering the health of those around me with the emission of second-hand smoke. In the 1990s, people might have said that I was wasting the resources of wood, phosphorus, and oxygen (as well as violating an anti-smoking ordinance). In the future, people may wonder why I use a match or smoke a cigarette at all because there may exist environmentally benign ways to accomplish my task. This may seem to be a simple example, but the same logic applies to more complicated examples. In particular, the same logic applies to basic business processes, materials, and objectives. Look at the smokestack in figure 1.7. *What do you see?*

Again, the answer will depend on who is observing it and when. In the 1950s, a smokestack was viewed favorably. People liked to look out the window and see a billowing smokestack. It meant jobs, economic progress, and industrial strength. But in the 1960s, the smokestack began to be viewed as something different and less desirable. It came to symbolize an ugly and smelly nuisance. In the 1970s, it represented the need for greater government controls on industrial pollution (such as the Clean Air Act). In the 1980s, it was viewed as a source of toxic pollution that could be hazardous to the health

Figure 1.7

What Is a Smokestack?

© *Kevin J. Fachetti. All rights reserved. Used with permission.*

of community members. In the 1990s, the smokestack came to symbolize wasted resources and money.[48] What will it mean in the twenty-first century?

Environmentalism redefines the way we view basic business processes, materials, and objectives. It influences the way we view basic business systems. Who are your competitors? Who are your partners? What is your product? What are your raw materials? What is your waste? The answers to all these questions are altered by the lens of environmental strategy. Consider the following examples of environmental strategy and the way basic concepts of the business system are redefined. Some are simple; others are more complex.

Who Are Your Competitors?

If you were an executive of an automobile-manufacturing firm, who would you consider to be your rivals in the market? Other automakers is clearly one answer. But environmentalism creates new forms of competition that are no less important than those based on products manufactured. To look at competition another way, one might ask, What is the best way to reduce automobile emissions? The answer could be one of two possibilities: (1) alter the engine design of the automobile or (2) alter the formulation of the gasoline fed to the engine. This has been the form of the debate over automobile emissions since it began in the 1960s. Early on, the oil industry won the debate with the requirement that catalytic converters be installed in new cars. Later, automakers won with the requirement that lead be removed from gasoline formulations. Even as recently as 1999, this battle has been waged. In June 1999, automakers infuriated oil refiners by asking the U.S. government to cut sulfur levels in gasoline to near zero to help them achieve future emission standards. In 2004, the EPA proposes to reduce tailpipe sulfur emissions from 300 parts per million to 30 parts per million.[49] These types of changes cost the respective industries significant amounts of money in research and production costs. The important consideration from this example is the reconfiguration of competitive dynamics. Automobile manufacturers were competing with oil companies for strategic advantage.

In the future, we may become witnesses to another, more intriguing reconfiguration of competition in the automobile industry. It centers on the emerging development of the zero-emission automobile. Again, to see new competitive possibilities, you must examine the way you view this new car. In effect, the zero-emission car will be run by computers, servomotors, and switching equipment. Is it a car with highly technical electronic equipment? Or is it a computer on wheels? The difference is significant in terms of which companies possess the complementary assets and core competencies to develop it. Amory Lovins believes that the future electric car (what he calls the "hyper-car") is more accurately described as the latter, a computer on wheels. Therefore, he concludes, it is not the big three automakers that should develop it but companies like Siemens AG, the Hewlett-Packard Company, and Motorola, Inc. They possess the competencies to develop the car's sophisticated circuitry, and their sales outlets can be developed through the growing marketplace on the Internet. One can already buy a Dell computer from home through the computer interface, he argues. And since automotive sales are already becoming standardized at dealers such as the Saturn Corporation, you could choose your car's color, style, and options through the World Wide Web and have it delivered to your door from the factory.

Who Are Your Partners?

Few environmental issues involve tensions more extreme than those between real estate development and endangered species protection. Yet environmentalists and developers have found ways to become partners in satisfying their mutual interests. For example, Riverfront Plaza, a retail outlet mall along the banks of the Kansas River in Lawrence, Kansas, was originally slated for construction in a nesting area for bald eagles. Through a negotiated settlement, the city of Lawrence established permanently protected easement areas on both sides of the river to preserve some of the best remaining habitat, planted new trees to replace those being lost, and enforced a no-entry zone along the outside walkway of the mall during the period when eagles are present in the greatest numbers. Subsequently, architects built one-way viewing windows facing the river, and these attracted customers to the mall.[50]

In Cleveland, Ohio, the city's 1993 Independence Day fireworks show threatened to harm a pair of nesting falcons. Potential conflicts were resolved through multiparty negotiations, which produced an alternative fireworks plan. As a result, the newly hatched falcons became the spotlight attraction of the show, benefiting the Tower City Center grand shopping mall and other downtown businesses.[51] Finally, a California developer proposed building a retail mall on land containing wetland habitat for the Sebastopol meadowfoam, a protected plant. After consultation with the U.S. Army Corps of Engineers and the U.S. Fish and Wildlife Service, the developer agreed to (1) establish a new Sebastopol meadowfoam colony on an off-site area and (2) acquire and protect additional habitat containing an existing natural population of the species.[52]

In other issues as well, environmentalism creates new and unusual alliances. In 1999, concerns about urban sprawl created a growing backlash against road and housing development. In that backlash, some traditional antagonists found themselves on the same side of the issue. For example, the Sierra Club and the National Rifle Association joined forces to stop expansion of Houston's George Bush Intercontinental Airport into the Katy Prairie, the largest winter home for migratory waterfowl in Texas and a popular hunting ground. Elsewhere, big-city mayors have allied with farmers to form special committees on land use. More than 1 million acres of farmland were lost between 1992 and 1999 while cities such as Detroit watched their population escape to the suburbs that rose up in its place.[53]

What Is Your Product?

The Raytheon Company has recently used environmental strategy to create a new market for its cold-war technologies, effectively turning "swords into plowshares." The company has contracted with the government of Brazil to use high-tech satellite surveillance technology to protect the largest rain forest in the world. Called the System for the Vigilance of the Amazon (SIVAM), the surveillance system will use a wide range of sensors—stationary radar devices, geophysical monitors, and satellites—to gather extensive data from the Amazon region.[54] This information will be processed centrally and distributed to numerous Brazilian government and independent agencies to help them manage land occupation and usage. The system is expected to ensure effective enforcement and border control; increase the accuracy of weather forecasting; assist in the detection, prevention, and control of epidemics; and improve air safety. For example, SIVAM will maintain surveillance over the Amazon's vast and remote areas to detect deforestation patterns caused by its citizens as well as illegal mining, logging, fires, and resource exploitation.

Beyond redefining product purpose, environmentalism can redefine product quality. For example, in the United States, product recalls are most often mandated by government agencies for products that have been determined to be unsafe. But in 1999, the General Motors Corporation and the federal government agreed to a recall of nearly half a million late-model Cadillac automobiles because they had faulty emission control systems. The settlement marked the first time that the courts ordered a recall of automobiles in order to curb pollution rather than to improve safety or dependability. The recall was expected to cost the company more than $30 million.[55]

What Are Your Raw Materials?

Many companies have begun to look to natural materials and natural systems for raw materials in developing products and processes. Various species of plants and animals differ both genetically and chemically, and the subtle distinctions among species found in different regions can provide needed components of new medicines and industrial products. Natural processes have made possible millions of years of evolution, adaptation, and diversification. As a result, organisms have fine-tuned anti-biologicals and other compounds that are effective in their own lives and could be helpful for ours. Nature has already done the testing; laboratories can only replicate this kind of testing, with high costs, and still cannot match the number of generations of product viability that evolution has provided. Hence, it is more cost-effective to look for new products in nature than in the artificial and costly laboratory environment. Many such products are now being exploited. This suggests a new perspective on the natural environment as a source of hidden treasures, which prudence would dictate we protect for future generations and future possibilities yet unseen.

For example, researchers at the Pacific Northwest National Laboratory have identified a microbe, *Sulfolobus acidocaldarius,* in the hot springs at Yellowstone National Park that breaks down the carbon-sulfur lattice in discarded rubber tires. It may hold the key to recycling the 2 billion to 3 billion tires presently stockpiled in the United States.[56] Another example is that of biopolymers, which are stronger and more lightweight and biodegradable than synthetic materials and can be derived from microbial systems, extracted from higher organisms such as plants, or synthesized chemically from basic biological building blocks. A wide range of emerging applications includes medical materials, packaging, cosmetics, food additives, clothing fabrics, water treatment chemicals, industrial plastics, absorbents, and even data storage elements.[57]

Some pharmaceutical companies have been exploring natural systems for potential new drugs. Digitalis, derived from the purple foxglove, saves the lives of 3 million heart disease sufferers per year in the United States.[58] The blood-clotting system of the ancient horseshoe crab produces proteins that are now being used to detect gram-negative sepsis, a potentially life-threatening condition caused by bacterial infection that affects more than 10,000 people each year.[59] The drug Taxol, one of the most promising new treatments for ovarian and breast cancers (which kill approximately 40,000 women per year in the United States), comes from the bark of the Pacific yew tree, found primarily in endangered ecosystems of the Pacific Northwest.[60] The rosy periwinkle, a native of a seriously endangered habitat in Madagascar, provides a critical component in the treatment of childhood leukemia and Hodgkin's disease.[61] The nearly extinct Houston toad produces alkaloids that may prevent heart attacks as well as an anesthetic more powerful than morphine.[62] The National Cancer Institute is studying four plant compounds that prevent replication of the HIV-1 and HIV-2 viruses. One is derived from the leaves and twigs of a tree in a Malaysian rain forest, and the other is derived from a tropical vine in the rain forest of Cameroon.[63]

The World Health Organization estimates that only about 5 percent of the world's known plant species have been investigated for their pharmaceutical properties.[64] So valuable are the potential medicinal benefits found in nature that pharmaceutical companies have started to invest in protection of biological diversity. For example, Merck & Company, Inc. and the Instituto Nacional de Biodiversidad (INBio), a nonprofit scientific institution in Costa Rica that promotes biological diversity, entered into an agreement in 1991 to catalog all plants and animals in Costa Rica. In exchange for the right to screen the results of this "chemical prospecting," Merck paid INBio $1 million up front and pays royalties on any drug developments. Ten percent of the initial fee and 50 percent of the royalties are used for conservation and biological diversity protection through an arrangement with the Costa Rican government.[65]

What Is Your Waste?

Is there money in your trash barrel? Ronald Spiegel, an engineer with the EPA, has found exactly that: money in landfills. Spiegel has developed a fuel-cell power plant that can burn the methane gas emitted from most landfills. The system filters impurities out of the landfill gas, converts the methane into carbon dioxide and hydrogen, and then combines the hydrogen with oxygen in a catalytic reaction that produces electricity. The emissions are primarily carbon dioxide and water. Spiegel believes that with this technology, it is possible to harness the country's 7,500 landfills and produce 4.5 billion watts of electricity, about enough to power a metropolis of approximately 5 million homes. The EPA and the Northeast Utilities Service Company are testing the prototype at a landfill in Groton, Connecticut.[66]

On a larger scale, electric utilities use scrubbers to remove sulfur and fly ash from the exhaust gases of their power plants. Typically, they have paid to dispose of these materials in landfills, but many are now finding markets for them, turning waste into a profitable product. Some companies buy the material to make construction products. The waste is high in calcium sulfate, or gypsum, which is normally mined as a feedstock for making materials such as wallboard and concrete. Farmers have also been buying the residue, called "scrubber sludge," and using it as fertilizer, particularly since sulfur restrictions were increased under the Clean Air Act Amendments of 1990. With its high sulfur content, the sludge has been found to increase crop yields and reduce polluted runoff by improving the soil's capacity to hold water. The Tennessee Valley Authority makes $6 million to $10 million annually on this by-product. The Indianapolis Power & Light Company sells about 300 tons per year from one plant, and some of its other plants are adjusting operating conditions to produce higher-quality sludge. As Jim Meiers, the utility's chief scientist, explained, "When you are getting paid for by-product, you can afford to spend more money on it."[67]

Opportunity or Threat? A Matter of Perspective

For some seasoned corporate veterans, environmental issues may have far exceeded what they consider to be reasonable or even conceivable. Many senior executives of today's corporations were new employees at the dawn of the modern environmental era, just four decades ago. They have seen environmental considerations evolve from a nonissue to an issue of central importance to the corporation. As a result, they may have experienced a significant degree of "battle fatigue" as these issues evolved to levels they may consider extreme. For example, one senior environmental health and safety manager at the Amoco Corporation complained: "I used to think that there would be an end to all this regulation. But, every time I say—What's left to regulate?—then we find something. Look at carpooling issues. How far will this go? Before we're done, I wouldn't be surprised if the oil industry will be subsidizing highway projects." Another executive expressed similar sentiments: "All I see is the complete frustration in the 1990s with the pure political nature of environmental regulations. There is no scientific, economic, or even environmental reason for some of this stuff. We've come to the point where we're saying, this is crazy, we've got to do something different."[68] Such executives may find themselves unable (or unwilling) to move beyond the zero-sum, win–lose perspective of environmental management, given the extent of change they have experienced in their careers.

Herein lies the opportunity for new managers who can see the changing business system and the strategic opportunities available through merging environmental and economic objectives. For them, stripping away the old mind-set of environmental management will reveal new opportunities for the corporation. Environmental strategy will be a logical component of corporate strategy. The purpose of this book is to help in this process.

Book Overview

The clues to understanding how environmentalism alters corporate strategy can be found by considering who is driving environmentalism in the business environment and how that pressure is changing basic conceptions of strategy, technology, and organization within the firm. This book explores these strategic questions in a structured and organized way. It is not intended to make the reader fully proficient in the structure of environmental law or the science of environmental hazards. Although such background material is presented as needed, the book focuses on the significance of these developments for corporate organization, markets, and strategy. It is not aimed only at managers with environmental interests. Every individual who wishes to engage in business management in the twenty-first century will need to have an appreciation of the implications of environmentalism for corporate activities and vice versa. What the reader will take away from this text is a grasp of the emerging complexity of environmentalism and its opportunities and limitations in the corporate enterprise. In the final analysis, environmentalism offers a new lens through which to view taken-for-granted conceptions of who is driving competitive and environmental concerns, the implications of those concerns for the corporation, how those implications alter product and process development and what their future form may be. Along these lines, the remainder of the book is divided into three parts.

Part II deals with the key *drivers* of corporate environmental management. The drivers are considered in five categories, each distinct in the type of pressure exerted. Chapters 2 and 3 look at domestic regulatory drivers and international environmental accords. Chapter 4 reviews the resource drivers, including buyers, suppliers, banks, shareholders, investors, and insurance companies. Chapter 5 broadens the scope of analysis to consider the market drivers of consumers, trade associations, competitors, and consultants. Finally, chapter 6 expands the analysis to consider the social drivers of environmental NGOs, the press, the courts, the community, academia, and religious organizations. In the end, it is not necessarily pressures from the natural environment to which firms respond directly. Rather, it is the demands for environmental protection articulated by key constituents of the firm's regulatory, resource, market, and social environments.

Part III examines the *corporate implications* of these drivers. It considers how environmentalism alters basic conceptions of competitive strategy (chapter 7) and organizational design (chapter 8). Chapter 9 then broadens the perspective to consider how institutions create both opportunities and limitations for environmental strategy. Environmentalism both necessitates corporate action by changing the business system and limits the form of that action through the inertia of that system. Environmental strategy must be developed with an appreciation for the external context in which it takes place.

The book closes with part IV, offering some final thoughts on competitive environmental strategy. Chapter 10 describes competitive environmental strategy within an institutional context. It presents two sectoral studies, one in which institutions create opportunities for strategic innovation and another in which institutions limit those opportunities. The chapter concludes with concrete examples demonstrating that environmental strategy must be developed with an eye toward the external business and social environments that are driving it. Chapter 11 wraps up with an overall discussion of competitive environmental strategy and draws connections with the emerging issue of sustainable development.

To help readers think more deeply about the core environmental issues developed in this book, additional readings are recommended at the ends of chapters. Further, boxes included in the chapters ask fundamental questions about the relationship between environmental protection and business strategy. The question for this chapter (see box 1.1) is as follows: Can business management be completely compatible with environmental protection? Others (listed at the front of the book) are similarly provocative. They come directly from a class I teach on environmental strategy, in which I require students to write a one-page position paper on each topic. I see these questions as challenges to the reader's fundamental beliefs about the relationship of environment and business. I hope you find these questions interesting and thought provoking as you consider the role of your corporation and your career in protecting the environment. The questions have no simple answers, but they should provoke careful thought and reveal new notions of how they can be addressed.

Box 1.1. Can Business Management Be Completely Compatible with Environmental Protection?

Before proceeding, we must consider an important question. The central premise of this book is that environmental issues can be compatible with business management, and to make them compatible, managers must recognize how they are translated through core business channels. But this is not a universally held opinion. Many believe that business management, as it is now defined, is completely incompatible with the goals of environmental protection, that to attempt to integrate environmental issues into business management is to disregard their complexity and the inability of present social structures to stop environmental degradation.[*] Some believe that much of our environmentally destructive behavior is supported by some very basic taken-for-granted beliefs of modern society and modern capitalism.[†]

For example, capitalist society has as one of its fundamental assumptions the human-centered view that unlimited progress is possible through the exploitation of nature's infinite resources. In the pursuit of that progress, organizations and individuals are perceived as independent, existing in a free market in which resource extraction and development are the right of the property owner to the exclusion of other social interests. Present management theory has been criticized for supporting these beliefs by promoting several unsustainable notions: an uncritical belief in the necessity of increasing economic growth; the perception of nature as a limitless sink; the notion of the supremacy of technological development in controlling natural systems; a belief in the social and physical autonomy of the firm; and the notion of the profit motive as a singular objective of the firm.[‡]

Instead of integrating environmental considerations into the business system, some argue that environmental considerations call for a complete restructuring of the capitalist system. They argue that the integration of environmentalism into present-day capitalism does not fundamentally change the social rules that are causing environmental problems and therefore will not affect their ultimate result. In "corporate environmentalism," the environment remains external to the economy, internalized through the application of norms and rules based principally on human utility and not ecological stability. Environmental studies professor Neil Evernden wrote: "The crisis is not simply something we can examine and resolve. We are the environmental crisis. The crisis is a visible manifestation of our very being, like territory revealing the self at its center. The environmental crisis is inherent in everything we believe and do; it is inherent in the context of our lives."[§]

(continues)

Box 1.1. *Continued*

This question is embedded both implicitly and explicitly in the arguments throughout this book. Attempting to answer it should challenge your basic notions of the future of the capitalist system and the future of the natural environment on which it is based. Should tomorrow's managers attempt to make environmental issues conform to the norms and beliefs of the existing business world? Or should they strive to reconstruct the beliefs of the business system to create new possibilities for resolving this important social issue?

* A. Schnaiberg, *The Environment: From Surplus to Scarcity* (New York: Oxford University Press, 1980); T. Gladwin, T. Freeman, and J. Kennelly, "Ending Our Denial and Destruction of Nature: Toward Biophysical Sustainable Management Theory," unpublished manuscript (New York: New York University, Stern School of Business, 1994).

† B. Allenby, "USA vs. SD: Can American Values and Sustainable Development Live Together in Peace?" *Tomorrow* 4, no. 8 (1998): 61.

‡ H. Daly and J. Cobb, *For the Common Good* (Boston: Beacon Press, 1994); H. Daly, *Steady-State Economics*, 2d ed. (Washington, D.C.: Island Press, 1991); T. Gladwin, J. Kennelly, and T. Krause, "Shifting Paradigms for Sustainable Development: Implications for Management Theory and Research," *Academy of Management Review* 20, no. 4 (1995): 874–907; F. Capra, *The Turning Point: Science, Society, and the Rising Culture* (New York: Bantam Books, 1982).

§ N. Evernden, *The Natural Alien: Humankind and Environment* (Toronto: University of Toronto Press, 1985), 128.

Further Reading

Hoffman, A. *From Heresy to Dogma: An Institutional History of Corporate Environmentalism.* San Francisco: New Lexington Press, 1997.

Hoffman, A., J. Gillespie, D. Moore, K. Wade-Benzoni, L. Thompson, and M. Bazerman. "A Mixed-Motive Perspective on the Economics versus Environment Debate." *American Behavioral Scientist* 42, no. 8 (1999): 1254–1276.

Palmer, K., W. Oates, and P. Portney. "Tightening Environmental Standards: The Benefit–Cost or the No-Cost Paradigm?" *Journal of Economic Perspectives* 9, no. 4 (1995): 119–132.

Porter, M., and C. van der Linde. "Green and Competitive: Ending the Stalemate." *Harvard Business Review*, September–October 1995, 120–134.

———. "Toward a New Conception of the Environment–Competitiveness Relationship." *Journal of Economic Perspectives* 9, no. 4 (1995): 97–118.

Walley, N., and B. Whitehead. "It's Not Easy Being Green." *Harvard Business Review*, May–June 1994, 46–51.

Part II

DRIVERS OF ENVIRONMENTAL PROTECTION IN A CHANGING BUSINESS CONTEXT

The twentieth century witnessed unprecedented economic growth and human prosperity. Global per capita income nearly tripled,[1] average life expectancy increased by almost two-thirds,[2] and people were significantly more literate and educated than their predecessors. Many of these improvements in the quality of life were driven by the accomplishments of industry. Advancing developments in medicine, materials, transportation, communication, and food production all emerged from the industrial sector. But since the 1960s, society has questioned some of the assumptions that support this technological growth, particularly as they pertain to the treatment of the natural environment. Today, we have reached a point in our social development at which quality of life is being redefined in terms that challenge two general assumptions of industrial and economic growth: that the environment is (1) an endless source of resources and (2) a limitless sink for wastes. In truth, it is industrial society as a whole that causes environmental problems; yet it is industry that often bears the burden of reducing their severity. Before discussing the drivers of environmental protection, it is important to examine briefly the kinds of activities these drivers seek to reduce.

The Environment as an Endless Source of Resources

In 1998, expenditures for public and private consumption reached an unprecedented $24 trillion, twice the level of 1975 and six times that of 1950. By contrast, in 1900, barely $1.5 trillion was spent on consumer goods and services.[3] To fuel this consumption, U.S. industry consumes a staggering 2.7 billion metric tons of raw material each year (not counting stone, sand, and gravel).[4] Worldwide development places equally significant demands on natural resources. Many resources are being extracted at levels that will inhibit future generations from satisfying their own needs.

Since 1980, tropical forestland, a critical component of the world's oxygen production system, has declined at an estimated rate of 59,500 square miles per year, an annual loss of an area nearly equivalent in size to the state of Florida. This translates into a disappearance rate of sixty-three acres per minute.[5] Each year, the world loses through erosion about 27.5 billion tons of topsoil, a resource necessary for world food production. [6] In the United States alone, 2.2 billion tons of soil in cropland was lost to erosion in 1992.[7] An estimated 11 percent of the earth's fertile soil has been eroded, chemically altered, or physically compacted enough to damage its original biotic function. Since 1950, worldwide water use has increased from 1,300 to 4,200 cubic kilometers.[8] With such growth rates, lack of freshwater is expected to affect as many as 2.9 billion people by the year 2020.[9] As many as 27,000 species of flora and fauna are estimated to be disappearing each year.[10] Scientists estimate that 4 to 8 percent of tropical forest species may face extinction by the year 2025, despite their unknown links to the complex ecosystem.[11] The best current global estimate of the maximum sustainable yield of marine fish is 62 million to 87 million metric tons per year, a level attained in the mid-1980s and surpassed since then. According to the Food and Agriculture Organization of the United Nations, four of the world's seventeen major fisheries are commercially depleted and nine more are in serious decline.[12] Unless decisive action is taken, the populations of many fish species will drop below levels necessary to ensure sustainable yields, leaving many fish-dependent human populations in search of other sources of food and economic livelihoods.[13] It is estimated that the area of wetlands in the continental United States decreased from 89 million hectares in 1780 to 42 million hectares in the 1980s, just 53 percent of the 1780 total.[14] This loss continues despite the importance of wetlands as purification and detoxification systems for aquatic environments and critical components of flood control. All of these problems will continue as world population, which hit 6 billion in late 1999, is expected to increase by 50 percent by 2050.[15]

The Environment as a Limitless Sink for Wastes

Beyond consuming natural resources at an unsustainable rate, industrial society places demands on the ecosystem through the emission of waste by-products from material use and manipulation. U.S. industry creates nearly 7 billion metric tons of solid waste annually through the extraction of raw materials.[16] Additionally, it releases or transfers off-site for treatment and disposal nearly 2.5 million metric tons of toxic chemicals created in the material development process[17] and emits more than 120 million metric tons of conventional air pollutants.[18] Further, there are roughly 1,500 abandoned hazardous waste sites in need of immediate attention on the Environmental Protection Agency's Superfund National Priorities List. That number could grow as high as 375,000 if a more comprehensive inventory is taken (to include the sites on the Hazard Ranking System, state cleanup sites, leaking underground storage tanks, and facilities used by the Department of Defense and the Department of Energy).

On a global scale, worldwide emissions of the greenhouse gas carbon dioxide have increased steadily. In 1950, world carbon dioxide emissions were 1.6 billion tons per year. By 1997, they had reached 7.0 billion tons per year. As a result, atmospheric concentrations have grown from 290 parts per million to 360 parts per million since the beginning of the industrial revolution in the middle of the nineteenth century.[19] The Intergovernmental Panel on Climate Change estimated that this has resulted in an increase in the earth's temperature of 1 degree Fahrenheit over the past century and could cause an increase of another 1.5–4.5 degrees Fahrenheit in the next hundred years.[20] This buildup is caused by economic growth that continues despite its potential to alter the world's climate. Commonly predicted effects include drier weather in midcontinent areas (including the U.S. Midwest), sea-level rise, more violent storms, and northward migration of vector-borne tropical diseases and climate-sensitive species.[21] Many species may not be able to migrate quickly enough and may become extinct.

A Changing Business Context

Historically, industrialized society has treated the environment as both a limitless source of resources and a limitless sink for wastes. Now, political, economic, market, and social systems are adjusting to change these beliefs. The question becomes, How do these adjustments enter the corporate consciousness? Part II of this book discusses the various drivers of competitive environmental strategy. As shown in figure II.1, they fall into four categories: coercive, market, resource, and social drivers. In the next chapter, we consider the specifics of government regulation for environmental protection, showing how this

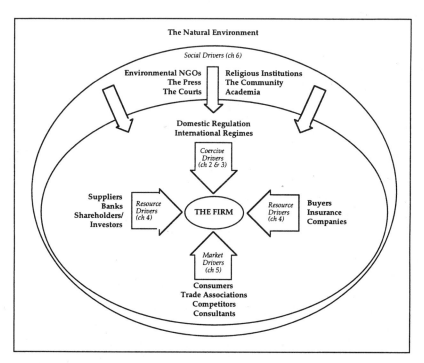

Figure II.1

Book Overview: Drivers of Environmental Strategy

area of corporate pressure is far from monolithic or precise. Opportunities for strategic regulatory response are becoming more and more plentiful. Then, in chapter 3, we consider the globalization of environmental concerns through establishment of international environmental accords. Finally, we delve into the sources of environmental pressures from the corporation's resource (chapter 4), market (chapter 5), and social networks (chapter 6).

Chapter 2

REGULATORY DRIVERS

Not surprisingly, most Americans believe that without government regulation, corporations would not attend to environmental issues. In a national survey on environmental issues, 94 percent of Americans said that they considered the Environmental Protection Agency to be necessary in today's economy.[1] But government pressures for environmental protection take many forms, and public opinion tends to overlook the complexity with which they presently drive corporate strategy. To understand this complexity, one must consider regulation in its evolving context. The format of regulatory mechanisms in the United States has shifted from strict command-and-control regulation in the 1970s to market incentives, voluntary programs, and criminal penalties today. The focus of those regulations has evolved through conservation and ecology in the 1970s; employee health, community relations, and public disclosure in the late 1980s; and pollution minimization and product stewardship efforts in the 1990s. The important point is that regulatory pressures are neither monolithic nor static. Their heterogeneity creates opportunities for different types of environmental strategy, and their dynamic trajectory points to a future of increasing uncertainty about which strategy will be most successful. But with this uncertainty comes greater opportunity for firms that can adapt to new environmental protections and regulatory mechanisms. This chapter examines regulatory pressures that are forming in the domestic arena; chapter 3 considers those pressures in the international context.

The Dawn of U.S. Environmental Regulation

The year was 1970. William D. Ruckelshaus, a rising political star in the Department of Justice, was named by President Richard Nixon to head the newly formed Environmental Protection Agency (EPA). The new organization's plan integrated nearly 6,000 employees from existing compartmentalized programs scattered among various departments in federal government agencies (see figure 2.1). Public attention was focused on Ruckelshaus and how the organization would get started. What should he do? How should he begin? What were his priorities and objectives? How were those objectives limited by existing political realities and technological understanding? This was an awesome challenge.

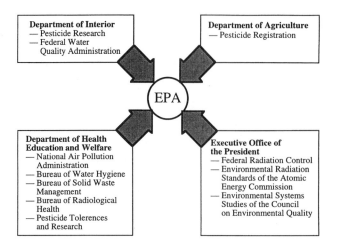

Figure 2.1

Functions Transferred to the EPA by Reauthorization Plan No. 3 of 1970

Source: Environmental Protection Agency, *The Guardian: EPA's Formative Years, 1970–1973* (Washington, D.C.: U.S. Government Printing Office, 1993), 6.

To understand how regulation became structured under Ruckelshaus's reign, one must consider the context of the time. Concern for environmental issues had been building since the early 1960s. Facilitated by widespread social activism in response to the Vietnam War, the environmental movement reached a critical mass that propelled it into the national agenda with the first Earth Day in April 1970. Politicians took notice of this large new constituency and began to add an environmental agenda to their election platforms. Even President Nixon's decision to form the EPA was more an effort to deflate the growing environmental strength of his political opponent, Senator Edmund Muskie, than evidence of a belief in the validity of the emerging social movement. Nixon associated the environmental movement with the anti-war movement, both of which he saw as reflections of weakness in the American character.[2]

With this as a backdrop, Ruckelshaus faced a daunting challenge in starting the country's environmental programs. But the decisions he made would create a legacy informing the way the issue would be framed over the next decades. The structure and format he established are still reflected in the regulatory programs we have today. In particular, much of the present state of corporate environmentalism can be traced back to three aspects of the initial formation of the EPA.

First, although many at the time recommended a complete restructuring of the nation's existing environmental programs—away from a media-segmented (separated by water, air, and land) focus and toward a holistic "intermedium" approach to protecting the environment—political realities forced the creation of the new agency through consolidation of existing compartmentalized programs into medium-specific offices for air pollution, water pollution, pesticides, radiation, and solid waste. An intermedium approach would have regulated an industrial facility as a unit, considering the effects of its operations on the environment as a whole. Unfortunately, time constraints and the organizational and cultural realities of forming an agency with 6,000 employees who were firmly entrenched in a media-based mind-set precluded the possibility of building a new regulatory framework from the ground up.

A second aspect of the original EPA that established future practices was the command-and-control format created by Ruckelshaus. The strong enforcement background he had acquired in his previous work as assistant attorney general for the Department of Justice carried over into his new position, and enforcement became the agency's primary focus. Ruckelshaus believed that once the government set standards and began to enforce them, industry would fall in line and the country's environmental problems would eventually disappear.[3] Even without this predisposition to strong enforcement, high public scrutiny and expectations would have demanded that the new agency establish its presence quickly and forcefully. During its first sixty days, the EPA brought five times as many enforcement actions as the agencies it inherited had brought during any similar period.[4] This focus on punishing polluters was justified on political grounds to establish credibility, but it also set an adversarial tone to the industry–government relationship that carries over to this day.

Third, the rudimentary understanding of environmental problems in 1970 led to a focus on prescript, technology-based standards. With air and water pollution their primary focus, the Clean Air Act of 1970 and the Federal Water Pollution Control Act of 1972 (amended in 1977 and renamed the Clean Water Act) mandated the installation of pollution abatement equipment deemed to be the best available technology (BAT). These technologies were fairly well known and required merely a financial investment for regulatory compliance. This reflected an optimistic technological-fix conception of the solution to environmental problems. The catchword for the early 1970s was *technology forcing,* wherein new federal rules would force industry to use new, pollution-free technology; it was expected that as new plants replaced old, the problem of pollution would be resolved.[5] Although later regulations would reflect performance-based standards, they still were usually based on best available technologies and therefore perpetuated the technology-forcing mind-set. In the end, this (1) media-segmented, (2) command-and-control, (3) adversarial, (4) technology-based approach to environmental regulation set the tone for the way environmental issues would be framed within both government and industry.

Command-and-Control Regulation

The EPA progressed through the 1970s developing the basic framework of environmental laws we have today (the environmental laws and their intent are briefly described in appendix A). As shown in figure 2.2, the pace of regulatory development was dizzying, both for the government in enforcement and for industry in compliance. This growth involved a continual redefining of the firm's environmental responsibilities in both scope and scale. Originally, the laws and statutes were geared to visible sources and manifestations of pollution. Actions to control them were viewed as protection of the ecosystem; public health was not a predominant concern. Later, regulatory requirements would be geared to more minute quantities of pollutants and be driven by a broader spectrum of concerns.

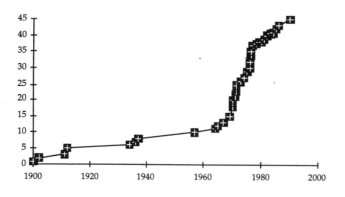

Figure 2.2

Trends in the Number of U.S. Federal Environmental Health and Safety Laws, 1900–1995

Source: J. Ausubel and H. Sladovich, *Technology and Environment* (Washington, D.C.: National Academy of Engineering, 1989).

In the second half of the decade, new laws began to transform the regulatory focus from one of ecological protection to one of human health protection. In 1974, the Safe Drinking Water Act (SDWA), the Toxic Substances Control Act (TSCA), and in 1976 the Resource Conservation and Recovery Act (RCRA) were signed into law. With these laws came a new responsibility for firms not only to the government but also to the health of their employees and community members. These regulations also increased the burden on industry to implement greater levels of environmental controls at steadily increasing costs.

Unfortunately for the EPA, the new legislations were also demanding an increasing enforcement presence. As shown in figure 2.3, the EPA's administrative and civil actions

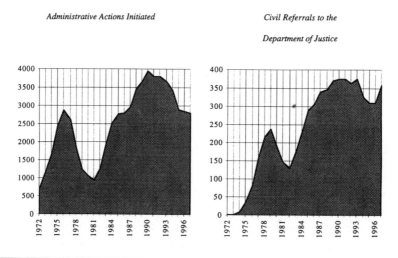

Figure 2.3

EPA Enforcement Activity, 1972–1997

Source: Environmental Protection Agency, *Enforcement and Compliance Assurance Accomplishments Report*, Report no. EPA-300-R-98-003 (Washington, D.C.: U.S. Government Printing Office, 1998).
(Figures are three-year rolling averages.)

increased rapidly through the decade, leading the agency's administrator, Douglas Costle, to complain, "The laws were written so that we would need a policeman at every corner."[6] By the late 1970s, the EPA was struggling under the weight of unrealistic objectives. No one had realized how complex the job of protecting the environment would be. Most thought that the big problems would be taken care of easily and that the remainder of the effort would be a matter of maintenance. That was not the case. Lawsuits, with environmentalists on one side and industry on the other, grew to be an unpleasant fact of agency life.[7] The antagonism between the EPA and industry was growing. Under the administration of President Jimmy Carter, the EPA attempted to reduce this tension by cutting back on enforcement, but it was too late. The confrontational relationship between the two had been established in the initial structure of the program and would not easily be reduced.

One event that would push these mounting tensions over the top was the discovery of 21,800 tons of toxic chemical waste beneath Love Canal, a residential neighborhood in Niagara Falls, New York, in 1978. The chemicals had been buried there thirty years before by the Hooker Electro-Chemical Company. But when the town built an entire neighborhood above the toxic waste dump, the residents were subjected to toxic hazards as the chemicals oozed into basements and emerged on school playgrounds. In 1978, the state and federal governments authorized the purchase of 803 homes and the relocation of their occupants (more detail is provided in chapter 6). The events at Love Canal changed the face of environmental problems from something that was slow to develop to something that could suddenly emerge from such seemingly benign sources as the ground beneath a private citizen's home.[8] It also changed the landscape of domestic environmental regulation and the relationship between the EPA and industry.

In response to widespread media coverage that fed on public fear of this new type of hazard, President Carter signed the Comprehensive Environmental Response, Compensation, and Liability Act (CERCLA or Superfund) into law in 1980. A controversial piece of legislation, Superfund held corporations liable for past actions in a way that departed from the prohibition of expost facto liability in American law—the principle that no one could be found liable retroactively for an act that was legal when undertaken. It also changed the role and responsibilities of the EPA. Going beyond the establishment of rules by which industry must conduct its affairs, the agency was now responsible for overseeing the cleanup of toxic wastes. The EPA could take steps to clean up an abandoned hazardous waste site and, under the clause of joint and several liability, sue one predominant party for the entire cleanup cost. This party could then seek the other responsible parties and recoup its costs in court. In taking on responsibility for the whole process, the EPA had become a contractor of services, establishing itself as project manager in the cleanup of abandoned hazardous waste sites and directly influencing the flow of corporate expenditures.

Superfund was viewed by industry as the most egregious of all environmental legislation. And with it, adversarial relations between industry and the EPA reached new levels. Although industry continued to look to the government to define society's expectations of its environmental management practices, it grew increasingly hostile toward and frustrated by the direction regulation was taking.

In 1981, President Ronald Reagan set environmental regulation briefly on a new track. Reagan's overall approach to public management was marked by severe budget cuts and regulatory reform of programs that restricted corporate activity. Environmentalism could not be missed by such an agenda, and with public attention to environmental issues at a ten-year low,[9] his initiatives gained early momentum. His newly appointed EPA administrator, Anne (Burford) Gorsuch, set about streamlining the myriad environmental laws and sought cooperation rather than confrontation with the regulated community in accomplishing her task. Even though both EPA enforcement and industry lawsuits had been on a decline under the Carter administration, Gorsuch slowed agency activity even further. In particular, Superfund activity ground to a halt.

Soon, closed meetings created an air of favoritism and secret deals, and Gorsuch's slashing of the EPA's budget and staff created a critical backlash among the public and subsequently within government. In 1983, Gorsuch and the head of Superfund, Rita Lavelle, were hastily removed from office, and Congress, empowered by the public backlash, renewed and strengthened RCRA (1984), Superfund (1986), the Safe Drinking Water Act (1986), and the Clean Water Act (1987). This strengthening was accompanied by renewed expectations for increasing administrative and civil actions, which continue to the present—see figure 2.3. But other forms of regulatory pressure also began to emerge.

Criminal Enforcement

Prior to 1982, most of the EPA's enforcement activity employed the tools of civil and administrative action. Even the worst environmental violations resulted in misdemeanor convictions. But beginning in 1982, criminal enforcement was added to the EPA inspector's tool kit. As shown in figure 2.4, growth in criminal enforcement was steady from 1982 until 1990 but then increased significantly with the adoption of federal sentencing guidelines that mandated specific punishments for various types of felonies and misdemeanors. The Pollution Prosecution Act of 1990 mandated that the EPA "increase the

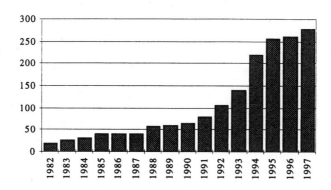

Figure 2.4

EPA Criminal Referrals to the Department of Justice, 1982–1997

Source: Environmental Protection Agency, *Enforcement and Compliance Assurance Accomplishments Report,* Report no. EPA-300-R-98-003 (Washington, D.C.: U.S. Government Printing Office, 1998).

number of criminal investigations" to at least 72 in fiscal year (FY) 1992, 110 in FY 1993, 123 in FY 1994, 160 in FY 1995, and 200 thereafter.

Criminal action is usually reserved for those who flout the law, cause massive environmental harm, or lie to the EPA. In one example, the Region V office of the EPA conducted an investigation of three officials at the P & H Plating Company in Chicago in 1989. The company had dumped 4,000 gallons of cyanide and cadmium waste into a floor drain, and the concentrated poisons had flowed through the sewers and into the Metropolitan Water Reclamation District of Greater Chicago's North Side Water Reclamation Plant, nearly closing it down. The poisons had run through the plant and been discharged first into the North Shore Channel and then into the North Branch of the Chicago River, where they killed an estimated 20,000 fish. Convicted of violations of the federal Clean Water Act were the president and owner of P & H, who had given the order to dump the waste (fifteen months in jail); the plant supervisor, who carried out the order (three years of probation); and the technical manager (the owner's wife), who conveyed the order to the supervisor (four months of work-release time and home confinement while continuing to run the company). The defendants complained that environmental compliance had already cost them $500,000, or 10 percent of gross sales, and that properly disposing of this batch of wastes would have cost them an additional $60,000. They were caught when a friend turned them in and won a $10,000 reward.[10]

Between FY 1982 and FY 1993, the Department of Justice recorded environmental criminal indictments against 1,203 defendants; 885 guilty pleas and convictions were entered. A total of $263 million in criminal penalties was assessed, and more than 461 years of imprisonment were imposed (of which more than 251 years accounted for actual confinement). Of the 1,203 defendants indicted, 339 were corporations and the remaining 864 were individuals. Of the 885 guilty pleas and convictions, 280 involved corporations and the remaining 605 involved individuals.[11] By 1997, the number of referrals to the Department of Justice reached 278 and the number of defendants charged had reached 322 per year, with 195 years of jail time sentenced.[12]

An Agency in Transition

Although Gorsuch's actions as EPA administrator were viewed as an attempt to slow down the agency, they reflected the growing complexity of the regulations then being developed and called attention to a need to restructure the system and move away from what had been established in 1970. In 1983, William Ruckelshaus was reassigned as EPA administrator to restore public trust. He focused on ways to integrate the existing segmented regulatory structure to make it less onerous for industry. This planted the seeds for continued reform that would carry through successive administrations. In the 1980s, administrator Lee Thomas focused on prioritizing regulatory items so that attention could be redirected to the areas where it was most needed (for example, away from abandoned hazardous waste sites and toward acid rain). These efforts represented a shift away from the incremental media approach adopted at the EPA's outset and toward increasing flexibility in an attempt to reconcile the economic and environmental objectives of the country. At the turn of the decade, administrators William Reilly and Carol

Browner continued this development by establishing market-based and cooperative programs between the agency and the regulated community. The EPA was now on a new tack, employing a wide variety of tools and techniques for gaining corporate environmental action.

Forcing Disclosure

One new form of environmental regulatory pressure arose from the power of knowledge. In response to the disastrous toxic gas leak in Bhopal, India, in 1984 (discussed in more detail in chapter 4), communities and environmental activists pressed the case that they had a right to know what was taking place within the walls of industrial plants in their midst. In 1986, the Emergency Planning and Community Right-to-Know Act (also known as Title III of the Superfund Amendments and Reauthorization Act of 1986) mandated that companies report the annual emissions of toxic chemicals at each of their U.S. facilities. The EPA compiles this information and publishes it in a database called the Toxics Release Inventory. Manufacturing facilities are required to report annual emissions into the environment of more than 600 toxic chemicals, including about 173 of the 188 hazardous air pollutants regulated under the Clean Air Act. Unfortunately, the program requires continual revision because emissions of the facilities required to file reports account for less than 10 percent of the estimated total airborne emissions of these pollutants.[13]

Regardless of this flaw, the program enables activists to apply new forms of pressure for increased environmental controls based on actual documentation of environmental discharges. Both communities and industry have become more aware of the volume of pollution being emitted and, by inference, more aware of their responsibility to reduce it. Thomas Lafferre, operations vice president for the Monsanto Company, wrote in 1990: "All of us are caught up in the myth of compliance . . . [but] if for example, you file a Title III report that says your plant emits 80,000 pounds of suspected carcinogens to the air each year, you might be comforted by the fact that you're in compliance with your permit. But what if your plant is two blocks from an elementary school? How comfortable would you be then?"[14]

The EPA uses the power of information in other ways to elicit corporate and community action. In 1998, under its Sector Facility Indexing Project, the agency began publishing on the World Wide Web a database of environmental infractions and inspections at 653 industrial facilities.[15] EPA administrator Browner commented, "We believe that providing the public with basic environmental information about their communities is one of the most powerful tools available for protecting health and the environment."[16]

Interestingly, recent attention to domestic terrorism has run head-on into environmental disclosure requirements. In 1998, the EPA decided not to post on the Web worst-case scenarios of harm to communities that could result from accidents at industrial facilities that handle hazardous chemicals. Under the Clean Air Act Amendments of 1990, companies were required to submit, beginning in 1999, a risk management plan (RMP) detailing quantities of specific hazardous chemicals stored on-site, accident prevention and emergency response plans, history of accidental releases, and an off-site consequence analysis (OCA) that includes the potential effects of worst-case spills on the surrounding community. The information will still be available to the public, but the agency concluded that the community's right to know through Web-based disclosure was overshadowed by the concern that such information makes it too easy for terrorists to cause catastrophic toxic releases.[17] In June 1999, the U.S. Senate passed a bill limiting public access to this information.[18]

Voluntary Programs

In a less confrontational format, the EPA also employs voluntary programs to encourage proactive industry efforts at pollution control. Although there are many examples of such programs, four are discussed here. The first is the Industrial Toxics Emissions Reduction Program, commonly referred to as the 33/50 Program. Under this program, participating companies agreed to reduce emissions of seventeen priority chemicals by 33 percent through mid-1992 and to achieve a further 50 percent reduction by 1995. One enticement used to gain participation was a national media campaign giving public recognition to member companies.

The second program, the Green Lights Program, was launched in January 1991 to encourage businesses to install energy-efficient lighting. Lighting accounts for 20 to 25 percent of electricity use in the United States, and the EPA estimates that efficient lighting could reduce the country's electricity demand by more than 10 percent, resulting in a net savings of $17 billion for ratepayers and a reduction of 202 million metric tons of carbon dioxide emissions. More than 1,900 corporations, hospitals, schools, utilities, and state and local governments have signed on to the program with the expectation that lighting upgrades will yield more efficient use of electricity while reducing electric bills. The average internal rate of return on investments in lighting upgrades by Green Lights partners is estimated to be 28 percent.[19]

The third program, the Common Sense Initiative (CSI), was launched in 1994 as an attempt to gain industry participation in developing standards for the industry as a whole rather than continuing a pollutant-by-pollutant approach to protecting the environment. In the program's first trial, the EPA worked with representatives from six pilot industries: automobile manufacturing, computers and electronics, iron and steel, metal finishing and plating, petroleum refining, and printing. Subcommittees were formed with representatives from industry, environmental organizations, labor unions, environmental justice groups, and federal, state, and local governments. They developed a blueprint for each industry based on six goals: review major rules and regulations as they apply to each industry; make pollution prevention a guiding principle inherent in the regulatory system; make environmental information easier for industry to provide and more accessible to the public; enforce flexibility to avoid punishing companies that are earnestly working to comply; improve the permitting process; and encourage technological development. EPA administrator Carol Browner called CSI "a fundamentally new way of protecting our environment."[20]

The final example is Project XL (Environmental Excellence and Leadership), a program established to give exemplary individual companies greater flexibility in achieving environmental objectives, provided they reduce discharges below current regulatory standards. The program does not involve modification of existing regulations but allows companies an alternative that they can choose on a voluntary basis. Building on the principles of the Common Sense Initiative, the program has five key components. First, an extensive environmental review of the participating facility is conducted to establish baseline conditions. Second, the facility develops an alternative strategy for emissions reductions to surpass existing standards. Third, the community is given an opportunity to provide input regarding the strategy. Fourth, the EPA approves the strategy, which will replace existing regulatory requirements. Finally, monitoring and reporting are carried out to audit progress with the strategy.

Market Incentives

In the late 1980s, the discourse on mainstream environmental policy, particularly within economic circles, focused on dismantling the command-and-control structure of regulation in favor of market incentives that entice firms to seek their own economic interests through protecting the environment. Although bottle-bill laws had been in effect since the early 1980s, the early 1990s witnessed the introduction of more aggressive market incentive programs that included deposit-refund systems, effluent taxes, and tradable permit schemes. The objective of these market incentive schemes is to place an economic price on pollution so that corporations can work the cost of the polluting activities into their strategic planning. Some observers believe that such a tactic involves moral issues that cannot be overlooked. Others counter that responses from a market system must employ market tools and that morals and ethics are not a consideration (see box 2.1).

Box 2.1. Is It Immoral to "Buy the Right to Pollute"?

Market incentives are designed to place a discreet economic value on the environment, as well as the measures corporations may use to protect it. In this way, the values of the market are brought to bear on protecting the environment. But some feel that market values are unable to capture the full value of the environment and therefore are inappropriate. These people see the underlying rationale for environmental protection as morally based. Therefore, they see as immoral any subjugation of environmental value to the interests of the economy. Environmental economists bristle at this line of reasoning. In fact, most environmental economists are loath to use the term "buy the right to pollute" and the connotation it presumes. This has been the form of an ongoing debate among scholars, most recently over the use of market incentives to reduce the threat from climate change. In 1997, the debate played out on the editorial page of the *New York Times*. Is it immoral to buy the right to pollute? Consider the views of these four academic experts.

It's Immoral to Buy the Right to Pollute[*]
Michael J. Sandel, Harvard University

At the conference on global warming in Kyoto, Japan, the United States found itself at loggerheads with developing nations on two important issues: The United States wanted those countries to commit themselves to restraints on emissions, and it wanted any agreement to include a trading scheme that would let countries buy and sell the right to pollute. The Administration was right on the first point, but wrong on the second. Creating an international market in emission credits would make it easier for us to meet our obligations under the treaty but [would] undermine the ethic we should be trying to foster on the environment.

Indeed, China and India threatened to torpedo the talks over the issue. They were afraid that such trading would enable rich countries to buy their way out of commitments to reduce greenhouse gases. In the end, the developing nations agreed to allow some emissions trading among developed countries, with details to be negotiated next year [in 1998].

The Clinton Administration has made emission trading a centerpiece of its environmental policy. Creating an international market for emissions, it argues, is a more efficient way to reduce pollution than imposing fixed levels for each country. Trading in greenhouse gases could also make compliance cheaper and less painful for the United States, which could pay to reduce some other country's carbon dioxide emissions rather than reduce its own. For example, the United States might find it cheaper (and politically palatable) to pay to update an old coal-burning factory in a developing country than to tax gas-guzzling sports utility vehicles at home.

Since the aim is to limit the global level of these gases, one might ask, what difference does it make which places on the planet send less carbon to the sky? It may make no difference from the standpoint of the heavens, but it does make a political difference. Despite the efficiency of international emissions trading, such a system is objectionable for three reasons.

First, it creates loopholes that could enable wealthy countries to evade their obligations. Under the Kyoto formula, for example, the United States could take advantage of the fact that Russia has already reduced its emissions 30 percent since 1990, not through energy efficiencies but through economic decline. The United States could buy excess credits from Russia, and count them toward meeting our obligations under the treaty.

Second, turning pollution into a commodity to be bought and sold removes the moral stigma that is properly associated with it. If a company or a country is fined for spewing excessive pollutants into the air, the community conveys its judgment that the polluter has done something wrong. A fee, on the other hand, makes pollution just another cost of doing business, like wages, benefits and rent.

The distinction between a fine and a fee for despoiling the environment is not one we should give up too easily. Suppose there were a $100 fine for throwing a beer can into the Grand Canyon, and a wealthy hiker decided to pay $100 for the convenience. Would there be nothing wrong in his treating the fine as if it were simply an expensive dumping charge? Or consider the fine for parking in a place reserved for the disabled. If a busy contractor needs to park near his building site and is willing to pay the fine, is there nothing wrong with his treating that space as an expensive parking lot?

In effacing the distinction between a fine and a fee, emission trading is like a recent proposal to open carpool lanes on Los Angeles freeways to drivers without passengers who are willing to pay a fee. Such drivers are now fined for slipping into carpool lanes; under the market proposal, they would enjoy a quicker commute without opprobrium.

A third objection to emission trading among countries is that it may undermine the sense of shared responsibility that increased global cooperation requires. Consider an illustration drawn from an autumn ritual: raking fallen leaves into great piles and lighting bonfires. Imagine a neighborhood where each family agrees to have only one small bonfire a year. But they also agree that families can buy and sell their bonfire permits as they choose. The family in the mansion on the hill buys permits from its neighbors— paying them, in effect, to lug their leaves to the town compost heap. The market works, and pollution is reduced, but without the spirit of shared sacrifice that might have been produced had no market intervened. Those who have sold their permits, and those who

(continues)

Box 2.1. *Continued*

have bought them, come to regard the bonfires less as an offense against clean air than as a luxury, a status symbol that can be bought and sold. And the resentment against the family in the mansion makes future, more demanding forms of cooperation more difficult to achieve.

Of course, many countries that attended the Kyoto conference have already made cooperation elusive. They have not yet agreed to restrict their emissions at all. Their refusal undermines the prospect of a global environment ethic as surely as does our pollution trading scheme. But the United States would have more suasion if these developing countries could not rightly complain that trading in emissions allows wealthy nations to buy their way out of global obligations.

What's Immoral?[†]
Robert Stavins, Harvard University

The ink is barely dry on the Kyoto protocol, but Michael J. Sandel argues that the agreement's emissions-trading provisions, supported by the Clinton Administration, will foster "immoral" behavior. Was it immoral when the United States used the tradable permit system among refineries to phase leaded gasoline out of the market in the 1980's more rapidly than anyone had anticipated and at a savings of $250 million a year? Is it now immoral that we are reducing acid rain by half through a tradable permit system among electrical utilities, reducing emissions (sulfur dioxide) faster than anyone had predicted and saving up to $1 billion a year for electricity consumers? Is that why the Environmental Defense Fund and others have worked so tirelessly and effectively to implement these emissions-trading programs?

Not If, But How Much[‡]
Eric Maskin, Harvard University

Michael J. Sandel neglects an important distinction in his argument against tradable emission credits. The examples he gives of immoral acts—throwing beer cans into the Grand Canyon or parking in spots reserved for the disabled—are discrete choices: one can do them or not do them, and society can therefore reasonably ban them outright. But virtually any manufacturing activity entails the creation of some pollution. So the question is not will we pollute, but rather how much. Further, if there is to be pollution, shouldn't we try to trade it off against economic consequences? Such a trade-off is facilitated by tradable rights.

Technology, Not Stigma[§]
Sanford Gaines, University of Houston

Michael J. Sandel invokes a moral argument against emissions trading in the context of reducing greenhouse gas emissions. Maintaining a moral stigma on pollution makes sense for hazardous substances where polluters have choices for reducing the pollution. But global warming is not such a situation. Does Mr. Sandel really believe he is behaving badly when he cooks his dinner, switches on a light or turns on a computer? These activities result in emissions of carbon dioxide. Or is it his utility that should be stigmatized, perhaps for not using nuclear power? To reduce greenhouse gas emissions, producers and consumers alike need to adopt new technologies. That's a perfect situation to use the power of the market. Mr. Sandel should reserve his moral outrage for those who don't even want the chance to buy the right to pollute because they refuse to accept that the planet can no longer afford cheap energy.

Source: The New York Times © 1998. All rights reserved. Used with permission.

[*] M. Sandel, "It's Immoral to Buy the Right to Pollute," editorial, *New York Times*, 15 December 1997, A19. Michael J. Sandel is a professor of government at Harvard Univer-

sity and author of *Democracy's Discontent: America in Search of a Public Philosophy* (Cambridge, Mass.: Harvard University Press, Belknap Press, 1996).

[†] R. Stavins, "What's Immoral?" letter to the editor, *New York Times*, 17 December 1997, A20.

[‡] E. Maskin, "Not If, But How Much," letter to the editor, *New York Times*, 17 December 1997, A20.

[§] S. Gaines, "Technology, Not Stigma," letter to the editor, *New York Times*, 17 December 1997, A20.

Deposit-Refund Systems

Most people are familiar with the format of deposit-refund systems through the bottle-bill programs prevalent in the United States. Under a deposit-refund system, consumers pay a surcharge when purchasing an item (in this case a bottled beverage), which is refunded when the used product or empty container is returned to an approved center. Such a system is intended to offset any financial incentive that may exist for improper disposal. It is important that the material on which the deposit is applied be largely unchanged through use to allow easy return and that the fee assessed be large enough to counter any financial incentive to dispose of the material in another way. Some candidates for a deposit-refund system include lead-acid batteries, used motor oil, and automobile tires.[21] A proposed deposit-refund system in Japan would require consumers to return household appliances for recycling. These would include television sets, refrigerators, washing machines, and air conditioners.[22]

Another important consideration in developing a deposit-refund system is the question of who should be responsible for accepting the waste material. Candidates include the original producer, the original retailer, a special redemption center, and the local municipality. Notice that two of these candidates presently collect bottles and cans in most states in the United States. Curbside recycling programs have flourished in recent years, yet bottle bills have been on the books, in most cases, for at least a decade. Although this variety of options has resulted in an increase in the number of people who "regularly recycle" bottles and cans, from 46 to 58 percent from 1990 to 1992 (and an increase in the number of people who recycle newspapers from 26 to 43 percent),[23] the redundancy has resulted in critics calling for the end of bottle bills in favor of total reliance on curbside recycling.[24]

Pollution Charges

The most direct way to impose a cost on pollution is through application of an effluent fee or emission fee. Rather than controls being imposed on specific pollution-generating activities or taxes assessed on the basis of amount of product created (such as the Superfund tax imposed per unit of chemical output), a fee could be imposed for every unit of pollution discharged into a river or into the air. One benefit of such a tax is that it can encourage a company to perform a cost–benefit analysis of reducing or eliminating the production of a certain waste stream. The difficulties lie in the government's ability to predetermine the level of tax necessary to drive specific reductions of a given pollutant. Nevertheless, one recently debated candidate for an emission fee is the reduction of carbon dioxide emissions to control global climate change.[25]

Marketable Permit Systems

Marketable or tradable permits can work in the same way as pollution charges, but with two caveats. First, such a program relieves the government of the responsibility for setting the level of the tax, relying on the market instead. Second, by going beyond the established standard, corporations can shift the tax to a subsidy paid by other companies. Explained simply, the government sets a goal for pollution control and companies are left to pursue it. Those that meet the standard are in compliance with the law. If a company does nothing more, this type of program has the same effect as the performance standards that have been in place since the 1970s. But companies are free to surpass the standard and receive credit for each unit of pollution reduction beyond that required by law. They may then bank these credits for use at a later date, or they may sell them to another company that is unable to meet the standard. Of course, the only reason why a company would buy credits is that the cost of meeting the standard is greater than the price of the permit. Such a transaction reduces the aggregate cost of pollution control with the same reduction in pollution.

To see exactly how this works, consider the following example. Two companies are in the business of making widgets: Old Soot Industries (OS) and Squeaky Kleen Inc. (SK). Each company produces 2,000 tons of pollution per year, as the present standard allows. But under a tradable permit program, a new standard is set at 1,500 tons per year. Because OS operates a very old plant, it costs the company more to reduce the pollution than is the case for SK, which has a brand-new, state-of-the-art plant. Specifically, OS's costs are $300 per ton and SK's are $200 per ton. If both companies are forced to achieve the same standard, the compliance costs of a reduction of 500 tons per year will be $150,000 (OS) plus $100,000 (SK), for a total of $250,000—see table 2.1.

But if SK reduces emissions to 1,000 tons per year at a total cost of $200,000 and sells the extra 500 tons of pollution to OS for $140,000, the total expenditures equal $200,000. For the same reduction in emissions, $50,000 is saved while incentives are created for the clean company to profit by shifting the cost burden to the dirtier plant. Compliance costs for the new, clean company are only $60,000, whereas those for the

Table 2.1. Compliance Costs *without* an Emissions Trading Scheme

	Old Soot Industries	Squeaky Kleen
Present emissions	2,000 tpy	2,000 tpy
New standard	1,500 tpy	1,500 tpy
Reduction	500 tpy	500 tpy
Costs	$300/ton	$200/ton
Total cost	($150,000)	($100,000)

Table 2.2. Compliance Costs *with* an Emissions Trading Scheme

	Old Soot Industries	*Squeaky Kleen*
Present emissions	2,000 tpy	2,000 tpy
New standard	1,500 tpy	1,500 tpy
Reduction	0 tpy	1,000 tpy
Costs	$300/ton	$200/ton
Total costs	$0	($200,000)
Trade of 500 tons	($140,000)	$140,000
Total costs	($140,000)	($60,000)

old, dirty company are $140,000—see table 2.2. Adding an additional wrinkle to the formula, individuals can purchase permits and retire them, thus driving up the cost of permits and ultimately decreasing the amount of pollution and increasing the cost of producing it.[26]

Do marketable permits work? Some complications can arise. First, if a region of the country is heavily populated by dirty industries that buy permits from other regions, there are localized increases in pollution. This creates equity issues in the distribution of polluting activities. Second, for some people, there may be a stigma associated with "buying the right to pollute," which would drive some to resist such programs. Some observers argue that buying pollution credits allows rich companies, individuals, and countries to pollute while those unable to afford such a "luxury" are forced to comply.[27] Others argue that market incentives are appropriate only in certain circumstances. Where there are serious public and environmental health issues, they argue that solutions should not be relegated to the market. Instead, they believe that outright bans are the only viable option (see box 2.2).

Box 2.2. Why Not Skip All the Complicated Compliance Schemes and Simply Ban Dangerous Chemicals?

Chlorine is the main component of some of the most controversial substances known to humankind, including banned substances such as chlorofluorocarbons (CFCs), polychlorinated biphenyls (PCBs), DDT, and dioxin. In their book *Our Stolen Future,*[*] Theo Colborn, Dianne Dumanoski, and John Peterson Myers advance the argument that synthetic chemicals (chiefly chlorine-containing compounds) mimic natural hormones such as estrogen and disrupt vital human biological processes such as fertility and fetal development. The authors argue that these so-called endocrine-disrupting chemicals, which include chemicals used in plastics, detergents, and pesticides, may be causing a decline in male sperm counts, an epidemic of breast and prostate cancer, and fetal effects that emerge later such as reduced intelligence, hyperactivity, and violent behavior. The book raises the question of whether we will poison ourselves to death unless some drastic action is taken. It prompted lawmakers to ask, How should a regulatory response be fashioned?

(continues)

Box 2.2. *Continued*

Not related to the issue of endocrine disruptor, the Environmental Protection Agency's Science Advisory Board (SAB) called for adoption of an integrated approach to environmental protection in 1999, moving away from a chemical-by-chemical approach to an aggregate approach to rule making.[†] Considering the issue of chlorine hazards and integrated rule making, should the agency develop some kind of program for the eventual elimination of chlorine rather than initiate incremental bans on chlorine-containing products (of which there are more than 15,000)? In cases in which the potential consequences are so severe and the prevalence of the hazard so pervasive, why not skip the complicated compliance schemes and simply ban the dangerous chemicals?

Is an all-out ban a reasonable way to protect the environment? Is virtual elimination of element 17 on the periodic table a rational approach? Many scientists argue that the data are not conclusive enough for them to state the effects of endocrine disrupters with certainty. Further, although synthetic chemicals can cause these effects, naturally occurring hormones in plants have the same effects. Economically, a ban on the substance would initiate widespread changes in the way society functions. Chlorine is a central component of the world market for synthetic materials. It is used in products as diverse as magnetic tape, surgical membranes, oil additives, electronic parts, pharmaceuticals, and flavoring extracts as well as in water disinfection.

Environmentalists worry that we are ignoring the signs of a dangerous threat similar to that identified in the early 1960s when Rachel Carson wrote about the dangers of harmful pesticides in *Silent Spring*.[‡] How might policy makers proceed? Could market incentives be a useful tool in phasing out chlorine compounds? Or in the face of such a potentially serious threat, should we not even try to balance economic and environmental considerations and simply take dramatic and decisive action? Can such a drastic effort bring about the best industrial and technological response?

[*] T. Colborn, D. Dumanoski, and J. P. Myers, *Our Stolen Future: Are We Threatening Our Fertility, Intelligence, and Survival? A Scientific Detective Story* (New York: E. P. Dutton & Company, 1996).

[†] "Panel Calls for New Approach to Environmental Protection," *Daily Environment Report*, 7 May 1999, A7.

[‡] R. Carson, *Silent Spring* (Boston: Houghton Mifflin Company, 1962).

Third, many companies may be unsure of how to trade in this type of commodity. To reduce transaction costs, a public auction of pollution permits is conducted every March by the Chicago Board of Trade. Yet executives in the oil, utility, and manufacturing industries may still be unfamiliar with the intricacies of commodity trading or feel unequipped to deal with them. This organizational resistance can translate into an opportunity for brokerage companies to offer their expertise to companies that need it. Cantor Fitzgerald Securities Corporation, for example, has positioned its Environmental Brokerage Services department to become the "hub" for the emissions allowance market. The company does not act as a principal by putting its own capital at risk but instead acts as an agent, collecting commissions for matching buyers and sellers in the secondary market for emission credits.[28]

Results have varied in the application of marketable permits. They were first applied, with great success, in the required phaseout of leaded gasoline in the 1980s. By allowing refiners to trade in lead permits, the program achieved its objective more rapidly than anticipated and at an estimated savings of $250 million per year. Other trading programs, such as a program developed in southern California, have found success at the local level. This innovative program uses an electronic trading system called Automated Credit Exchange (ACE), which allows participating companies, such as the Unocal Corporation and the Chevron Corporation, to log on to the electronic trading floor and make trades themselves. During one weeklong trading session in 1997, 2.9 million pounds of smog was traded, at a value of about $2.2 million. Credit prices during the session ranged from $.02 per pound for that year to more than $1 per pound for the credits to pollute in 2000. Participants were allowed to buy and sell credits for as far in advance as 2010.[29]

However, in the control of sulfur dioxide emissions under the Clean Air Act Amendments of 1990, marketable permits have performed below expectations.[30] Economic models predicted that utilities with a greater potential to reduce emissions would do so, collect permits for their overcompliance, and sell them to other utilities to make additional profits. However, companies began by overcomplying with the regulations and stockpiling the permits in anticipation of using them later, to keep their aging plants open when the standards became more stringent in 2000. The average market price for a ton of sulfur dioxide fell steadily from $250 in 1992 to $140 in 1995 to a mere $68 in 1996.[31]

But as 2000 approached and the standards became tighter, the permits increased in value. In 1997, a flurry of trading drove the average price back up to $100 as speculation caused some to begin to snatch up the low-priced permits.[32] In 1999, the Chicago Board of Trade announced a record $53 million in pollution trading transactions. Spot allowances that could be used immediately totaled 150,010 allowances; spot allowances for use in 2006 totaled 125,000. (Each spot bid allows the owner to emit one ton of sulfur dioxide.) The highest price for a spot allowance was $230, with an average overall price of $207. The American Electric Power Company (AEP) was the largest purchaser, accounting for 49.6 percent of the bids.[33]

One reason why the permit prices initially remained low was the unexpectedly low cost of low-sulfur coal. Utilities could meet the Clean Air Act standards either by installing scrubbers at a cost of $100 million or more or by switching their fuel source from high- to low-sulfur coal. Contrary to economic forecasts, prices of low-sulfur coal did not rise but actually fell to as low as 12 percent below prices for high-sulfur coal. Although nationwide coal production hit a record 1.05 billion tons in 1999, almost 1,000 mines closed during the 1990s, nearly all of them east of the Mississippi River, where high-sulfur coal is found.[34] With the shift in fuel source, production of high-sulfur coal in the long-dominant East fell by 14 percent in the 1990s while production of low-sulfur coal in the West jumped by 26 percent. It was a double-edged sword: Some environmentalists lamented that the switch to low-sulfur fuel, although better for air quality, encouraged the use of strip mining, the dominant method for mining low-sulfur coal in the West.

Regulatory Compliance and Environmental Strategy

By employing such a wide range of compliance mechanisms, the EPA operates in a slightly schizophrenic manner, using both the stick and the carrot to prompt corporate environmental action as well as various methods in between: threatening extreme penalties (criminal enforcement), dictating standards (command and control), appealing to the profit motive (market incentives), seeking cooperative partnerships (voluntary programs), and imposing embarrassment (forced disclosure). Corporate executives must find ways to maneuver through this complicated minefield.

In one route, capitalizing on the opportunities created by cooperative programs and flexible options, companies are striving to convince the EPA to loosen its grip even further. In 1990, the Amoco Corporation made an argument for more flexibility through the results of a research partnership it undertook with the EPA to study possibilities for reducing pollution at its refinery in Yorktown, Virginia. (To add credibility to the effort, the environmental research group Resources for the Future was commissioned for external peer review.) It was a bold step for an oil company to allow both a regulating agency and an environmental group access to one of its major refineries. Many inside the firm (and inside the industry) speculated that this would expose Amoco to increased scrutiny by enforcement agencies and activists. Despite these fears, Amoco executives felt vindicated because the study showed tremendous opportunities for more cost-effective solutions to environmental problems through flexible regulatory control.

At a cost of $2.3 million (of which Amoco paid 70 percent and the EPA paid 30 percent), Amoco executives discovered that greater regulatory flexibility would allow for greater reductions in emissions while reducing costs. Specifically, Amoco could achieve the level of emission reductions required by the Clean Air Act but at one-quarter of the cost—$10 million versus $40 million. This could be achieved if the company were allowed to choose where the money should be spent rather than responding to EPA-dictated standards. Empowered by these results, Amoco's EH&S vice president challenged EPA control, arguing that "if you give this company a mark on the wall and tell them to go for it, I have no doubt as to their capability to achieve it."[35] The Yorktown example also empowered others to argue that environmental regulation is too prescriptive and can be, at times, contrary to environmental objectives.

Whereas the Amoco Yorktown example revealed the potential benefits of creative regulatory controls, a project carried out by the Unocal Corporation revealed how they can work in practice. Unocal operates a refinery in the Los Angeles Basin, an area with some of the most stringent controls on hydrocarbon and nitrogen oxide emissions. Through a collaborative effort with the state of California and the general public, Unocal found an economically efficient solution to its compliance challenge. Rather than following prescribed standards for reducing emissions at its facilities, the company achieved mandated emission reductions at a reduced cost through a car-scrapping business. Unocal established a program in 1990 to purchase older, higher-polluting pre-1971 vehicles at $600 apiece and destroy them. By measuring the tailpipe emissions of each vehicle and extrapolating the amount of miles the vehicle would have been driven, the company calculated that it had removed nearly 13 million pounds of pollution per year at one-tenth the cost and in one-tenth the time that would have been expended had the reductions been made at the refinery.[36] Unocal incorporated the unit that operates the program (called ECO-SCRAP, Inc.) and now sells its services on the open market. Any company in the Los Angeles Basin that must reduce its emissions of airborne hydrocarbons and nitrogen oxides can commission ECO-SCRAP to retire an equivalent number of old cars instead.

This kind of creativity will become central to a strategic response to environmental protection as regulations become more flexible over time. Some companies will find opportunities in such flexibility and uncertainty, whereas others may continue to resist. As time goes on, resistance will increasingly be a luxury. For example, some countries are pushing regulations that will place the burden of pollution control entirely on the corporation. The Norwegians have mandated that manufacturers take back electronic products, and, as mentioned earlier, the Japanese have proposed mandated take-back for household appliances. In Sweden, regulations now require the country's automakers, the Volvo Car Corporation and Saab Automobile AB, as well as importers to take back and recycle their cars when they reach the end of their useful life. The industry must recover 85 percent of the materials in these cars through reuse, recycling, or incineration, with energy recovery, by the year 2002, and the amount rises to 95 percent in 2015. The current European Union (EU) average is about 75 percent.[37] In 1999, EU ministers followed suit, approving End-of-Life Vehicle (ELV) legislation, which requires that carmakers take back vehicles beginning in January 2001 for new cars and 2006 for all cars.[38] Developing an effective strategic response will involve a complete redefinition of the materials used to make an automobile and the processes by which it is constructed. In effect, it represents a redefinition of the business of making automobiles.

This kind of economic transformation is not unlike those that are under way at all times. For example, as consumer needs change and technology advances, certain industries face new competitive environments, some declining while others rise to fill their places: The typewriter industry was virtually eliminated by the computer in the early 1980s; the compact disc replaced the phonograph album in the mid-1980s; the 1984 dissolution of the Bell System wrought structural changes in the telecommunications industry. Environmental protection represents just such a shift, moving us away from the purely exploitive view of the environment that carried us through the past century and toward a stewardship view incorporating a new blend of interests that will carry us through the next century. These new interests are indicative of the evolving nature of business and the economy.[39]

Corporate managers can resist or lament this evolution, or they can accept its inevitability, assessing its meaning and capitalizing on the opportunities it creates. This is a challenge that innovative companies will aggressively pursue. As one former refinery manager for Amoco explained, "When we push for more flexible [regulatory] options, I'm taking a lot on faith. I have to believe that we have engineers who know our processes a lot better than some 25 year old [EPA] engineer in Cincinnati or at Research Triangle Park."[40] Framing the necessary changes as a market adjustment, these process engineers will be able to find strategic opportunities that those who remain in the environmental management mind-set overlook.

Conclusion

Regulation takes many forms in both its focus and its format. One can no longer think of regulatory compliance as a clearly defined and precise notion. Regulatory controls (on both the domestic level and the international level) are growing in complexity, and this change is being promoted by both government and industry. Since 1995, the EPA has been set on a series of "high-priority and significant actions aimed at improving the current regulatory system and laying the groundwork for a new system of environmental protection." These efforts are designed to "achieve better environmental results through the use of innovative and flexible approaches to environmental protection" and to "make it easier for businesses to comply with environmental laws by offering them compliance assistance and incentives to prevent pollution at its source."[41] Supporting such a move, the Global Environmental Management Initiative,[42] a collective of representatives from leading corporations, released a report in 1999 suggesting that incentives be used in tandem with traditional command-and-control regulation to obtain better environmental results.[43]

In response to both internal and external pressures, domestic regulations are expanding in scope and utilizing mechanisms that trigger responses more central to the core objectives of the firm. This creates strategic challenges for the firm. For example, in the face of a marketable permit program under the Clean Air Act Amendments of 1990, should the chief executive officer of a major U.S. utility consider trading in the commodity market of pollution permits? The answer has significantly more strategic considerations than does a mechanical response to standard command-and-control formats. The repertoire of possible actions is greater, and the anticipated outcome is less certain.

In the end, with this uncertainty comes either threat or opportunity. Corporate managers who remain fixed on the notion of environmental management may see only a threat, but for those who adopt a strategic approach, opportunities that were previously hidden will become visible. Environmental regulation need not be viewed purely as a restraint on market activities; rather, it can be seen as a tool for working to achieve market growth.

Further Reading

Brown, L. *State of the World.* New York: W. W. Norton & Company, 1998; published annually.
Brown, L., C. Flavin, and H. Kane. *Vital Signs.* New York: W. W. Norton & Company, 1998; published annually.
Environmental Protection Agency. *The Guardian: EPA's Formative Years, 1970–1993.* Washington, D.C.: U.S. Government Printing Office, 1993.
———. *The Guardian: Origins of the EPA.* Washington, D.C.: U.S. Government Printing Office, 1992.
———. *U.S. EPA Oral History Interview No. 1: William D. Ruckelshaus.* Washington, D.C.: U.S. Government Printing Office, 1993.
———. *U.S. EPA Oral History Interview No. 2: Russell E. Train.* Washington, D.C.: U.S. Government Printing Office, 1993.
Hahn, R., and R. Stavins. "Incentive-Based Environmental Regulation: A New Era from an Old Idea." *Ecology Law Quarterly* 18, no. 1 (1991): 1–42.
Landy, M., M. Roberts, and S. Thomas. *The Environmental Protection Agency: Asking the Wrong Questions.* New York: Oxford University Press, 1990.
Portney, P., ed. *Public Policies for Environmental Protection.* Washington, D.C.: Resources for the Future, 1990.

Tietenberg, T. *Environmental and Natural Resource Economics.* New York: HarperCollins Publishing Company, 1992.

World Resources Institute. *World Resources.* New York: Oxford University Press, 1998; published annually.

Chapter 3

INTERNATIONAL DRIVERS

Regulatory pressures do not stop at national borders. Just as goods and services are traded increasingly in global markets, environmental concerns are transferring increasingly across international borders. This transfer creates some challenging questions regarding environmental protection and business strategy, both domestically and abroad. For example, are free trade and environmental protection incompatible? Do trade agreements such as the General Agreement on Tariffs and Trade (GATT) and the North American Free Trade Agreement (NAFTA) transfer jobs and facilities to countries with less stringent standards? Do they challenge national sovereignty in defining domestic environmental legislation? Are international environmental agreements a form of "eco-colonialism," a type of trade barrier, or the proper establishment of international protocols for protecting the global commons? All of these questions permeate discussions of environmental strategy in the international arena. To address them, we begin by analyzing the basic justification for international "free" trade—the Ricardian model of comparative advantage.[1]

Comparative Advantage, Trade, and Environmental Protection[2]

The principle of comparative advantage is built on two basic notions. First, countries trade because they are different from one another in terms of labor, capital, and resources. Through trade, they can benefit from these differences by reaching an agreement that allows each country to do what it does comparatively well. Second, countries trade in order to achieve economies of scale in production. That is, if each country produces a limited range of goods, it can produce each of these goods on a larger and more efficient scale than would be possible if it tried to produce everything.

Consider an example of two countries—Merlot and Angus. Merlot has steep, fertile valleys for growing grapes. Angus has open, grassy plains for raising cattle. Each country could produce both wine and beef, but the relative costs would be quite different. Beef produced in Merlot would be more expensive and of poorer quality than that produced in Angus. Wine produced in Angus would be more expensive and of poorer quality than that from Merlot. In a world of no trade, the consumers in each country would pay more for a lower-quality dinner of steak and wine than they would in a world of free trade. By exploiting each country's comparative advantage, Merlot could produce primarily wine, and Angus, primarily beef. The price of each good would be reduced, overall quality would increase, and through international trade, the citizens of each country would pay less for a better evening meal.

This is a very simple example of the way free trade works in theory. In a real-world context, the issue is, of course, more complex. In the real world, a broad range of goods and services are traded among countries with various cultures, values, standards, and needs. The issue of environmental protection is central to these differences. Countries prioritize economic and environmental issues differently in trying to achieve an improved quality of life. To understand the implications of these differences, Jagdish Bhagwati of Columbia University notes that we must draw a distinction between two kinds of international environmental problems, those that are intrinsically domestic and those that are intrinsically transnational.[3] For example, the pollution of the Great Salt Lake, which lies entirely within the borders of the United States, is a problem that is intrinsically domestic. The migration of sulfur dioxide emissions from power plants in the American Midwest to eastern Canada and their precipitation as acid rain is a transnational problem. The inequity of the latter case clearly requires cooperative, multilateral solutions among trading partners. But the development of solutions in the former case is where free-trade issues become problematic.

Intrinsically domestic environmental problems evoke economic concerns among trading partners. The problem is that, although comparative advantage increases competition and competition decreases costs, costs can be decreased in two ways: first, by increasing efficiency, and second, by lowering standards (on pollution control, worker safety, child or slave labor, wages, health care, and so on).[4] Industry fears that a disparity in environmental standards among countries will allow an unfair comparative advantage for businesses in countries with the lowest standards. Environmentalists fear that this disparity will encourage environmental hazards to migrate to developing countries as these countries are forced to accept them for the trade dollars they provide (see box 3.1).

Box 3.1. How Far Should Free Trade Go with Respect to the Environment?

If comparative advantage exploits the advantages a country possesses in providing cheaper goods and services, should this notion be extended to the disposal of pollution? Should a country with the resources to dispose of toxic pollution exploit its comparative advantage in the world marketplace? This very notion was suggested in an internal memorandum from Lawrence Summers, chief economist for the World Bank, to some colleagues in December 1992. Its contents were published, much to the embarrassment of the World Bank, in the *Economist.*[*] The language may be a little coarse, but the merits of the argument are challenging on purely economic terms.

> Just between you and me, shouldn't the World Bank be encouraging more migration of the dirty industries to the LDCs [less developed countries]? I can think of three reasons:

(continues)

Box 3.1. *Continued*

(1) The measurement of the costs of health-impairing pollution depends on the forgone earnings from increased morbidity and mortality. From this point of view a given amount of health-impairing pollution should be done in the country with the lowest cost, which will be the country with the lowest wages. I think that the economic logic behind dumping a load of toxic waste in the lowest wage country is impeccable and we should face up to that.

(2) The costs of pollution are likely to be non-linear as the initial increments of pollution probably have very low cost. I've always thought that under-populated countries in Africa are vastly inefficiently low [sic] compared to Los Angeles or Mexico City. Only the lamentable fact that so much pollution is generated by non-tradable industries (transport, electrical generation) and that the unit transport costs of solid waste are so high prevent world-welfare-enhancing trade in air pollution and waste.

(3) The demand for a clean environment for aesthetic and health reasons is likely to have very high income-elasticity. The concern over an agent that causes a one in a million change in the odds of prostate cancer is obviously going to be much higher in a country where under-5 mortality is 200 per thousand. Also, much of the concern over individual atmospheric discharge is about visibility-impairing particulates. These discharges may have very little direct health impact. Clearly trade in goods that embody aesthetic pollution concerns could be welfare-enhancing. While production is mobile the consumption of pretty air is a non-tradable.

The problem with the arguments against all of these proposals for more pollution in LDCs (intrinsic rights to certain goods, moral reasons, social concerns, lack of adequate markets, etc.) could be turned around and used more or less effectively against every bank proposal for liberalization.

In a subsequent letter to the *Economist*, Summers clarified his position, stating that it "is not my view, the World Bank's view, or that of any sane person that pollution should be encouraged anywhere, or that dumping of untreated toxic wastes near the homes of poor people is morally or economically defensible. My memo tried to sharpen the debate on important issues by taking as narrow-minded an economic perspective as possible."[†] His argument presents a critical challenge to those who support both free trade and a clean environment. Can the quandary of his argument be resolved while satisfying both sets of objectives?

[*] "Let Them Eat Pollution," *Economist*, 8 February 1992, 66.

[†] L. Summers, "Polluting the Poor," letter to the editor, *Economist*, 15 February 1992, 6.

Free-trade proponents counter that economic growth and environmental protection go hand in hand and that economic growth must precede environmental controls. As standards of living rise, people will gain both the resources to maintain a clean environment and the desire to do so. Without a financial injection from economic development, they argue, developing countries will never have the opportunity to address the basic issues of living standards before addressing environmental concerns. So as free trade raises the standard of living among trading partners, there is a "harmonizing up" of environmental standards and a leveling of the playing field. Supporters of this argument point to countries such as Germany and Japan, where the toughest environmental regulations correlate with some of the highest standards of living in the world.[5] In one study conducted at Princeton University, researchers found that in cities around the world, sulfur dioxide pollution fell as annual per capita income rose (with the exception of countries where per capita income was below $5,000).[6]

But industry, labor unions, and environmentalists jointly express concern about the time required for the harmonizing-up process. Even if economic standards do rise over the long term, they argue, both domestic business and the environment will be at a serious disadvantage in the short term. The U.S. carbon and steel alloy industry, for example, spends as much as 250 percent more on environmental controls as a percentage of gross domestic product than do its competitors in other countries.[7] Many observers fear that to counter this disadvantage, businesses will be forced to move to locations where environmental standards and costs of production are lower. The debate over environmental protection and free trade boils down to concerns about ensuring a level playing field while establishing standards for protecting the environment.

From here, the issue becomes even more complex. Where should this level playing field be set? Should Kenya be spending its limited resources for environmental protection on issues important to the United States (such as protection of endangered species and cleanup of hazardous waste sites) or issues important to Kenya (such as clean drinking water and sanitary sewage systems)? Even if two countries share the same environmental objectives, the specific pollutants and methods of control they focus on will very likely differ. For example, to improve the health of local communities, Mexico has a greater social incentive than does the United States to spend more on preventing dysentery than on reducing lead emissions from automobiles. Values are not universally accepted across national boundaries, and the important question is which values should prevail. No country possesses a "monopoly on virtue."[8] Americans place importance on protecting northern spotted owls; Indians consider the cow to be sacred; animal rights activists have no preference for one over the other and would probably support a ban on all endangerment (and slaughterhouses). At what point is the imposition of one country's environmental values on another proper protection of the common environment, and at what point is it eco-colonialism? Conversely, must a country with strict environmental standards justify those standards to countries with less stringent standards through an international governing body? These are the fundamental challenges of integrating environmental concerns into international trade. With this as a backdrop, we will first consider the environmental implications of several international trade agreements and then examine some international environmental agreements that are now in force.

International Trade Agreements[9]

There are three primary international trade agreements that have environmental implications. GATT is by far the oldest and most far reaching of these agreements and is discussed first, followed by an overview of the European Community and NAFTA.

General Agreement on Tariffs and Trade and the World Trade Organization

Created as a branch of the United Nations after World War II, the General Agreement on Tariffs and Trade (GATT) is both the framework and the governing institution for most international trade. In 1995, GATT was replaced by the World Trade Organization (WTO). The WTO's central premise in establishing fair and free trade is that of nondiscrimination. Simply put, WTO members are not allowed to take actions that discriminate between domestic products and imports, between goods sold in the home market and goods that are exported, and between imports of different countries. Countries may remain in compliance with the WTO while imposing a wide range of environmental product policies (such as command-and-control regulations, market incentive schemes, eco-labeling requirements, subsidies on "green" products, and even bans on "nongreen" products) as long as they are applied in a nondiscriminatory way. The WTO prohibits countries from developing domestic policies "which would constitute a means of arbitrary or unjustifiable discrimination between countries where the same conditions prevail, or a disguised restriction on international trade." These include measures "necessary to protect human, animal or plant life or health" and measures "relating to the conservation of exhaustible natural resources if such measures are made effective in conjunction with restrictions on domestic production or consumption."[10]

One notable dispute involving the WTO (GATT at the time), the dolphin–tuna case, demonstrated how the principles of the agreement would be applied to environmental protection. In 1991, the U.S. Department of Commerce imposed an embargo on tuna from Mexico, Venezuela, Vanuatu, and other countries because their by-catch of dolphins (dolphins killed in the process of harvesting the tuna) violated the terms of the Marine Mammal Protection Act of 1972 (MMPA). Yellowfin tuna tend to swim underneath schools of dolphins in tropical waters of the eastern Pacific Ocean. Fishermen round up the dolphins along with the tuna and then throw the dolphins overboard, usually dead. The MMPA prohibits persons or vessels under U.S. jurisdiction from taking any marine mammal in connection with the harvesting of fish. Importation of tuna harvested in tropical eastern Pacific waters is prohibited unless (1) the exporting country adopts regulations in conformity with U.S. regulations and reduces the incidental taking of marine mammals to no more than one and one-fourth the U.S. rate or (2) the exporting country restricts the use of purse seine fishing nets (which indiscriminately catch both tuna and dolphins) and demonstrates significant reductions in incidental dolphin mortality. Easily the largest tuna-fishing fleet in the tropical eastern Pacific belonged to Mexico, and the U.S. market was a very important outlet for its tuna.

Mexico complained to GATT, and a three-person arbitration panel sided with Mexico. The panel argued that the MMPA was inconsistent with GATT's nondiscrimination principle. A country had no right, the panel ruled, to enforce processing restrictions on other countries when those processes have no effect on the product itself. Furthermore, since the tuna was caught in international waters, panel members believed that the United States had no jurisdiction to enforce standards regarding animal health or conservation.[11] Further, since it was impossible for Mexican fishermen to know before the U.S. catch was made whether or not they were over the established one and one-fourth taking rate, the measures were deemed too unpredictable to be consistent with GATT. The restrictions were deemed to constitute trade protection rather than dolphin preservation and were nullified.

In short, GATT, or the WTO, recognizes four ways in which domestic regulations may be set such that they are not a restraint of trade: (1) the true intention of a regulation must be to protect the environment and not a local business; (2) a country may not impose restrictions in excess of what is necessary to achieve its stated objectives; (3) a country may not set standards that have no scientific basis; and (4) the standards must focus on aspects of the product and not on the process for developing it.

This last criterion was again put to the test in 1998, and again environmental protection lost. In April of that year, the WTO ruled that the United States could not ban the importation of shrimp from countries that do not protect endangered sea turtles from deadly entrapment in fishing nets. The United States requires domestic fishermen to use turtle-excluding devices (TEDs) that allow the large reptiles to pass through the nets unscathed and has negotiated agreements and provided funding to several countries for their adoption. However, the governments of India, Thailand, and Malaysia filed a complaint, calling the import ban a restriction on free trade, and the WTO agreed, arguing that the United States had no ground for imposing restrictions on fishing processes. The country could impose restrictions only if the characteristics of the product itself were somehow in question. Conservation groups pressed the administration of President Bill Clinton to defy the decision, arguing that the WTO was subverting domestic environmental policy (in an odd alliance of interests, conservative Republicans echoed the conservationalists challenge).[12]

In general, environmental NGOs remain critical of the WTO's influence on environmental protection. First, it challenges national sovereignty in developing stringent domestic standards. Leaders of the NGOs fear that if the harmonizing up of environmental standards predicted by free-trade proponents does not occur, pressure from foreign countries (supported by domestically disadvantaged companies) will create pressures to harmonize domestic environmental regulation down to the lowest common denominator. Since scientific data are rarely certain, the WTO creates a mechanism for programs based on such evidence to be opened to subjective analysis and critical foreign challenge. Hard-won domestic environmental victories, then, may be lost in the name of international trade equity. Second, the requirement that national environmental measures be nondiscriminatory with respect to trade may rule out any attempt at balancing environmental and commercial objectives. In principle, a particular policy could be argued to give rise to environmental benefits outweighing the costs of trade restrictions, but this would not be consistent with the goals of the WTO.[13] In the wake of the shrimp–sea turtle decision in 1998, environmentalists have requested international talks aimed at reshaping the way the WTO balances environmental and free-trade issues. In 1999, the organization's director-general called for the creation of a World Environment Organization as a legal counterpart to the WTO.

European Union

In 1987, the Single European Act gave the European Union (EU) explicit power to enforce environmental regulations throughout the entire union. The commission established by the act has passed regulations on eco-labeling and has taken up topics such as voluntary eco-audits for private companies, packaging and packaging waste, end-of-life vehicle regulations, emissions standards, and carbon taxation. In the "EC 1992" initiative, member states established a European Environmental Agency and harmonized standards with environmental implications, including those for animal and plant health and industrial products. Members may choose to impose higher standards than those followed by the rest of the community, but such measures are subject to a "rule of reason" and must not restrict trade among member states any more than is absolutely necessary for the attainment of their legitimate purposes.[14] Disputes among EU members are referred to the Court of Justice of the European Communities.

North American Free Trade Agreement

Approved by Congress in 1993, the North American Free Trade Agreement (NAFTA) was established to foster free trade among Mexico, Canada, and the United States. A part of the agreement called the North American Agreement on Environmental Cooperation (NAAEC) (otherwise known as the "environmental side-agreement") established a commission to negotiate environmental cooperation among the three countries. The NAAEC "recognizes the right of each party to establish its own levels of domestic environmental protection and environmental development policies and priorities" but has a stated objective to "promote economically efficient and effective achievement of environmental goals." Domestic environmental regulations may be challenged by any party if they create an "unnecessary obstacle to trade between the Parties" without fulfilling any "legitimate objective." These objectives include "(a) safety, (b) protection of human, animal or plant life or health, the environment or consumers, including matters relating to quality and identifiability of goods or services and (c) sustainable development." This list is similar to the exemptions specified by the WTO, with the exception of quality of consumer goods and sustainable development. Parties are encouraged to resolve complaints not related to enforcement in a "mutually satisfactory" manner through "consultations."[15] If consultations are unsuccessful after 60 days, an arbitration panel hears the case and may recommend an action plan, monetary penalties, or suspension of NAFTA benefits (trade sanctions). The numerous opportunities for amicable resolution (such as a 180-day cooling-off period) make fines or trade sanctions improbable.

International Environmental Agreements

Just as international agreements have been set to foster world trade, others have been established specifically to foster environmental protection. Some of these run afoul of free-trade considerations. In a 1991 study for the GATT Secretariat, 17 of 127 multilateral environmental agreements were found to have implications for trade. Three of these—(1) the Convention on International Trade in Endangered Species of Wild Fauna and Flora (CITES), (2) the Montreal Protocol on Substances That Deplete the Ozone Layer, and (3) the Basel Convention on the Control of Transboundary Movements of Hazardous Wastes and Their Disposal—were considered to "break the GATT's rule that no country must treat one trading partner worse than another, by imposing more restrictive trade provisions on non-signatories than apply to signatories."[16] This section provides an overview of each of these international environmental agreements as well as three others—(4) the International Tropical Timber Agreement, (5) the International Code of Conduct on the Distribution and Use of Pesticides, and (6) the Kyoto Protocol to the United Nations Framework Convention on Climate Change.

Convention on International Trade in Endangered Species of Wild Fauna and Flora (1973)

International agreements to protect wildlife date back to 1933 and the Convention Relative to the Preservation of Fauna and Flora in Their Natural State. But it is the Convention on International Trade in Endangered Species of Wild Fauna and Flora (CITES) that is the most comprehensive and best known. The treaty prohibits importation and exportation of endangered species or their body parts. The list of species covered is decided by majority vote among the signatories (which numbered 120 in 1993).[17] Parties to the convention are obliged to enforce it by penalizing countries and individuals that trade in or possess endangered flora and fauna. U.S. implementation of CITES is covered in the Endangered Species Act of 1973, the 1978 modifications to the Fishermen's Protective Act (Pelly Amendment), and the High Seas Driftnet Fisheries Enforcement Act (1992).

In 1992, six countries in southern Africa petitioned the CITES Secretariat for permission to allow limited killing of elephants (at a sustainable level, at which the herd could replace the lost animals) in order to generate funds for further preservation efforts, but the majority of signatories denied the petition. In 1994, President Clinton imposed a ban on wildlife and fish products from Taiwan under the Pelly Amendment because Taiwan was participating in trade of rhinoceros horns. Because Taiwan is not a member of the WTO, there was no recourse for testing the trade sanction for WTO consistency.

Montreal Protocol on Substances That Deplete the Ozone Layer (1987)

In 1987, twenty-four countries negotiated the Montreal Protocol on Substances That Deplete the Ozone Layer, setting into motion the production phaseout of chemicals that destroy the earth's ozone layer, most prominently chlorofluorocarbons, or CFCs. Signatories had to require domestic producers and users to halve emissions by 1999. Largely hailed as an example of successful cooperation among countries (its success was made easier by the small number of producers to be regulated), the Montreal Protocol is now yielding positive results. Concentrations of ground-level CFCs have been detected to be decreasing. Given the time necessary for these gases to rise into the stratosphere, scientists now predict a peak in ozone destruction early in the twenty-first century, after which time the ozone layer should begin to recover.

The Montreal Protocol is important not only for its environmental benefits but also for the cast of characters involved in the negotiations. What has been hailed as an example of global cooperation is also an example of competition in the global environmental arena between chemical producers allied with their respective governments, particularly with Imperial Chemical Industries PLC and the British government on the one side and E. I. du Pont de Nemours and Company and the U.S. government on the other. The resultant treaty had significant implications for the product markets of these large corporations, and government officials found it in their national interest to influence the treaty to benefit their domestic industries.[18] The spheres of business strategy, government industrial policy, international trade, and environmental protection all came together in the negotiation of this treaty.

The economic effects of the ban are also becoming visible as consumers find it more difficult to obtain CFC-12, or Freon, on which many air-conditioning systems rely. Given the basic economic laws of supply and demand, this has driven the price of existing Freon stocks to historically high levels. Where law makes commodities scarce, criminals have tried to capitalize on the unsatisfied demand. In 1997, U.S. federal officials indicted fifteen individuals and three businesses for smuggling Freon in San Diego, Houston, Los Angeles, Miami, Philadelphia, and Savannah, Georgia. Along the U.S.–Mexican border, officials acknowledged that smuggling of CFCs ranked second behind smuggling of narcotics as a source of black market profits.[19]

Basel Convention on the Control of Transboundary Movements of Hazardous Wastes and Their Disposal (1989)

The basic objectives of the Basel Convention on the Control of Transboundary Movements of Hazardous Wastes and Their Disposal are to (1) limit exportation and importation of hazardous wastes unless safe disposal is ensured and (2) ban the trade of hazardous wastes between convention signatories and nonsignatories unless the parties have a bilateral agreement consistent with the principles of the convention. Twenty nations signed the agreement in 1992, but as of 1999 the United States had yet to ratify it. In principle, the convention is an attempt to encourage countries to treat hazardous wastes at home whenever possible. In practice, the convention requires that signatories notify and receive written approval from recipient countries of intended shipments of hazardous waste. The treaty places environmental responsibility on the exporter of the waste, who is required to ensure that the receiving country can dispose of it properly. If the shipment is found to have been improperly disposed of, the convention requires the shipment's return to the country of origin. One major flaw in the treaty is that it provides no ironclad definition of hazardous waste. Each country is allowed to apply its domestic definition, and these vary widely. Germany, for example, does not consider a waste to be hazardous if it is intended for recycling.[20] In 1995, steps were taken to amend the Basel Convention by formalizing an unofficial decision to go beyond the regulation and ban the trade of hazardous wastes between developed and developing countries. The amendment proved controversial, with some countries concerned that the ban would prevent the trade of wastes bound for legitimate recycling operations.[21]

International Tropical Timber Agreement (1983)

The International Tropical Timber Agreement (ITTA) calls for the sustainable management of tropical forests. But given the ambiguity in defining the term *sustainable* in general, specific guidelines on how this should be achieved were not developed until 1990. Despite these guidelines, the agreement has created controversy regarding its effects on world trade in timber. In 1985, both Indonesia and the Philippines banned exportation of domestically cut logs. The EU objected on the ground that this violated the WTO's nondiscrimination clause by giving preference to domestic pulp, paper, and wood mills, which would not have to compete with foreign interests in acquisition of raw material. In 1992, Austria passed a law requiring that timber from tropical forests be labeled as tropical, in an attempt to stem the deforestation of tropical rain forests. Malaysia and Indonesia protested that this discriminated against wood from tropical forests but not wood from temperate regions.[22]

Closely linked to the ITTA, the Intergovernmental Panel on Forests was formed at the United Nations Conference on Environment and Development (UNCED), held in Rio de Janeiro in June 1992, to stem the decrease in the world's forests. The panel originally established a nonbinding declaration of principles for preserving dwindling forests that lacked specific targets and compliance monitor programs. But since 1990, fifteen European Union countries and Canada have pushed for talks on a binding convention. Much of the developing world (with the support of the United States) resists such measures, fearing that they might limit trade and economic growth.[23] As of 1999, the issue had yet to be resolved.

International Code of Conduct on the Distribution and Use of Pesticides (1985)

The International Code of Conduct on the Distribution and Use of Pesticides establishes a baseline standard for the testing, labeling, packaging, storage, disposal, distribution, and advertising of pesticides in international trade. This requirement is largely a response to the exportation of pesticides (such as DDT) that may be banned in the country of origin. Similar to the Basel Convention, it requires the exporting country to obtain prior informed consent from the importing country before shipments of pesticides can take place. Exporting countries are required to disclose any existing restrictions on products to be shipped. However, unlike the situation under the Basel Convention, the exporter need not ensure that the pesticide is used properly. The importer maintains the right to make an independent judgment regarding the risks and benefits of the pesticide's use as they relate to domestic conditions.[24]

Kyoto Protocol to the United Nations Framework Convention on Climate Change (1997)

As a follow-up to the 1992 United Nations Framework Convention on Climate Change, which called for voluntary stabilization of emissions of atmospheric greenhouse gases, the United Nations convened the Third Conference of the Parties (COP-3) in Kyoto, Japan, in 1997 to negotiate a set of binding protocols. Of primary concern was emissions of carbon dioxide (CO_2), but also included were methane (CH_4), nitrous oxide (N_2O), and tropospheric (near-surface) ozone (O_3). The basis of the COP-3 meeting was a 1995 statement by the Intergovernmental Panel on Climate Change that "the balance of evidence suggests a discernible human influence on the global climate" and that by increasing the content of greenhouse gases in the atmosphere, humankind was raising the earth's temperature through the "greenhouse effect."[25] Hypothesized consequences included a rise in sea level, increased severity of storms, the spread of tropical diseases, and adverse effects on human health.

Diplomats from more than 160 countries met and approved a treaty that would require developed countries to reduce their emissions to 6 to 8 percent below 1990 levels, starting in 2008. The United States is required to reduce its emissions by 7 percent, and the EU countries face an 8 percent reduction. Two innovative mechanisms written into the treaty are market incentives and joint implementation, which allow the purchase and sale of pollution credits across national borders and investment in carbon dioxide reductions in foreign countries in lieu of reduction credits at home. The logic is similar to the tradable permit program for sulfur dioxide (SO_2) under the Clean Air Act Amendments of 1990—if it costs $100 per ton to eliminate carbon dioxide emissions in the United States and $5 per ton to eliminate them in China, joint implementation will allow U.S. companies to make the Chinese investment and receive domestic credit[26] (see chapter 2 for a more detailed discussion of emission credits). The original treaty did not require the participation of developing countries, a caveat that will have tremendous trade implications (and that many believe will make its ratification by Congress doubtful—as of 1999, the treaty had not been ratified by the United States). One aim of continued negotiations is to bring developing countries into the emissions reduction protocol.

Other Types of International Environmental Institutions

International agreements on environmental issues are not restricted to multilateral treaties. Other institutions have been established to promote voluntary adoption of environmental technology and management practices. Two of these are discussed here.

Global Environment Facility and Multilateral Fund for the Implementation of the Montreal Protocol

The Global Environment Facility (GEF) and the Multilateral Fund for the Implementation of the Montreal Protocol (MFMP) were both established to provide financial and technical support for compliance with international environmental agreements. Administered under the auspices of the United Nations Development Programme (UNDP), the United Nations Environment Programme (UNEP), and the World Bank, they support projects in developing countries that address ozone depletion, global warming, biodiversity, and pollution in international waters. Between its founding in 1991 and 1999, GEF has funded more than 500 projects in 120 countries for a total investment of more than $2 billion. Co-finance of these projects from other sources, public and private, exceeded $5 billion.[27]

ISO 14001 Standards

Established by the International Organization for Standardization (ISO), based in Geneva, Switzerland, ISO 14001 is a set of voluntary standards that integrate environmental responsibility into corporate management procedures.[28] Specifications and guidelines are being established by committees made up of representatives from companies such as the IBM Corporation, the Eastman Kodak Company, and British Telecommunications PLC. They are designed to ensure a uniform approach to handling environmental affairs among companies around the world. It is important to note that these are management standards and not specific performance goals. Firms are required to adopt the standards and earn ISO certification in order to do business in certain multinational markets, such as the European Union. The standards generally involve planning, implementation and operations, checking and corrective action, and management review. By late 1998, more than 5,500 organizations had obtained certifications worldwide (see figure 3.1), an increase from 1,491 in 1996.

There are differing views of whether the ISO program is a success. Although certifications are rising rapidly, many observers are concerned that U.S. companies have shown little initiative in getting certified. As of 1999, the Environmental Protection Agency had not even endorsed the program. Yet there are signs that ISO certification will become more valuable in the future. Several European banks and insurance companies, including Deutsche Bank AG, have announced that they will give preferential treatment to companies with ISO 14001 certification. Individual companies such as Daimler-Chrysler are requiring all suppliers to be certified. In the United States, New Hampshire and Wisconsin have pledged more regulatory flexibility for companies that are certified.

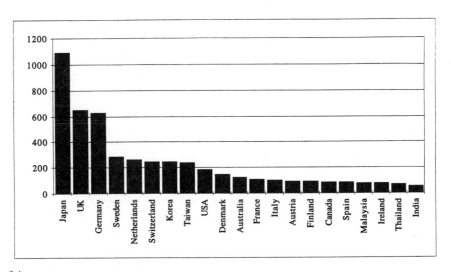

Figure 3.1

ISO 14001 Certifications by Country, 1998

Source: "Marketing and Management Stats," *Tomorrow* 8, no. 6 (1998): 16. © *Tomorrow* magazine. All rights reserved. Reprinted with permission.

Only countries with fifty or more certifications are shown. Countries with fewer than fifty certifications included Singapore, Norway, Brazil, China, Argentina, Indonesia, New Zealand, the Philippines, Hungary, South Africa, Hong Kong, Mexico, Egypt, Turkey, Belgium, the Czech Republic, Poland, Slovenia, Slovakia, and Israel.

The most active development appears to be in Asia, where a survey by Nihon Keizai Shimbun, Inc. found that half of all Japanese companies expect to be certified. China has required that all relevant government agencies seek ISO 14001 certification. Many of these companies have U.S. subsidiaries that may take similar action. Mitsubishi Electric USA has committed to have its roughly half-dozen plants certified by 2000.[29] Skeptics question whether corporations can be trusted with self-policing, even when it is overseen by independent third-party auditors. Others wonder whether the program will actually improve environmental operations or whether it will conflict with environmental management systems already in place. This has led some companies, such as Procter & Gamble (P&G), to steer clear of the standard. A P&G spokesman commented, "We did not want to be associated with the ISO 14001 bureaucracy, but to focus instead on ISO 14001's real intent: having a good [environmental management system] in place." Whether certified or not, this is how some executives are viewing the benefits of the program. It has been estimated that for every company that registers, ten to fifteen others are implementing the standard without seeking registration.[30]

Will the standards bring competitive advantage to companies that adopt them? In 1998, they got their first test in consumer markets. The 1998 Volvo S80 was the first product in the world to get the ISO's type III eco-label, certifying "greenness" in four categories: environmental management, manufacturing, vehicle operation, and recycling.[31] The market response has yet to be measured.

Other Types of International Environmental Pressure

Just as the domestic regulation discussed in chapter 2 varies in its mechanisms from the carrot (market incentives) to the stick (criminal enforcement), international environmental pressures vary in their mechanisms. Companies that conduct international business affairs in ways that deviate from norms that are accepted either in other countries or within their own country can meet with swift and unpleasant reprisal.

For example, the ministers from Russia and the Group of Seven (G7) leading economies (the United States, France, Germany, Italy, Japan, Canada, and the United Kingdom) agreed in 1998 to form a process for cracking down on international environmental crime. Presently, illegal trade in banned products such as endangered species, ozone-depleting substances, and hazardous wastes is estimated to be very lucrative, with a value of nearly $20 billion per year. Britain's deputy prime minister, John Prescott, went so far as to call for the equivalent of an Interpol for environmental crime.[32]

Beyond such formalized mechanisms, informal pressures can push transnational environmental issues onto the political agenda. One example involves the long-running dispute between the United States and Canada over how to divide the steadily declining salmon catch off the Pacific coast shared by the two countries. When negotiations stalled in 1997, Canadian fishermen took matters into their own hands. More than 200 of them refused to allow the Alaskan ferry *Malaspina* to leave port at Prince Rupert, British Columbia, 1,000 miles north of Vancouver. By lashing their ships together and forming a floating barricade at the mouth of the harbor, they stranded 328 passengers and 71 vehicles for three days. A similar but much shorter blockade had been staged in 1995.

The Canadian fishermen believed that U.S. fishermen were taking three to four times more sockeye salmon than was allowed by the 1985 Pacific Salmon Treaty. Many of these fish spawn in Canadian waters but migrate through Alaskan waters and are harvested in huge numbers by U.S. commercial fleets. The state of Alaska retaliated by filing a $2 million lawsuit against the fishermen and demanding that they provide $3 million in bonds or face seizure of their boats.[33] In turn, British Columbia filed a lawsuit seeking $300 million in damages from the United States, contending that U.S. fishermen were profiting from treaty violation. Trade and environmental negotiations are ongoing.

In another example, a 1993 class action lawsuit was filed against Texaco, Inc. in New York on behalf of seventy-seven Amazonian Indians and settlers, seeking $1.5 billion to repair damage to Ecuador's rain forest and compensate families who live there. Twenty years earlier, Texaco had begun drilling for oil in the lush forests. One by-product of the drilling process is heavy metal–tainted wastewaters that rise with the oil. In the United States, oil companies force these wastes back underground, at a cost of more than $1 million per well. In Ecuador, however, the wastes were stored in large lagoons. In 1991, Texaco turned the sites over to a local interest, Petroecuador, which still operates the wells. But in the ensuing years, it became known that the lagoons were leaching arsenic, lead, and heavy metals into the region's streams and rivers. The attorney who filed the case argued that Texaco "went abroad, created a low standard of environmental protection unique to the country and made billions," a fortune that is now "being paid by the indigenous people of Ecuador." One central aspect of this case is the question of whether Texaco took advantage of a poor country with few environmental laws to produce cheap oil using a low environmental standard.[34] More important, can companies be held liable in the United States for practices that are legal in the countries in which they take place? Can they be held liable years after their involvement in the site has ended? As of 1999, the case was still pending.[35]

Viewing these examples as indicative of future trends toward increasing environmental pressures in the international arena, some forward-looking oil companies have sought to leave a lighter footprint in the rain forest. In an effort to avoid punishing scrutiny from environmental and human rights groups, embarrassing boycotts, tarnished corporate images, and the development of stiff new laws, Shell, Inc. and the Mobil Corporation went to extreme lengths to make sure that the environment and local villagers were protected in their $3 billion Camisea Project, a natural gas exploration and development project in Peru.[36] Camisea is an ambitious forty-year project to extract vast reserves of natural gas from a region of the country accessible only from the air or water. Located 350 miles southeast of Lima, the fields contain an estimated 11 trillion cubic feet of natural gas and 600 million barrels of condensates, a liquid form of gas. The region is also unusually rich in plant and animal life and is home to about 5,000 indigenous Indians. Because Camisea is such a massive project in such a visible and vulnerable area, the companies "are bending over backwards to do the right thing," according to Isabel Tafur, director of hydrocarbons for Peru's Ministry of Energy and Mines; she said that "they know their every move is being watched."[37]

Shell, the majority partner, began conducting the project as if it were an offshore operation on an oil rig. Workers were shuttled to the work site by air and were forbidden to have contact with the local villagers. Previous contact between oil workers and locals had been blamed for a devastating influenza epidemic. Every visitor received at least eleven vaccinations, most of which were aimed at protecting local residents. Further, Shell pledged not to build any roads in the region. Instead, the company brought 10,000 tons of equipment to the main base using Hercules cargo aircraft and Chinook helicopters. The Chinook, which uses a sling to haul everything from bulldozers to steel pipe, costs $10,000 per hour to stay aloft. At the drilling site, the company installed a variety of equipment designed to allow reuse of potentially toxic waste mud and rock cuttings. Whatever it could not reuse, recycle, or treat, the company compacted and hauled out. There was plenty of skepticism about the genuineness of Shell's "change of heart," and executives understood such distrust, given the oil industry's poor history in the region. Thus, to help give the program credibility, Shell signed up New York–based Pro-Natura USA and Lima-based Red Ambiental Peruana to monitor how well the companies maintained these high standards.[38]

Despite Shell and Mobil's efforts to portray the project as a model of sustainable development, they were unable to win the approval of important environmental activists in the United States and Peru. As a result, Shell pulled out of the project in July 1998. The company was especially vulnerable to criticism after its human rights problems in Nigeria and its environmental problems with the Brent Spar oil rig in the North Sea (see chapter 6). (In 1995, environmentalist Ken Saro-Wiwa and eight other Nigerian activists were executed by the Nigerian government for their protests of oil drilling in their native Ogoni homelands. Allegations of collusive ties between Shell and the Nigerian military government in suppressing Ogoni environmental and political autonomy movements caused international protests.) Without support from the environmental and human rights communities, the public relations costs of proceeding with the Camisea Project would have been too high for a company already under international scrutiny. Since signing the Camisea license agreement in 1996, Shell and Mobil had invested about $250 million in drilling preparations. The plans to cancel the largest natural resource investment in Peru's history came as a blow to that country, which had been banking on the project to be a major catalyst for economic development. The fields had been expected to start producing gas in 2001 and had been expected to net more than $8 billion for Peru over the next ten years in tax revenues, wages, and investments. Shell estimated that the fields would have produced gas for about forty years.[39]

Despite this setback, Mobil continued work on a project in Peru's biologically diverse Tambopata River valley. To ensure success, the company entered into a partnership with Conservation International (CI) to study the long-term environmental and social effects of seismic exploration and exploratory drilling. Beginning in 1996, Mobil work crews supplied CI researchers with transportation and access to enable them to conduct extensive studies beyond the traditional "footprint" of the project work sites. CI undertook ecological profiling of the area as part of a broader environmental impact assessment of operations, and it was also able to counsel Mobil about rerouting paths and helicopter pads to avoid sensitive ecosystems. As with the Camisea Project, the company did not build any roads into the sensitive region and ferried in supplies and workers by helicopter. CI will continue to work with the project, documenting its environmental performance and, as appropriate, distributing the results to other companies as a benchmark of best practices.[40]

Conclusion

Corporate executives cannot remain focused on domestic standards alone in developing effective environmental strategies. International standards are expanding in their range of control and their ability to transfer environmental issues across national boundaries. This globalization of environmental issues has significant implications for business management. In effect, world markets are being transformed by environmentalism. Will these transformation processes be enough to adequately offset resource scarcity and environmental destruction? Many environmentalists believe that environmental degradation is inevitable given continuing consumption patterns and population growth. The question of whether there are limits to economic growth has fueled a lively debate that began 200 years ago and continues today (see box 3.2).

Box 3.2. Are There "Limits to Growth" in the World Economy?

The development of international accords is driven by the need to manage the global "commons"—resources that are used and depleted by all. But a central question in managing those commons boils down to whether the market system can offset future scarcity of resources or whether more draconian measures are in order. To consider this issue, we must go back to 1798, when Thomas Robert Malthus wrote his famous "Essay on the Principle of Population,"* in which he argued for the first time that there may be limits to the carrying capacity of the earth. He reasoned that the rate of growth of the human population exceeded the rate of growth of food production. Eventually, he predicted, we would face limits to growth and, ultimately, starvation. Although his calculations were sound, his conclusions were not because he failed to anticipate the technological advancements in pesticides, fertilizers, and commercial farming techniques. Yet his central argument has remained in many forms, with many supporters and detractors. One noted dissenter was Julian Simon, a noted economist and professor who spent much of his professional life debating scientists, demographers, and other academics who argued that humankind was stretching the resources of the earth to the breaking point. He died in February 1998 and left behind an interesting legacy in this debate.

In his book *The Ultimate Resource,* Simon argued that (1) over the long term, "the relative measures of scarcity—the costs of natural resources in human labor, and their prices relative to wages and to other goods—all suggest that natural resources have been becoming *less* scarce over the long run"; (2) although pollution is a problem, "on the average we now live in a less dirty and more healthy environment than in earlier centuries"; and (3) although each additional child born into the world is a burden on social systems, particularly in the first fifteen to twenty-five years of life, "an additional person is also a boon. The child or immigrant will pay taxes later on, contribute energy and resources to the community, produce goods and services for consumption of others, and make efforts to beautify and purify the environment. . . . The real population problem, then, is *not* that there are too many people or that babies are being born. It is that others must support each additional person before that person contributes in turn to the well-being of others."†

(continues)

Box 3.2. *Continued*

The essence of Simon's optimistic view of the future is contained in two predictions he made in *The State of Humanity*, a book he edited for the Cato Institute. First, he wrote, "humanity's condition will improve in just about every material way. Second, humans will continue to sit around complaining about everything getting worse." He argued that humankind would rise to any challenges and problems by devising new technologies not only to cope but to thrive. He wrote, "Whatever the rate of population growth is, historically it has been that the food supply increases at least as fast, if not faster."‡

Simon's views were widely contested by members of the academic and scientific community, who believed firmly that the increasing world population strains the earth, causing excessive pollution and overconsumption of natural resources. "Most biologists and ecologists look at population growth in terms of the carrying capacity of natural systems," wrote Lester Brown, president of the Worldwatch Institute. "Julian was not handicapped by being either. As an economist, he could see population growth in a much more optimistic light."

In contrast to Simon's views, Donella Meadows, Dennis Meadows, and Jørgen Randers provided another perspective in their books, *The Limits to Growth* and *Beyond the Limits*, arguing that "human use of essential resources and generation of pollutants has surpassed sustainable rates. . . . Unless there are significant reductions in material and energy flows, the world faces an uncontrolled decline in per capita food output, energy use and industrial production. . . . In order to avoid this decline, growth in material consumption and population must be eased down at the same time as there is a rapid and drastic increase in the efficiency of materials and energy use."§

The critical factor they identified as driving resource depletion to unsustainable levels was "overshoot," which has three underlying causes. First, the pace of depletion is very rapid. Second, there exists some sort of limit beyond which depletion should not go. Third, there is a difficulty in detecting and controlling the rate of depletion as it approaches or passes this barrier. Whether it be fishery extraction, ozone depletion, or greenhouse gas emissions, overshoot will prevent us from knowing the damage we have done by surpassing the limits of these systems until we have already done so. Incomplete information, delayed feedback loops, slow response time, inattention, and unavoidable momentum may render us unable to prevent fishery collapse, the growth of the ozone hole, and uncontrollable climate change.

Their book does not end on such a pessimistic note. It argues that corrections are possible before collapse occurs. But it is not the market system as presently constructed that will warn us of the necessity to make these corrections. Although the market system must be relied on for social change, they argue, many other organizational devices will also be necessary to bring about a different future. "Although there are limits to growth, there need be no limits to development." An altered market system must incorporate "concerns for carefully balancing our long and short term goals and emphasizing equity and quality of life."

The debate between these two perspectives on limits to growth took an interesting turn in 1980. Julian Simon entered into a highly publicized bet with Paul Ehrlich, the Stanford University ecologist whose 1968 best-selling book *The Population Bomb*‖ predicted that one-fifth of humanity would starve to death by 1985. Ehrlich and two colleagues from the University of California at Berkeley responded to an article Simon had written for *Science* magazine titled "Resources, Population, Environment: An Oversupply of False Bad News." In that article, Simon challenged anyone to a bet that the price of any natural resource would be lower, not higher, on a mutually agreed-on date. Ehrlich and his colleagues took the bet, believing that rising demand for raw materials by an expanding global population would limit supplies of nonrenewable resources and drive prices up. Ehrlich boldly accepted Simon's "astonishing offer before other greedy people jump[ed] in."‡

The Ehrlich group bet $1,000 on the expected rise in prices of five metals—chrome, copper, nickel, tin, and tungsten. Simon agreed to the challenge, betting that the metals would decrease in price. If the combined prices of the metals in 1990 turned out to be higher than $1,000 (in 1980 dollars), Simon would pay the difference in cash. If prices fell, the Ehrlich group would pay him. During the decade, world population grew by more than 800 million, the greatest increase in history, and the store of metals did not get any larger. Yet in the fall of 1990, with the price of the metals down sharply, Ehrlich was forced to concede the bet and mail Simon a check for $576.07. Simon wrote a thank-you note offering to raise the wager to as high as $20,000, based on any other resources over any time period. Ehrlich declined the offer.

Does this bet settle the issue? Who is right? Are resources becoming more scarce? Will market signals and human ingenuity resolve resource depletion? Should we be worried about resource scarcity, or will markets create solutions when needed? This debate between market economists and Malthusian environmentalists will continue long into the future. At its core lie the questions of whether there is a limit to growth and whether human systems are responsive enough to detect and offset the damage they inadvertently create.

* T. Malthus, "An Essay on the Principle of Population" (1798), reprinted in *British Society and Politics*, ed. J. F. C. Harrison (New York: Harper & Row, Publishers, 1965).

† The quotations in this paragraph are from J. Simon, *The Ultimate Resource* (Princeton, N.J.: Princeton University Press, 1981), 3.

‡ The quotations in this and the next paragraph are from K. Gilpin, "Julian Simon, Sixty-Five, Optimistic Economist, Dies," *New York Times*, 12 February 1998, D21.

§ The quotations in this paragraph and the following two paragraphs are from D. Meadows, D. Meadows, and J. Randers, *Beyond the Limits* (Post Mills, Vt.: Chelsea Green Publishing Company, 1992), jacket, xix, and jacket, respectively.

‖ P. Ehrlich, *The Population Bomb* (New York: Ballantine Books, 1968). The quotation by Paul Ehrlich at the end of the paragraph is from K. Gilpin, "Julian Simon, Sixty-Five, Optimistic Economist, Dies," *New York Times*, 12 February 1998, D21.

Further Reading

Bhagwati, J. "The Case for Free Trade." *Scientific American*, November 1993, 42–49.

Daly, H. "The Perils of Free Trade." *Scientific American*, November 1993, 50–57.

———. *Steady-State Economics*. 2d ed. Washington, D.C.: Island Press, 1991.

Ferrantino, M. "A Brief Description of International Institutional Linkages in Trade and the Environment," Office of Economics, Working Paper No. 94-11-A. Washington, DC: U.S. International Trade Commission, 1994.

Maxwell, J., and S. Weiner. "Green Consciousness or Dollar Diplomacy? The British Response to the Threat of Ozone Depletion." *International Environmental Affairs* (winter 1993): 19–41.

Meadows, D., D. Meadows, and J. Randers. *Beyond the Limits*. Post Mills, Vt.: Chelsea Green Publishing Company, 1992.

———. *The Limits to Growth*. New York: Universe Books, 1972.

Preston, L., and D. Windsor. *Rules of the Game in the Global Economy: Policy Regimes for International Business*. Boston: Kluwer Academic Publishing, 1992.

Reinhardt, F., and E. Prewitt. *Environment and International Trade*. Case Studies, no. 794018. Boston: Harvard Business School Press, 1994.

Simon, J. *The Ultimate Resource*. Princeton, N.J.: Princeton University Press, 1981.

Zaelke, D., P. Orbuch, and R. Housman. *Trade and the Environment: Law, Economics, and Policy*. Washington, D.C.: Island Press, 1993.

Chapter 4

RESOURCE DRIVERS

How much is nature worth? It would seem a bizarre question—perhaps, to some, even offensive. But thirteen economists, ecologists, and geographers ventured not only to ask the question but also to answer it in a 1997 issue of the journal *Nature*.[1] Natural systems perform valuable and practical services for the earth's life-support systems, such as flood control, soil formation, pollination, food and timber production, provision of raw materials for new medicines, and maintenance of a favorable climate. Because human welfare depends on these functions, the researchers decided that it was time that their value was considered in economic decision making. Based on an analysis of seventeen ecosystem services, they determined a value for nature estimated at $16 trillion to $54 trillion per year, with a likely figure of at least $33 trillion.[2] Many environmentalists bristled at the idea of placing an economic value on nature, but the researchers used their conclusion to highlight an important point. If one compares the figure with the $18 trillion world gross national product (GNP), the value of all the goods and services produced by people each year, it becomes clear that the services provided by nature exceed the services provided by the human economy. Protection of nature, they argued, should therefore be given greater importance in relation to our own economic considerations.

With such large dollar figures at stake, is nature really peripheral to our economy? Is the environment merely an externality to the market system? Are companies provoked into protecting the natural environment only through the imposition of government regulation? Increasingly, an awareness of the economic value of the natural environment is creeping explicitly into business systems. It is happening through an appreciation for the value of the services that the environment provides and a transfer of that appreciation through resource, market, and social forces.

For example, in 1997, the city of New York embarked on an ambitious five-year, $660 million program to protect the natural ecosystems surrounding its precious upstate reservoirs. City officials recognized that microorganisms purify the city's water supply as the water percolates through the soil of the Catskill Mountains. Further development within the watershed would both diminish that filtration capacity and introduce new contaminants that would have to be removed later. Recognizing the economic value of this ser-

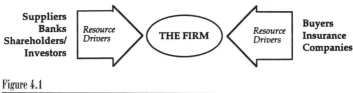

Figure 4.1

Resource Drivers of Environmental Strategy

vice, the city began purchasing thousands of acres of land around the reservoirs and restoring the soil's natural function. The cost of buying the land was estimated to be far less than the anticipated $4 billion needed to build a new filtration plant.[3]

The city's action represents one way in which organizations are recognizing the value of the natural environment to their operations. Other organizations may see economic opportunity in reducing hazardous or toxic materials in their processes. Still other organizations may see economic value in reducing their exposure to environmental liability through environmentally hazardous activities (such as crude oil transport). All organizations are concerned with the economic costs of regulatory controls and penalties. Just as a pebble dropped in a still pond creates waves, as organizations integrate environmental considerations into their decision making, they also transfer those considerations to other organizations through business and social interactions.

Corporations are part of a complex system, interacting with one another through a variety of channels. Although domestic and international regulations are extremely influential in driving corporate environmental strategy, they do not represent the full extent of the pressures. Recalling figure II.1, firms are controlled by value-chain pressures from organizations that are critical for process inputs and outputs, market pressures from organizations with which they compete and cooperate, and social pressures from organizations that act as thought leaders. In each of these realms of corporate activity, environmental considerations are becoming an integral part. Chapters 2 and 3 covered the coercive pressures of domestic regulation and international regimes; this chapter addresses resource drivers in the value chain of buyers and suppliers, insurance companies, banks, shareholders, and investors (see figure 4.1).

Buyers and Suppliers

Organizations that control the acquisition of raw materials and the consumption of products can be highly influential in the way a firm conducts its operations. When members of a firm's value chain begin to attach environmental considerations to the supply and consumption of a firm's process materials, environmentalism becomes translated into a core business concern of resource acquisition, processing, and sale. To assess the presence of environmental pressures within the business environment, we begin by considering the role of buyers and suppliers.

In decision making about environmental strategy, the environmental effect of a product is the sum of the environmental effects of each input and output along the value chain. Companies become tied to one another. If one company introduces a toxic material into the process, all companies must consider how the material should be handled. Further, if a company toward the end of the value chain is receiving a signal from consumers that the product is environmentally destructive, it must impose restrictions on its suppliers in order to remove it. Companies are now considering the effects of the actions of other companies up and down the value chain on their environmental activities.[4]

For example, the Dow Chemical Company has adopted, as one of its guiding principles, cradle-to-grave management of its products and by-products. The company's rationale is, "If it's our product, and in the eyes of some from the day we make it until the day someone else discards it, we had better be ready with some preventive customer and user support before it becomes anybody's problem."[5] To support this rationale, the company imposes rigid standards on all contractors who provide materials that enter the product stream. Levi Strauss & Company has also developed strict sourcing guidelines for selecting contractors that go beyond the traditional focus on price, quality, and delivery time. Beginning in 1992, the company began requiring that contractors comply with Levi Strauss's environmental principles, even if it meant paying higher prices. The company also offered generous timetables, loans, and volume guarantees for contractors who met their requirements. In turn, many contractors believed that meeting these requirements and having Levi Strauss as a client was helpful in attracting new customers.

More than just reducing liability, linking environmental attributes to supplier and buyer relationships can reduce overall costs that are shared among all partners. For example, E. I. du Pont de Nemours and Company's films business, DuPont Polyester Films and DuPont Polyester Resins & Intermediates, set up a reverse distribution network for recycling the polyester film it manufactures and sells. The company has developed a process by which the material can be infinitely regenerated into virgin-quality product and has enlisted customers in the process. DuPont saves 25 percent of the cost of buying new raw materials, and customers save money by not having to pay for disposal of the waste material.[6]

Greening the supply chain can also bring competitive advantage by identifying ways in which environmental improvements also improve the quality of the product or the efficiency of the production process. Although conventional wisdom may hold that most innovation is carried out by manufacturers, a study by Eric von Hippel, a professor at the Massachusetts Institute of Technology Sloan School of Management who specializes in innovation management, showed that innovation often originates with users and suppliers, who at times know more about the attributes of the product and raw material than does the manufacturer.[7] For example, von Hippel found that in the production of scientific instruments, 77 percent of innovation was developed by users, and in the production of wire termination equipment, 56 percent was developed by suppliers.[8]

This lesson was not lost on Procter & Gamble (P&G), which in the late 1980s began to consider the recycling of waste packaging in direct response to user concerns and interests. To successfully implement the program, the company turned to its suppliers for help in altering packaging materials to ensure a continuous stream of high-quality recyclable material.[9] Today, P&G uses recycled material in more than 200 packages. One Tide detergent refill bag has 70 percent less packaging than a cardboard box of the same size. P&G's concentrated detergents have saved 304 million pounds of packaging material since 1992, according to the company's annual report. Tom Rattray, associate director of environmental quality for Procter & Gamble, said: "We're not doing it because it sells soap in Cincinnati. We're doing it because it's the right thing to do and saves money."[10]

Making packages smaller is not as simple as it sounds. Manufacturers must weigh the money saved by use of fewer materials against reduced shelf presence, greater vulnerability to damage, and the heightened possibility that shoplifters will steal the smaller items. An efficient package that satisfies all these concerns requires input from all partners in the supply chain. Toward that end, S. C. Johnson & Son, Inc. sought to gain more direct value-chain input by hosting an environmental symposium in 1991 designed to initiate joint efforts between the company and representatives of fifty-seven of the largest international suppliers to help it reach its environmental goals.[11]

S. C. Johnson's initiative is representative of changes throughout the industry; most producers have decreased packaging. Cardboard package housing for deodorant containers has all but disappeared. Many toothpastes and cough and cold formulas have similarly shed outer cardboard shells. Laundry detergent is increasingly found in concentrated formulas and refills.

In the end, corporations are turning to suppliers and buyers in an attempt to minimize the adverse environmental effects of their products through process and material alterations. All of them form the continuous stream of the value chain as goods and services are contributed to the process of product development. Each of these organizations faces environmental constraints of its own, whether through regulatory, social, or economic pressures that are particular to that company's interests. Any company can look upstream and downstream in the value chain and recognize that environmental influences diffuse throughout its exchange relationships.

Insurance Companies

Insurance companies are now equating environmentally risky operations with increased financial risk and are beginning to apply environmental criteria to minimize risk in their underwriting practices. The risks of environmental liability are pushing insurance companies to demand sound environmental practices before a policy is written.

The connection between environmental risk and financial risk was first made by U.S. insurance companies in the early 1980s in response to two pressures. First, growing liability over Superfund cleanups was increasingly drawing insurance companies into providing coverage for cleanup costs. Although insurance companies were arguing that cleanup costs fell outside traditional liability coverage, juries were producing different interpretations. For example, the Hartford Accident and Indemnity Company was required to pay investigation and cleanup costs associated with groundwater contamination at the Broderick Wood Products site in Denver, Colorado. The court chose to overrule the pollution exclusion in the company's policy. This case set a precedent with the verdict rendered in favor of the insured.[12]

The second driver of insurance companies' concerns about environmental liability was a heightened awareness of the potential financial magnitude of an environmental calamity. The precipitating event for this awakening occurred on December 3, 1984, when approximately forty-five tons of methyl isocyanate (MIC) gas escaped from two underground storage tanks at a Union Carbide Corporation pesticide plant in Bhopal, India. In the leak's aftermath, 2,000 people had died and another 300,000 had been injured.[13] In March 1985, the government of India took Union Carbide to court; in January 1989, it won a mediated settlement of $470 million.[14] The scope of the accident and the exposure of Union Carbide's insurance underwriters served to alter the structure of insurance liability coverage.

Beginning in 1987, the state of corporate environmental coverage became very confused and the number of lawsuits between insurance carriers and industry grew rapidly as liability limits became disputed.[15] According to industry analysts, this was due to a broad change in insurance policy coverage as well as a change in the form of environmental incidents. First, there was generally a condition in policies that pollution must be "sudden and accidental" to be covered under most general liability contracts. This condition excluded the newly emerging and slowly developing problems of waste site remediation and leaking underground storage tanks. Second, after 1986, general insurance coverage became more strict with the creation of pollution exclusion clauses. Pollution protection as separate coverage became more difficult and expensive to acquire. According to a 1988 General Accounting Office (GAO) report, "the number of insurers writing pollution insurance, the number of policies written, and the total pollution liability coverage decreased dramatically from a 1984 peak. Simultaneously, the average premium increased as much as 11 times its 1982 level. Insurance contracts became more limited in their coverage and in some cases provided no real protection to operators from financial losses arising out of pollution damage."[16] Many policies written became "claims made" policies, meaning that claims could be made only during the term of the policy. This offered no protection for a policyholder hit with a claim after the term of the policy.

David Dybdahl of Caroon and Black Environmental Insurance Services described three reasons why insurance companies were uneasy about getting involved in pollution coverage. First, claimants did not have to prove a cause-and-effect relationship between an event and ensuing environmental damage. This concern was supported by the courts' interpretation of strict liability. Second, plaintiffs could "sue for the moon" on the basis of unspecified effects or fear of future damages. Third, the courts appeared to have shifted the burden of proof onto the corporation to prove that it was not responsible for third-party injuries.[17] Today, U.S. insurers face an estimated $2 trillion in pollution cleanup and asbestos-related claims.[18] They are still cautious about policy applications with environmental considerations and are attempting to make corrections.

More recently, environmental considerations are creeping into more broad forms of risk underwriting, many beyond just pollution control. In November 1995, the insurance industry developed a Statement of Environmental Commitment with the support of the United Nations Environment Programme (UNEP). As of 1998, the document had enjoyed rapid buy-in from insurers (mostly from Europe, Canada, and Japan), with seventy-eight official signatories making a commitment to include the environment as a value driver in underwriting decisions. The document's preamble affirms that signatories will "work together to address key issues such as pollution reduction, the efficient use of resources and climate change."[19] In the face of scientific uncertainty regarding environmental concerns, particularly the uncertainty surrounding climate change, the UNEP document states: "We recognize the precautionary principle, in that it is not possible to quantify some concerns sufficiently, nor indeed reconcile all impacts in purely financial terms. Research is needed to reduce uncertainty but it cannot eliminate it entirely."[20]

UNI Storebrand, a large Norwegian Insurance Company, has begun putting some of these principles into practice, refusing coverage to companies that fail to assume environmental responsibilities. Carlos Joly, a former Storebrand senior vice president for Environmental Policy and Investments, said: "We're foregoing premium income, but the loss from accidents, spills and so on would not be tolerable. Even at a higher premium, we wouldn't want the business. . . . Demonstrably better environmental performance leads to lower environmental risk, which leads to lower premiums. Companies with lower environmental risk are beginning to pay lower premiums, all else equal."[21]

Insurance companies' decisions go to the core of corporate decision making in several ways. First, their underwriting practices act as consulting recommendations, influencing the way companies handle their environmental affairs. Second, if companies choose not to adopt insurer-recommended practices, they will find their business costs raised through higher premiums. Third, insurance companies can refuse to cover certain environmental risks, such as gradual pollution, thereby discouraging the practices that create them. And fourth, the premiums received by these companies contribute to large amounts of investment capital, which can be used to sway financial markets.[22]

In this last area, insurance companies have begun to drive changes in the way corporations respond to global climate change. An important driver is a relatively new industry that is one step removed from corporate decision making as discussed so far: the reinsurance industry. One of the more aggressive reinsurance companies, Swiss Re, reported in 1994 that "the more quickly and radically the global climate changes, the more [that] extreme weather patterns could cause damage which [would] not only pose a threat to individual citizens, families and enterprises but could also jeopardize whole cities and branches of the economy and—on a global scale—entire states and social systems. In brief: damage which had better not be risked because it can no longer be handled."[23] Many in the insurance industry are beginning to question whether, in light of climate change implications, their interests are contrary to the interests of those who sell carbon fuel or use it in large quantities. One view now gaining support in the industry is that insurers should lobby for policies that reduce the weather-related risks of climate change.[24] These risks are beginning to have quantifiable costs.

In 1998 alone, weather-related disasters such as fires, floods, storms, and droughts caused approximately $89 billion in economic losses globally. This surpassed the previous record of $60 billion in 1996.[25] During the first three quarters of the year, the U.S. insurance industry alone had weather-related claims for more than $8 billion.[26] Insurers worry that climate change could cause substantial losses in the years ahead, and this concern is driving some companies to invest in environmentally sound projects. For example, in 1997, Swiss Re invested $2.75 million in SunLight Power International Holdings, Inc., a start-up company planning to install 1 million photovoltaic systems in developing countries over the next seven years, for a carbon dioxide offset of nearly 6 million tons over a twenty-year period. Swiss Re's investment decision followed on the heels of a similar $2 million investment in photovoltaic systems spearheaded by Rolf Gerling of the Gerling Insurance Group.[27]

Banks

One important component of the supply chain is capital. Corporations need financial support to continue operations, support expansion plans, and direct new ventures. As capital markets begin to press environmental performance criteria as part of their loan-granting procedures, environmental performance is translated into cost-of-capital considerations within the firm. As one major source of capital, banks have been slow to pick up on the environmental considerations of their lending practices. Recently, that has begun to change. This change, particularly in the United States, has been triggered by a growing number of court cases in which banks have been held liable for the actions of their borrowers. To limit that risk, they are beginning to include environmental considerations in their lending decisions.

For example, today no one can purchase property without first conducting an environmental audit to determine whether there are any hidden environmental liabilities from previous owners. Brownfields—development sites in urban settings that have been previously used and may contain hidden environmental hazards (as opposed to greenfields, which are development sites on previously unused land)—can present both serious opportunities and serious threats. If due diligence is not properly applied and environmental hazards are discovered after the loan is granted, a bank could lose the entire loan as what was considered a benign property is found to contain hazardous or toxic wastes. Once discovered, environmental problems can limit the available options for servicing a troubled loan. If a bank chooses to manage a long-term bailout of a troubled firm and assumes any kind of management control to accomplish this task, interpretations by the courts of what constitutes an owner-operator may expose the bank to environmental liability.[28] This concern is particularly critical under the Comprehensive Environmental Response, Compensation, and Liability Act (CERCLA), which, although it exempts lenders from being classified as owners, has excepting circumstances that have been pursued in the courts. To avoid such liability, a Texas bank disavowed a foreclosure on an oil refinery site in 1986 after learning that it might become liable for its cleanup under CERCLA.[29] On the other hand, the environmental aspects of brownfield development can create economic opportunities because brownfields are often cheaper to develop, provided that the environmental risk is appropriately identified and minimized. Either way, both brownfield and greenfield development proposals are highly scrutinized by banks for potential environmental hazards.

Beyond examining the merits of the individual proposal, some banks are beginning to look at the practices of the applicant, equating poor environmental performance with high financial risk. More so than regulation, environmental constraints from sources of capital go to the core of corporate decision making and push the firm to consider strategic responses to environmental concerns. This kind of thinking is becoming international in scope. The European Bank for Reconstruction and Development (EBRD) wrote into its establishing agreement that it will promote in the full range of its activities environmentally sound and sustainable development. [30] In April 1995, the government of Brazil required all banks and credit institutions in the country to grant loans only for projects that take environmental effects into consideration. In 1992, UNEP coordinated a declaration of environmental commitment by the banking industry similar to that of the insurance industry. Signatories have made a commitment to incorporate environmental factors into their daily business practices. The declaration's principles state that environmental responsibility is "a fundamental aspect of sound business management" and that "environmental risks should be part of the normal checklist of risk assessment and management."[31] By 1995, the number of signatories had reached 123 as banks recognized that they could save money and attract new customers (and employees) by integrating progressive environmental considerations into their operating practices. In a survey of European banks, fifteen respondents said that they offered discounted rates to environmentally responsible companies, shaving as much as fifty basis points from the rate and halving the fees.[32]

Feeling left out by the distinctly European focus of the environmental banking initiatives of the United Nations, North American bankers launched the Western Hemisphere Bank Advisory Group to include institutions engaged in commercial and investment banking, fund management, leasing, and insurance in developing a set of environmental operating principles. The core organizing group includes the Bank of America Corporation, Salomon Inc., and the Royal Bank of Canada.[33]

Shareholders and Investors

Shareholders and investors are powerful forces for change within the corporation. In the cause of the environment, they have been wielding that power since the late 1980s both through shareholder voting and by directing capital investment. Beginning in 1989, shareholders began to file environmental proxy resolutions at annual board meetings.[34] One major force driving this new form of pressure was the Coalition for Environmentally Responsible Economies (CERES), which enlisted investors who controlled more than $100 billion to support only those companies that subscribed to a list of principles of environmental protection. CERES was formed in 1989 as a collaboration between socially responsible investors and representatives of several prominent environmental organizations. The organization's first step was public announcement of the Valdez Principles (now called the CERES Principles), a set of ten guidelines for environmentally responsible behavior; then it solicited companies to endorse the principles.[35] As of 1998, CERES had enlisted 158 signatories, including Fortune 100 companies such as the General Motors Corporation, the Polaroid Corporation, the Bethlehem Steel Corporation, and Sunoco, Inc.[36]

When companies would not sign on voluntarily, CERES investors filed proxy resolutions at annual stockholder meetings that would put to an open vote a set of environmental concerns. Up from only three in 1989, forty-three environmental resolutions were filed in 1990, and a mean of sixty have been filed yearly since then. Originally, such resolutions were proposals to sign the CERES Principles. More recently, votes have dealt with such issues as establishment of environmental policy committees, revised health and safety policies, toxic wastes in ethnic and minority communities, control of carbon dioxide emissions, and elimination of the use of specific compounds.

CERES is not the only impetus for investor action. In June 1999, the Sinsinawa Dominican Sisters (a religious order with operatives in the United States, Bolivia, Guatemala, and Trinidad) used their 100 shares of stock to force the Occidental Petroleum Corporation to reconsider its oil exploration program. The company was preparing to drill for oil in Colombia, on land occupied by the U'wa Indians. In fact, members of the 5,000-member U'wa tribe considered the land to be so sacred that they vowed that if drilling proceeded, they would walk off a 1,400-foot cliff in the Andes. Aided by environmental activists and the Internet, the Dominican sisters won shareholder approval of a plan to hire an outside company to analyze the potential effects of the U'wa suicide threat on the company's stock.[37]

The power of investment capital is now becoming an important tool for environmentalists. According to Julie Tanner, senior financial services analyst for the National Wildlife Federation, the organization has been "training people all around the world about the role of financial institutions and where they can find points of leverage."[38] In 1999, a precedent-setting shareholder resolution was introduced at the annual meeting of Morgan Stanley Dean Witter. The resolution, endorsed by 5 percent of the shareholders, requested the board of directors to consider the environmental risks of underwriting and lending. In particular, the resolution pointed to the controversial Three Gorges Dam in China, which environmentalists fear will cause an environmental catastrophe. The resolution warned of a possible boycott of both the company's brokerage business and its Discover credit card. Similar resolutions were filed at Salomon Smith Barney Holdings, Inc. and Merrill Lynch & Company, Inc. seeking a halt to underwriting projects associated with the dam.[39]

Beyond the use of investor voting to change corporate behavior, the capital from investment funds is an area in which the connection between environmental performance and cost of capital has more of a history. In the late 1980s and early 1990s, environmental considerations became a new and exciting part of the investment market. "Wall Street Likes What It Sees" claimed one headline in 1989.[40] "The U.S. environmental market is a good investment with tremendous potential for growth," another article stated.[41] In the early 1990s, Wall Street analysts took strong notice of the growth in environmental markets. The number of interested investors prompted an outpouring of public offerings, including those of environmental funds run by the Oppenheimer Global Fund, Fidelity Investments, Freedom Capital Management Corporation, Merrill Lynch, New Alternative, Progressive, and SFT. These funds tended to focus on the large environmental firms, particularly those that operated landfills and collected household trash and other nonhazardous garbage. But by the early 1990s, this euphoria had worn off. Recently, investment managers have not been drawn as strongly to "green" investments.

For example, a 1994 White House report stated:

> A spokesperson for the investment banking industry recently testified
> before Congress that in 1988 nearly every major investment firm

planned to commit at least 10 percent of its portfolio to environmental businesses. By 1993 fewer than 15 percent had done so, and less than 10 of these had invested in technology. In 1991 the venture capital industry, with $40 billion under management, invested in five new technology firms. Many venture capitalists cite uncertainty about the regulatory process as a central reason for reluctance to invest in the environmental industry. Uncertainty about whether a particular technology will be approved or endorsed by regulators adds a significant and difficult-to-analyze dimension to the riskiness of investment projects.[42]

Today, although the chief executive officers and chief financial officers of an increasing number of firms have recognized the positive links between environmental performance and financial performance, capital markets for the most part continue to view the environment either as only a liability or as financially immaterial when considering a corporation's strategy and performance. To change this thinking, a number of forums have been established by the World Business Council for Sustainable Development, the United Nations Environment Programme Financial Institutions Initiative, the Aspen Institute, and other institutions to advance the dialogue between the corporate and analytical communities. In 1998, the New York Society of Security Analysts, Inc.—the world's largest and most influential society of investment professionals—launched "Uncovering Value," a series of environmental seminars designed to examine how progressive corporate environmental practices contribute to a company's performance, profitability, and growth.[43]

Supporting such a rationale, some studies have found a positive correlation between environmental and economic performance. The Alliance for Environmental Innovation reviewed seventy studies and concluded that companies that outperform their peers environmentally also outperform them on the stock market by as much as two percentage points. ICF Kaiser International, Inc. found a similar correlation in a study of 300 of the largest public companies in the United States.[44] Companies with high scores on environmental criteria were "lower-beta stocks," meaning that they were less risky investments and would thus enjoy a lower cost of capital and ultimately a higher stock price.[45] Although empirical studies that link environmental and financial performance are growing, Wall Street investors remain skeptical. They see a general lack of rigor, a potential for biases on the part of the investigators, and difficulty in establishing a firm cause-and-effect relationship between environmental and financial performance.[46] Still, some have been able to turn this proposed correlation into actual financial success.

In 1996, the global ethical and environmental investment fund industry numbered thirty funds in the United Kingdom, fifty-three in the rest of the European Union, and thirty-seven in the United States (of the latter, seven were "true" environmental funds).[47] But performance varies among them according to portfolio selection criteria. On the whole, their performance has been less than impressive.[48] In 1995, only one U.S. fund listed by the Social Investment Forum, a trade group for social managers, beat the 37.58 percent growth rate of the Standard & Poor's 500. During that year, the average return

on a $100 investment for thirty-six environmental and ethical funds was $114.16, compared with the *Financial Times*–S&P Index figure of $119.07. Over the four-year period
from 1992 to 1996, a $100 investment in a selection of European "green" funds would
have grown on average to $136.87, compared with the *Financial Times*–S&P Index fig-
ure of $144.48.[49]

However, exceptions are emerging. Some investment funds have begun to find a successful formula by moving away from using the environment as an absolute screen and
instead balancing environmental criteria with other financial criteria in their portfolio
management procedures. In 1996, UNI Storebrand and Scudder Kemper Investments
jointly created the Storebrand Scudder Environmental Value Fund. Scudder screens a
company's financial performance; Storebrand checks its environmental performance.
Stocks that pass both screens are included in the fund. This includes companies such as
the Sony Corporation, DuPont, and the Minnesota Mining and Manufacturing Company (3M). Starting with $10 million of Storebrand's money, the fund appreciated by 51
percent in its first two years, outperforming the Morgan Stanley Capital International
World Index by more than eight percentage points.[50] Translating environmental performance into risk reduction, Jan-Oluf Willums, a Storebrand senior vice president, stated,
"We will not market this as a green fund, but as a good financial returns fund with limited risk."[51]

Amy Domini directs the Domini Social Equity Fund, which focuses on companies
that score high on a broad range of social issues. The fund excludes companies involved
in alcohol, tobacco, gambling, nuclear power, or weapons and includes companies with
good records on the environment, diversity, and employee relations. Domini believes that
her fund has outperformed the S&P Index because her screening process eliminates
companies with problems and includes companies of better financial quality. According
to Domini, "one thing this does is introduce a bias toward more visionary management."[52]

Although none of the case studies just described can claim a cause-and-effect relationship between environmental performance and financial performance, a correlation
between the two is a powerful indicator of future success. The primary logic of this new
breed of fund is not that environmental factors should predominate over financial factors. Rather, they should be included as ways to assess how well a company is run. Environmental performance becomes a proxy for managerial and financial performance.
These funds will avoid environmentally sound companies whose stocks seem fully valued. Moreover, they are not investing only in "green" companies, such as solar energy or
wind power companies. Instead, they are buying stocks that represent "best of class" in
basic industries such as paper and steel manufacturing. These companies, according to
fund managers, manage their environmental affairs more responsibly than their industry
competitors and will very likely manage their overall operations more responsibly as well.
This will lead to greater returns. According to fund manager Jackson Robinson with
Winslow Management Company, "some of the best investment opportunities are environmentally sensitive companies in otherwise 'dirty' industries."[53]

UBS Brinson, for example, now offers two funds in which both financial performance and environmental performance are considered in investment decisions, and in 1997 the company enjoyed a return of 24 percent, compared with the 22.4 percent return of the Morgan Stanley index. Ingeborg Schumacher, an associate director for UBS Brinson, commented, "An eco-efficient company is making efficient use of its resources, and that's probably a strong signal that it is well managed as a whole."[54]

Still, this message remains a tough sell on the rest of Wall Street. One easily identifiable obstacle is that reliable environmental data are much harder to come by than sound financial data. Environmental performance reports vary widely from one company to the next. They are generally written in a language that differs from the standard financial terminology with which financial analysts are comfortable, and there is no standard for the way they should be written. To correct this disconnection and bridge the gap between measurement of environmental performance and measurement of financial performance, CERES is pushing for reliable environmental reporting. Of the ten original CERES Principles, one outlined requirements for public disclosure of environmental performance. Now moving beyond its initial mandate of gaining buy-in to its guiding principles, CERES has made the major thrust of its program the development of uniform and reliable statements for reporting environmental performance. Although such reporting was nonexistent prior to 1990, a multitude of corporate environmental report formats have developed independently around the world. For example, a 1997 survey by the accounting firm KPMG LLP found that although 87 percent of these reports included quantitative data, only 20 percent included tangible targets and deadlines. A minuscule 15 percent were verified by a third party—a legal requirement for annual reports in conventional accounting. Further, the measurement criteria for these reports varied widely, with some reporting in pounds, others in tons, and others in percentages.[55] Only 60 percent of the reports adjusted their data for production levels, a necessary criterion for comparing firms of various sizes.[56] The executive director of CERES, Robert Massie, believes that environmental reporting today is where financial reporting was decades ago. Through its Global Reporting Initiative (GRI), his organization is trying to bring together and harmonize these standards and shape them into one set of coherent, consistent global standards.

If GRI is successful, there will likely be a snowball effect, as environmental and financial measures of corporate success continue to merge. Looking to the future, some suggest a change in views of fiduciary responsibility for pension fund managers. Those who do not take advantage of environmental criteria in their investment decisions may someday be charged with negligence. Companies that perceive this change not only can remain ahead of the curve but also can influence its outcome. The Aspen Institute reported:

> As strategies derived from or driven by the environment are increasingly viewed as opportunities to enhance return on investment, fund managers will have a fiduciary responsibility to consider how companies have incorporated environmental factors into their business decisions. . . . Companies that act first to identify and define the strategic environment/business connection may influence how the financial community views and acts on environmental information, and this

could have a significant impact on the companies' share price and cost of capital.[57]

In 1999, the Pacific Lumber Company and its parent, the Maxxam Corporation, witnessed first hand how it's environmental posture and performance could have a dramatic and sudden effect on its share price. In March, the federal government and the state of California agreed to pay the company $480 million for its holdings of the largest privately owned grove of ancient redwoods in the world. The company also agreed to restrictions on the way it would harvest trees on its remaining 211,000 acres. The deal to protect the Headwaters Forest, about 10,000 acres in northern California's Humboldt County, was ten years in the making and nearly fell apart in the final days and minutes. But investor pressure was influential in bringing it to completion. With the contract due to expire on Tuesday, March 2, the boards of Pacific Lumber and Maxxam voted unanimously on Friday, April 26, to reject the proposal. On Monday, the first stock-purchasing day after the rejection of the deal was announced, Maxxam stock tumbled. After the deal was signed on Tuesday, two minutes before it was to expire, the stock rose by 24 percent.[58] The company claims that the drop in stock price was not influential in its decision making. Whether that is true or not, this dramatic market response is a signal that investors notice and value environmental protection as an economic variable in their investment decisions.

Conclusion

As these examples illustrate, every firm is connected to others in the value chain that supply materials, product outlets, and capital. While a firm struggles with its own environmental issues, each of these other organizations is doing the same. They all share demands for regulatory compliance, risk management, and consumer demand. As a result, these concerns are passed from one organization to the next, thereby normalizing environmental concerns up and down the value chain. As the organization comes under pressure from different players, these concerns become transformed. From buyers and suppliers, environmentalism becomes an issue of resource acquisition, processing, and sale. From insurance companies, environmentalism becomes an issue of risk management. From banks or shareholders and investors, these concerns become an issue of capital acquisition and cost of capital. When organizations alter their investment and underwriting protocols to avoid environmentally mismanaged companies, they alter the flow of capital markets, which directly alters corporate practice. The connection between good environmental performance and low financial risk or high financial performance is being made. Each of these sources of pressure directly affects the way the corporation handles its environmental affairs as well as what kinds of environmental performance it expects from its business partners. As pressures increase, a question that necessarily arises is whether market drivers can ever fully offset environmental damage or whether some form of strict control will be necessary (see box 4.1). In the next chapter, we consider additional environmental business pressures tied to the market.

Box 4.1. Can the Market System Protect the Commons?

The tragedy of the commons is a phrase coined by Garrett Hardin in a famous 1968 article in the journal *Science*. In the excerpt that follows, he lays out his explanation of the concept and closes with a challenging and provocative solution for avoiding the tragedy. In his article, he is discussing overpopulation, but the argument can be expanded to any form of commons that involves business management.

The Tragedy of the Commons[*]
Garrett Hardin

The tragedy of the commons develops in this way. Picture a pasture open to all. It is to be expected that each herdsman will try to keep as many cattle as possible on the commons. Such an arrangement may work reasonably satisfactorily for centuries because tribal wars, poaching, and disease keep the numbers of both man and beast well below the carrying capacity of the land. Finally, however, comes the day of reckoning, that is, the day when the long-desired goal of social stability becomes a reality. At this point, the inherent logic of the commons remorselessly generates tragedy.

As a rational being, each herdsman seeks to maximize his gain. Explicitly or implicitly, more or less consciously, he asks, "What is the utility to me of adding one more animal to my herd?" This utility has one negative and one positive component.

1) The positive component is a function of the increment of one animal. Since the herdsman receives all the proceeds from the sale of the additional animal, the positive utility is nearly +1.

2) The negative component is a function of the additional overgrazing created by one more animal. Since, however, the effects of overgrazing are shared by all the herdsmen, the negative utility for any particular decision making herdsman is only a fraction of −1.

Adding together the component partial utilities, the rational herdsman concludes that the only sensible course for him to pursue is to add another animal to his herd. And another; and another . . . But this is the conclusion reached by each and every rational herdsman sharing a commons. Therein is the tragedy. Each man is locked into a system that compels him to increase his herd without limit—in a world that is limited. Ruin is the destination toward which all men rush, each pursuing his own best interest in a society that believes in the freedom of the commons. Freedom in a commons brings ruin to all. . . . The commons, if justifiable at all, is justifiable only under conditions of low-population density. . . .

. . . No technical solution can rescue us from the misery of overpopulation. . . . At the moment, to avoid hard decisions many of us are tempted to propagandize for conscience and responsible parenthood. The temptation must be resisted, because an appeal to independently acting consciences selects for the disappearance of all conscience in the long run, and an increase in anxiety in the short. The only way we can preserve and nurture other and more

(continues)

Box 4.1. *Continued*

precious freedoms is by relinquishing the freedom to breed, and that very soon. "Freedom is the recognition of necessity"—and it is the role of education to reveal to all the necessity of abandoning the freedom to breed. Only so, can we put an end to this aspect of the tragedy of the commons.

The question then becomes, Will business ever find it in its interest to protect the commons? Or will draconian measures always be necessary for its protection? The answer has important implications for the question of whether the market system can prevent destruction of the commons or whether government regulation will always be necessary to control market excesses. *New York Times* columnist Peter Passell, for example, argues that one way to prevent overfishing is to privatize the fisheries. He argues that "if the right to catch a fixed percentage of the annual harvest were assigned to individual fishermen, the problem of the commons would be solved. Incentives to overfish would dissolve—indeed, those with quotas would have a strong stake in sustaining the fishery, much the way owners of farmland have a stake in preventing erosion."[†] Is this a reasonable approach? Can the market system accommodate protection of the commons?

[*] G. Hardin, "The Tragedy of the Commons: The Population Problem Has No Technical Solution; It Requires a Fundamental Extension of Morality," *Science* 162 (13 December 1968): 1243–1248. © 1968 American Association for the Advancement of Science, All rights reserved. Used with permission.

[†] P. Passell, "One Answer to Overfishing: Privatize the Fisheries," *New York Times*, 11 May 1995, D2.

Further Reading

Aspen Institute. *Uncovering Value: Integrating Environmental and Financial Performance.* Queenstown, Md.: Aspen Institute Publications Office, 1998.

Cairncross, F. *Costing the Earth: The Challenge for Governments, the Opportunities for Business.* Boston: Harvard Business School Press, 1991.

Elkington, J., J. Hailes, and J. Makower. *The Green Consumer: You Can Buy Products That Don't Cost the Earth.* New York: Viking Press, 1990.

Jablonski, J., and L. Pasquini. *Prosper through Environmental Leadership: Succeeding in Tough Times.* Albuquerque, N.M.: Technical Management Consortium, 1994.

Repetto, R., and D. Austin. *Relating Environmental Performance to Shareholder Value: An Approach Based on Fundamentals.* Washington, D.C.: World Resources Institute, 1999.

Schmidheiny, S., F. Zorraquin, and World Business Council for Sustainable Development. *Financing Change: The Financial Community, Eco-Efficiency, and Sustainable Development.* Cambridge, Mass.: MIT Press, 1996.

Chapter 5

MARKET DRIVERS

Drivers in the value chain such as insurance companies, banks, and investors go to the core of corporate financial decision making. However critical drivers are also emerging from a wide-ranging group of market constituents with concerns beyond the acquisition, processing, and distribution of resources. These constituents are driving companies to consider environmentalism in their market strategies (see figure 5.1). For example, to appeal to customers' environmental interests, the Shell Oil Company and BP Amoco have begun testing solar service stations. The first Shell test stations—two in Germany and two in the Netherlands—service electric cars, with any remaining energy going back into the local power grid. BP Amoco's test stations, still in development, will use solar power to provide conventional service.[1] In the package delivery industry, United Parcel Service of America, Inc. has developed an environmentally friendly letter-sized envelope. The package is bleach-free, is produced with 80 percent postconsumer recycled fiber, and is reusable.[2] Given the positive consumer response, the Federal Express Corporation has announced a similar packaging system. Even the lingerie market has seen "green" competitors. Tokyo-based Triumph International Overseas Ltd. has developed a line of lingerie made from recycled plastic bottles. Approximately three and one-half 1.5-liter bottles go into the making of one brassiere, according to the manufacturer.[3] In each of these examples, market competition has focused on environmental considerations. To look more closely at the dynamics of such competitive pressures, in this chapter we consider how consumers, competitors, trade associations, and consultants introduce environmental concerns into the business environment.

Consumers

When considering the value chain, attention should be paid to the role of the end consumer in driving environmental considerations within the firm. If consumers demand environmentally friendly attributes in products, firms will respond to environmental issues as a market opportunity. But pinning down the exact status of environmental consumerism is a difficult challenge. One way to capture environmental market demand is

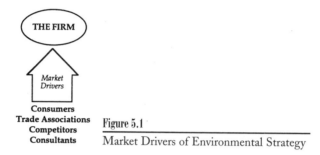

Figure 5.1

Market Drivers of Environmental Strategy

to observe trends in public opinion. When one looks back over the past two decades, a trend is very clear. Since the early 1980s, there has been a significant and steady increase in both public awareness of the seriousness of environmental problems and support for environmental protection.[4] With the twentieth anniversary of Earth Day, in 1990, the emergence of the environmentally conscious consumer was first noted. Although public concern for the environment has been on a slight decline since a 1992 peak,[5] the environmental consumer has remained a confusing presence.

The power of this purchasing bloc is a much-debated issue. Beyond indicating general attention to the issue, public opinion polls show that people care about the environment and claim that they will allow that concern to affect their buying decisions. In response to a 1989 survey, 77 percent of Americans claimed that a company's environmental reputation affected what they bought.[6] A 1995 poll showed that 76 percent of Americans were willing to pay twenty-five cents per gallon more for pollution-reducing gasoline.[7] However, opinion polls and actual buying practices are not tightly linked. It is widely believed that even though consumers claim otherwise, they will not pay a premium price for environmentally friendly attributes. Conventional wisdom suggests that the best that marketers can expect is that when goods provide comparable value (and are comparably priced), environmental attributes can break the tie.

But "green" consumers are a complex, heterogeneous subsegment of the general consuming public. There are several ways to try to understand how this segment behaves. First, one can think of these consumers in terms of the extent to which they will allow values to drive their buying decisions. In 1990, S. C. Johnson & Son, Inc. commissioned Roper Starch Worldwide Inc. to carry out such an analysis by developing a technique to identify and classify individuals with respect to their behavior toward the environment. Roper Starch identified five distinct groups: (1) "true-blue greens," (2) "greenback greens," (3) "sprouts," (4) "grousers," and (5) "basic browns."[8]

- The *true-blue green* is a true environmental activist and leader. True-blue greens have "strong personal concerns about the environment, and they are convinced that individual actions can make a difference in helping to protect and improve the environment."[9]
- The *greenback green* expresses "commitment to the environment by his/her willingness to pay significantly higher prices for green products. But, unlike the true-blue greens, they are not likely to get involved in pro-environment activities, such as recycling, that could consume much of their time."[10] People in these first two categories qualify as real environmental consumers.

- Those in the third group, *sprouts,* show "middling levels of concern about environmental problems, but their involvement in certain kinds of environmentally responsible activities can be rather high."[11] This is the swing group.
- The final two groups could be considered nonenvironmentalist in nature. The *grousers* are "relatively uninvolved in pro-environmental activities, and they justify their indifference by citing factors beyond their control. By nature, they tend to believe that environmental problems are caused by others and not themselves."[12]
- Finally, the *basic browns* are the least environmentally active. "While they might be concerned about pollution problems, they are convinced that their individual behavior can't make a difference in solving these problems. Thus, unlike the grousers, they do not feel the need to rationalize their lack of effort."[13]

The S. C. Johnson–Roper Starch study indicated that the two extremes and the middle grew over time in the United States while the intermediate classifications shrank. Basic browns grew from 28 percent in 1990 to 35 percent in 1993; true-blue greens grew from 11 to 20 percent, and sprouts grew from 26 to 31 percent.[14]

Beyond value differentiation, there is also demographic differentiation.[15] Certain segments of society display environmentalist behavior more than others:

- *Gender.* Women are generally more environmentally aware than men. One survey shows that women are more willing than men to exchange money for lower pollution (39 percent versus 32 percent).[16]
- *Age.* Children tend to be the most environmentally aware age group. The second most aware is the age group from 36 to 45. In one survey, 44 percent of those between 18 and 34 years of age were willing to pay more for environmental protection, compared with 23 percent of those aged 65 and older.[17]
- *Education and income.* Environmentally driven consumerism tends to increase with both education and income levels. More affluent and more highly educated people are more likely to select products on the basis of their environmental attributes. One survey indicated that 28 percent of high school graduates were willing to pay more for lower-polluting gasoline, whereas 48 percent of those with some college education and 45 percent of college graduates were willing to do so.[18]
- *Urban versus rural.* People in urban centers tend to allow environmental considerations to affect their buying decisions more than do people in rural areas. Environmental consumerism tends to be highest on the East and West Coasts and lowest in the South.
- *Political affiliation.* Democrats (40 percent) were more willing to pay an extra twenty-five cents per gallon of gasoline to help clean the environment than were Republicans (30 percent).[19] Table 5.1 shows the correlations between demographic characteristics and S. C. Johnson's five consumer segments.
- *Nationality.* Environmental consumerism also differs from one country to the next. As shown in figure 5.2, S. C. Johnson and Roper Starch applied their behavioral characteristics model to Mexico, the United States, and Canada.

Finally, one might differentiate "green" consumers according to the issues or products that "strike a personal chord" and therefore alter buying decisions. One market segment

Table 5.1. Demographic Composition of Five Environmental Consumer Segments

	Total Public	True-Blue Greens	Greenback Greens	Sprouts	Grousers	Basic Browns
Sex						
Male	47%	40%	52%	48%	44%	52%
Female	53%	60%	48%	52%	56%	48%
Median age	41	42	35	43	40	40
Median income (thousands of dollars)	28	34	33	30	27	20
Education						
Less than high school	19%	10%	11%	14%	17%	33%
High school graduate	38%	30%	27%	40%	44%	40%
Some college	24%	32%	34%	26%	26%	17%
College graduate or more	18%	27%	29%	20%	13%	10%
Occupation						
Executive/professional	16%	23%	24%	17%	15%	10%
White collar	18%	29%	13%	21%	24%	15%
Blue collar	26%	20%	30%	24%	26%	30%
Marital status						
Married	57%	66%	58%	60%	53%	49%
Single	43%	34%	42%	40%	47%	51%
Children under 13	34%	39%	37%	30%	36%	33%
Region						
Northeast	21%	25%	16%	22%	25%	18%
Midwest	25%	27%	22%	26%	21%	25%
South	33%	25%	31%	27%	30%	46%
West	20%	23%	31%	25%	23%	11%

Source: S. C. Johnson/Roper (1993) *The Environment: Public Attitudes and Individual Behavior, North America: Canada, Mexico, United States,* p. 46. Commissioned by SC Johnson (a leading multinational company with operations in nearly 60 countries worldwide) and conducted by Roper Starch (Racine, Wis.: SC Johnson & Son, Inc.) © 1993. All rights reserved. Used with permission.

that has recently enjoyed phenomenal success is organic foods—foods that are free from artificial preservatives, coloring, irradiation, synthetic pesticides, fungicides, ripening agents, fumigants, and growth hormones and that are harvested with sustainability in mind. Sales of organic foods nearly doubled in the five-year period from 1989 ($3.9 billion) to 1994 ($7.6 billion). Similarly, sales of bottled water nearly tripled from 1984 (933 million gallons) to 1995 (2.87 billion gallons). In 1991, there were 195 health-food supermarkets across the United States; by the end of 1994, there were 650.[20]

Hoping to cash in on the growing interest in "green" products, companies are using the environment as a marketing point to an increasing extent. Up from only 3 percent in 1988, the proportion of new products using environmentalism in their marketing campaigns reached 12 percent in 1991, and the percentage has continued to grow. To increase the marketing potential of green products, several organizations are attempting to establish certification programs in order to inform consumers of which products pass their

United States

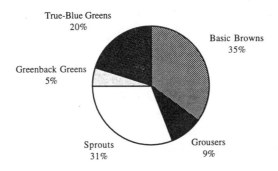

True-Blue Greens
20%

Basic Browns
35%

Greenback Greens
5%

Sprouts
31%

Grousers
9%

Canada

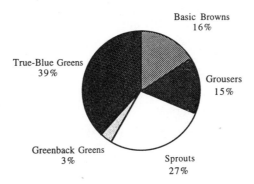

Basic Browns
16%

True-Blue Greens
39%

Grousers
15%

Greenback Greens
3%

Sprouts
27%

Mexico

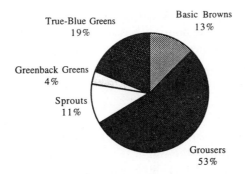

True-Blue Greens
19%

Basic Browns
13%

Greenback Greens
4%

Sprouts
11%

Grousers
53%

Figure 5.2

Profile of Five Environmental Consumer Segments in the United States, Mexico, and Canada, 1993

Source: S. C. Johnson/Roper (1993) *The Environment: Public Attitudes and Individual Behavior, North America: Canada, Mexico, United States,* pg. 35. Commissioned by S. C. Johnson (a leading multinational company with operations in nearly 60 countries worldwide) and conducted by Roper Starch (Racine, Wis.: S. C. Johnson & Son, Inc.) © 1993. All rights reserved. Used with permission.

standard. These organizations charge a fee to research a product's attributes, and if the product is found suitable, they award it an official stamp of approval (much like the Good Housekeeping Seal of Approval certification).[21] Although their influence on "green" consuming has not yet been fully verified, some of the more prominent certification programs include the Green Seal program in the United States (formed in 1990),[22] the European Union Eco-label program (1992),[23] the Swedish Society for Nature Conservation's Good Environmental Choice program (1987),[24] Taiwan's GreenMark Program (1992),[25] Zimbabwe's Environment 2000 Program (1991),[26] the Canadian Environmental Choice Program (1988),[27] the Korean Environmental Labelling Association's Eco-Mark program (1992),[28] the Eco Mark Program of the Japan Environment Association (1989),[29] Germany's Umweltzeichen, or The Blue Angel (1978),[30] Environmental Choice New Zealand (1992),[31] Ecolabelling Norway's Nordic Swan Label program (1989),[32] and the Dutch Milieukeur (Environmental Hallmark) program (1992).[33]

Although these programs are designed to encourage markets that already exist, some companies are attempting to use "greenness" to capitalize on markets that have yet to materialize. For example, several states (including Massachusetts and California) have passed legislation to deregulate the utility industry. That will force the industry to compete in what will rapidly become a commodity market. Lower prices will dominate—that is, unless a company can differentiate its power to gain a price advantage. The Enron Corporation is banking on that differentiating factor being "green" power. The company has invested heavily in wind and solar power as the dominant components of its power portfolio. According to Enron's surveys, 75 percent of Americans would pay more for energy generated from renewable sources: 24 percent would pay 2 percent more, 26 percent would pay 5 percent more, and 20 percent would pay 10 percent more. These figures are supported by other surveys in which 73 percent of Americans said they would pay five cents more for a gallon of gasoline if the higher price would "significantly reduce global warming." When the suggested price increase was raised to twenty-five cents per gallon, 60 percent said they would be willing to pay.[34] In 1998, Enron signed a sole source contract with Patagonia, Inc., an outdoor clothing manufacturer based in Ventura, California, to provide 100 percent of the energy needed by its fourteen California facilities (roughly 1 million kilowatt-hours per year) from wind energy. To provide this energy, Enron will install a 16-megawatt wind plant near Palm Springs. This announcement followed announcements from Toyota Motor Sales, U.S.A., Inc. and Working Assets, an environmentally minded long-distance telephone carrier, that they would purchase renewable energy from other providers.[35]

Other companies are trying to use "greenness" to create markets as well. For example, the average consumer differentiates wool according to the quality of the fiber. But is there a way to differentiate it by the way it is produced? Some sheep ranchers in the western states of Montana and Idaho believe that there is, and they have found environmentalism the aegis under which to do it. In 1997, several ranchers banded together to form the Growers' Wool Cooperative, a consortium that sells "predator-friendly" wool.

Coyotes pose a significant threat to the stability and safety of sheep herds; ranchers have estimated losses of $35 million per year to coyote predation. For more than a century, the preferred solution has been to shoot the coyotes. From 1990 to 1997, federal trappers killed more than 600,000. But some segments of the general population see this as environmentally irresponsible, believing that coyotes serve a useful function within a balanced ecosystem. In response, some ranchers have found that certain animals (such as llamas, dogs, and burros) can be mixed in with the herd to run off the profit-eating predators. Economic benefits have emerged from the reduced time needed to watch over the sheep as well as their increased survival rate. The cooperative hopes to sell its wool for as much as $2 per pound, a $1 premium over the prices ranchers usually get at traditional outlets. The cooperative has contracted with home-based knitters in Montana to manufacture its line of wool sweaters, hats, and blankets. The Nature Conservancy has been enlisted to help and has agreed to feature the cooperative's products in its catalog.[36]

Even if companies can integrate environmental attributes into their products, the next challenge in gaining market acceptance may be developing environmental literacy in the general public. For example, although some Americans state that they would pay more for power generated from "green" energy sources, do they really know what is green? Is hydroelectric energy green? Some say that it is, but others point to the damage dams do to spawning fish. Is wind power a green energy source? Again, although some say that it is, others point to the hazards wind generators create for the thousands of birds that are killed in their propeller blades. Even when the issues are not so muddled as these examples, there is confusion on the part of the American public. In a survey by the Enron Corporation, for example, nearly 6 percent of respondents considered coal to be a renewable energy source.

To measure environmental literacy, the National Environmental Education and Training Foundation (NEETF), in collaboration with Roper Starch, conducts an annual survey titled "National Report Card on Environmental Attitudes, Knowledge and Behaviors." Each year, the survey reveals persistent myths and misinformation in the public's environmental knowledge. In the seventh survey, conducted in 1998,[37] NEETF found that a majority of people think (incorrectly) that energy in the United States is produced in ways that do not pollute the air, mostly at hydroelectric plants. Only one person in three sees coal burning as an issue of concern. Nearly half think that factory discharges are the main cause of water pollution. Only one in five could identify the leading factor, runoff from the land. Just one in six know that the 30,000 tons of spent nuclear fuel in the United States is being stored on a temporary basis. A majority assumes (incorrectly) that a government agency screens all household chemicals.[38] The persistence of these kinds of myths impedes the development of policy to solve environmental problems. It also creates the need for a strong educational program for any company that wishes to capitalize on "green" attributes in its products.

Competitors

When competitors make the environment an issue in their strategies or challenge the environmental components of other companies' strategies, environmentalism is translated into a competitive issue. For example, oil companies and automobile manufacturers have long been challenging each other over the proper mechanism for reducing automobile emissions. Automakers have pushed government to mandate alterations in the formulation of gasoline, and oil companies have pushed for alterations in engine design and the installation of catalytic converters. The outcome of this exchange has significant cost implications in each industry and has, at times, caused very pointed accusations and challenges. In January 1972, friction between the two industries erupted when an executive of the General Motors Corporation argued publicly that unleaded gasoline should be priced two to four cents per gallon lower than regular. Concurrently, a broader debate flourished over the merits of catalytic converters and their associated need for fuel with low lead and sulfur content.[39]

Beyond competition among companies over environmental initiatives, battles can be fought over the form of environmental regulation. For example, early Superfund cleanups in the 1980s were based on cap-and-contain technologies. Hazardous wastes were contained on-site by means of impermeable caps covering them to prevent rainwater infiltration and drain systems surrounding them to limit contaminant migration. An entire market of specialized contractors developed to provide these caps and drain systems. However, the Superfund Amendments and Reauthorization Act of 1986 (see appendix A) mandated stringent cleanup standards with a preference for permanent solutions that significantly reduced waste volume, toxicity, and mobility and that encouraged alternatives to land disposal. Companies that had perfected cap-and-contain proficiencies watched their market eliminated with a shift in regulatory preference. Further, companies with Superfund liabilities watched the cost of those liabilities increase dramatically with imposition of the more stringent standards.

These kinds of strategic implications of government regulation are playing out in more recent debates over flexible regulatory options, such as Project XL (Environmental Excellence and Leadership), discussed in chapter 2. Such a regulatory shift will allow some companies to find compliance strategies that are consistent with their own economic strategies and that will therefore allow them to reduce compliance costs and improve the bottom line. This regulatory format will have a significant competitive component in the industry as companies that are better able to find efficient responses to government requirements increase their competitive success. Other companies, however, may not be so adaptable and may not wish to see such a shift. They may not possess the skills and knowledge to turn regulations into a source of competitive advantage. In some cases, inefficient command-and-control regulations may have attractive benefits such as the creation of a barrier to entry for new competitors or an unsustainable drain on resources for smaller competitors. With inefficient regulations, compliance becomes a spending game in which the company with the deepest pockets wins.

Government is not the only arena in which environmentalism becomes a competitive issue. Companies have begun "benchmarking" themselves against other companies that have better environmental records and that enjoy the benefits of better environmental performance. Searching for industry best practices regarding the environment has become an important part of many companies' environmental strategy. Interestingly, the boundaries of what constitutes a competitor often blur in this kind of analysis. Although investors may be beginning to consider best-in-class considerations in their determination of environmental leaders, companies themselves seem to compare themselves across the board. An oil company, for example, may benchmark itself not only against other oil companies but also against chemical, consumer product, automobile, and forestry companies. In this kind of comparative analysis, certain companies (such as the Dow Chemical Company, the Interface Corporation, and British Petroleum) emerge as leaders and others as followers in setting the standards and industry norms regarding the environment. There is at times a first-mover advantage in the development of environmental programs that others feel compelled to emulate. An executive of the Amoco Corporation stated, "A leader in this arena can not only reap the benefits arising from a satisfied public and 'green' investors but can also put considerable pressure to catch up on the competition."[40]

For example, in late 1997 the Toyota Motor Corporation stunned the international automobile industry and stirred increasing commitment within the industry to produce more fuel-efficient automobiles when it unveiled the seventy-mile-per-gallon "parallel" hybrid Prius in Japanese markets. This spurred renewed enthusiasm where previously there was little. Prior to the unveiling of the Prius, American automakers had joined forces with the oil and coal industries in a lobbying campaign against the Kyoto Protocol to the United Nations Framework Convention on Climate Change, an international agreement to limit global warming. Their chief executive officers met with President Clinton and warned him that the technologies did not yet exist to make the necessary advances and that he should not sign any such treaty. In December, the Clinton administration endorsed the Kyoto Protocol, Toyota introduced the Prius, and executives of major automakers began to shift their perspectives. At the North American International Auto Show in January 1998, John Smith Jr., chairman and chief executive officer of the General Motors Corporation (GM), proclaimed that "no car company will be able to thrive in the 21st century solely with the internal-combustion engine." William C. Ford, Jr. chairman of the Ford Motor Company's finance committee (later to became chairman of the board), announced that there was "a compelling business case to be made" that the first automaker to reach the market with a reasonably priced alternative-fuel vehicle would win a significant competitive advantage.[41] GM announced that it hoped to have a car powered by a fuel-cell engine ready for production by 2004 and a hybrid to compete with Toyota's Prius by 2001. The race for a new technology in automobile propulsion was spurred by the threat of controls to prevent global warming, mandates from several states for a zero-emission vehicle (California, Massachusetts, New York, and Vermont), and, most important, the strategic action of a major competitor, Toyota.

In another example from 1997, the British Petroleum Company (BP) precipitated a major shift in corporate positions on global climate change. John Browne, the company's chief executive officer, made an unprecedented announcement in a speech at Stanford University that *(a)* he believed that action was necessary to respond to the climate change issue, *(b)* his company would make significant investments in solar energy toward that end, and *(c)* the company would voluntarily institute new programs to monitor greenhouse gas emissions and would unilaterally reduce their volume by 10 percent. By being the first to break ranks with industry groups opposed to the Kyoto Protocol (such as the Global Climate Coalition), BP received tremendous accolades from the press, environmentalists, and government. The benefits in public reputation, employee morale, and government influence were enormous. Oddly, this was a statement that some other oil company executives would not have found it difficult to make. Amoco, for example, had long been heavily involved in the development of photovoltaic cells. (It is interesting to note that analysts of the merger between BP and Amoco pointed out that "both also operate in the niche area of solar energy and will pose a challenge to that market's leader, Germany's Siemens AG.")[42] Conversely, it was also a statement that some companies could not make. Thus, by being first, Browne both saw and influenced the direction of public, nongovernmental organization, government, and international opinion. He set his company on a path that others will be pressured to follow. Some may find this new direction to be consistent with their current strategies; others may not. In any event, BP was central in determining that new direction. The company's defection from the Global Climate Coalition, for example, has been followed by other notable defections (e.g., by Shell).

Competition regarding environmental performance is strong within the hotel industry, driven in part by concerns about resource efficiency at a time when hotel capacity has increased (by 25 percent through the 1990s). Hilton International CO, for example, instituted an environmental program that has reduced annual electricity and water use by 30 percent, waste generation by 25 percent, and gas consumption by 60 percent. Between 1990 and 1997, May Fair Inter-Continental London reduced its energy consumption by 27 percent. In 1996, the energy budget for Inter-Continental Hotels and Resorts was $74 million, $6 million less than in 1995, despite its opening new properties around the world. Resource reductions such as these are obtained through new air-conditioning and energy management systems, fluorescent lighting retrofits, low-flush toilets, gray-water systems, and, perhaps most important, training of staff members to rethink and reduce consumption on a daily basis. The India-based Taj Group of Hotels, which operates hotels in regions where water is at a premium, has instituted an environmental initiative to ensure that wastewater is treated and reused for such purposes as gardening and use in cooling towers. The initiative also mandates the installation of water meters and low-flush toilets and improved water maintenance. These measures have led to water use reductions of as much as 35 percent at some hotels.[43]

Beyond realizing direct savings in operational costs, can these hotels set industry standards to gain competitive advantage from these initiatives? The Taj Group has launched an environmental magazine, *Eco-Taj*, aimed at communicating best practices in the hotel industry. On the industry level, the International Hotels Environment Initiative has been established, with financing from member organizations, to communicate best practices even further. The group produces an environmental action guide for hotels, conducts workshops and conferences worldwide, produces reports on environmental best practices and ecologically friendly products, and publishes *Green Hotelier* magazine. Are consumers paying attention? Holiday Inn Worldwide includes hotel guests in its environmental initiative, allowing them to choose between reusing towels and linens and getting new ones.[44] In contrast, Inter-Continental tries to keep its environmental initiative low-key, fearing that guests might not equate such measures with a luxury hotel experience. Many hotels, however, are reconsidering such a stance, particularly in light of the demographic research suggesting that people want to see businesses become more environmentally responsible and that this desire increases with income level.

In general, how do consumers react to the environmental claims of large multinational companies such as BP, Hilton, and GM? Often, it is a challenge for these companies to gain widespread endorsement for their environmental positions; in many cases it is the smaller companies, such as Ben & Jerry's Homemade Holdings, Inc., Patagonia, Body Shop International PLC, and Tom's of Maine, Inc., that are the more prominent examples of firms gaining competitive advantage by employing environmental strategies. Consumers and the public generally associate small consumer products companies with "green" consciousness. This creates a serious dilemma for corporate strategists in determining how to position their companies in terms of the environment (see box 5.1).

Box 5.1. Is "Green" Marketing Really Greenwashing?

Does "green" marketing work? Does it reflect a legitimate effort to accurately portray the "greeness" of a company? Or is it merely a public relations ploy to increase market share by convincing consumers to spend more money on material consumption and thereby increasing environmental degradation? Several factors may influence the success of green marketing. For example, does it merely play on the biases people already have regarding a particular company? Can it work for a chemical company as well as it does for an ice cream manufacturer? Or do people naturally distrust large multinational corporations and therefore distrust their environmental claims? Marianne Jennings presented an interesting view of green marketing in a 1995 article in the *Wall Street Journal.* One question that emerges in her essay is whether there are risks to wearing the environmental mantle too proudly. When companies do this, they become targets for critics who seek to discredit their efforts.

Confessions of a Business Ethicist[*]
Marianne M. Jennings, Arizona State University

Join me in reciting the business ethics litany: no use of animals in product testing; benefits for "domestic partners"; some emotion for the rain forests; refusal to do business (except for women's conferences) in China; affirmative action quotas; and, well, you can guess the rest. Profess your devotion to the politically correct agenda, and you are praised in perpetuity. So politically charged is the field that a recent issue of *Business Ethics* suggested boycotts of businesses, including Kinko's Copies, that advertised on Rush Limbaugh's show. In the following issue, a Kinko's mea culpa appeared; it would not happen again.

I had fallen for the agenda myself. In my ethics classes I extolled Anita Roddick's Body Shop for years: natural cosmetics; "Products for People Tested by People: first-world wages for Third World products." Even when Jon Entine's damaging expose of the Body Shop's false advertising claims and other ethical lapses were published in *Business Ethics,* readers wrote to protect its appearance. Ben Cohen of Ben & Jerry's resigned from the editorial board. I wrote to Ms. Roddick's husband, Gordon, Body Shop's chairman, with my "Say it isn't so!" plea. The firm responded by attacking Mr. Entine, countering some points, but affirming others.

While I was busy teaching about the Body Shop's product testing and exotic sources, franchises were suffering from direct competition from the company's catalogue sales. Mr. Roddick's memorandum of response also acknowledged use of synthetic colorings, fragrances and preservatives.

(continues)

Box 5.1. *Continued*

Ben & Jerry's Homemade Inc. had also charmed me. After all, it produced an ice cream called Rainforest Crunch with official rain forest nuts and berries, used all natural ingredients, and sent a percentage of profits on sales to charities. But through the company's self-audit, which was eventually released to shareholders and the public, I learned that Cherry Garcia contained sulfur dioxide preservatives. And it was margarine, not butter, in some flavors. Further, financial performance was not so hot, and the laid-back, socially responsible firm was facing stiff competition. There is more to running an ethical business than agendas. Small things like shareholders.

The ethics agenda brands certain industries as unethical, per se. Oil and water and business ethics don't mix. There is a side to the story of the Exxon *Valdez* spill that partially mitigates Exxon. The spill was not as great and was not handled as poorly as the media depicted, but this is rarely mentioned in business ethics. Dow Corning will never again gain the restoration of reputation it deserves following the new studies that debunk the relationship between breast implants and certain diseases. Audi was tarred and feathered in the 1980's for an alleged sudden acceleration problem. The federal government eventually released a study concluding there was no sudden acceleration problem: Owners were using the wrong pedal!

Dupont budgets $20 million each year for mammograms and flu shots for employees. Through ergonomics, exercise and dieting, Dow Chemical has reduced employee sprains and strains by 90 percent. Tenneco feeds its 1,500 pipeline workers a low-fat diet. These progressive actions and firms are not described in business ethics literature.

The agenda is set. The questions are not asked. The presence of a social agenda overpowers the simple issues in business ethics. Is animal testing as critical as the fair and honest treatment of franchisees? Is commitment to the rain forests as important as truth in labeling? Are contributions to centers against sexual assault as important as fairness to shareholders? Ryka Inc., a manufacturer of women's athletic shoes, was known for its founder, Sherl Poe, and its contributions to fighting violence against women. When the business didn't take off, Ms. Poe signed to sell Ryka to L.A. Gear Inc. Under the terms of the failed merger, the Ryka shareholders would have gotten 25 to 30 cents a share. Ms. Poe's take would have been a $1.3 million contract. One shareholder asked, "How could a company with such strong ideals make such an unfair deal?" The operative words are "strong ideals." Have we business ethicists defined "strong ideals" correctly?

We have equated certain social goals with business ethics. While we may wish to believe that commitment to social issues is a good measure of ethical conduct, it is not an absolute determinant of fairness and honesty. The social responsibility agenda of business ethics sets the standards and lists acceptable firms. Yet, who checks to see that these firms have in fact not simply developed a marketing plan easily designed and executed to maximize their return using the ethics agenda?

No one is checking. Not the investment firms that tout socially responsible clients and investments. Not those of us academics dedicated to the field of business ethics. Not the media, enamored of anyone who spouts "green" or "cultural diversity." No one asks the hard questions about values. Kinko's "Rush Limbaugh" ads are an ethical issue, but not for Kinko's. They are an issue for business ethicists: Political views are not an appropriate measure of business ethics.

* M. Jennings, "Confessions of a Business Ethicist," *Wall Street Journal,* 25 September 1995, A14. Reprinted with permission of Marianne M. Jennings and *The Wall Street Journal,* © 1995, Dow Jones & Company, Inc., All rights reserved. Used with permission.

Some industries have found that consumer perceptions can be more easily changed through a joint effort. The chemical industry, through its Responsible Care program (discussed later in this chapter), has been the most visible in this regard. It has produced television and print advertisements describing how much the industry has done to reduce pollution and how much it still needs to do. The American Plastics Council adopted a similar program and moved favorability ratings from 52 to 65 percent in four years by publicizing what it was doing about pollution. Other industries, such as the pharmaceutical, steel, aluminum, cotton, beef, pork, and milk industries, have done the same. Will consumers respond to this kind of message, given the messenger?

In 1997, oil company executives faced this question. Lobbying for an advertising campaign, Kenneth Dickerson, senior vice president for the Atlantic Richfield Company (ARCO), highlighted some impressive facts for the previous decade: atmospheric lead concentrations were down by 78 percent; carbon monoxide was down by 37 percent; sulfur dioxide was down by 37 percent; particulates were down by 22 percent. He attributed these to real-time monitoring of industrial facilities, significant reductions in stationary source emissions, and cleaner-burning fuels in cleaner-running vehicles such that twenty new cars in 1997 produce the tailpipe emissions of one new car in the 1960s. Yet the general public continues to hold the oil industry in low esteem. In surveys of public opinion regarding corporate environmental attributes, oil companies consistently rate significantly lower than all other industries combined.[45] In the end, the oil executives decided to cancel the proposed advertising campaign, concluding that the general public would not believe them.[46]

Trade Associations

In 1986, the Chemical Manufacturers Association (CMA) began to debate its larger role in mending the public image of the chemical industry following events such as the disaster in Bhopal, India. At that time, the Canadian branch of the CMA began to recognize that all companies shared a common problem and instituted a program called Responsible Care, which binds its members to a set of principles designed to improve environmental performance. The industry was the first to recognize a common interest in protecting the environment—an individual firm cannot stand out as clean in an industry that is perceived as dirty. This message was brought home poignantly when the Dow Chemical Company conducted public surveys around its Canadian plants to find out the geographic scope of its "green" reputation compared with that of the rest of the industry. The disturbing answer was that the company's reputation extended only three kilometers around its plants. All the company's efforts to improve its environmental reputation were for naught because the reputation of the industry as a whole was dominant.

To correct this problem, company executives pressed the Canadian branch of the CMA to develop a set of environmental standards for all member companies to adopt. The U.S. branch of the CMA quickly followed suit, with the board voting unanimously to adopt the program, and in January 1989, member companies officially signed on. The program was formally announced in April 1990 when the CMA took out full-page advertisements in major newspapers around the United States to coincide with the 1990

Table 5.2. Summary of Ten Industry Environmental Programs

Industry	Program	Year Formed	Compliance	Third-Party Audit	Public Disclosure
Chemical	Responsible Care	1990	Compulsory[a]	No	Yes
Oil	STEP[c]	1990	Voluntary	No	Yes
Automobile	APPP[d]	1991	Voluntary	No	No
Lead	PSP[e]	1991	Voluntary	No	No
Paper	3P[f]	1991	Voluntary	No	Yes
Textile	E3[g]	1992	Voluntary	No	No
Printing	EMP[h]	1992	Mandatory[b]	Yes	No
Printing	GPP[i]	1993	Voluntary	No	No
Dry-cleaning	IFICP[j]	1994	Mandatory[b]	No	No
Forestry	SFI[k]	1995	Compulsory[a]	No	No

Source: A. Hoffman, "The Many Faces of Environmental Stewardship," *Chemical Week* 157, no. 1 (1995): 65. © 1995 Chemical Week Associates. All rights reserved. Used with permission.
[a]With membership.
[b]With sign-up.
[c]STEP = Strategies for Today's Environmental Partnership (American Petroleum Institute).
[d]APPP = Great Lakes Automotive Pollution Prevention Project (American Automobile Manufacturers Association).
[e]PSP = Product Stewardship Program (Lead Industries Association, Inc.).
[f]3P = Pollution Prevention Partnership (Wisconsin Paper Council).
[g]E3 = Encouraging Environmental Excellence (American Textile Manufacturers Institute).
[h]EMP = Environmental Management Program (Printing Industries of America, Inc.).
[i]GPP = Great Printers Project (Printing Industries of America, Inc.).
[j]IFICP = IFI Certification Program (International Fabric Institute).
[k]SFI = Sustainable Forestry Initiative (American Forest and Paper Association).

celebration of Earth Day. The advertisement in the *New York Times* appeared on April 11, 1990, included the names of 170 chemical firms as supporters, and outlined the 10 guiding environmental principles that are now a mandatory requirement for membership in the CMA, which represents 90 percent of the country's basic industrial chemical manufacturing capability.

If imitation is the sincerest form of flattery, it would seem that many think the CMA's idea is a good one.[47] Since the program was unveiled, the model of Responsible Care has become the norm. Similarly designed programs are flourishing in other industries, such as the petroleum, printing, textile, paper, lead, and automobile industries. Like Responsible Care, these programs are built on the belief that a company's environmental reputation depends on the reputation of the entire industry. The following sections provide nine additional examples. Along with the CMA's Responsible Care program, they are summarized in table 5.2.

American Textile Manufacturers Institute (ATMI): Encouraging Environmental Excellence (E3)

The Encouraging Environmental Excellence (E3) program of the American Textile Manufacturers Institute is a national, voluntary initiative that calls for companies in the textile-manufacturing industry to adopt a ten-point plan to improve the environment.

These points include establishment of corporate environmental policy and goals, detailed auditing of facilities, an outreach program for suppliers and customers, and employee education and community awareness programs. Perhaps more so than in other industries, the drive for the program appears to have been initiated by downstream users. Companies such as Levi Strauss & Company and L. L. Bean, Inc. have begun to choose their vendors on the basis of environmental performance. Companies accepted into E3 receive a seal of approval and permission to use the E3 logo on their hangtags. Beyond addressing public relations concerns, however, the industry is tackling some serious technical issues: developing dyes that require less water; coming up with processes that do not use formaldehyde; producing more fabrics with organic cotton, recycled polyester, and eco-friendly fibers; and gaining market acceptance of unbleached fabrics.

Wisconsin Paper Council (WPC): Pollution Prevention Partnership (3P)

The Wisconsin Paper Council established its Pollution Prevention Partnership (3P) as a statewide cooperative between the council and the Wisconsin Department of Natural Resources. The 3P program focuses on pollution prevention projects that are technically and economically feasible for the paper industry to undertake. Its founders state that it is cost–benefit driven. The 3P program currently involves twenty-seven firms and forty-three facilities and encompasses air emissions, wastewater discharges, and solid and hazardous waste production. It began with two tasks, which have been completed: cataloging industry emissions for the years 1987 through 1992 to establish a baseline for future reductions, in line with the requirements of Title III of the Superfund Amendments and Reauthorization Act of 1986 (see appendix A), and targeting substances for potential pollution prevention and source reduction. On the basis of the 1992 levels, releases of seven major contaminants were set for reduction by an average of 40 percent by 1999. Although technology development and transfer is the primary thrust, work is under way for a supplier outreach program. Founders of the program state that cooperation from chemical suppliers in particular is needed if 3P is to succeed. "If some of their chemicals are not environmentally friendly," said the WPC's president, Thomas Schmidt, "we want their help in coming up with alternative products."[48]

American Forest and Paper Association (AF&PA): Sustainable Forestry Initiative (SFI)

The American Forest and Paper Association's Sustainable Forestry Initiative (SFI) is a national program that establishes detailed guidelines for member companies to reforest harvested land promptly, provide wildlife habitat, improve water quality and ecosystem diversity, and protect forestland of special ecological significance. By January 1996, all 400 AF&PA members were to have been in compliance with the SFI program's twelve guidelines as a condition of membership. These companies account for 95 percent of paper production and 65 percent of solid wood production in the United States and own 90 percent of the country's industrial forestland. Beyond the technical requirements, there are requirements for community outreach and public reporting.

Printing Industries of America, Inc. (PIA): Environmental Management Program (EMP)

The Environmental Management Program (EMP) is designed to provide information about minimizing the adverse environmental effects of printing. It is sponsored by the Printing Industries of America, Inc. (PIA) and 3M and administered by PIA and its local affiliates. Aimed at small printers, the program is focused primarily on regulatory compliance through the implementation of standard operating practices. A self-study segment that involves reviewing a manual on major environmental regulations is followed by a self-administered test. The participating company is then visited by a PIA affiliate for an independent site visit. After completing the program, printers receive a 3M-PIA environmental management certificate. This certification is renewed every two years by a plant audit. By 1995, 600 printers had begun the process and 15 had achieved full certification.

Printing Industries of America, Inc.: Great Printers Project (GPP)

The Great Printers Project (GPP) is a joint initiative of the Environmental Defense Fund, PIA, and the Council of Great Lakes Governors. Its first task has been to unite representatives from government, industry, labor, and environmental groups to focus on environmental protection goals for the printing industry. Primarily technical in its objectives, the project seeks to make pollution prevention the guiding environmental principle not only for lithographic printers but also for suppliers and customers, regulators, and providers of financial and technical assistance in the Great Lakes region. Four of the eight Great Lakes states are serving as pilots in implementing the GPP recommendations. Simultaneously, work groups have been organized to develop specific standards and practices regarding consolidated reporting procedures, "green" marketing, measurement and evaluation procedures, technical and financial assistance, and technology transfer.

American Automobile Manufacturers Association (AAMA): Great Lakes Automotive Pollution Prevention Project (APPP)

The Great Lakes Automotive Pollution Prevention Project (APPP) is a voluntary program closely related to the Great Printers Project in its focus on the Great Lakes. It is a cooperative venture between the American Automobile Manufacturers Association (AAMA), the Michigan Department of Natural Resources—representing the eight Great Lakes states—and the big three domestic auto producers. Its primary goals are to identify the persistent toxic substances that have measurable adverse effects in the Great Lakes region; reduce the generation and release of those contaminants; promote pollution prevention through technology transfer between the automobile industry and its suppliers; and address regulatory barriers to pollution prevention. In its first year, the APPP reduced toxic releases into the Great Lakes by 20 percent. Adjustment to reflect production volumes reveals that releases have been lowered by 28.9 percent, to less than two pounds per automobile manufactured.

Lead Industries Association, Inc. (LIA): Product Stewardship Program (PSP)

The Product Stewardship Program (PSP) is an initiative of the Lead Industries Association, Inc. (LIA) designed to provide technical support and promote four primary objectives: assist companies that use lead products in reducing lead levels in the blood of workers; establish a program for primary and secondary smelters to prevent childhood lead exposure in local neighborhoods; encourage increased lead recycling; and provide information about issues related to lead use. The PSP is primarily an information transfer program, and member companies may adopt the LIA standards on a voluntary basis.

American Petroleum Institute (API): Strategies for Today's Environmental Partnership (STEP)

Perhaps the program most closely modeled after the CMA's Responsible Care program, Strategies for Today's Environmental Partnership (STEP) is a set of eleven guiding environmental principles that were incorporated into the bylaws of the American Petroleum Institute (API) in 1990. For the most part, these reflect verbatim the CMA's ten guiding principles. However, in contrast with the Responsible Care program, acceptance of the STEP requirements is voluntary.

International Fabric Institute (IFI): IFI Certification Program (IFICP)

The International Fabric Institute (IFI) Certification Program (IFICP) is significantly different from the other programs discussed here in one important aspect: given that dry cleaners are generally small operations, the program certifies not individual plants but individual operators. Each year, the IFI distributes a self-study guide on environmentally sound dry-cleaning procedures. Eight hundred dry cleaners took the first exam in 1994, and 1,000 were expected at the second exam, in the fall of 1999. Those who pass the exam receive certificates that are valid for three years.

Some of the major criticisms of these programs center on three issues:

1. *Enforcement.* Many programs threaten expulsion of member companies that do not comply with their requirements, but they do not make clear whether or how they will carry out such a threat. Many observers believe that without enforcement mechanisms, the programs are impotent. The AF&PA's Sustainable Forestry Initiative, sensitive to this concern, earned credibility early when several members left the trade association after refusing to sign on to the environmental program.
2. *Third-party accountability.* If the progress reports of these programs are developed exclusively by member companies, there is a question as to whether they can be trusted. Many believe that external audits by third-party organizations are the only way to ensure reliability.
3. *Transparency.* Some programs do not require public disclosure of participants' environmental performance. Many observers believe that the central aspect of these programs should be public disclosure of the hazards and opportunities of environmental initiatives. Regardless of these criticisms, the reality is undeniable that industries are banding together and influencing the environmental practices of their members.

As a final note, industry groups not only can set rigid standards for their members; they also can influence the direction of technological advancement in regard to the environment. For example, production of energy-efficient refrigerators was encouraged through a competition sponsored by a consortium of utility companies in 1992. Under the "golden carrot" program, appliance giants such as the Whirlpool Corporation and Frigidaire Home Products competed to build a superefficient, environmentally friendly refrigerator that would beat the Department of Energy's existing standard by 25 to 50 percent. The winner would take home a $30 million prize.[49] After a year of development, Whirlpool was declared the winner for a design that used no chlorofluorocarbons (CFCs) in its refrigerant as well as an improved compressor, better insulation, and a computer-chip-controlled defrosting system that adjusts the length and frequency of power-consuming defrost cycles.[50]

Consultants

Environmental consulting did not exist as a specialized field prior to 1970. Since then, its purpose has historically been to help companies comply with complex government regulations. Consultants are a conduit through which rules of thumb, standard operating procedures, and best industry practices are transferred among companies. As such, they can both perpetuate existing perspectives on the environment and spread new ones. For example, virtually all of the more than $13 billion spent on environmental equipment and services to industry and government in 1992 went to control, analysis, form filling, or remediation, with only a minor fraction going to pollution prevention.[51] This institutionalized preference in spending was perpetuated by a consulting industry that thrived on the market for pollution control and regulatory compliance services to the exclusion of pollution minimization and waste reduction. This carried over into the corporate mind-set where consulting services were offered.

More recently, that mentality has begun to change. In the early 1990s, companies began to adopt a more proactive stance regarding environmental issues. For this reason, they began to look for different types of consulting services to help them get out of the "regulatory rotary" and integrate environmental concerns into their economic strategies. As a result, the consulting industry, typically dominated by science- and technology-based firms that provided services such as wastewater cleanup and hazardous waste treatment, began to shift toward satisfying the demand for more management-based services. To provide these services, management consulting firms such as McKinsey & Company, Deloitte and Touche LLP, and Arthur Andersen began to join the traditional ranks of environmental companies such as Camp Dresser & McKee Inc. (CDM) and CH2M HILL, Inc. in offering environmental services. These firms began to offer more comprehensive services to reduce pollution. However, in the mid-1990s, their numbers dropped off. It turns out that comprehensive services including both technical and managerial services were difficult to develop. The management consulting firms found that it was more difficult to acquire the technical services and client base to supplement their management services than it was for the technically based companies to acquire management services.

The late 1990s saw significant contraction in the environmental consulting industry. As companies became smarter about reducing pollution within plant walls and regulators continued to shift away from command and control and toward the "carrot" of market-based services, the need for environmental consulting based on discrete technical solutions dropped off. Between 1994 and 1996, the number of environmental consulting firms in New England, a region traditionally rich in such services, declined by 27 percent.[52] One direct reason cited for the decline was a lack of significant new legislation, federal or state, creating new requirements. As companies have begun to understand the regulations, there has been less of a need for consulting services to help interpret them. Another reason is an extraordinarily large number of mergers of consulting firms. In 1997 and 1998, five major merger and acquisition transactions occurred,[53] with companies whose revenues were valued at more than $3 billion, or about 20 percent of the environmental consulting industry. In 1993, a large firm in this industry was considered to be one that had annual sales in the range of $100 million. In 1998, that number reached $1 billion.[54]

With this contraction, consulting services are beginning to shift toward other areas. For example, pending regulations that will allow companies to self-audit their environmental programs rather than go through lengthy permitting process (such as Project XL) will create new demand for environmental consultants. Today, traditional environmental engineering companies such as Metcalf & Eddy, Inc. and CDM are developing management proficiencies to provide the comprehensive services that management consulting firms cannot. Within these companies, new vice president positions are emerging in areas such as sustainable development. Their goal is to supplement the companies' technically based services with management and policy services.

Conclusion

When consumers include environmental concerns in their purchasing decisions, the issue of environmental protection is translated into an issue of market demand. When competitors use the environment as a strategic issue or challenge the way others use it, the issue is translated into one of competitive strategy and growth of market share. When trade associations see opportunities in presenting a united front on environmental affairs, the issue becomes one of industry reputation or external and government relations. Finally, when consultants prescribe strategic programs that incorporate elements of environmental protection, they (like the other entities in this list) act to disseminate best practices and spread common perceptions of corporate responsibility toward the environment. The next chapter examines how social drivers can alter business practice through yet other business channels.

Further Reading

Cairncross, F. *Green, Inc.: A Guide to Business and the Environment*. Washington, D.C.: Island Press, 1995.
DeSimone, L., and F. Popoff. *Eco-Efficiency: The Business Link to Sustainable Development*. Cambridge, Mass.: MIT Press, 1997.

Frankel, C. *In Earth's Company: Business, Environment, and the Challenge of Sustainability.* Stony Creek, Conn.: New Society Publishers, 1998.

Hirschhorn, J., and K. Oldenburg. *Prosperity without Pollution: The Prevention Strategy for Industry and Consumers.* New York: Van Nostrand Reinhold, 1991.

Leggett, J., ed. *Climate Change and the Financial Sector: The Emerging Threat—the Solar Solution.* Munich: Gerling Akademie Verlag, 1996.

Morrison, C. *Managing Environmental Affairs: Corporate Practices in the U.S., Canada, and Europe.* New York: Conference Board, 1991.

Chapter 6

SOCIAL DRIVERS

In 1995, the Shell Oil Company was preparing to retire its twenty-two-year-old Brent Spar oil platform off the coast of Norway, which had reached retirement age and was no longer useful to the company. The plan was to tow the 420-foot rig into the North Sea and sink it. Actually, that was the plan until the environmental group Greenpeace got wind of the company's intentions. The group argued that sinking the rig would destroy life on the seabed both from the impact of the structure and from the toxic chemicals that it claimed were still on board. To make its point, the group staged the most expensive protest in its history. It hired ships to shadow the rig as it was towed out to sea and hired helicopters to place protesters on board and hang banners as it was moored 250 miles off Aberdeen, Scotland. Most important, it engaged in a vigorous communications and media campaign to mobilize public concern. The campaign raised public emotions to such a pitch that there was a Europe-wide boycott of Shell products and there were firebomb and shotgun attacks on Shell filling stations.

Would sinking the Brent Spar have caused an environmental hazard? Greenpeace argued that the rig contained more than 5,000 tons of oil and other toxic substances that would create an environmental catastrophe if released into the ocean. The organization pushed for Shell to decommission the platform on dry land rather than turn the North Atlantic Ocean into a dump site. Shell countered that less than fifty tons of oil residue remained on board and that dropping the steel hull to the ocean bottom would be environmentally beneficial, creating a reef to support sea life.

In the end, Shell reconsidered its disposal strategy. But after that reconsideration, Greenpeace was forced to retract its claims about the Brent Spar's toxic cargo, was criticized by news editors for using manipulative tactics, and was charged by the Advertising Standards Authority with misinforming the public. Shell disposed of the rig by dismantling it and turning it into a ferry quay for a Norwegian fjord. The environmentally friendly option will cost Shell 43 million British pounds, compared with the original cost of 4.5 million pounds for dumping at sea. As a result of the incident, the company has opened discussions with Greenpeace and is undertaking a campaign to change its cul-

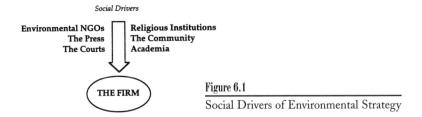

Figure 6.1

Social Drivers of Environmental Strategy

ture of secrecy regarding internal decision making, which has precluded interactions with environmental groups in the past.

For Shell, the only issue is not whether or not sinking the rig would have created an environmental hazard. What is of equal or even more importance is that the company learned of the environmental group's importance in driving public opinion. Although environmental issues have a technical component directed by regulatory, resource, and market pressures, they also have a social component. The sinking of the Brent Spar might have been a technically feasible option both economically and environmentally, but public pressure can be more influential in deciding the final outcome. Decision makers must actively manage constituents in their external social environments in order to develop effective and successful operating strategies. Constituents in the social system can mobilize public sentiment, alter accepted norms, and change the way people think about the environment and the role of the corporation in protecting it. This chapter considers the social drivers of environmental nongovernmental organizations (NGOs), the community, the press, the courts, academia, and religious institutions (see figure 6.1).

Environmental NGOs

One prominent actor to consider in the discussion of any environmental issue is the environmental nongovernmental organization. Its influence on corporate operations cannot be denied. What is even more important, however, is the diversity of methods and channels by which NGOs exert this influence. They undertake scientific research, conduct public protests, engage in corporate alliances, and influence press coverage and public opinion. Their influence can be direct as well as indirect; based on science, policy, law, or economics; and confrontational or cooperative. This diversity makes the environmental NGO a complicated entity for industry to understand and negotiate with. Although environmental NGOs could have been discussed in any of the previous chapters because they drive regulation on the domestic and international levels and alter resource and market relationships in the business environment, they are discussed here because of their pervasive effects in changing societal norms and beliefs.

In 1989, 5,817 organizations calling themselves environmental groups filed for tax-exempt status under section 501(c)(3) of the Internal Revenue Code. Of these, 1,578 (27 percent) filed tax returns with financial data showing an average budget of $721,000 per organization and total expenses of $1.1 billion.[1] In 1992, 17 organizations in this latter group (see table 6.1) (1 percent) commanded nearly 50 percent of the group's total expenses.[2] Despite their common label as environmental groups, this group of organiza-

Table 6.1. Membership and Budgets of the Seventeen Largest Environmental Groups, 1992 and 1998

		1992		1998	
Organization	Year Founded	Membership (Thousands)	Budget[a] (Millions)	Membership (Thousands)	Budget[b] (Millions)
The Nature Conservancy	1951	588	$101	900	$131
National Wildlife Federation	1936	6,200	$71	4,400	$96
World Wildlife Fund	1961	800	$60	1,200	$60
Greenpeace USA	1971	2,000	$50	500	$37
National Audubon Society	1905	600	$44	600	$44
Sierra Club	1892	650	$35	550	$43
Environmental Defense Fund	1967	200	$18	300	$24
The Wilderness Society	1935	310	$17	255	$15
Natural Resources Defense Council	1970	170	$16	350	$27
Water Environment Federation	1928	38	$13	40	$14
National Parks and Conservation Association	1919	300	$9	350	$14
Air & Waste Management Association	1907	13	$8	17	$8
Defenders of Wildlife	1947	80	$6	180	$7
Friends of the Earth	1969	50	$4	35	$3
Izaak Walton League of America	1922	54	$2	40	$2
Citizens for a Better Environment	1971	30	$2	30	$2
Environmental Action	1970	20	$2	10	$1
Total		12,106	$458	9,757	$528

[a]Gale Research Inc., *The Encyclopedia of Associations*, 28th ed. (Detroit: Gale Research, 1993).
[b]Gale Research Inc., *The Encyclopedia of Associations*, 34th ed. (Detroit: Gale Research, 1999).

tions is extremely diverse in methods and interests. In this respect, the term *environmentalist* may be a misnomer, lumping many varied interests, such as wildlife conservation and pollution control, into one category.[3] Some of the organizations are staffed with lawyers and scientists and work within existing institutions to bring about corporate and social change (e.g., the Natural Resources Defense Council and the Environmental Defense Fund). Others remain outside those institutions, relying on less professionally oriented staffs and working in a more confrontational style (e.g., the Public Interest Research Groups and Greenpeace). Various environmental groups also define the issue on vastly different terms. For example, with its goal of promoting zero economic and population growth, Earth First! differs dramatically from The Nature Conservancy, which seeks to protect the environment through integration of environmental and economic concerns.

Membership in U.S. environmental groups is stronger in the West and Northeast and lower in the South and Midwest. Figure 6.2 reveals membership concentrations using the location quotient, a statistic that relates local and state membership to the national average.[4] The highest per capita number of memberships in environmental groups is found in northeastern states such as Vermont, Connecticut, Maine, Massachusetts, Maryland, and New Hampshire and western states including California, Oregon, Hawaii, and Washington. With the exception of North Carolina, Virginia, and Florida,

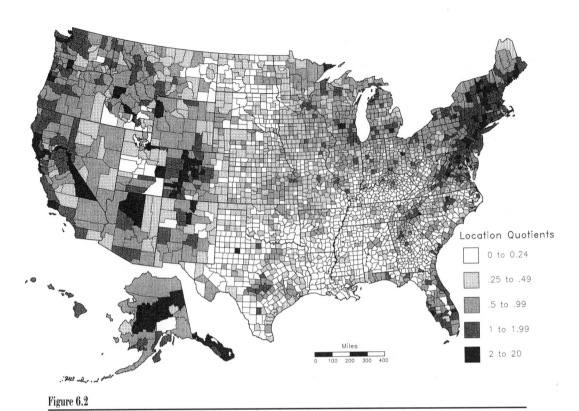

Figure 6.2

County-Level Membership in Environmental Organizations, 1994

Source: T. Wikle, "Geographical Patterns of Membership in U.S. Environmental Organizations," *Professional Geographer* 47, no. 1 (1995): 41–48. © 1995 Blackwell Publishers. All rights reserved. Used with permission.

Note: A location quotient is a statistic that relates local and state membership to the national average.

states in the South have low membership ratios. Membership in environmental groups grew steadily in the early 1980s and more rapidly in the late 1980s. From 1988 to 1990, membership in the sixteen largest environmental groups grew from 6.5 million to more than 10 million, a rate equal to that of the entire 1980s. In 1992, membership had peaked for many organizations and had remained steady or even dropped off for some.[5]

Just as the Environmental Protection Agency (EPA) has become multidisciplinary in its methods of driving corporate environmental action, environmental NGOs have become diverse in their methods. To begin with, as exemplified by the Environmental Defense Fund's 1970s slogan "Sue the bastards," lawsuits continue to be a mainstay of the NGOs' tool kit. In 1993, environmental NGOs were involved in more than fifty federal-level lawsuits, in nearly 95 percent of those cases acting as plaintiff against either the EPA or industry. As figure 6.3 shows, that trend is growing.

NGOs also continue to employ more direct forms of activism, such as protests, with great success. For example, in 1998 the Rainforest Action Network won concessions from Mitsubishi Motor Sales of America, Inc. and Mitsubishi Electric USA to curb pollution and help protect rain forests. The NGO agreed to stop its protests at trade shows

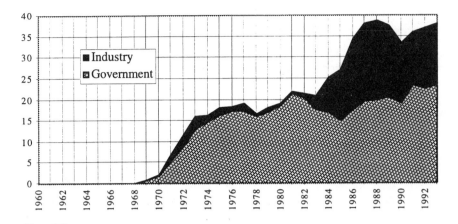

Figure 6.3

Federal-Level Lawsuits Involving Environmental Groups, 1960–1993

Source: A. Hoffman, *From Heresy to Dogma: An Institutional History of Corporate Environmentalism* (San Francisco: New Lexington Press, 1997).

(Figures are three-year rolling averages.)

and its eight-year-long boycott efforts. The two companies, with combined annual revenues of about $6 billion, agreed to stop using any products, such as paper and packaging, made from old-growth and otherwise rare forests. Furthermore, the companies agreed to eventually eliminate all wood products from their operations through such steps as using paper made only from agricultural waste and plant materials such as kenaf (a fast growing plant that produces a high-quality fiber) rather than trees. The agreement does not involve Mitsubishi's main wood products unit, which dropped out of the negotiations. The Rainforest Action Network intends to continue its aggressive tactics and boycotts against this unit of the company as well as against Mitsubishi's foreign operations.[6]

MacMillan Bloedel Ltd., one of Canada's largest forest products companies, found itself facing similar protests in 1993. Activists staged what was then Canada's largest civil protest to call attention to the company's logging and clear-cutting practices in the controversial old-growth areas of the coastal rain forest of British Columbia. In 1998, the company reversed its position, announcing plans to phase out clear-cutting within five years and pursue forest certification. The company also agreed to increase the conservation of its old-growth forests and replace clear-cutting with more environmentally friendly techniques.[7]

These agreements are indicative of the growing importance of environmental NGOs, their elevated status providing them a seat at the bargaining table. With this seat comes increasing legitimacy with business leaders. Moving from strictly confrontational relations, leaders of business and environmental NGOs are starting to work together cooperatively to find solutions that make both economic and environmental sense. So, beyond legal challenge, cooperation and integration of environmentalists and industrial companies is growing. First, as shown in table 6.2, environmentalists are finding themselves at board-level positions in major multinational corporations.

Table 6.2. Environmentalists on Corporate Boards

Company	Environmental Director	Affiliation
Ashland Inc.	Patrick Noonan	President, Conservation Fund
Atlantic Richfield Company (ARCO)	Frank Boren	Conservation fellow, World Wildlife Fund, Conservation Fund
Chevron Corporation	Bruce Smart	Senior counselor, World Resources Institute
E. I. du Pont de Nemours and Company	William Reilly	Former administrator, Environmental Protection Agency (EPA)
Exxon Corporation	John Steele	Senior scientist, Woods Hole Oceanographic Institution
Monsanto Company	William Ruckelshaus	Former administrator, EPA
Union Carbide Corporation	Russell Train	Chairman, World Wildlife Fund; former administrator, EPA

Source: L. Cahill and S. Engelman, "Bolstering the Board's Environmental Focus," *Directors and Boards,* fall 1993, 23–25.

Second, alliances between industry and NGO activists are becoming more common. The earliest was perhaps the National Wildlife Federation's Corporate Conservation Council in 1982. More recently, the most prominent example is the 1990 alliance between the McDonald's Corporation and the Environmental Defense Fund (EDF). The two groups worked together to develop an alternative to polystyrene clamshell containers in which the chain served its food. Now companies such as Ashland Inc., The Goodyear Tire & Rubber Company, the Eastman Kodak Company, AT&T, the Monsanto Company, the Dow Chemical Company, and others are also getting into the game.[8] Even the United States Golf Association has found an ally in the National Fish and Wildlife Foundation for integrating wildlife conservation and golf course design and operation. Formalizing this consulting role for the NGO, EDF (in conjunction with The Pew Charitable Trusts) has developed a project called The Alliance for Environmental Innovation to help individual companies find optimal solutions to environmental problems. To maximize its institutional effectiveness, the alliance works only with market leaders and companies toward the end of the value chain.[9] In this way, they hope to change to norms in entire industries by convincing the market leader to adapt environmental interests.

In surveying companies to determine why they would choose to develop such alliances, The Conference Board found that "corporate use of best practices has become mainstream in environmental management. EH&S leaders seeking feedback on political, not only business, situations are finding that alliances are becoming a viable route to invoke these responses."[10] Companies surveyed also found strategic benefits in terms of improved access to political and strategic information, enhanced abilities for communication with stakeholders, and opportunities to achieve conflict resolution with environmentalists. The most prominent outcomes of these alliances were improved community relations (reported by 61 percent of respondents), improved political or strategic information (52 percent), and improved environmental programs (46 percent).[11] Table 6.3 shows the results of The Conference Board's survey, detailing the percentage of respondents reporting particular outcomes and benefits from their alliance experiences. Table 6.4 shows the results of a 1997 *Green Business Letter* survey of businesses' attitudes about

Table 6.3. Key Conclusions of Managers' Survey of Corporate–NGO Alliances (Percentage of Respondents Who Agreed with the Stated Value)

1. What Were the Reasons for the Alliance?

Good corporate citizenship	68%
Community relations	56%
CEO/top management commitment	52%
Positive media value	35%
Shared technical information	32%
Response to a crisis	27%

2. What Were the Outcomes of the Alliance?

Improved community relations	61%
Improved political/strategic information	52%
Improved environmental programs	46%
Better scientific/technical information	39%
Award/recognition programs	38%
Conflict resolution	37%
Higher employee morale	35%
Improved processes or products	22%
Increased profitability	16%
Marketing advantage	15%

3. What Were the Critical Elements to Initiating the Alliance?

Tangible short-term benefits	90%
Equal power bases	90%
Common goals or commitment	68%
Trust between partners	61%

4. What Were the Obstacles to Building the Alliance?

Insufficient time or resources	75%
Conflicting interests among partners	47%
Need for secure company information	40%
Lack of confidence in outcome	39%

5. How Was the Alliance Project Evaluated?

Evaluated on an informal basis	75%
Evaluated with other initiatives to mainstream the alliance	47%
No effort made at evaluation	40%
Evaluated through formal measurement	39%

Source: L. Orti, *Environmental Alliances: Critical Factors for Success* (New York: Conference Board, 1995), 9. © 1995 The Conference Board. All rights reserved. Used with permission.

Table 6.4. How Corporate Executives Rate Ten
Environmental NGOs as Alliance Partners

Group	Rating
The Nature Conservancy	4.33
World Wildlife Fund	4.07
National Wildlife Federation	3.96
National Audubon Society	3.90
Council on Economic Priorities	3.74
Environmental Defense Fund	3.73
Natural Resources Defense Council	3.25
Rainforest Action Network	3.08
Sierra Club	2.88
Greenpeace	1.85

Source: Green Business Letter, Sleeping with the Enemy:
What Business and Activist Groups Really Think about
Working Together (Washington, D.C.: Tilden Press, 1997),
4. © Tilden Press, Inc., All rights reserved. Used with
permission.
Ratings were made on a scale of 1 to 5, with higher numbers reflecting more positive impressions by companies
about a group's partnership potential. Although they are
not listed here, the report noted that the Center for
Marine Conservation, Conservation International,
Friends of the Earth, the Rainforest Alliance, the Rocky
Mountain Institute, and the World Resources Institute
were also given high marks.

various environmental groups as alliance partners. The survey indicated that the most attractive group for corporate alliances was The Nature Conservancy.

However, in entering into such alliances, NGOs run the risk of being perceived as co-opted. Legitimacy and credibility are the most critical assets possessed by NGOs, and their contribution to an alliance is exactly that credibility. Since environmental groups are harsh critics of corporate polluters, their assistance in managing environmental issues can confer legitimacy, helping a company avoid any future criticism from the general public and other groups. But this puts the credibility of the NGO at risk, something that many are unwilling to do. In one illustrative example, the General Motors Corporation (GM) entered into a partnership with the Environmental Defense Fund (EDF) to study a wide range of air pollution problems in its manufacturing operations. To protect the legitimacy of EDF, the organization was not paid for its services, and GM was expressly forbidden to use EDF's name in any advertisements. In return, EDF gained a direct influence on the actions of this large organization. For GM, the alliance contributed strategic insights into environmental management practices while legitimating the company's efforts.

Corporations are not the only focus of environmental consultancy. NGOs are also forming alliances with or disseminating information to nontraditional partners such as the health care industry, financial institutions, and the general public, thereby triggering corporate change through a variety of channels. For example, the World Resources Institute (WRI) is working to integrate environmental concerns into the field of accountancy. Accounting is the language of business and, as yet, remains somewhat disconnected from the corporate changes imposed by environmentalism. To fill this gap, the WRI created the Total Cost Accounting Project to improve internal data collection and analysis practices for identifying environmental costs.

The Environmental Defense Fund is aiming its information dissemination efforts at the general public and local community groups with its development of the "Scorecard" World Wide Web page.[12] The Web page allows a user to input a zip code and find out "what chemicals are being released into your neighborhood environment by manufacturing plants, which of these chemicals are potentially the most harmful, and what companies are responsible." The page entices users to "use our maps to see how close these polluting facilities are to your home, your workplace, or your children's schools." Interest in this information was so high that the day the page went on-line, it was forced to shut down temporarily because of the volume of inquiries.

Showing increasing sophistication in understanding what drives corporate behavior, environmental NGOs have also begun to train their sights on the banking industry. Their goal is to alter the funding of development projects around the globe by influencing the role of finance and capital in their development. In 1998, two financial training courses in Washington, D.C., drew more than fifty NGOs from more than thirty countries. The course was taught by consultants Hewson Baltzell of Innovest Strategic Value Advisors, Inc. and John Ganzi of the Environment & Finance Enterprise and was sponsored by Friends of the Earth and the National Wildlife Federation. "We need to make a quantum leap from Washington to Wall Street," explained Michelle Chan-Fishel, international policy analyst for Friends of the Earth.[13]

Taking that sophistication directly to the marketplace, environmentalists have also funded technological innovation and market innovation projects. For example, NGOs have long focused on diesel buses, which are responsible for inordinate amounts of urban air pollution. The Natural Resources Defense Council fought a lengthy campaign with the city of New York to gain the acceptance of hybrid buses that use electric motors and natural gas, thereby greatly reducing the emissions that are standard with diesel-powered buses. In 1999, New York's Metropolitan Transportation Authority announced that it would buy 500 new buses that run on compressed natural gas and electricity to replace nearly 15 percent of the city's 3,600-bus fleet. The city of Boston and Logan International Airport followed with a similar pledge.[14] The research, design, and assembly of the new buses have been supported by public and private partnerships that include the environmental nonprofit organization Northeast Advanced Vehicle Consortium, the New York Power Authority, and the General Electric Company.

The Community

As former Speaker of the House of Representatives Tip O'Neill stated, "All politics is local," and so, too, can it be for environmental issues. Similar in tactics to the environmental NGO, activism at the community level can be quite powerful and influential in driving corporate and government action. The first formative example of neighborhood environmental activism occurred in the late 1980s when the residents of Love Canal, a neighborhood in Niagara Falls, New York, mobilized the community, the national media, the federal and state governments, and corporations to respond to the health threat posed by chemical contaminants under their homes.

The history of Love Canal dates back to the 1890s, when entrepreneur William T. Love began digging a canal that would connect the upper and lower Niagara River to provide power for his "city of the future." Economic hard times derailed his efforts, however, and the canal was abandoned. From 1942 until 1953, the canal was owned by the Hooker Electro-Chemical Company (it is now owned by the Occidental Chemical Corporation) and used as a dump for 21,800 tons of toxic chemical waste, including many known and suspected carcinogens. In 1953, under pressure from the city of Niagara Falls, which was trying to accommodate a rapidly expanding population, Hooker covered the wastes with clay and sold the sixteen-acre parcel to the Niagara Falls School Board for $1, with a stipulation in the deed that hazardous chemicals were buried at the site. Ignoring that warning, the board built an elementary school on top of the site, and the city permitted homes to be constructed at its edge. The ensuing road and sewer construction punctured the protective clay cap over the canal. To make matters worse, the New York State Department of Transportation built the LaSalle Expressway along the southern end of the property, thereby preventing the migration of groundwater. By the mid-1970s, the chemicals, buried twenty years before, had literally come to the surface as what has been described as a "chemical bathtub" overflowed.

What followed was a nightmare for local residents and an education in activism and government action for the country. The federal government responded to the chemical bathtub overflow with a series of weak-willed efforts, but it was the actions of the Love Canal Homeowners Association—led by housewife Lois Gibbs—that brought national attention to the situation through some very visible protests. In 1978, President Jimmy Carter responded to the protests by declaring a federal emergency, the first ever involving a non-natural environmental disaster. That same day, New York's governor, Hugh Carey, announced that the 239 homes closest to the canal would be bought by the government and subsequently destroyed. Residents of Love Canal were not satisfied with these actions, however, and they continued their activism. In May 1980, a group of home owners took two EPA officials hostage for five hours to pressure the government into carrying out further evacuations. Two days after this incident, President Carter issued his second emergency declaration and offered federal funds to buy an additional 564 homes in what is now called the Emergency Declaration Area (EDA). Residents of all but 72 of the homes elected to move. Largely in response to the events at Love Canal, the Comprehensive Environmental Response, Compensation, and Liability Act (CERCLA or Superfund) was signed into law on December 12, 1980.[15]

Today, Lois Gibbs is director of the Center for Health, Environment and Justice (formerly the Citizens Clearinghouse for Hazardous Waste) in Falls Church, Virginia, where she leverages her Love Canal experience to help other neighborhood activists organize and fight localized pollution. She is part of a growing grassroots movement in the United States that is forcing the localization of environmental issues. Mark Dowie, in his book *Losing Ground,* calls this the "fourth wave" of the environmental movement and argues that many of the national environmental organizations are "courting irrelevance" by losing touch with the fundamental constituency who must live with the environmental problems of our society. "The central sentiment that will define the next generation," he argues, "is, quite simply, a sense of justice."[16]

This type of community-level, justice-based environmentalism can have significant implications for corporate facility siting and operations. In particular, two movements have been changing the way companies approach development decisions, each of them linked to the local community's empowerment regarding the kind of industrial activity that takes place in its midst. The first movement is the environmental justice movement. Particularly in urban areas, communities are becoming more aware of and active regarding a combination of environmental and civil rights issues. Industrial activity in urban centers unfairly affects the low-income people who generally inhabit them, and these urban residents are gaining a stronger voice in deciding the fate of such developments. The second movement is the "not in my backyard" (NIMBY) syndrome, which some say is now more accurately described as NOPE ("not on Planet Earth"). Much like the environmental justice movement, this is a movement of empowered local citizens deciding what kind of development will or will not take place in their community. They can stall expensive investments and cripple corporate portfolios.

To engage communities regarding these concerns, many of the trade association programs listed in table 5.2 require community outreach as a condition of participation. The CMA's Responsible Care program, for example, requires members "to recognize and respond to community concerns about chemicals" and the adverse effects of operations, products, wastes, and services and "to counsel customers on the safe use, transportation, storage and disposal of chemical products."[17] Some companies even go so far as to organize citizen advisory panels. Their purpose is to invite representatives of nearby communities to provide input on how the plants should be operated so as to maintain a positive community relationship. In return, by establishing close community ties, companies find it easier to hire top-quality local employees, and they face less resistance in expanding existing facilities and siting new ones. This is a far cry from the corporate mentality of the 1970s, in which people outside the borders of the plant had no legitimate voice on operations taking place within the plant.

The Press

The news media have long played an important role in bringing environmental issues to the fore of public and industrial concern. In some cases, their role has been not only informing but also directing public debate. One study found evidence of agenda-setting effects from media coverage of toxic waste issues, not just on public opinion but also on the attitudes of policy makers.[18] For example, it is widely argued that the media were strongly influential in placing the Love Canal disaster on the national agenda.[19] The environmental group Greenpeace has understood the importance of the media for years, staging lavish displays and protests designed to appeal to news editors and thereby attract public attention and sway public opinion. In its highly publicized attack on the Shell Oil

Company's plan to sink the Brent Spar oil platform, the group leveraged the power of the media to force the company to dismantle the rig in dry dock instead.

Acting almost as advocates, many business journals now recognize environmentalism as a critical business issue and publish analyses of best industry practices and top environmental leaders. For example, *Fortune* magazine published an article in 1993 listing the "ten leaders" (such as AT&T, Apple Computer, Inc., and the Dow Chemical Company) and the "ten laggards" on environmental issues (such as the Louisiana-Pacific Corporation, E. I. du Pont de Nemours and Company, Monsanto, and BP America).[20] What criteria were used? The magazine ranked each company on twenty key environmental areas, such as toxic releases, percentage of reduction in those releases, and comprehensiveness of the company's environmental program. The results of this survey and the prominence of the resulting article created a form of public reward and censure for corporate environmental activities.

Some within the press even acknowledge taking an active political role in developing environmental awareness. Teya Ryan, senior producer of Turner Network Television's *Network Earth*, stated: "I think the environment may be one area where you can say that advocacy journalism is appropriate, indeed vital. . . . At some point, balanced journalism simply does not give them the answers, it gives them issues. . . . Can we afford to wait for our audiences to come to its conclusions? I think not."[21] As Jerry Hayes, former president of the Council on Packaging in the Environment, pointed out, "The media doesn't just report the news, it helps create it."[22]

With such influence, the press can both help and hurt the efforts of environmental activists (or corporations). In 1997, for example, recycling advocates were expressing frustration with the media. At the time, the percentage of aluminum and plastic being recycled was dropping, and steel recycling remained flat. Jerry Powell, editor of *Resource Recycling* magazine, said he believed that it was because of decreased press coverage: "The reminders aren't out there anymore, because the media don't think this is a story."[23] David Mazzarella, editor of *USA Today*, commented, "Five years ago recycling seemed to affect most people's lives, but now most people see it as a routine thing."[24]

The problem, according to Joby Warrick, environmental reporter for *The Washington Post*, points to the growing importance of environmental journalism as a differentiated field: "[The] environment is a massive beat, and on any day there are 10 or 15 reports or news conferences that take priority."[25] The Society of Environmental Journalists was formed in 1990 in response to this trend, and it presently has a membership of more than 800 in all sectors of news reporting. Today, environmental issues transcend the arena of specialized reporting in the science and government sections and can be found in the business, international, and domestic pages—virtually everywhere in the newspaper.

The Courts

The courts are considered separately in this chapter because their decisions define operating norms for the proper management of corporate affairs. For example, when one customer spills hot coffee on his lap, takes the matter to court, and receives a large monetary award, all coffee houses begin to check their coffee temperature and place warnings on their coffee cups. After the *Exxon Valdez* oil tanker ran aground in Prince William Sound in 1989, spilling 10.8 million gallons of crude oil from Alaska's North Slope, the Exxon Corporation was forced to pay more than $5 billion in legal settlements. In the wake of this settlement, most oil companies took a careful look at the safety records of their oil transport procedures and their level of preparedness to handle a major incident.

The courts provide a forum for initiating corporate change. Case outcomes can have reverberating effects throughout an industry, and civil lawsuits against industry in regard to environmental issues have been growing steadily in the United States since 1982.[26] Persons who believe that they have been injured by an environmental hazard can pursue common-law remedies through four types of legal action: trespass, nuisance, negligence, and strict liability—collectively referred to as "toxic torts." A *trespass* action may be brought by a plaintiff who owns a parcel of land that has been physically invaded by some environmental hazard so as to injure the rights of the landowner. For example, in 1982 O. H. Materials was sued for its accidental release of an acid cloud during cleanup of the Drake Chemicals site in Lock Haven, Pennsylvania; payments totaled $133,000.[27]

A *nuisance* action is used to defend the right to use one's property free from disturbance or interference from activities carried on by others on another property. The most common remedy obtained in a nuisance suit is abatement of the nuisance. For example, a nuisance action was used to force a disposal company to stop depositing hazardous waste in a municipal landfill (*Village of Wilsonville v. SCA Services*)[28] when the local community convinced the court that the company's activity was harmful to the environment.

In a *negligence* action, the plaintiff must show that the defendant was obligated to conform to a specific standard of due care, that the defendant failed to do so, that an injury occurred, and that the lack of due care was the proximate cause of the injury. These cases are most successful when the temporal delay between the act of negligence (e.g., a chemical release) and the injury is brief. One thing that makes these types of lawsuits of particular concern for industry is the definition of the standard for due care. Industry best practices regarding environmental issues are changing rapidly, and courts can hold companies liable for activities that, even though legally compliant, do not conform to the standards of trade associations or competitors.

Strict liability is considered to be the most viable action for plaintiffs to pursue. There are several formulations of strict liability. The first formulation holds a party strictly liable for damage caused by a "non-natural" use of land. For example, in *Rylands v. Fletcher*, the court found the defendant liable for the escape of water impounded on his land into a neighbor's mine shaft, even though the defendant was not found to be negligent. A second formulation holds defendants strictly liable for injuries caused by "ultrahazardous" activities. A third formulation determines strict liability by analyzing six factors: degree of risk, likelihood of great harm, ability of third parties to protect themselves by exercise of reasonable care, commonness of usage, appropriateness of location, and value to community versus risk of harm.[29]

Two important aspects of each of these areas of environmental liability that distinguish them from other high-risk industrial activities (such as bridge or tunnel building) are (1) the long-term, latent aspect of the injuries and (2) the scale of damages that can be awarded. Medical injuries, such as a preponderance of cancer or leukemia in a specific geographic location, take a long time to develop. Therefore, industrial defendants may be held liable long after activities have been completed. Furthermore, even if the injury is detected early, the scope of the injury and the size of the subsequent award are extremely vague and open to subjective reasoning by the courts. This may leave companies open to unlimited liability. Thus, toxic torts introduce a more important dimension to corporate risk management than the mere need to reduce regulatory burdens. Corporate environmental strategy requires a time horizon extending well into the future so that future standards can be anticipated and the company can be protected from latent and potentially massive liability.

Academia

Shifting norms regarding the role of environmentalism in society can be seen on college campuses across the country. The study of environmental management in colleges and universities appears to be on the upswing. One article in the *Boston Globe* noted that "the mainstream environmental movement may be faltering, but interest and involvement in ecological issues appear to be booming on college campuses."[30] Tomorrow's workforce is being influenced by a growing number of environmental courses offered at schools of business, engineering, science, journalism, law, and public policy.[31] Demand is growing faster in some areas than in others. For example, between 1989 and 1992, enrollment in environmental engineering programs in the United States jumped by more than 25 percent, and it continues to climb.[32] On the other hand, although roughly 100 of the country's 700 business schools offered elective courses on the environment in 1997,[33] the World Resources Institute noted that "only 16 percent of schools report integrating environment into core or departmental requirements, thus only a few MBAs truly receive environment-business training."[34] But on the whole, today's young people are being educated about the environment in ways that are far different from the way previous generations were taught. Academia is becoming an important force in shaping the evolution of environmentalism and, in particular, its integration into the practices and objectives of the modern corporation.

Beyond the classroom, there is a growing trend toward student environmental activism. For example, in 1994, students at Dartmouth College, Tufts University, Williams College, and Wellesley College succeeded in pressuring their administrations to divest their financial holdings in Hydro-Quebec, a Canadian utility company engaged in a hydropower project that environmentalists criticized for flooding large areas of northern Quebec.[35] Academic research on environmental issues also is growing, supported by new research outlets and new sources of funding. New journals focusing on research and the environment are gaining readership and popularity, such as *Business Strategy and the Environment, Industrial and Environmental Crisis Quarterly, Total Quality Environmental Management, Pollution Prevention Review, Sustainable Development,* and *Tomorrow.* With respect to funding, research support provided by government programs is growing. For example, the Partnership for Environmental Technology Education (PETE) is a joint program of the Department of Energy, the EPA, and the Department of Defense to support linkages between community colleges and federal laboratories to advance the training of environmental technicians and engineers.

This growing concern for environmental awareness is also emerging at other levels of the educational system. Today, thirty-one states require school systems to incorporate environmental concepts into courses at most grade levels, and some even require special training in environmentalism for teachers. Some high schools are teaching courses in ecology for which students can receive college credit.[36] From 1992 until 1997, the EPA spent $13 million on environmental education, giving grants to approximately 1,200 school projects.[37] Vice President Al Gore's Global Environmental Education Initiative is designed to involve children throughout the world in monitoring environmental quality, thereby teaching them about global environmental issues while training them to use scientific instrumentation to gather and analyze data.[38] In support of such initiatives, environmental groups such as the World Resources Institute and the Environmental Defense Fund are developing curricula to help high schools integrate environmental education into their programs. Gaylord Nelson, a former U.S. senator and founder of Earth Day, stated, "We won't forge a sustainable society until we have nurtured a generation that is imbued by a guiding environmental ethic."[39]

Religious Institutions

In considering how future views about the environment will materialize, we must consider one final actor in the development and permanence of environmentalism in society: religious institutions. Religious institutions help shape values and norms at both the individual and societal levels. Religion is one institution that can alter people's behavior by directly affecting their values and beliefs. So important is religion in changing people's behavior toward the environment that Aldo Leopold lamented in his famous 1949 work *A Sand County Almanac* that no important change in people's ethical appreciation of nature (what he called a "land ethic") could ever be accomplished "without an internal change in our intellectual emphasis, loyalties, affections and convictions. The proof that conservation has not yet touched these foundations of conduct lies in the fact that philosophy and religion have not yet heard of it."[40] Leopold looked forward to an extension of moral judgment that would address maltreatment of the land, which in his day was considered morally neutral. Indeed, in his day, religious teaching and scripture (particularly those of the Western traditions) appeared to support maltreatment of the environment. Many look to the book of Genesis as the origin of the West's ecological troubles. Australian historian John Passmore sums up this critique:

> The Lord created man, so Genesis certainly tells us to have "dominion over the fish of the sea, and over the fowl of the air, and over the cattle, and over all the earth and over every creeping thing that creepeth upon the earth" (1:26). This has been read not only by Jew but by Christian and Muslim as man's charter, granting him the right to subdue the earth and all its inhabitants. And God, according to Genesis, also issued a mandate to mankind: "Be fruitful and multiply and replenish the earth and subdue it" (1:28). So Genesis tells men not only what they can do, but what they should do—multiply and replenish and subdue the earth. God is represented, no doubt, as issuing these instruc-

tions before the Fall. But the Fall did not, according to the Genesis story, substantially affect man's duties. What it did, rather, was to make the performance of those duties more onerous. After the Flood . . . God still exhorted Noah thus: "Be fruitful, and multiply, and replenish the earth" (9:1). But he then added two significant riders. The first rider made it clear that men should not expect to subdue the earth either by love or by exercise of natural authority, as distinct from force: "And the fear of you and the dread of you shall be upon every beast of the earth and upon every fowl of the air, upon all that moveth upon the earth and upon all the fishes of the sea: into your hand they are delivered" (9:2). The second rider—"every moving thing that liveth shall be meat to you" (9:3)—permitted men to eat the flesh of animals. In the Garden of Eden, Adam, along with the beasts, had been a vegetarian, whose diet was limited to "every herb bearing seed . . . and every tree, in which is the fruit of a tree yielding seed" (1:29). Now, in contrast, not only the "green herb" but all living things were handed over to Adam and his descendants as their food.[41]

Referring to such religious foundations, UCLA historian Lynn White wrote in 1967 that our ecological problems derive from "Christian attitudes towards man's relation to nature which are almost universally held," attitudes that lead us to think of ourselves as "superior to nature" and to be "contemptuous of it, willing to use it for our slightest whim." He doubted that changes in those attitudes could occur unless "orthodox Christian arrogance towards nature" were somehow dispelled, and he viewed science and technology as being so imbued with Christian "arrogance" that "no solution for our ecological crisis can be expected from them alone."[42]

Today, the context for the biblical verses at which White leveled his criticism is fundamentally different. Our technological and social structures now threaten the survival of various plant and animal species and the overall stability of the ecosystem on which we depend for survival. Our newfound ability to alter the global environment has forced us to reexamine the way we value the environment and our role in interacting with it.[43] In an observation reminiscent of Aldo Leopold's 1949 lament, Garrett Hardin pointed out that "the morality of an act is a function of the state of the system at the time it is performed. Using the commons as a cesspool does not harm the general public under frontier conditions, because there is no public; the same behavior in a metropolis is unbearable. A hundred and fifty years ago a plainsman could kill an American bison, cut out only the tongue for his dinner, and discard the rest of the animal. He was not in any important sense being wasteful. Today, with only a few thousand bison left, we would be appalled at such behavior."[44]

Indeed, with today's changing context, the world's religions are changing their views of the morality of behavior toward the environment. In 1991, the Presbyterian Church placed environmental concerns directly into the church canon, thus making it a sin to "threaten death to the planet entrusted to our care."[45] In its new catechism in 1994, the

Roman Catholic Church equated environmental degradation with theft from future generations.[46] Reversing traditional views of humankind's superiority over nature, the catechism redefines the morality of our treatment of it:

> The seventh commandment (Thou Shalt Not Steal) enjoins respect for the integrity of creation. Animals, like plants and inanimate beings, are by nature destined for the common good of past, present, and future humanity. Use of the mineral, vegetable, and animal resources of the universe cannot be divorced from respect for moral imperatives. Man's dominion over inanimate and other living beings granted by the Creator is not absolute; it is limited by concern for the quality of life of his neighbor, including generations to come; it requires a religious respect for the integrity of creation.[47]

In 1997, His All Holiness Ecumenical Patriarch Bartholomew I, spiritual leader of the world's 300 million Orthodox Christians, linked specific ecological problems with sinful behavior. He announced that "for humans to cause species to become extinct and to destroy the biological diversity of God's creation, for humans to degrade the integrity of the Earth by causing changes in its climate, water, its land, its air, and its life with poisonous substances—these are sins."[48] Pointing out that "excessive consumption may be understood from a world view of estrangement from self, from land, from life and from God," he used his comments to specifically target the issue of climate change: "Many are arguing that someone else should address the problem, or that they should not have to take serious action unless everyone else does. . . . This self-centered behavior is a symptom of our alienation from one another and from the context of our common existence."[49]

This kind of thinking is not foreign to many non-Western religions. For example, the first of the basic Buddhist precepts counsels those pursuing the path to liberation to avoid destroying life, and Buddhism fosters a worldview that emphasizes the interdependence of all beings. His Holiness Tenzin Gyatso, the Fourteenth Dalai Lama of Tibet, wrote that "every living being, whether animal or human, has an innate sense of self" and that relations with one's fellow human beings, animals, and insects "should be based on the awareness that all of them seek happiness, and none of the them want suffering. All have a right to happiness, a right to freedom from suffering. . . . All are interdependent in creating our joy and happiness."[50] Many Native American traditions tie this concept of interconnectedness to a responsibility for future generations. Audrey Shenandoah, elder of the Eel Clan of the Onondaga Nation, explained: "We are responsible for seven generations in my tradition. Our leadership must not make decisions that are going to bring pain or harm or suffering to seven generations in the future. As individuals, we have the same mandate."[51]

Although these non-Western religious traditions, which incorporate an awareness of the interconnectedness of nature, are increasing in popularity, it is the Western religions, from which much ecological damage has originated, that are dominant in the developed world. Thus, a shift in Western religious thought goes to the core of the world's dominant technological and social development. There are, of course, dissenters. Today, some religious scholars dispute the existence of any theological imperative—either in the Bible or in non-Western traditions—to support the notion that environmental protection is a religious issue. Others worry that preaching the environmental message threatens to put trees and animals ahead of people and before God as the center of the universe. "There is a certain pantheistic element in all this," warned the Reverend Robert P. Dugan Jr. of the National Association of Evangelicals.[52]

Despite such dissent, changes in religious thought are being mobilized into social and political action. In 1996, evangelical groups rallied support for reauthorization of the Endangered Species Act of 1973, calling it "the Noah's ark of our day," while questioning Congress's apparent attempt to "sink it."[53] Supported by surveys showing that 78 percent of Americans believed that "because God created the natural world, it is wrong to abuse it,"[54] the winter 1996 issue of *Green Cross*, a Christian environmental quarterly, focused on the "implications of Christian responsibility to protect species."[55] In 1998, twenty-two members of the National Council of Churches of Christ—a coalition of Protestant, Greek Orthodox, and Catholic religious leaders—rallied to support the Kyoto Protocol to the United Nations Framework Convention on Climate Change, sending a letter to President Clinton pledging to work to get the treaty implemented because it is "an important move towards protecting God's children and God's creation."[56] The National Religious Partnership for the Environment—a coalition of the National Council of Churches of Christ, the United States Catholic Conference, and the Coalition on the Environment and Jewish Life—also vowed to lobby U.S. senators to support the treaty.[57]

Applying religious pressure even to shift consumer behavior, the Episcopal Diocese of California adopted a resolution in 1998 instructing all eighty-seven Episcopal churches in California to buy clean, renewable energy. In 1999, the Commonwealth Energy Corporation and the North American Coalition on Religion and Ecology (NACRE) announced the formation of the Greensmart Renewable Energy Project to promote the benefits of "green" power. NACRE encouraged the more than 30,000 religious organizations and other nonprofit organizations in California to demonstrate their environmental commitment by switching to electricity generated by renewable energy sources.[58]

In the end, it is clear that religious thought and values regarding the environment are being debated and altered. Through debate, environmental protection is being adopted as a fundamentally religious and moral issue. Religious leaders of many traditions are searching individually and jointly to find ways for society to live in the natural world that promote sustainable development.[59] They are a potent force in shifting social thought, and they often use their influence to drive social change in other sectors, including politics and business. With changes in religious values relating to the environment come changes in the foundations of human conduct. Although such changes represent only the beginning of the full "internal change in our intellectual emphasis, loyalties, affections and convictions" sought by Aldo Leopold, they point to the certainty of continued change in the societal values that are the basis of our regulatory, market, economic, and social systems, of which the firm is a part.

Conclusion

In this and the previous four chapters, we reviewed a wide range of external pressures for increased corporate environmental performance. These pressures range from the coercive to the market based to the socially based. Underlying them all, there is a fundamental generation shift occurring. Although public opinion regarding the environment may fluctuate with the saliency of the issue, the institutions by which society guides its behavior are shifting beneath our feet. Rollbacks in regulatory standards and diversions of public attention may slow the pace of environmental advancement, but broad-scale cultural change relating to environmentalism is taking place and quite likely cannot be stopped. The way society views environmental issues today is far different from the way society viewed them just ten years ago. More important, the way future generations view the issue will be far different from the way we view it today.

The Conference Board noted that the drivers of environmental responsibility today come from within the corporation "as younger managers and their families begin making demands on top management that previous generations would never have dared to do."[60] The employees entering today's corporations are also the investors, consumers, environmentalists, community members, bankers, insurance agents, and churchgoers discussed in this chapter and the previous ones. While society is shifting, so, too, is the workforce that is running today's corporations. Managers cannot deny or avoid this fact and will find that corporate programs that are out of alignment with the shift taking place in society will have a difficult time becoming accepted within the organization.

At the core of all this is a shift in values. It can be seen in corporate action and in the values that drive decision making within corporations, government agencies, environmental NGOs, and the courts. An instillation of values comes through the market system but is driven by a baseline evolution in fundamental values. Consider the landmark decision by the Federal Energy Regulatory Commission in 1998, when it refused for the first time in history to renew the license of a working hydroelectric dam that the owners, the Edwards Manufacturing Company, wished to keep operating. Further still, the commission ordered the company to tear down its 917-foot dam straddling the Kennebec River in Augusta, Maine, arguing that the hindrance the dam posed to the migratory sturgeon, salmon, striped bass, and other fish as they struggle upstream to spawn far outweighed the benefit it provided in electricity generation. The 3.5-megawatt dam produced only one-tenth of 1 percent of Maine's electricity. To avert a lengthy court challenge from the company, an agreement was reached in May for environmentalists, other dam operators, and a Maine shipbuilder to help pay the $8 million to $10 million cost of demolition, which began on July 1, 1999. Although the decision was labeled a "special case" by the commission, it served as a worrying precedent for other dam owners. Hydroelectric power provided for 14 percent of the country's energy needs in 1998, and over the next fifteen years, about 550 dams were expected to come up for relicensing. Many of them, particularly in western states, hinder the spawning routes of migratory fish.

The shift in values relating to the environment penetrates all aspects of the business system. The story of Interface, Inc., the leading producer of commercial carpet (discussed in the next chapter), provides a case in point. Interface's decision to lease rather than sell carpets, thereby reducing or eliminating its use of virgin materials, represents a dramatic shift in corporate values. The company's chief executive officer, Ray Anderson, claims he wants to "pioneer the company of the next industrial revolution."[61] Robert Shapiro, chief executive officer of Monsanto, said he believes that "we're entering a time of perhaps unprecedented discontinuity. Businesses grounded in the old model will become obsolete and die. At Monsanto, we're trying to invent some new businesses around the concept of environmental sustainability."[62] And John Browne, chief executive officer of the British Petroleum Company, announced that "it is a moment for change and for a rethinking of corporate responsibility."[63]

In an on-line rebuttal to commentary on his determination that nature is worth $33 trillion, Robert Costanza wrote that "the point is that one cannot state a value without stating the goal being served."[64] And such goals lie within the intentions and values of individual constituents of society and the business environment. The chapters in part II described some of the many constituents imposing new goals and new values on the corporation. For readers who see value in nature beyond the needs and interests of specific constituents, this may be an incomplete analysis (see box 6.1). For the corporation, it is important to consider that these constituents are part of a system that brings environmental issues into the realm of business concerns. The system is in dynamic motion and it is important to consider the trajectory of that motion. Just as we may view the environmental norms, standards, and practices of the previous generation as primitive and naive, future generations will look back in wonder at the wasteful environmental practices we maintain today. Cultural change is in motion throughout society and is not likely to stop. This process of change has altered the past and present norms by which corporations have had to act and will alter the way those firms will have to act in the future.

Box 6.1. Is There Inherent Value in Nature?

What is missing from the discussion in the past five chapters? Is the environment valuable only if someone places some utilitarian value on it? This is an intriguing question that brings the discussion of business and environment into the domain of values and ethics. In arguing that market mechanisms and institutional demands will drive corporate environmentalism, one could be making the assumption that nature has no value other than its utility to these stakeholders. Should we protect the environment for its own inherent value? Or must we protect it for the utilitarian benefit of humankind, in both present and future generations? This question first became an issue in the United States at the beginning of the twentieth century as a war of words and ideals emerged over the water needs of the city of San Francisco and the sanctity of one of the country's most beautiful national parks, Yosemite National Park.

In 1906, San Francisco suffered the worst earthquake in its history. But worse than the earthquake were the fires that followed. As water supplies ran dry, the fires consumed much of the city. In the wake of the disaster, the mayor of the city made a secure public water supply one of his most important priorities. Lying west of the city was the Hetch Hetchy Valley in Yosemite National Park. With its steep cliffs, narrow opening, and abundant water flow, the valley was an ideal site for a dam.

This was happening at the same time that the country was rediscovering nature as something valuable to its identity. An avid hunter and fisherman, President Theodore Roosevelt embodied that ideal. During his presidency, he tripled the amount of land in national forests, named five new national parks, and established the USDA Forest Service. Although it was clear that national forests were to be used for natural resource extraction as well as conservation purposes, the status of the national parks had not yet been established or tested. The debate over whether to put the water needs of San Francisco over the preservation of a natural wonder took seven years to resolve and involved newspapers, politicians, and the public nationwide.

Between 1906 and 1913, there were eight congressional hearings on the issue. Representing the two sides of the debate were John Muir, the great naturalist writer, and Gifford Pinchot, the first head of the Forest Service. The two men represented polar opposite views, and both had the ear of the president in this debate. To John Muir, damming the Hetch Hetchy meant sacrilege against nature and against God. He wrote: "Hetch Hetchy valley is a grand landscaped garden, one of nature's rarest and most precious mountain temples. Dam Hetch Hetchy, as well dam for water tanks the people's cathedrals and churches. For no holier temple has ever been consecrated by the heart of man."* He railed against dam supporters (whom he called "Satan and company"), writing: "These temple destroyers, devotees of ravaging commercialism, seem to have a perfect contempt for nature. And instead of lifting their eyes to the God of the Mountain, lift them to the almighty dollar."† With words and sentiments such as these, Muir was able to appeal to the conscience of Americans and mobilize support for the idea that this wilderness should be left alone.

For Gifford Pinchot, on the other hand, nature equaled resources. He wrote a speech for President Roosevelt that said, in part: "The fundamental idea of forestry is the perpetuation of forest by use. Forest protection is a means to protect and sustain resources." Pinchot believed in "multiple use" of the national parks, which would allow for hunting, fishing, grazing, forestry, watershed protection, and preservation of wilderness values. In fact, he could not fathom the idea that utilitarian values should not drive the country's land-use policies. He wrote: "As for me, I have always regarded the sentimental horror of some good citizens at the idea of using natural resources as unintelligent, misdirected and short-sighted. . . . The question is so clear that I cannot understand why there's been so much fuss about it. The turning of the Hetch Hetchy into a lake will not be a calamity. In fact, it will be a blessing. It is simply a question of the greatest good to the greatest number of people."‡

In the end, Roosevelt sided with Muir in his heart. But as politician and president, he sided with Pinchot. Although most of the country's newspapers condemned the dam, Congress granted final approval for it in 1913. However, though the valley now lies submerged, the debate over its fate left an indelible mark on American politics and the American psyche. Since Hetch Hetchy, no comparable intrusion into national parks has occurred, and in 1916, the National Park Service Organic Act was passed, granting measures of protection for the rest of the system.

But the debate over inherent versus utilitarian value in nature continues today. For example, the debate over oil drilling in the Arctic National Wildlife Refuge (ANWR) has raged since the 1970s. Are we to place the value of a pristine environment such as ANWR—one that almost no human will ever see—over the utilitarian needs of the United States for energy security? Should we find a way to balance the two and allow limited drilling excursions into this vast wilderness? Are we to subordinate nature to our technological society, or are we to subordinate our material needs to the preservation of wild places? The debate rages on.

---

* L. Hott and D. Garey, *The Wilderness Idea: John Muir, Gifford Pinchot, and the First Great Battle for Wilderness,* videotape documentary (Santa Monica, Calif.: Direct Cinema Limited, 1989).

† Ibid.

‡ Ibid.

Further Reading

Collett, J., and S. Karakashian, eds. *Greening the College Curriculum: A Guide to Environmental Teaching in the Liberal Arts.* Washington, D.C.: Island Press, 1996.

Fastiggi, E. *Catalyzing Environmental Results: Lessons in Advocacy Organization–Business Partnerships.* Boston: Alliance for Environmental Innovation, 1999.

Hott, L., and D. Garey. *The Wilderness Idea: John Muir, Gifford Pinchot, and the First Great Battle for Wilderness.* Videotape documentary. Santa Monica, Calif.: Direct Cinema Limited, 1989.

Kempton, W., J. Boster, and J. Hartley. *Environmental Values in American Culture.* Cambridge, Mass.: MIT Press, 1995.

Leopold, A. *A Sand County Almanac, and Sketches Here and There.* New York: Oxford University Press, 1949.

Long, F., and M. Arnold. *The Power of Environmental Partnerships.* New York: Dryden Press, 1995.

Orti, L. *Environmental Alliances: Critical Factors for Success.* New York: Conference Board, 1995.

Passmore, J. *Man's Responsibility for Nature: Ecological Problems and Western Traditions.* New York: Charles Scribner's Sons, 1974.

Pillar, C. *The Fail-Safe Society: Community Defiance and the End of American Technological Optimism.* Berkeley: University of California Press, 1991.

Rockefeller, S., and J. Elder, eds. *Spirit and Nature: Why the Environment Is a Religious Issue.* Boston: Beacon Press, 1992.

Part III

NEW "RULES OF THE GAME"

The social responsibility of business is to increase its profits. So states the criticism of "socially responsible business" as it has been since Milton Friedman first wrote these words in 1970. Any company, he wrote, making

> expenditures on reducing pollution beyond the amount that is in the best interests of the corporation or that is required by law in order to contribute to the social objective of improving the environment . . . [is engaging in] pure and unadulterated socialism. . . . There is one and only one social responsibility of business—to use its resources and engage in activities designed to increase its profits so long as it stays within the rules of the game, which is to say, engages in open and free competition without deception or fraud.[1]

Others have continued the argument. William Meckling and Michael Jensen wrote that the efforts of advocates for social responsibility are thinly veiled attempts to gain control of the governance structures of the firm. In their words, "The term 'social responsibility' has the advantage, from the standpoint of its proponents, that it disguises what they really have in mind; namely, that managers should deliberately take actions which adversely affect investors in order to bestow benefits on other individuals."[2]

This book does not contradict these critical views. Corporations are in business to increase their profits, and managers should take actions that benefit their investors. But the "rules of the game" have changed. Managers acting in the best interests of their investors must now consider environmental protection in their decision making. Environmental protection has moved out of the realm of socially responsible management (or even simple regulatory compliance) and entered the realm of strategic business management. This movement is driven by the concerns of constituents (or individuals), which include investors as well as many others. What twenty years ago was driven primarily by pressures separate from core business objectives is now driven by a host of interests that strike at the core of business decision making. As shown in figure III.1, the issue of environmental protection is imposed on the firm by a diverse array of core business con-

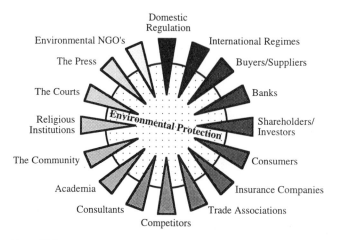

Figure III.1

Environmental Strategy as a Composite of External Business Drivers

stituents. Managers who remain fixated on regulation or public opinion to guide their environmental activities will lose their focus on the real changes within the business environment. As an issue of corporate concern, environmental protection has become much more complex and requires a more sophisticated view to be managed effectively. To consider it driven solely by "advocates for social responsibility" is missing the full extent to which environmental protection has become a part of the business environment.

The drivers in figure III.1 vary in their importance and influence. They also vary in the degree to which their importance is changing. For example, chapter 2 looked at the dynamic state of regulation and examined how these pressures are becoming both more extensive in their influence and more ambiguous in their methods. Increasingly, regulation will allow greater flexibility and therefore greater opportunity for corporations to tailor response strategies in ways that blend with, rather than constrain, their competitive strategies. Compliance strategy of the future must include ways to reduce corporate cost effects and therefore improve the bottom line above and beyond the costs imposed by a command-and-control mind-set.

Next, chapter 3 looked at the proliferation of international environmental accords. Companies may choose to develop dual environmental strategies for domestic and foreign operations, but in the future that will be increasingly inefficient. Rather than acting as a constraint, however, the globalization of environmental issues tends to create opportunities for companies that are able to transcend standard environmental problems and find a synergy between their environmental and global competitive strategies.

Looking beyond such coercive pressures, chapters 4–6 examined the environmental drivers in the firm's market, economic, and social realms. It is not just governing bodies that create environmental demands. Increasingly, environmental concerns are becoming infused into the relationships between firms and buyers, suppliers, consumers, competitors, trade associations, insurance companies, shareholders, investment funds, financial institutions, environmental NGOs, local communities, individual citizens, the press, consultants, and employees. As this lengthy list should make clear, the firm is part of a complex web of interrelationships. This web is becoming increasingly integrated with environmental demands and their expectations. The definition of what constitutes a "green" company continues to expand as external pressures for corporate environmental action become more diverse and demanding. Corporations are finding that satisfaction of environmental concerns is tied to the economic concerns presented by each of these business linkages. To see that the environmental aspect of these linkages will become more pronounced, one need only observe the growing infusion of environmental concerns within educational and religious institutions. This pattern forms the foundation of norm and value development in human societies, and the permanence of environmentalism in the educational and religious institutional regimes serves as assurance of its permanence in other institutional regimes that they support.

In short, part II discussed how the business environment has changed and therefore why companies must consider environmentalism as a strategic issue. It addressed the initial question posed in this book: *What are the sources of environmental pressures?* In part III, we consider what this actually means. We address the second question posed by this book: *What are the corporate implications of environmental issues?* The question has three components. First, chapter 7 considers the way in which environmental protection alters the objectives of competitive and technology strategy. Chapter 8 then discusses how such a change in strategy requires an alteration in organizational structure and culture. Finally, chapter 9 places these changes in the context of the broader social and business environment to examine how institutions can limit or set the pace of strategic change.

Chapter 7

ALTERING STRATEGIC OBJECTIVES

It is not enough simply to identify the source of pressures for corporate environmental action. To learn from this knowledge, it must be applied. It is important to understand what it means for the corporation. From this understanding emerges the realization that environmental effects on the firm translate into its fundamental business concepts. As insurance companies impose environmental pressures on the firm, the issue ceases to be one of environmentalism and becomes one of risk management. As competitors apply environmental pressure, the issue becomes one of strategic direction and market growth. With investors, it becomes an issue of capital acquisition, and so on. In effect, environmentalism is becoming less and less an environmental issue. The firm's business channels are being altered to bring environmentalism to managerial attention through avenues related to marketing, accounting, finance, and the like. Environmental strategy incorporates many layers of core business objectives. In each case, the firm has a preexisting model and language with which to conceptualize the issue and formulate a response. By realizing this "fit," firms can begin to see environmental issues as strategic issues, directed no longer by external societal interests but rather by internal strategic interests, as shown in figure 7.1.

It becomes evident that the business manager need not even believe in the validity of certain environmental issues to take them seriously as a business concern. What matters is that key business constituents possess that concern and are translating it through core business channels. By identifying key business constituents whose interests align with the environmental objectives of the corporation, managers within the corporation can find ways to merge environmental strategy and business strategy and create value for the corporation. Managers must focus on identifying, measuring, and communicating about—both internally and externally—business value derived from the integration of environmental protection and economic growth.[1] This is the essence of competitive environmental strategy.

Competitive Strategy

To structure where such value can be found, the Global Environmental Management Initiative (GEMI) has developed a framework of six areas of value-creating opportuni-

131

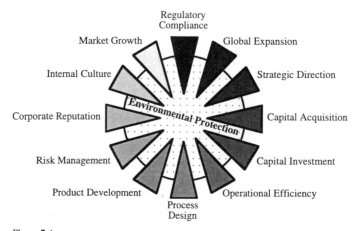

Figure 7.1

Environmental Strategy as a Composite of Internal Business Interests

ties for environmental strategy: regulatory compliance, operational efficiency, risk management, capital investment, market growth, and strategic direction.[2] To these six can be added two others related to technology strategy—process development and product design. Each of these areas can be linked to specific constituents discussed in the previous five chapters, and each is discussed in the section that follows.

Value in Regulatory Compliance

Certain environmental performance standards and activities are required by company policies and government regulations. Although these activities are typically viewed by managers as a cost of doing business, they in fact provide fundamental value to business. With increasing flexibility allowed for compliance programs, corporate executives must recast their perspectives of compliance in terms that support their overall competitive strategy. A well-designed compliance program can provide numerous benefits, including those detailed in the following three areas.

Protection of the License to Operate

National, state, and local governments impose environmental, health, and safety requirements on corporations that do business within their jurisdictions. Compliance with these requirements adds real value. Safeguarding the health and safety of workers, communities, and the environment is essential to securing the public trust to continue operations, expand, and innovate. Without this trust, governments can impose more stringent requirements and communities can stifle development plans.

Avoidance of Penalties

Failure to ensure compliance can bring about significant costs in the form of business fines, permit denials, plant shutdowns, and legal fees—all of which directly affect the bottom line. Although it is impossible to precisely document avoided costs, numerous environmental managers have found the estimation of such costs to be useful in translating environmental value into competitive value.

Increased Flexibility with Regulators

A record of strong and effective compliance can earn even greater flexibility with regulators, which enables operations to make needed changes more quickly. Investors are beginning to see the benefits this can create as greater flexibility translates into shorter development times, lower cost of capital, and lower insurance rates.

Value in Operational Efficiency

At the operations level, competitive environmental strategy should focus on finding new ways to do more with less. The key is to alter the use of resources. By reducing total resource inputs, hazardous inputs, and undesirable by-products, it is possible to lower the costs of production and compliance as well as waste disposal and management costs. The three R's—reduce, reuse, and recycle—represent a hierarchy for approaching material use strategies. Thus, environmental initiatives can enhance operational efficiency in numerous ways.

More Efficient Resource Use

Yield and resource utilization rates can be improved by reducing the amount of resources used per unit of product produced. This approach, often called process optimization, involves changing processes to minimize resource requirements in manufacturing.

Minimization of Wastes

Wastes, emissions, and discharges mean higher disposal costs as well as increased regulatory reporting costs, a greater potential for spills, and unacceptable health and safety risks. Reducing the amount of off-quality product has a triple effect: saving inputs, reducing wastes, and producing more product to sell.

Reduced Costs of Hazard Management

Identifying opportunities to eliminate the use of hazardous materials in production processes reduces the costs of engineering and control measures. This can translate into lower risk, which can translate into lower insurance premiums and lower threat of worker injury lawsuits. A simple rule is this: If you don't use it, you can't spill it, your workers can't be exposed to it, and you can't be held liable for it.

Enhanced Process Innovation and Reduced Maintenance Costs

Pollution prevention activities can reveal other opportunities for streamlining, and even eliminating, process elements and maintenance requirements. Many corporate environmental professionals report that creative pollution prevention and waste minimization programs often result in significant process improvements because they permit a fresh look at accepted practices and procedures.

Increased Productivity and Morale

Improved working conditions can increase productivity. For example, addressing issues regarding indoor air quality and noise has been demonstrated to reduce absenteeism and improve staff morale. Similarly, in some cases energy-efficient lighting upgrades have boosted worker productivity by to 5 to 7 percent. Further, companies with high-quality environmental programs and few adverse effects on the environment have noted a greater ability to recruit and retain high-quality employees.

Value in Risk Management

Reducing environmental risks can help a firm avoid significant costs across many areas of corporate activities. Four are listed below.

Reduced Costs of Emergency Response

Proactive environmental management can minimize or prevent both the short- and long-term costs of accidents, spills, and releases. In the short term, companies can begin to scale back portions of their emergency preparedness programs that become obsolete after hazards are eliminated. Over the long term, proactive measures and effective plans can reduce response and cleanup costs while minimizing costs arising from regulatory penalties, litigation fees, and legal settlements.

Reduced Remediation Costs

Improving the management of remediation projects can reduce ongoing operational costs and help close out remediation projects ahead of schedule.

Reduced Product Liability Costs

Addressing environmental, health, and safety concerns at the product design stage can reduce the potential for adverse effects resulting from product use, misuse, or disposal. This can reduce liability exposure in tort law as well as waste disposal risks.

Reduced Insurance Premiums

Limiting environmental risk exposure for employees, contractors, and customers can directly lower corporate insurance costs. As discussed in chapter 6, more and more insurance companies are considering these issues when pricing coverage.

Value in Capital Investment

Companies spend millions of dollars servicing the long-term life-cycle costs of capital investment and design decisions. The environmental implications of capital investments such as the purchase of new sites, construction of facilities, and start-up or redesign of manufacturing lines and new products can have significant business consequences. Managers can add value by providing critical environmental information early in the capital budgeting and decision-making processes. By integrating environmental considerations into the capital acquisition and change processes, it is possible to realize a number of benefits, four of which are discussed below.

Reduced Uncertainty of Corporate Transactions

Due diligence activities can identify potential environmental liabilities associated with property acquisitions and divestitures, directly affecting prices. Brownfield redevelopment, for example, can result in strategic business and tax advantages. However, many refuse to consider such an undertaking because of the environmental hazards involved. Managers must take the initiative to educate peers and managers in other departments about ways to take advantage of these opportunities.

Reduced Time to Market

Intervening early to secure permits and address regulatory requirements can remove obstacles to new product commercialization and production expansion. Competitive environmental strategy can also play a key role in overcoming community opposition to construction or expansion of facilities by initiating communication with local residents and addressing their concerns.

Improved Equipment Acquisition Decisions

In purchasing departments, environmental considerations can inject energy efficiency and pollution prevention criteria into purchasing decisions for office equipment, machinery, and vehicle fleets. These considerations can reduce life-cycle operating costs and improve a company's image while protecting the environment.

Encouragement of Sustainable Design in Facility Construction

Companies can lower lifetime operating expenses and adverse environmental effects of new facilities by incorporating environmental considerations into their design at the outset. Sustainable design techniques such as use of recycled and nontoxic building materials and components, energy-efficient lighting and climate control systems, and native plantings can reduce utility and maintenance costs and improve working conditions and productivity. It can also benefit the company's public image.

Value in Market Growth

Competitive environmental strategy can enhance the marketability of products and services. Consumer demand for environmentally friendly products and consumer interest in environmentally responsible companies are on the rise. These market pressures are felt not only by consumer products companies; high environmental performance standards also are increasingly expected of vendors and suppliers. Thus, environmental initiatives, such as the three listed below, can reap a number of benefits related to market growth.

More Beneficial Supplier Relationships

Corporate environmental professionals can work with suppliers to reduce costs and risk and can win supply contracts with other companies by implementing proactive environmental management systems. Environmental considerations become one more aspect of the value offered by a company.

Enhanced Environmental Attributes of Products

Companies can appeal to environmentally conscious consumers by using recycled and recyclable materials, eliminating hazardous product constituents, and reducing adverse environmental effects of products and services.

Safeguarding of Corporate Image and Brand Names

In many industries, environmental performance has become a lightning rod for public inquiry and consumer decision making. Word of environmental shortcomings travels fast though the press and other channels, influencing consumer preferences, spurring boycotts, and in some cases affecting the bottom line. A solid environmental record enhances public perceptions of a company and can improve the marketability of its products and services.

Value in Strategic Direction

Competitive environmental strategy can expose valuable information and insights that can influence overall strategic decision making. This can manifest itself in a number of ways.

Influence on Product Mix

Documenting the true environmental costs and risks of certain products can illuminate strategic opportunities in shifting resources to more profitable and environmentally benign activities. Environmental drivers such as consumer preferences and regulatory incentives can prompt companies to enter new business areas through strategic acquisitions.

Monitoring and Management of Strategic Issues

Regulatory initiatives, public attitudes, media attention, and community concerns can alter a corporation's image and financial performance. Competitive environmental strategy involves monitoring these trends, alerting management when corporate interests might be affected, and considering external relations activities to offset or direct them.

Redefinition and Expansion of Markets

As markets and industries rapidly change, corporate environmental attributes and performance can help secure new markets and protect existing ones. Strategic decisions to invest in product redesign to enhance recyclability, for example, can win market share where new regulations, such as product take-back, penalize competitors. In this way, environmental initiatives can spur the innovation that builds new markets.

Modification of the Business Mission

There may be strategic advantage in modifying the core mission of the company to include environmental themes. Corporate focus on themes of sustainability and innovation "for achieving a better world" can demonstrate commitment to long-term value creation.

Technology Strategy

Each of the areas of enhanced value just discussed has one overarching objective—reduced adverse environmental effects from materials processing within the corporation. As such, competitive environmental strategy must have at its core a technological strategy in the development of new processes and the design of new products. Each will be discussed in turn.

Value in Process Development

One way to reduce the environmental consequences of company operations is to alter the manufacturing process. Process improvements can include (1) changing the raw materials of production, (2) changing the products of production, (3) changing production technology and equipment, (4) improving production operations and procedures, and (5) recycling waste within the plant. Examples of environmentally driven cost reduction and quality improvements can be as complex as adding additional seals to storage tanks to reduce vapor losses or as sophisticated as altering process conditions (e.g., temperature, pressure, or reactant mix) to use raw materials more efficiently. But such opportunities are not universally available across industries; some industries find their options for process improvements more limited than do others.

For example, opportunities for process innovation in the oil industry are quite limited. Although gasoline, the primary feasible product, is theoretically available from other raw materials such as shale or coal, crude oil currently remains the only economically viable source. Likewise, the processes used to convert the raw material into product, such as catalytic cracking, hydrogenation, and distillation, are largely defined and open to only limited modification. Substitutions in acids and catalysts are possible, but their effects are slight. As a result, opportunities for source reduction are quite limited.

The chemical industry, on the other hand, has been a leader in pollution prevention efforts through changes in equipment, products, and raw materials. For example, solvent recovery has presented the industry with a clear opportunity to minimize emissions on the basis of cost consciousness. Similarly, reduction of wastewater (which accounts for a major portion of the industry's waste stream) has been accomplished through alterations in the product mix at the plant, the type of processing done, and the complexity of operations.

Going to the furthest extreme, some industries with concerns for very high product purity and material yield, such as the pharmaceutical industry and the producers of some food products, can achieve near-zero emission processes. Kirin Brewery Company, Ltd., for example, one of the largest beer and beverage companies in Japan, successfully converted its fifteen Japanese factories into zero-waste factories, saving the company more than $4 million in operating costs from 1992 to 1998. The Environmental Protection Agency has identified and ranked U.S. industries in which opportunities tend to exist for reductions in waste or toxicity, as shown in table 7.1.

Opportunities for process-focused pollution prevention such as those listed in table 7.1 often become visible only through shifts in present economic equations or future projections. For example, one raw material—water—that was once considered virtually lim-

Table 7.1. Industrial Pollution Prevention Opportunities by Industry

Industry	Opportunity
Textiles	Recovery of dyes and scouring agents from wastewater
Wood preserving	Investigations of new, less toxic preserving agents
Pulp and paper	Improved recovery of coated stock; restoration of fiber strength in recycled paper; process changes/improvements
Printing	Minimization in prepress photographic chemistry through the use of computer technology; solvent recovery
Chemical	Solvent reuse; substitution
Plastic	Segregation of scrap plastics; compatibilization
Pharmaceutical	Solvent reuse; substitution
Painting	Low- and non-VOC[a] painting techniques; improved application technology
Ink manufacturing	Low- and non-VOC inks; elimination of metallic pigments
Petroleum exploration and refining	Improved recovery of usable oil from drilling muds and processing wastewaters
Steel	Reuse of tar decanter sludge and electric arc furnace dust; reuse of recovered calcium fluoride
Nonferrous metals	Isolation of arsenic contamination to allow reuse of stack dusts; improved hydrometallurgical processes, minimizing sulfur oxide emissions
Metal finishing	Noncyanide plating systems; improved chemical recovery from cyanide plating processes
Electronics	"Clean" fabrication techniques that eliminate or minimize degreasing solvent use
Automobile refinishing and repair	Reductions in solvent loss in various operations
Laundry and dry-cleaning	Improved solvent recovery

Source: Environmental Protection Agency, *Industrial Pollution Prevention Opportunities for the 1990s,* EPA Contract no. 68-C8-0062 (Washington, D.C.: U.S. Government Printing Office, 1991), 2–3.
[a]VOCs are volatile organic compounds.

itless is becoming increasingly expensive, and Americans reduced their use of it by about 9 percent from 1980 to 1995 (see figure 7.2). Water used for electric power generation fell by 5 percent; industrial use decreased by 35 percent; and farm use of water per acre of irrigated land fell by 16 percent (while the land under irrigation remained relatively constant).[3] Much of these reductions can be attributed indirectly to increasing standards for water discharge purity and more directly to business economics. As regulatory standards and water prices have increased and technologies have improved, it has become less expensive to recycle water or reduce water use than to remove pollutants and impurities

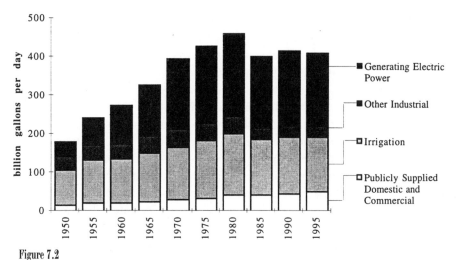

Figure 7.2

Water Use in the United States, 1950–1995

Source: U.S. Geological Survey, reported in W. Stevens, "Expectations Aside, Water Use in U.S. Is Showing Decline," *New York Times,* 11 November 1998, A1, A16.

before discharge. Companies that continue to use a great deal of water will find the economic disadvantages increasing over time.

One industry that has been particularly hard hit by the increasing costs of water use is the forest products industry. In the 1970s, the average pulp and paper plant discharged 40 million gallons of contaminated water into streams and rivers. By the 1990s, most plants were discharging one-quarter of that volume while also improving the purity of that discharge by as much as 80 to 90 percent.[4] In fact, several companies, such as the Weyerhaeuser Company, look forward to the day when their discharges will approach zero. Although regulation has been one driver, some companies see reduced water use as a source of strategic advantage driven by community concerns—as population grows and demand for drinking water increases, industrial users may find their access to water taxed or limited. Others are driven by concerns about liability and regulatory crackdowns. In 1992, Weyerhaeuser was sued for $1 billion by local landowners for the release of dioxin, a by-product of the paper-bleaching process. In 1991, the owners of two paper mills in Eureka, California, agreed to pay $5.8 million in penalties for polluting local beaches with dioxin. These concerns precipitated a federal initiative to reduce dioxin discharges, which forced investments of as much as $20 million per paper mill.[5]

To reduce dioxin-related liabilities, many paper manufacturers have altered production processes to use less reactive bleaching agents such as chlorine dioxide instead of chlorine gas. A few, such as the Louisiana-Pacific Corporation and the Union Camp Corporation (now merged with International Paper), have eliminated the use of chlorine compounds entirely. This results in not only cleaner discharges but also less corrosive wastewater that is more cheaply recycled back into plant operations. The Champion International Corporation has formed a joint venture with Wheelabrator Water Technologies Inc. and Sterling Pulp Chemicals, Ltd. called the Closed Loop Alliance to develop water-recycling technologies for papermaking processes and market them to the rest of the industry.[6] These technologies save costs in water use and discharge. They can also increase profits by recovering chemicals from tree residues that traditionally would have been discharged, such as turpentine, which can be sold, and others that can be burned for fuel.

Although the paper industry has long been the focus of environmental pressures, the electric utility industry is facing some new process concerns as deregulation increasingly becomes a reality. In the past, utilities were shielded from the financial risks of a competitive market and were able to recoup costs for pollution control by passing them along to customers. But with deregulation, that luxury will be eliminated and environmental costs will be factored into a company's process costs. Some electricity marketers, such as the Enron Corporation and Green Mountain Energy (now called GreenMountain.com), believe that consumers will prefer to buy their energy from utilities that maintain an environmentally balanced resource mix (employing such technologies as solar and wind power). Others believe that the inevitable increase in environmental standards will make polluting emissions a financial liability in the eyes of the investment community.

Of considerable concern are carbon dioxide emissions in the face of potential controls to mitigate climate change. In 1997, Fitch Investors Service, one of the top three U.S. credit services (now part of Fitch IBCA, Inc.), issued a report on PSI Energy, Inc. indicating "concern" about its "dependence on coal-fired generation" and "the potential of the company being affected by any future limits of emissions, including carbon dioxide."[7] Some estimate that limits on carbon dioxide emissions will cost the electric utility industry more than $60 billion annually.[8] The Natural Resources Defense Council (NRDC) has attempted to quantify the distribution of this liability and financial risk among the various power companies. As shown in figure 7.3,[9] the NRDC's index calculates a utility's financial risk on the basis of volume of emissions per dollar of operating revenue. NRDC researchers expect that environmental liability will translate directly into competitive liability in the emerging deregulated marketplace.

One final example of an industry altering its processes to reduce adverse environmental effects is the automobile industry's progress in pollution reduction. In any given automobile production plant, the major source of airborne emissions has traditionally been the painting and coating operations. But between 1988 and 1996, automakers reduced emissions, chiefly of xylene and xylene-based chemicals, by 20.6 million pounds.[10] For the Ford Motor Company, this amounted to a reduction from 16.5 pounds of reportable chemicals per vehicle produced (under the Environmental Protection Agency's Toxics Release Inventory) in 1988 to just 6.5 pounds in 1996. The primary reason for the reductions is the company's transition from solvent-based paints to water-based paints. The General Motors Corporation began the switch in 1990, and executives hope to have most, if not all, of the company's operations switched to water-based paints by 2004.[11]

Going deeper to reduce pollution in the automobile production and repair process, in 1999 Ford announced its intention to become the world's largest recycler of automobile parts. By acquiring existing recyclers and developing central recycling centers, the company expects to increase its annual revenues by $1 billion.[12] Each year in the United

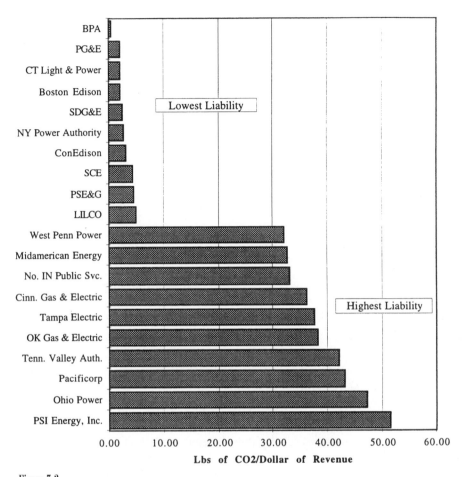

Figure 7.3

Environmental Liability Rankings of U.S. Electric Utilities

Source: R. Cavanagh and Natural Resources Defense Council, "Global Energy, Emissions, and Regulatory Outlook" (presentation at the Fourth Aspen Energy and Environment Roundtable, Aspen, Colo., 25 September 1997); © 1997 Natural Resources Defense Council. All rights reserved. Reprinted with permission.

(Rankings reflect pounds of carbon dioxide emitted per dollar of electric revenues in 1995.)

States, about 11 million vehicles are sent to junkyards, and about three-quarters of those are recycled or stripped of parts for reuse. Ford's goal is to recycle or reuse at least 90 percent of every vehicle and use the Internet to sell parts (such as windshields, body panels, engines, and transmissions) and recycled materials to repair shops and its own suppliers. The project is being driven by expectations of increased automobile recycling regulations (already a reality in Europe) as well as demands by insurance companies for use of cheaper used parts in automobile repairs. According to industry estimates, repair shops are presently able to find used parts only about 10 percent of the time.[13] With an on-line inventory of parts, customers should not have to wait as long for repairs and may pay less for them.

This is a strategy that Comprehensive Automotive Reclamation Service of Maryland

Inc. has been using since 1996. The company has developed a high-tech "de-assembly line" that recycles 95 percent of each car and efficiently distributes the parts to repair shops. The company earned more than $10 million in revenues in 1999 and opened a new branch that year in Stamford, Connecticut.[14]

Eventually, Ford plans to link its recycling division with its entire value chain as part of a larger plan to be involved in the life cycle of vehicles beyond development and assembly. By incorporating recyclability concerns into the initial automotive design with the expectation that the company will see that automobile again at the end of its usable life, this type of system redesign holds the promise of "closing the loop" on automobile manufacturing. As more countries pass automobile take-back laws, the early development of recycling and reclaiming competencies will prove to be a distinct competitive advantage.

Value in Product Design

Process innovation is only one way to visualize technology strategy. Process improvements are the primary focus when a dominant product design exists and competitors fine-tune their processes to compete in predominantly commodity-based markets, where margins are low and price is a deciding factor. Innovation becomes focused on perfecting process technology. This focus continues until the process is retired or there is a change in the parameters by which the quality of the product or process is judged. At this point, attention shifts to product design.[15]

In general, product design follows a trajectory that resembles an S-curve, as shown in figure 7.4. Early in the research process of a new technology (the lower left end of curve *A*), theoretical and empirical knowledge must be generated, research questions hypothesized, and technical problems uncovered. At this early stage, the pace of technological improvement on some specified performance parameters is slow. But with the accumulation of data and the development of a technological track record, progress increases, technological improvements become more easy to accomplish, and development moves up the S-curve. Once the technology becomes known and its attributes are accepted in the marketplace, improvements in the technology are rapid. The path of incremental improvement along a single innovation curve involves satisfying performance parameters that are set and established. As a result, technological advances do not take place in a haphazard fashion but occur in a systematic manner on what are called "innovation avenues."[16] Technological development becomes shaped by societal forces that lead from one technology to the next (such as the 286 computer chip leading to the 386 chip, and so on).

After reaching a peak of technological performance improvement, technology begins to be constrained by its limits and the rate begins to slow in the face of diminishing returns (the upper right end of curve *A*). At this point, either competitors focus on process improvements or a technological shift occurs. In the latter case, a new technology rises to replace the old and we move to a new technological S-curve, labeled *B* in figure 7.4. The jump from one curve to the next is called a discontinuity, and the difference between the curves is the set of performance parameters being satisfied by the product

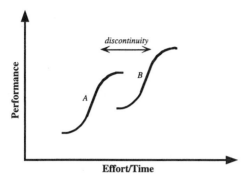

Figure 7.4

Technology Development Follows an S-Curve

Source: R. Foster, "Timing Technological Transitions," in *Technology in the Modern Corporation,* ed. M. Horwich (Woburn, Mass.: Pergamon Press, Inc., 1986). © Pergamon Press. All rights reserved. Used with permission.

development process. For example, the shift from solid-state electronics to vacuum tubes represents a radical innovation and a technological discontinuity.

Environmental concerns alter the performance criteria in the technological S-curve. They can drive incremental innovation along the existing innovation curve or cause jumps through radical innovation to a new curve. Whereas the design objectives of a given technology may include parameters such as speed, comfort, and aesthetics, environmentalism may introduce new parameters such as amount of pollution produced, amount of water used, amount of toxic materials included, and recyclability. By the inclusion of such new parameters, existing innovation avenues are altered or new ones are created. Either way, the pattern of technological development shifts. These shifts will decide winners and losers in technological development. Companies that can successfully steer innovation patterns toward precise parameters that complement their proficiencies will reap the benefits of environmentalism's infusion into the development process.

For example, the federally mandated corporate average fuel economy (CAFE) standards have prompted incremental improvements in the internal combustion engine that have cut the U.S. automobile fleet's fuel intensity by half since 1965 and have cut emissions by 97 percent since 1970. To extract further reductions from the present technological pattern, a coalition of seven U.S. federal agencies, twenty federal laboratories, and the big three auto manufacturers formed the Partnership for a New Generation of Vehicles (PNGV). The partnership spent nearly $400 million in the period 1995–1999 and was funded with $50 million in fiscal year 1999. Its goal is to produce a car with three times the fuel efficiency of today's midsize sedans by improving the existing emission technology of the internal combustion engine. New types of fuel-recycling systems, combustion ratios, fuel mixtures, and computer technology can help to improve fuel economy along the existing technology track. These involve innovation along the existing innovation S-curve. But many observers are beginning to wonder whether it is time for a new technological paradigm.

In 1997, the race for an alternative-fuel vehicle had taken on some very interesting dynamics and the industry found itself facing a new S-curve. Spurred on by pressure from environmental nongovernmental organizations (NGOs) and advancements by several automakers, the California legislature approved a standard by which 2 percent of cars sold in the state must be zero-emission by 1998 and 10 percent by 2003. (The first requirement was rescinded.) In response, the General Motors Corporation (GM) began leasing its EV1, the world's first mass-produced electric car, in markets in the American Southwest in the spring of 1997. The EV1 was intended to satisfy the California standards for a zero-emission vehicle and is filled with technological marvels that help it reduce aerodynamic drag and weight. Although it has met with poor sales performance, the $35,000 EV1 balances high performance (acceleration from 1 to 60 miles per hour in 9 seconds; 137 horsepower; 0.19 aerodynamic drag coefficient) and low maintenance costs ($80 over three years) with limited driving range (70 miles in the city, 90 miles on the highway).[17] The limited range highlights the major drawback of the vehicle—a lead acid battery. Regardless, GM introduced a possible shift from one curve to another while at the same time attempting to introduce new parameters into the design criteria for a cleaner car. Although the car may not become the answer to our transportation needs, its design may influence the parameters by which other cars are designed in the future. Moreover, because GM now holds dozens of patents for features of the EV1, the company is technologically poised to drive the way those design parameters are standardized.

In the fall of 1997, the Toyota Motor Corporation introduced a competing technology that threatened to drive technological development along a different innovation avenue. The Prius is a hybrid vehicle (half electric, half gasoline powered) that gets 70 miles per gallon while cutting carbon dioxide emissions by 50 percent and other emissions by as much as 90 percent.[18] Initially sold only in Japanese markets, the "parallel" hybrid automobile uses an electric motor to power the car until it reaches a speed of 12 miles per hour, the point at which gasoline-engine emissions are highest. At that point, a 1.5-liter gasoline engine starts up and seamlessly becomes the main power source. (The alternative, a "series" hybrid, uses the gasoline motor to generate electricity, which runs the wheels.) The electric motor also operates when maximum power is needed, as when climbing a hill. When it is running, the gasoline engine also recharges the batteries, eliminating the need for external recharging. The sticker price for the car is $20,000, which industry experts say is less than the cost of production and is Toyota's attempt to gain first-mover advantage in marketing and manufacturing. This would allow Toyota to gain the necessary skills to present a formidable force in the race to develop a clean car and to attempt to define (for consumers and regulators) the parameters by which a successful clean car will be judged. Toyota plans to introduce a hybrid in the United States by 2000.

The introduction of the Prius precipitated an innovation race for alternative-fuel vehicles among the other automakers. More powerful than the government regulation that spurred development of the EV1 (sales of which have been disappointing), Toyota's competitive challenge has spurred rhetoric from chief executives and investment dollars from corporate strategists. The American Honda Motor Company, Inc., for example, plans to unveil its hybrid, the Insight, in late 1999. At the North American International Auto Show in 1998, GM's chairman and chief executive officer, John Smith Jr., announced that "no car company will be able to thrive in the 21st century solely with the internal combustion engine."[19] But which technology will be the answer? Beyond electrics and hybrids, other technological avenues are emerging, the most promising of which is the fuel cell.

A fuel-cell automobile runs on electricity produced from the chemical reaction of hydrogen and oxygen, with water as the only by-product. Daimler-Benz AG, at the forefront of this technology, formed a joint venture with Ford and the leading fuel-cell maker, Ballard Power Systems Inc. of Vancouver, British Columbia, to begin jointly producing as many as 100,000 cars per year by 2004. GM and Toyota have developed a similar pact.[20] Recognizing that no infrastructure exists for distributing hydrogen, Chrysler, taking a different approach, has been working on a fuel cell that uses gasoline to produce the hydrogen required by the fuel cell. In the fall of 1997, Arthur D. Little, Inc. and the Department of Energy jointly developed the first-ever gasoline-powered fuel-cell electric engine for the automobile.[21]

In each of these cases—electric, hybrid, and fuel cell—innovation is presently low on the S-curve, but if one technology emerges as dominant and innovation reaches the middle portion of the curve, a leapfrog effect will occur, bringing about drastically improved fuel economy by diverting technological development along a different track, away from the internal combustion engine. In the end, those who can determine the timing and direction of the S-curve shift by defining new design parameters will reap success in the technology race. GM's vice chairman, Harry Pearce, stated: "Fuel cells have strong potential to be the best long-term solution. . . . Our fuel-cell vehicle gets 80 miles per gallon and has a driving range of 300 miles."[22] Ultimately, the dominant design will be that of the vehicle that can satisfy the multitude of design parameters on which automobiles have traditionally been judged and the newly emerging environmental parameters on which they will increasingly be judged.

The race for a clean automobile does not rest solely with the drivetrain. Other companies have gone further in attempting to redefine some of the basic notions of the automobile and its role and purpose. For example, in 1997, the World Future Society forecasted that "future cars will not only create less pollution but many actually destroy it. A catalytic coating technology on the surface of cars can reduce ambient sir and vehicle pollution. Using this technology, cars designed to take in air will clean up smog around them."[23] In 1999, Volvo became the first auto company to make this forecast a reality with the introduction of the Volvo S80 which is the first car capable of destroying smog-producing ozone. The automobile is equipped with a specially coated radiator that converts as much as 75 percent of the ozone passing through it into oxygen. The PremAir catalyst system, designed by the Engelhard Corporation, costs only about $50—a small fraction of the $40,000 price tag for the automobile.[24] Although the company will gain no regulatory benefits for the device, Volvo anticipates benefits in reduced urban air pollution and increased consumer interest.

PSA Peugeot Citroën is also exploring an innovation for introducing electric vehicles into urban centers, where they are needed most. Recognizing that urban centers are also places where consumers are less likely to have the space or the desire to own an automobile, the company developed a system called TULIP (Transport Urbain Libre Individuel et Public) that allows consumers to own a remote-control unit rather than the car itself. In Paris, customers can walk down to the local TULIP car station and check out a car. They are charged for mileage and can return the car either to the station where they checked it out or to any of the other TULIP stations situated throughout the city.[25]

Major urban centers have been searching for other solutions to their air pollution problems. China in particular holds the dubious honor of having five of the ten cities with the worst air pollution in the world. At times, these cities are so blanketed in smog that satellites cannot locate them. Much of this air pollution is generated by scooters with highly polluting two-stroke motors. President Clinton announced in 1998 that the Export-Import Bank of the United States would provide $50 million in loans for clean energy projects to help improve China's air quality.[26] Some U.S. companies have seen this pollution and financial support as a signal of a major market opportunity. Among them is the Vectrix Corporation, a start-up company in Newport, Rhode Island, that has developed an electric-powered scooter. Designed to carry two people, the Vectrix scooter can accelerate from zero to 50 miles per hour in about 5 seconds, reach speeds of 60 miles per hour, and travel as far as 70 miles on a charge, making it competitive in design characteristics to gasoline-powered scooters.[27] Priced between $4,500 and $6,000 (helmet included), the unit will compete with models in the upper end of the $17 billion worldwide market for gasoline-powered scooters.

Value in Product Design and Process Development

The examples so far have treated product and process innovation separately. But that differentiation is artificial, and the lines between the two can be ambiguous. Some opportunities emerge around technologies in which the product and the process are intertwined. One example is automobile tires. Tires make up less than 2 percent of the country's trash by weight, an amount comparable to disposable diapers and cat litter.[28] But for entrepreneurs, their presence looms much larger. Roughly 250 million tires are scrapped each year, adding to a present-day stockpile of 2 billion to 3 billion. New tires sell for more than $50 apiece and weigh roughly eighteen pounds. But after a mere quarter-inch of tread is worn off, the tire is discarded. These tires are extremely resource intensive to make and, unfortunately, cannot yet be recycled. Vulcanization, a process developed by Charles Goodyear in 1839, mixes rubber and sulfur under heat and pressure and makes tires hard and long lasting. The process is widely believed to be irreversible.

In attempting to resolve this problem, three questions must be considered. First, of course, is there a way to overcome the vulcanization process and develop a tire that is recyclable? Second, is there a way to develop a tire that does not require the disposal of eighteen pounds of material when only two pounds are worn out? Third, is there a way to put the existing stockpile of waste tires to good use? Many people have attacked the third opportunity, but none have found the solution. Some ideas include grinding them up for use in roadbeds, tying them together for use as offshore reefs, and using them as building material. The Yellow Cab Shoe Company even uses old tires as soles for its shoes.[29] Today, the primary use of old tires is as fuel for cement kilns and industrial boilers. Unfortunately, this does not make use of the energy and materials that originally went into making the tires. It is tremendously wasteful in the overall analysis of the life of the materials. Extracting a higher use from used tires would represent an increase in both business and environmental benefits.

Ultimately, if successful, technologies that are effective at minimizing or eliminating adverse environmental effects while improving the corporate bottom line will be indistinguishable from other technological advances within the corporation. For example, the Cycloid Company has developed a new product called the "continuous tire pressure maintenance system" that continually monitors and maintains truck tire pressure.[30] By keeping tires at their proper operating pressure, the system can reduce exhaust emissions by improving fuel mileage by 5 percent or more, reducing waste and raw material usage by extending the life of the tires by as much as 30 percent. The system also saves the driver as much as $1,100 per rig per year in fuel costs and more than $4,000 per tire set per rig. Is this an "environmental" technology? The trucker probably buys it not for its environmental attributes but for its economic attributes. Yet the technology is funded with venture capital from the environmental technologies fund of First Analysis Corporation. The lines between environmental and economic attributes are blurred.

Technology Types and Innovation Trends

All of the examples discussed thus far have represented ways to reduce the adverse environmental effects of corporate operations. But just as the drivers of environmental pressures evolve over time, so, too, do the technological needs they are satisfying. To provide a glimpse of how such technologies might evolve in the future, the National Science and Technology Council (NSTC) divides environment-related technologies into four categories—avoidance, monitoring and assessment, control, and remediation and restoration.[31] The following is the NSTC's overview of those categories.

AVOIDANCE

Avoidance technologies avoid the production of environmentally hazardous substances or alter human activities in ways that minimize damage to the environment. These technologies include equipment processes; process sensors and controls designed to prevent or minimize the generation of pollutants, hazardous substances, and other damaging materials; and technologies used in product substitution or in recycling and recovery of useful raw materials, products, and energy waste streams. These activities usually encompass the use of energy-efficient technologies and clean, high-efficiency energy production technologies, practices, and equipment. They might involve product substitution or the redesign of an entire production process. Avoidance can be achieved by operational changes, including the use of materials, practices, and procedures that reduce or eliminate waste, or institutional changes, including employee training programs, total quality management programs, just-in-time inventories, "green" procurement policies, full-cost accounting, and life-cycle analysis. Avoidance may include incremental changes to existing manufacturing infrastructure, such as replacement of volatile organic compounds with aqueous cleaning systems, use of more efficient motors or lighting, or substitution of a less hazardous intermediary. But it may also involve substantial changes in industrial infrastructure, such as near net shape casting, no-coke steelmaking, or entirely redesigned processes (design for environment). Such extensive changes in production processes usually require the development of a new attitude toward doing business. They are labeled with different names in various sectors of the economy. Examples in the manufacturing sector are *design for the environment* and *green design*. In agriculture, the descriptive phrase is *sustainable agriculture systems*.

MONITORING AND ASSESSMENT

Monitoring and assessment technologies are used to establish and monitor the condition of the environment, including the releases of pollutants and other natural or anthropogenic (human-made) materials of a harmful nature. These technologies include the design, development, and operation of monitoring instrumentation, with associated quality assurance and risk evaluation aspects. Monitoring and assessment systems encompass microsensors, chemical sensors, biosensors, space- and aircraft-based remote sensors, ground-based mobile platforms for sensors, sampling services, automation systems for tracking pollutant levels, and advanced techniques for data collection and analysis. These systems may be strategically established to provide information of broad international interest, such as climate change effects on a global or regional scale. They may also be very specific, as in the case of a dedicated detector used to ensure compliance by tracking the levels of a hazardous chemical in an effluent. Alternatively, they may be quite general, as in the case of employing the services of analytical and control laboratories to help identify pollutants at sites contaminated with unknown substances.

CONTROL

Control technologies render hazardous substances harmless before they enter the environment. These technologies may include treatment of pollutants or anthropogenic materials to eliminate or reduce environmental and human health hazards, or they may include reduction of volume or mobility of pollutants or waste materials to make subsequent management more effective. An example is the use of precipitators in fossil fuel–based power plants to remove particulates from waste gas streams. Subsequent treatment of the pollutants is often required after their removal from the process streams. Another example is the use of catalytic converters on automobiles to convert combustion by-products to less harmful substances prior to exhausting them. Other control technologies (also called "end-of-pipe" technologies) include incineration, separation, oxidation, reduction, bioprocessing, absorption, filtration, and neutralization.

REMEDIATION AND RESTORATION

Remediation technologies are those that render harmful or hazardous substances harmless after they enter the environment. These technologies include eradication, encapsulation, and other cleanup technologies that either remove the risks associated with harmful wastes or make the wastes more manageable. An example is the use of bioprocessing to convert polychlorinated solvents found in contaminated groundwater to compounds such as water, carbon dioxide, and salts. Restoration technologies embody methods designed to improve ecosystems that have declined as a result of naturally induced or anthropogenic effects. As a result, the natural ecosystem processes are restored and sustained, as are their contributions to other ecosystems, human populations, and global cycles. Examples include reforestation and the creation of wetlands and artificial reefs. Ideally, remediation and restoration activities work together to return waste sites to useful purposes. Other examples of these technologies include chemical transformation, incineration, groundwater recharge, soil augmentation, waste extraction, in-situ treatment techniques, and waste stabilization.

Innovation Trends

As shown in figure 7.5,[32] the National Science and Technology Council sees remediation technologies as presently dominant in the market but projects that they will eventually be replaced by avoidance technologies. The report by the NSTC states: "During the early part of the next century, investments in remediation will have cleaned up a large portion of existing hazardous waste sites. Intensified expenditures in technologies to avoid environmental harm will have paid off significantly. . . . By 2040 most industries will be approaching a zero-discharge goal, but some control technologies may still be required to deal with residual discharges into the environment."[33] In focusing on technology strategy for the long term, company executives must consider this evolution in corresponding investment patterns.

At present, it would appear that opportunities are wide open in avoidance technologies because attention is being focused on other sectors. There are 45,000 firms in the

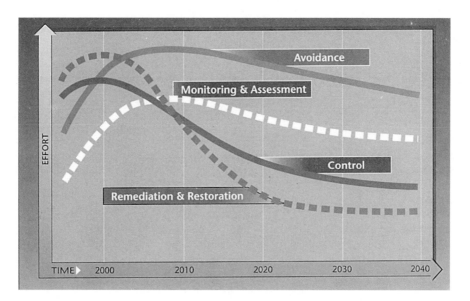

Figure 7.5

Technology Development Scenarios by Segment, 1995–2040

Source: National Science and Technology Council, *Technology for a Sustainable Future: A Framework for Action* (Washington, D.C.: Office of Science and Technology Policy, 1994), 3.

U.S. environmental technology sector. That sector enjoyed a $186 billion market in 1997,[34] whereas the global market is estimated at $468 billion.[35] (The other two major markets include western Europe, at $137 billion, and Japan, at $89 billion.[36]) But presently, much of these expenditures is devoted to pollution management rather than pollution prevention.[37] Industry trends show that from 1989 until 1998, process and prevention technology claimed less than 1 percent of technology revenues, but it also had the greatest growth rate, surpassing the average of all environmental technologies by over six times—see table 7.2. Future projections show this growth rate leveling off but still remaining strong in comparison with the growth rates of other sectors.

In sum, environmental considerations are becoming increasingly important in the

Table 7.2. Environmental Technology Markets: Revenue and Growth, 1989–2002

Environmental Industry Segment	Average Annual Growth	Revenue (Billions of Dollars)		Projected Annual Growth	Projected Revenue (Billions of Dollars)	
	(1989–1998)	1989	1998	(1999–2002)	1999	2002
Services						
Analytical services	−2.0%	1.5	1.1	0.8%	1.1	1.1
Wastewater treatment works	3.2%	19.2	25.3	3.7%	26.3	29.3
Solid waste management	4.8%	24.2	35.9	2.7%	36.9	39.8
Hazardous waste management	0.6%	5.7	5.7	−2.9%	5.5	5.0
Remediation/industrial services	1.1%	10.3	11.4	0.9%	11.6	11.7
Consulting and engineering	4.5%	10.5	15.2	−0.4%	15.2	15.1
Equipment						
Water equipment and chemicals	4.9%	12.8	19.1	6.2%	20.0	24.6
Instruments and information systems	11.2%	1.6	3.4	3.5%	3.5	3.9
Air pollution control equipment	3.4%	12.1	16.2	2.7%	16.6	18.0
Waste management equipment	2.2%	8.2	10.0	2.2%	10.2	10.9
Process and prevention technology	23.3%	0.3	1.0	7.0%	1.1	1.4
Resources						
Water utilities	5.2%	18.8	28.5	3.2%	29.4	32.3
Resource recovery	3.2%	12.0	15.9	3.1%	16.4	17.8
Environmental energy sources	8.1%	1.6	2.9	6.0%	3.1	3.6
Total industry	3.8%	138.8	191.5	3.0%	196.9	214.6

Source: Environmental Business International, Inc. San Diego, Cal. © 1997. All rights reserved. Used with permission.

direction of technology strategy, whether by altering product performance criteria and spurring incremental innovation along the existing S-curve, by altering innovation avenues to such an extent as to cause discontinuous shifts, or by altering process performance parameters and spurring improvements in process development patterns. New questions now arise for the corporate manager: How can one understand the overall trajectory of environmental pressures? Is there a way to move beyond the continual pressures of the external constituency and consider the fundamental driving factors of corporate concerns for the environment? How might a business manager proactively develop technologies that will remain ahead of the technological demands of environmentalism? The next section will consider these questions.

Competitive Environmental Strategy in Focus

There are many examples today of companies incorporating environmental protection into their competitive and technology strategies. However, because the definition and expectations of what constitutes a "green" technology and the unknown implications of those technologies continue to evolve, it proves difficult to judge whether these companies are on the right track. Before closing this chapter, we will look at two examples of environmental strategy and consider their merits and their risks.

Altering Natural Systems through Biotechnology: The Monsanto Company

Page eight of the Monsanto Company's 1996 annual report reads:

> Today, more than five-and-a-half billion people populate our planet. Roughly one billion of those people live in developed countries under economic systems that allow them to earn a comfortable living. Another one-and-a-half billion in emerging economies are within reach of a solid standard of living; they can aspire to a better future. Three billion—most in the least developed nations—face poverty. Economic systems worldwide are adjusting to these aspirations of greater wealth for more people. But the global environment is less adaptable. Today's productive systems will not work as well as more people seek higher standards of living based on current practices of agriculture and industry that are environmentally unsustainable.[38]

The report explains how Monsanto holds one solution to this problem. Is this just some slick marketing campaign by a standard chemical company? Monsanto has invested heavily in what it sees as the future of the company: "Information technology and biotechnology are the most promising tools we have today to create better lives for more people on a sustainable basis."[39]

In 1996, the company spun off the core of the firm, the chemical business, with annual sales of approximately $3 billion. Left behind was what is called a "life sciences" company with annual sales of some $6 billion—half from agricultural products, the rest from pharmaceuticals and food ingredients. The firm, under the leadership of chief executive officer Robert Shapiro, has pinned its hopes on becoming the main provider of agricultural biotechnology, which the world will need in the future if it is to feed itself without destroying the environment in the process.

World population is growing by about 1.5 percent annually, with roughly 90 million people being added to the globe each year. In 1990, the world's population was 5.3 billion. By 2025, it could reach 8.5 billion.[40] In a little more than two decades, farmers will need to produce 50 percent more food than they do now, just to keep up with population demand.[41] Many observers believe that the world's resources are finite and that without dramatic improvements in the way we utilize agricultural resources, a crisis is unavoidable. Thomas Malthus was the first to point out this scenario when he wrote several essays on population growth and food supply in the early nineteenth century.[42] He foresaw an eventual collision between the food needs of an increasing population and the fixed amount of available land on which to grow that food. However, Malthus failed to foresee improvements in agricultural productivity through fertilizers, pesticides, herbicides, and managed monocultures. Today, many believe that Malthus may not have been correct in his absolute predictions, but his overall thesis remains sound. Agricultural advances have only delayed the inevitable overlap—that is, before the advent of biotechnology.

Monsanto's first agricultural biotechnology product offering is "Roundup Ready" soybeans. Soybean crops are particularly sensitive to outside influences such as disease and pesticides. Yet Monsanto has developed a genetically altered strain of soybeans (as well as a second crop, canola) that is able to survive direct application of the company's popular Roundup herbicide. The results are impressive, with farmers claiming as much as fivefold increases in crop yield. This strain of soybean is only the tip of the iceberg. The company sees the market for genetically altered seeds growing from $450 million in 1995 to as much as $7 billion in 2005. Societal benefits of such technologies could be the development of seed strains that can thrive in desert or saline conditions, where the world's poor presently cannot sustain necessary levels of agriculture.

The stock market is very definitely behind Monsanto's advance. The company's stock rose from $14 per share in 1995 to $39 in 1997 to $52 in 1998. In January 1998, the stock was trading at an enormous price-to-earnings ratio of 66. Clearly, the company's sustainable development strategy opens up new possibilities for avoiding Malthus's dire prediction while increasing the company's bottom line.

However, there are critics who believe that proponents of the new technology are not fully cognizant of its full systemic effects. Leaders of many environmental NGOs are unconvinced by the argument that biotechnology is essential to feeding the world's growing population. They are critical of this argument as maintaining a reductionist mind-set that seeks technical fixes for one aspect of the system's problems but fails to address the entire system and the issues that created the problems in the first place. They argue that a shift from chemical fixes to informational and biological fixes will not solve any problem if the problem continues to be conceived in the same way.[43] Beyond the systemic aspect of the problem, the Union of Concerned Scientists has voiced concern about the systemic effects of the solution. These scientists fear that pests thwarted by Monsanto's efforts will eventually adapt and become a new and more potent menace.[44] This concern, coupled with uncertainties about the safety of genetically altered food (such as milk from cows treated with Monsanto's bovine growth hormone, Posilac), has led Greenpeace to organize protests charging that these products are being introduced too fast and that the world's consumers are becoming unwitting guinea pigs to test their safety. (The U.S. government does not require special labeling of the soybeans, for example.) To alleviate fears that some varieties of genetically altered corn will speed the evolution of pesticide-resistant insects, Monsanto announced in 1999 that it would require farmers to grow sizable areas of corn that is not genetically engineered along with the new crops.[45]

Finally, there are those who fear that biotechnology will have harmful effects on the future of the farmer. In a critical essay in the *New York Times* editorialist Veryln Klinkenborg warns "For thousands of years, farmers have looked for better varieties of the crops they plant, and for all but the last half a century or so, farmers have been the principal means of improving crops . . . farmers have controlled the genetic material on which their livelihoods, as well as America's food supply, depended."[46] But when farmers enter into a contract with Monsanto over Roundup Ready soybeans they agree to several restrictions. They will use only Roundup herbicide. They will not hold any portion of the harvest as seed for the next year. On the grounds of intellectual property rights, the company wants the farmer to pay for the specialized seeds yearly. (As an alternative, the company has undertaken controversial research into "terminating" seeds, seeds that will not reproduce.) Moreover, the company reserves the right to inspect farms to ensure that they comply with these requirements. Some see this as a further shift of economic and technological power from farmers to agricultural corporations, reducing farmers to what one agricultural foundation calls "bioserfdom," the once independent farmers having become mere suppliers of labor.[47] The question then becomes whether this shift is best for the health of the land and the people who make their living from it.

European consumers have been the toughest to convince about the merits of genetically altered vegetables. In fact, Monsanto has become a hated company in Europe because of its prominence in the genetic engineering field (Europe's Zenaca Group PLC and Novartis AG have kept a low profile). Often referred to as the "Frankenstein food giant" and "biotech bully boy" by the English press, the company has drawn criticism from Prince Charles, Paul McCartney, and Norman Baker, a member of Parliament. Consumers and critics are wary of the health effects of bioengineered foods to such an extent that their animosity is beginning to affect trade between Europe and the United States. A significant percentage of American crops, particularly soybeans, is now grown with genetically engineered seed.[48]

As these concerns should make clear, the questions about technological development, and particularly the environmental aspects of biotechnology, are difficult ones. Our knowledge on many levels is insufficient to develop complete and comprehensive answers. In fact, it may be safe to say that we will never completely understand all aspects of the ecosystem and the effects of our technology on it (see box 7.1). But as the Monsanto example illustrates, opportunities emerge from the application of technological development to environmental problems. And with each new opportunity comes a whole new series of questions that await answers. With each expansion of our reach comes a new understanding of the limitations of our understanding of its effects.

Box 7.1. Is Technology the Solution or the Cause of Environmental Problems?

Biologist and Pulitzer Prize winner René Dubos, in his classic article "Symbiosis between Earth and Humankind," wrote that we are to be stewards of the environment:

> The earth is to be seen neither as an ecosystem to be preserved unchanged nor as a quarry for selfish and short-range economic reasons, but as a garden to be cultivated for the development of its own potentialities of the human adventure. The goal of the relationship is not the status quo, but the emergence of a new phenomena and new values. Millennia of experience show that by entering into a symbiotic relationship with nature, humankind can invent and generate futures not predictable from the deterministic order of things, and thus can engage in a continuous process of creation.[*]

Rachel Carson might have countered that Dubos's statement epitomizes what she referred to as the "arrogance of man." Although Carson did not oppose technological development (or even the industrial application of organic chemistry), she believed strongly that "man's grasp must be well within his reach."[†] In arguing for a cautious temperament, she argued for a balance between the needs of humankind and the needs of the ecosystem:

We are not being truly civilized if we concern ourselves only with the relation of man to man. What is important is the relation of man to all life. This has never been so tragically overlooked as in our age, when through our technology we are waging war against the natural world. It is a valid question whether any civilization can do this and retain the right to be called civilized.[‡]

In another book, she continued:

> The "control of nature" is a phrase conceived in arrogance, born of Neanderthal age of biology and philosophy, when it was supposed that nature exists for the convenience of man. The concepts and practices of applied entomology for the most part date from that Stone Age of science. It is our alarming misfortune that so primitive a science has armed itself with the most modern and terrible weapons, and that turning them against insects has also turned them against the earth.[§]

Renowned conservationist Aldo Leopold concurred when he wrote, "Ability to see the cultural value of nature boils down, in the last analysis, to a question of intellectual humility."[‖]

Environmental writer Bill McKibben believes that in the end, technology can never be the solution to environmental problems. He argued:

> The environmental optimists are wrong: there is no market-oriented technological fix. Simply and radically, people have to change their lives. . . . More money makes reducing smog easier, because you can afford to build *better* cars; more money makes dealing with the greenhouse effect harder, because you can afford to buy *more* cars. So the dream that we will grow rich enough to turn green is simply that—a dream, and one that will turn into a nightmare if we try to follow it. We face tough choices. The most pragmatic realism, rooted in the molecular structure of CO_2, demands electric cars. It also demands nothing less than heresy: an all-out drive for deep thrift, for self restraint, for smaller families. Brute objectivity requires new ideas about what constitutes

sufficiency: smaller homes, more food grown locally, repair instead of replacement.[#]

So how do we solve environmental problems? Which perspective is correct? Can we use technology to improve on ecological systems? Do we have no choice but to try, given the growth of society and the legacy of environmental damage already done? Can new technologies reverse the ecological damage caused by the old ones? Or are we on a technological track, an innovation avenue, that will lead to unavoidable environmental destruction? Will our reach always exceed our grasp? Or can we develop a system whereby we use technology to develop a better balance with nature? Is technology the answer to our environmental problems?

[*] R. Dubos, "Symbiosis between the Earth and Humankind," *Science* 193 (1976): 462.

[†] "The American Experience: Rachel Carson's *Silent Spring*" (Boston: Public Broadcasting System, 1993), video.

[‡] R. Carson, *Silent Spring* (Boston: Houghton Mifflin, 1962), 297.

[§] Speech in acceptance of the Schweitzer Medal of the Animal Welfare Institute, 7 January 1963. P. Brooks, *The House of Life: Rachel Carson at Work* (Boston: Houghton Mifflin Company, 1972), 316.

[‖] A. Leopold, *A Sand County Almanac, and Sketches Here and There* (London: Oxford University Press, 1949), 200.

[#] B. McKibben, "Not So Fast," *New York Times Magazine*, 23 July 1995, 24, 25.

Shifting from a Product to a Service Focus: Interface, Inc.

In applying the ecological principle of interdependence to environmental technology, Physicist Fritjof Capra and business executive Gunter Pauli see a resultant shift of focus from objects to relationships. This entails a shift in emphasis to the objectives of technology and the services it provides. Do people living in cities want to own automobiles? Or do they want freedom of movement, which can be satisfied when a taxi driver owns the car and provides the service? When people say they want to own a television set, are they saying that they want to buy a cathode-ray tube and printed circuit boards or that they want to watch the ball game, a movie, or the soaps?[49] According to Capra and Pauli, "the manager of a car company should say: We are not in the business of selling cars; we are in the business of providing mobility. This will include cars, but also trains, bicycles, buses, and—above all—integrated systems of these means of transportation. Similarly, the managers of an oil company should say: We are not in the business of selling oil; we are in the business of satisfying our customers' energy needs."[50] Some oil companies have begun to consider this question as they face ever-increasing restrictions on the legitimacy of fossil fuels.

Amory Lovins, L. Hunter Lovins, and Paul Hawken believe that a shift from selling products to delivering services involves reinvesting in natural capital to restore, sustain, and expand the planet's ecosystem. Because natural capitalism is both necessary and profitable, it will subsume traditional industrialism, the authors argue, just as industrialism subsumed agrarianism. And the companies that are furthest down the road will have the competitive edge.[51]

One company that has taken this kind of thinking to heart is Interface, Inc., the largest maker of commercial carpet. In 1995, the company, led by chief executive officer Ray Anderson, set out a goal of producing zero waste and using zero oil while maintaining a healthy profit. Employees examined every process for potential savings. They developed a way to make carpet using 10 percent less nylon, and they pressured suppliers to develop "greener" processes. By the end of 1997, Interface was claiming to have saved $25 million through pollution reduction while attracting customers and architects. The company posted record revenues of $1 billion in 1997.

The most innovative step the company made was based on the ecological principle of interdependence. Interface now offers an Evergreen Lease that allows building owners to rent rather than buy carpet. Focusing on services rather than objects and operating on the premise that customers do not "wake up in the morning and say: I want to own a piece of nylon," Interface provides and maintains carpets and then replaces them as they wear out, carting away and recycling the old carpet. As James Hartzfeld, Interface's research director, said, "Durable goods are really just valued for the service they deliver." The company is now in the business of selling services, not goods.[52]

Like Monsanto, Interface is embarking on an interesting and exciting way to employ technology, solve environmental problems, and improve the company's bottom line. But is recycling always the best solution from a systemic perspective? The question is a difficult one, just like the unending question, Which is better for the environment: cloth or disposable diapers? Does carpet recycling serve both human and ecological systems? Each year, nearly 2 million tons of old carpeting goes to landfills, where it constitutes 1 percent of the entire municipal solid waste load. Keeping carpets out of the landfill is clearly good for the environment. But how much energy is required to recycle them? Recycling requires the development of an efficient industrial system in order to minimize costs and environmental effects. For example, shipping old carpets to the few existing recycling facilities is costly in time, energy, and fuel. Those few recycling facilities represent a capital investment that requires sufficient feedstock to operate in a cost-effective fashion. In 1997, E. I. du Pont de Nemours and Company's recovery facility in Chattanooga, Tennessee, operated inefficiently at about one-quarter capacity because it was not receiving enough used carpets. With or without efficiency considerations, the recycling process itself can be energy and material intensive. Sorting and handling also add costs to the process. Many carpets look and feel alike, but most have unique formulations, possibly making them incompatible with recycling. To ease this problem, the Carpet and Rug Institute is developing a seven-part universal coding system that describes a carpet's components to recyclers.[53]

As Monsanto found, the integration of ecological concerns with technology development raises questions as it answers them. In the United States, our society's continuing need for new products, our unending curiosity in exploring new issues, and our emerging role as ecological stewards pushes us toward new configurations of industrial systems and new technologies to support them. With each new vista comes a new understanding of the problems we have created and the solutions they require.

Conclusion

In the final analysis, environmental issues represent an important dimension in triggering a market or industrial transition, like those in which the computer industry eliminated the typewriter in the early 1980s, the compact disc replaced the phonograph album in the mid-1980s, and the 1984 dissolution of the Bell System caused structural changes in the telecommunications industry. Environmental problems indicate long-term problems in maintaining a sustainable ecosystem and economy. They warn of the need to diversify, innovate, and change to ensure the long-term competitiveness of an industry and the resource base on which it is built. The signal for the transition comes through business constituents that are sensitive to these warnings and are able to mobilize changes within the market, such as government agencies, environmental NGOs, insurance companies, suppliers, investors, and consumers. As market expectations shift and technological development advances, certain industries face demise and others rise to fill their place. As a result, in such transitions there will always be those with an interest in resisting and trying to delay such market transformations and those who will capitalize on them. There will always be winners and losers, the difference between them determined by their strategic positioning with respect to the issue.

For example, some logging companies were hurt by restrictions on timber supply from federal lands in the Pacific Northwest resulting from protection of the northern spotted owl in the early 1990s. But some companies have successfully adapted and prospered under species protection programs, engaging the government and environmentalists in development plans through habitat conservation plans (such as the Weyerhaeuser Company and Plum Creek Timber Company, Inc.) or implementing sustainable forestry techniques. The Collins Pine Company of Portland, Oregon, for example, earned certification from Scientific Certification Systems and the Forest Stewardship Council for its sustainable management practices. Employing 100- to 130-year rotations in its 92,000-acre Collins Almanor Forest, the company is adapting to the changing economic nature of the industry while reaping attractive supplier preferences at The Home Depot.[54] (In 1997, amid great controversy, The Home Depot discontinued the relationship because Collins Pine could not meet the inventory needs of the chain.[55])

Companies must anticipate market changes and decide what strategic track to take. To develop the strategy, they must consider the form of environmental pressures on the basis of who is applying them. Will governments implement regulations that allow companies adequate flexibility to respond strategically? Will consumers respond by buying environmentally sensitive products? Will insurance companies cut back on investments in and underwriting of pollution-intensive industries? Will competitors take advantage of first-mover opportunities by adopting programs for early pollution reductions? All of these questions will determine what kind of strategy a firm must take.

At the heart of the strategic questions and at the intersection of environmental protection and economic growth is a debate over the fundamental role of the corporation in society and the technology it employs. This debate comes at a critical juncture in our history. We live at a time when the consequences of our technological and economic systems reach far beyond those of generations before. In listing the six important trends for the twenty-first century, historian Paul Kennedy makes an important distinction between the environmental dangers of today and those of yesterday. More than just localized pollution effects, he warns, "the environmental crisis we confront is quantitatively and qualitatively different from anything before, simply because so many people have been inflicting damage on the world's ecosystem during the past century that the system as a whole—not simply its various parts—may be in danger."[56]

Because of our newfound power over the biosphere of the entire planet, we must, by necessity, adopt a steward's role in developing technologies that meet the expanding needs of present generations while considering the needs of those in the future.[57] But as the late philosopher Hans Jonas warned more than twenty years ago, "For such a role of stewardship no previous ethics has prepared us—and the dominant, scientific view of *Nature* even less. Indeed, the latter emphatically denies us all conceptual means to think of nature as something to be honored, having reduced it to the indifference of necessity and accident, and divested it of any dignity of ends."[58] Since our thirst for technological development is not likely to subside, markets are evolving to incorporate interests that will drive that development in a way that will not strain our balance within the natural system.

This role of steward may not necessarily be a role to which many of us are suited or fully capable of understanding. But as Stephen Jay Gould wrote, humans "have become, by the power of a glorious evolutionary accident called intelligence, the stewards of life's continuity on earth. We did not ask for this role, but we cannot abjure it. We may not be suited for it, but here we are."[59] To accept this role, we will have to defy much of what has driven the historical goal of technological development, the domination of nature as inanimate and separate from ourselves. C. S. Lewis captured the extent to which this belief is ingrained in our belief structures when he wrote: "We reduce things to mere Nature *in order* that we may 'conquer' them. We are always conquering Nature, because 'Nature' is the name for what we have, to some extent, conquered."[60]

As one of society's most powerful forces, business will play a role in meeting this challenge. Society will demand that it does. But what lies at the center are two important shifts. The first is an awareness of ourselves as part of a complex system of natural and human systems. With this acknowledgment comes an appreciation of the fact that every technological development may have consequences far beyond our scope of reason. The second is an awareness that technology alone will not bring about environmental solutions. Behavioral change will also be necessary. As discussed in the chapters that follow, organizational and institutional changes must accompany any efforts at merging our technological advancements with our ecological systems.

Further Reading

Capra, F., and G. Pauli, eds. *Steering Business toward Sustainability*. New York: United Nations University Press, 1995.

Carson, R. *Silent Spring*. Boston: Houghton Mifflin Company, 1962.

Dubos, R. "Symbiosis between the Earth and Humankind." *Science* 193 (1976): 459–462.

Global Environmental Management Initiative (GEMI). *Environment: Value to Business*. Washington, D.C.: GEMI, 1999.

Hawkins, P., A. Lovins, and H. Lovins. *Natural Capitalism: Creating the Next Industrial Revolution.* New York: Little, Brown and Company, 1999.

Jonas, H. "Technology and Responsibility: Reflections on the New Tasks of Ethics." *Social Research* 40 (1973): 31–54.

National Science and Technology Council. *Bridge to a Sustainable Future.* Washington, D.C.: Office of Science and Technology Policy, 1995.

———. *Technology for a Sustainable Future: A Framework for Action.* Washington, D.C.: Office of Science and Technology Policy, 1994.

Reinhardt, F. *Down to Earth: Applying Business Principles to Environmental Management.* Boston: Harvard Business School Press, 1999.

Schmidheiny, S., and World Business Council for Sustainable Development. *Changing Course: A Global Business Perspective on Development and the Environment.* Cambridge, Mass.: MIT Press, 1992.

Smart, B. *Beyond Compliance: A New Industry View of the Environment.* Washington, D.C.: World Resources Institute, 1992.

Chapter 8

STRATEGY ORIGINATES
WITHIN THE ORGANIZATION

Imagine that you have been given the task of improving the environmental performance of a major petrochemical corporation. Where would you start? Does the core of your strategy lie in technological development? Would you order that all tankers be double hulled? Would you install equipment at drilling operations to recover usable oil from drilling mud and processing wastewater? Or would you begin by analyzing how environmental concerns fit within the reward systems, structural responsibilities, and organizational culture of the corporation? These are important questions that highlight an important fact—although environmental concerns have reached the level of a strategic concern for corporations, opportunities for environmental strategy will not materialize unless organizations are structured to identify them. Environmental strategy is not primarily a technological or an economic issue; more important, it is embedded within the behavioral and cultural aspects of the firm.[1] Although technological and economic activity may be the direct cause of environmentally destructive behavior and may enable or drive environmental change, it is the culture of the organization that guides the development of that activity.[2] And just as an organization's existing competitive strategies are the product of history and culture, so too will be the environmental strategy.

Seeing the importance of this connection, the Environmental Protection Agency (EPA) mandated organizational changes as part of an enforcement action against the United Technologies Corporation (UTC) in 1993. The EPA fined UTC a record $5,301,910 for violations of federal and state laws regarding hazardous waste and water pollution control. As part of the settlement, UTC was required to (1) implement an extensive multimedia environmental audit of all twenty-six of its New England facilities and (2) hire a management consultant to make management improvement recommendations for achieving compliance with every major environmental law at all of its facilities. An EPA press release stated, "This is one of the most extensive environmental audits ever agreed to in an enforcement action . . . by this settlement we have not only corrected past problems, but have also acted to assure future violations will be deterred."

Perhaps one of the most contentious environmental issues of our day, global climate change is considered by many as likely to have a crippling effect on economic development. Yet some see an answer not in expensive new technologies but in an alteration in the way we view the problem and its solution. Amory Lovins of the Rocky Mountain Institute is one of the more controversial thinkers on this topic; his ideas serve as a provocative starting point in considering the organizational implications of environmental strategy. In his view, controls on climate change will not cost money but will actually save money. This view is based on the notion that the obstacles to clean technologies are not in technological development. Instead, he sees organizational barriers to the adoption of existing technologies or the development of engineering parameters that will minimize energy use (see box 8.1).

Box 8.1. Do the Solutions to Environmental Problems Lie in Technological or Organizational Innovation?

In May 1997, nearly fifty senior executives met at Northwestern University to discuss the emerging issue of global climate change. The following December, the Kyoto Protocol was signed in Kyoto, Japan, calling for the developed countries of the world to limit their emissions of carbon dioxide. But at the time of this meeting, the future of that treaty was far from certain and opinions ranged widely on whether it should come to fruition. Opening the discussion, Tim Wirth, undersecretary of state for global affairs and chief U.S. negotiator, proclaimed, "The debate about the existence of climate change is over; there is now broad scientific consensus that we humans are having a major impact on our planet's climate."[*] The next speaker, Steven Percy, chairman, chief executive officer, and chief financial officer of BP America, supported Undersecretary Wirth's comments: "We [at BP] acknowledge two facts: first, CO_2 concentrations are rising; second, world temperatures are rising. We feel that the body of scientific opinion now weighs in favor of a connection between the two. While there's still a lot of uncertainty around the timing and consequences of that connection, we can no longer discount the possibility of that connection or of serious consequences. So we, as a company, believe that it is time for action and action on our part."[†]

Roger Stone, chairman, president, and chief executive officer of Stone Container Corporation, then presented a counterargument and challenge to them both:

> With all respect to Undersecretary Wirth, I, for one, do not believe that the science debate is over. I'm curious to know why we as a nation or a world are pursuing a policy that would radically change the way we manufacture our products, potentially burden us with unnecessary technology costs and ultimately deprive the U.S. paper industry of its global competitive advantage. And to do all that without any compelling evidence that such a policy change is needed or any benefit is derived. I believe there is considerable scientific uncertainty that increases in CO_2 emissions have resulted in an increase in global temperatures. And I am concerned that we are blindly accepting a policy that would result in permanent and destructive changes to our economy.[‡]

The final opening remarks came from Amory Lovins, vice president and director of research for the Rocky Mountain Institute, and they proved a controversial and thought-

(continues)

Box 8.1. *Continued*

provoking discussion point, not only for the executives taking part in this dialogue but for everyone who considers the technological and cultural aspects of environmental issues. He began: "I find myself both in sympathy and in disagreement with all three of the previous speakers. If I heard correctly, they all like to do things that make money and make sense; they all like flexibility; and they all assume that protecting the climate will cost more than what we're doing now. I'd like to suggest that actually protecting the climate will be highly profitable rather than costly if we do the cheapest things first; and that pursuing that profit motive will put industry in its rightful place as the largest part of the solution."

He continued:

> There is some very good news about the climate problem: we do not need to worry about how the climate science turns out or whether this is a real problem or not because we ought to do the same things about it anyway just to save money. [The Rocky Mountain Institute] had a 97 percent energy saving by retrofitting an office air-conditioning system, and it became more comfortable. We just got a 92 percent energy saving on a pumping system in a Chinese carpet factory just from using big pipes and small pumps instead of small pipes and big pumps.
>
> The obstacles to achieving this profitable resolution are not technological or economic. Rather, they are cultural and procedural. They are what economists call "market failures"—the silly rules and practices that do not mean anyone is dumb, but rather that the normal way we do things does not let us use energy in a way that saves money. Obsolete rules-of-thumb used throughout engineering practice are typically wrong by half to one order of magnitude compared with whole system life-cycle optimization, because they're optimizing a little piece of the system and therefore pessimizing the whole system. Most of our building design is "infectious repetitis," not real engineering or architecture at all— partly because architects and engineers are rewarded for what they spend, not for what they save. Similarly our utilities, in almost every jurisdiction, are rewarded for selling more energy and penalized for cutting your bill. We have split incentives between builders and buyers of equipment or buildings, and between landlords and tenants. If you invest to save energy in your operations or home, you probably want your money back about ten times as fast as utilities want their money back from building power plants. This ten-fold difference in discount rate is equivalent to about a ten-fold price distortion.[§]

Lovins's arguments center on the idea that there are "$20 bills [lying] on the ground" but no one has taken the initiative to pick them up. In his view, hidden opportunities await managers who can look beyond the cultural and institutional barriers of the organization or society. But this notion challenges the beliefs that business managers act rationally and that environmental solutions are technically and economically complex. Taking issue with this challenge, Paul Portney, president of Resources for the Future, countered: "I'm willing to make a concession to Amory. It is that markets are not as perfect as at least some people in the economics profession sometimes suggest that they are. If I could just get you to concede that business men and women are not as stupid as you persistently suggest that they are. The notion that we have to put a gun to business men and women's heads to get them to take advantage of all this free money is silly."[||]

At the root of this exchange are questions that challenge us all. Do the solutions to environmental problems lie in changing our cultural and institutional norms? Does finding them require expensive new technologies? Will this search create a drain on economic growth or give it a boost? Or do the opportunities in environmental strategy involve merely seeing environmental protection and economic growth from a new perspective?

Source: Lexington Books, © 1998. All rights reserved. Used with permission.

* T. Wirth, "The Scientific Debate Is Over: Now the International Community Must Respond," in *Global Climate Change: A Senior Level Dialogue at the Intersection of Economics, Strategy, Technology, Science, Politics, and International Negotiation,* ed. A. Hoffman (San Francisco: New Lexington Press, 1998), 127.

† S. Percy, "A Call for Action," in Hoffman, *Global Climate Change,* 134.

‡ R. Stone, "A Call for Restraint," in Hoffman, *Global Climate Change,* 140.

§ A. Lovins, "Energy Efficiency, the 'No-Regrets Policy,' and Market Failures," in Hoffman, *Global Climate Change,* 194–196.

|| P. Portney, "The Role of Research and Development in Setting Collaborative Climate Change Goals," in Hoffman, *Global Climate Change,* 174.

Environmental Strategy and the Organization

A shift from environmental management to environmental strategy requires a concurrent and supporting shift in organizational culture, structure, reward systems, and job responsibilities. Managers must focus on developing an organizational culture that will encourage a merger of environmental and economic interests in the decision making of its employees. But what does the "green" firm look like? How does a firm efficiently integrate environmental protection into its structure and culture? In this chapter, we first consider the goal of organizational design and then examine present-day realities and obstacles to achieving that goal.

Organizational Goals

Effective organizational strategy must focus on diffusing environmental responsibilities throughout the organization. To understand the rationale behind this statement, begin with the notion presented in chapters 2 through 6—what twenty years ago was driven primarily by pressures separate from core business objectives is now driven by a host of constituents whose interests strike at the core of business decision making (as shown in figure 7.1). In chapter 7, the connection between these drivers and the strategic objectives of the corporation was made. These external constituents redefine environmental issues in terms that reflect their own interests, terms with which the corporation may already be familiar. In each case, the firm has a preexisting model and language with which to conceptualize the issue and formulate a response. By realizing this "fit," firms can begin to see environmental issues as strategic issues, directed no longer by external societal interests but rather by internal strategic interests.

In this chapter, we make the final connection between the strategic interests of the firm and the organizational departments established to handle those interests. Environmental strategy is really a composite of core organizational functions (see figure 8.1). External constituents making environmental demands do so in their own strategic language and from their own perspective. These demands are brought to the attention of the organization through the functions to which they are traditionally connected and whose language and perspectives they share. To develop an effective strategic response, the firm must push environmental responsibilities to those functional levels, which are, in fact, best equipped to handle them. In a company that integrates environmental strategy, environmental concerns will diffuse from the periphery of specialized departments to the core of the organization's functional competencies. Through this process, the work roles and functions of the various departments will be transformed within the organization.

Given this diffusion process, those seeking a career in environmental strategy will need to develop an applicable set of skills and crafts and an appropriate professional path (see appendix B for a list of environmental information resources). In the future, firms will look less for environmental specialists and more for environmental generalists—not for people who know only environmental affairs but for those who can articulate environmental issues in the language of the finance, accounting, and marketing constituents that are exerting pressure. The converse will also ring true. Those seeking a career in other areas of business management will find environmentalism becoming a necessary component of their job skills, becoming integral to the conceptual framework of their decision-making processes.

Some firms today are adding environmental issues to the list of performance measures at promotion and bonus time. Executives are finding that tenure in environmental affairs is an important step in their promotion path and an important component of their ability to understand the full range of issues facing the corporation. Similarly, some business schools are beginning to include environmental considera-

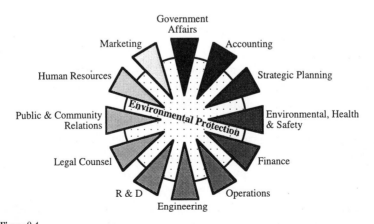

Figure 8.1

Environmental Strategy as a Composite of Internal Functional Responsibilities

tions in degree programs, either through specific course offerings or by infusion of environmental topics into standard course requirements.[3] In this way, students are often taught environmental management not simply as an adjunct to their management studies but as an integral component of accounting, finance, marketing, strategy, process design, and product development. Even the business press, including both newspapers and journals, is reporting on environmental issues with increasing regularity. Overall, the culture of environmental protection is merging with the culture of business.

Over the long term, external environmental pressures will become more diverse and more demanding, and as the issue of environmental protection gets larger, as represented by the circle in figure 8.1, so too will the functional "slices" of this circle. The proportion of environmental concerns falling to the environmental health and safety (EH&S) department will diminish. Environmentalism will continue to diffuse throughout the organization, affecting the culture of nearly every department. As this diffusion process continues, there will be less need for an exclusive corporate environmental affairs department and more reliance on an environmental structure that integrates the skills of all operating and support departments. Although an environmental department's role will not disappear, it will function more as an agent of internal change—that is, it will (1) interpret changes in environmental regulations and external demands, (2) set internal direction and responses, (3) facilitate change and integration, (4) measure performance, and (5) communicate internally and externally. With this functional change, the centrality of its function to corporate practice will continue to diminish. The more important environmental work will fall to the broadly diffused management staff in pursuit of internally defined environmental goals.

This progression follows the historical trajectory of environmental management. The evolution from end-of-the-pipe treatment in the 1970s to waste minimization in the 1980s to pollution prevention in the early 1990s and product stewardship in the late 1990s involved a progressive shift in the departmental knowledge base away from environmental management and toward engineering management and product design. It is an inevitable result of the EH&S department's origin, purpose, and function. It is, in effect, a natural evolution in management from the disconnected environmental ignorance of the 1960s to the integrated environmental awareness of the new century. In effect, environmental managers are destined eventually to work themselves out of a job.

Taken to its extreme outcome, environmentalism should ultimately disappear into the cultural foundations of the corporation, just as the drive for profit and quality has. It will be implicit in the organizational structure and individual roles of each of the firm's members and departments. No profitable company must overtly remind its employees that the corporate objective is to make a profit. Similarly, a company that has achieved a reputation for first-class quality need not overtly advise its employees to perform their duties with quality in mind. These concerns become ingrained in the everyday practices of the firm so as to disappear from conscious awareness and become part of the unconscious.

Likewise, in developing the most efficient and effective response to environmental demands, the corporate manager is challenged to translate environmental considerations into concerns that resonate with the central objectives of the firm. Environmental concerns must be presented as strategic issues and pushed up to the executive level, down to the operating line, and across functional lines. However, for both cultural and institutional reasons, this change in mind-set will prove a difficult challenge. Firms will have to break down the structures and beliefs that have been built up over the past three decades and then establish new norms and values to replace them. That brings us to consider the present realities of environmental management within many firms.

Organizational Realities

The problems that led to the mandated organizational changes at the United Technologies Corporation are similar to problems found in many corporations. Because of structural and cultural barriers, companies have not been able to integrate their environmental and economic decision-making processes, perpetuating the notion that environmental issues are something outside the realm of basic business concerns. For example, after the establishment of environmental regulations in 1970, most corporations adopted a government-centered approach to handling environmental issues through a division of responsibilities within the organization. Separate environmental affairs departments were developed and often kept organizationally isolated from core departments. Their objectives were to ensure that the corporations remained in compliance with the law so that the operating core could remain focused on maximizing profits, buffered from external interference.[4] Environmental considerations of toxicity, pollution, and resource-use reduction were not considered relevant to the primary objectives of the corporation. Solutions to environmental problems that could be mutually beneficial to both the environment and the bottom line were thus excluded because of structural arrangements.

Such structural limitations create communication breakdowns throughout the organization. A 1995 survey by Arthur D. Little, Inc. identified lack of integration among departments as a major roadblock to the effective management of corporate environmental issues.[5] Departments within an organization often do not or cannot communicate their interests or opportunities to one another. For example, the federal government buys its buildings with one budget and operates them with another. Any up-front cost increases may be overlooked despite their potential to minimize operating expenses and yield short payback horizons.[6] In a similar way, most corporations pay for energy costs out of overhead expenses. Thus, even though small, incremental reductions can yield large, company-wide paybacks, most firms overlook them as individual departments remain unaware of their economic effects and focus instead on investments that increase output or market share.[7]

When asked to list the primary obstacles to industrial expenditures on environmental programs, many corporate managers ranked the accounting department at the top of the list.[8] Environmental protection costs are generally listed as a liability and not an asset on balance sheets, even if expenditures result in decreased compliance and disposal costs, savings in other areas such as improved public relations, or liability and regulatory reduction. Department managers are often shielded from incentives to seek more efficient solutions to environmental problems because environmental costs are billed not to the department but to corporate overhead.

A collaborative case study carried out by the Dow Chemical Company and the Natural Resources Defense Council revealed organizational breakdown as the primary inhibitor of the adoption of pollution prevention initiatives at one Dow facility, despite the projection that the company might save more than $1 million per year by eliminating 500,000 pounds of waste. Since the program was not required for the purposes of environmental compliance, it was not of central interest to production engineers, whose main priorities were capacity building, and did not appeal to business line personnel with profit-and-loss authority. Therefore, the project was not implemented. These personnel were more interested in maximizing profit for their business through yield improvements than through waste minimization.[9]

Beyond structural limitations to the free flow of information, the language, rhetoric, objectives, and external constituencies of the various departments also limit the identification of strategically important environmental actions.[10] For example, environmental management staff members often take for granted that the value of their strategic environmental programs is apparent. Therefore, in communicating that value, they fail to adopt the business metrics and lexicon employed in other parts of the organization. Return on investment (ROI) and earnings per share (EPS) remain the most common business validation metrics, yet most environmental managers do not provide such economic cost–benefit analyses of environmental initiatives when attempting to gain budgetary approval. Making the boundaries even more impermeable, environmental managers often use non-business-related phrases and acronyms such as pounds of toxics, biological oxygen demand (BOD), notice of deficiency (NOD), environmental impact statement (EIS), and life-cycle assessment (LCA), which may be familiar to their external constituencies but serve to distance other business managers from environmental matters.[11]

Organizational Change Management

How does the corporate manager overcome these organizational realities and restructure the motivations and cultural objectives of the entire organization? In developing a strategy for change management, two overarching guidelines must be kept in mind. First, according to leadership professor John Kotter, in the more successful cases, "the change process goes through a series of phases that, in total, usually require a considerable length of time. Omitting steps creates only the illusion of speed and never produces a satisfying result. And second, a critical mistake in any of the phases can have a devastating impact, slowing momentum and negating hard-won gains."[12] A road map of these phases, depicted in figure 8.2, can be segmented into a four-phase general process[13] subdivided into a series of eight critical steps.[14]

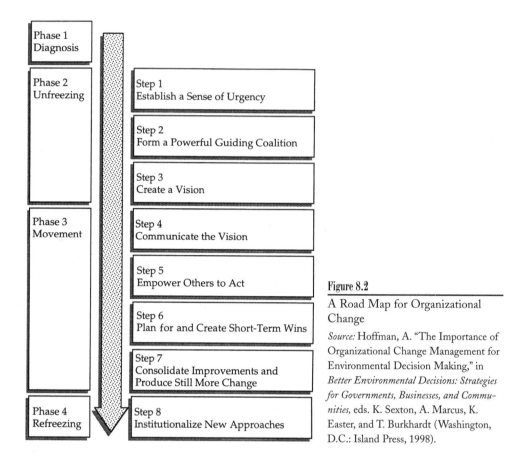

Figure 8.2

A Road Map for Organizational Change

Source: Hoffman, A. "The Importance of Organizational Change Management for Environmental Decision Making," in *Better Environmental Decisions: Strategies for Governments, Businesses, and Communities,* eds. K. Sexton, A. Marcus, K. Easter, and T. Burkhardt (Washington, D.C.: Island Press, 1998).

Phase One: Diagnosis

The first phase of any change process is that of diagnosis: realizing that change is necessary and then deciding what strategic actions to take in response to critical external signals. To remain connected to these external signals, many firms participate in boundary-spanning activities with organizations that are sensitive to changes in the environment. These activities can involve the following types of interaction:

1. *Business–business relationships.* Examples can be seen in the Public Environmental Reporting Initiative (PERI), the Chemical Manufacturers Association's Responsible Care program, the American Petroleum Institute's Strategies for Today's Environmental Partnership (STEP) program, the International Chamber of Commerce's Business Charter for Sustainable Development, and the World Environment Center (WEC).
2. *Business–government relationships.* Examples include the Common Sense Initiative, the 33/50 Program, the Amoco Corporation's Yorktown project, and Project XL (Environmental Excellence and Leadership).
3. *Business–environmental NGO relationships.* Examples include the Keystone Center, the Global Tomorrow Coalition, the Global Environmental Management Initiative

(GEMI), the Coalition for Environmentally Responsible Economies (CERES), and individual alliances between corporations and environmentalists, such as the alliance between the McDonald's Corporation and the Environmental Defense Fund and the Save the Tiger initiative between the Exxon Corporation and the World Wildlife Fund.

Through such collaborations, corporate managers can remain connected to vital sources of information, including both external signals for change and available options for organizational change management.

In selecting a solution that is tailored to the distinct needs of the individual organization, a careful analysis of the organization's purpose, structure, internal relationships, reward structures, and leadership systems must be undertaken. In short, any diagnosis of the firm's culture must consider its specific needs and proficiencies. Any attempt simply to overlay an externally devised formulaic program will merely create the illusion of change without providing any lasting substance. Thus, the diagnostic phase is a stage of careful reflection in which questions specific to the distinct demands, needs, and capabilities of the organization are considered. Boundary spanning will help trigger this diagnosis, but the challenge for the manager comes in interpreting these external signals and tailoring a strategic response.

It is not necessarily the heroic chief executive officer who will facilitate the process of diagnosis and change but rather what John Katzenbach and his colleagues call "real change leaders."[15] In turning the evolving demands for environmental performance into a strategic advantage, it is the managers located at key organizational pressure points who will manage the process of making the organization more effective and efficient in handling environmental affairs. These managers are "the linchpins connecting three critical forces for organizational change and performance: top leadership aspirations (what are we trying to become?); workforce energy and productivity (how will we climb the mountain?); and the marketplace reality (what do our target customers truly seek, and what can and will our potential competitors really do?)."[16]

Phase Two: Unfreezing

Once the formulation of a strategy is developed, the second phase, unfreezing, prepares the organization for change. Organizational change is likely to encounter resistance (examples of which will be discussed later), and the unfreezing phase is designed to decrease this resistance and gain buy-in from the organization regarding the necessity of change. The unfreezing stage comprises three fundamental steps: establishing a sense of urgency, forming a powerful guiding coalition, and creating a vision.

Establish a Sense of Urgency

No process of change will succeed if the members of the organization do not clearly understand why the change is being made and what importance it holds for the organization. One obvious way in which an organization can be motivated into action is through a crisis or an organizational jolt. Clearly, a disaster on the scale of the 1984 toxic gas release in Bhopal, India, by the Union Carbide Corporation or the 1976 dioxin release near Seveso, Italy, by a chemical company owned by the Roche Group (formerly Hoffman-La Roche) will garner support for change, but a manager typically will not be confronted with (or desire) such an empowering event.

Successful managers will initiate change by taking a hard look at their company's competitive situation, market position, technological trends, and financial performance. This may involve developing a strong audit program, identifying the weaknesses in the present organization, assessing the full range of environmental risks, and calculating the costs of poor environmental programs that do not offset these risks. Only when the environmental agenda is tied to these core business interests will a process of organizational change be accepted. For example, support for an alteration of the Amoco Corporation's environmental strategy was gained in the late 1970s when an internal report forecast $500 million in environmental expenditures over the next five to ten years. Most insiders were shocked at the scale of this estimate, and it served as a wake-up call regarding the need for change within the organization.[17] At other times, consultants can act as triggers of external change, producing a report that highlights the necessity for change. More commonly, a government enforcement action will precipitate action. In rare cases, managers may even manufacture a crisis to initiate change. In one such case, a division president commissioned a customer satisfaction survey, knowing that the results would be negative, and then embarrassed the organization into changing by making those findings public.[18] Once a significant percentage of the staff believes that business as usual is unacceptable, the process of change can begin.

Form a Powerful Guiding Coalition

Major renewal programs start with one or two central proponents. But without a sufficiently powerful core of supporters, the effort will very likely fail. One of the initial active supporters must be the head of the organization. Without such top-level support, the change process will lack legitimacy. With this in mind, chief executive officers of major corporations have made public pronouncements of their companies' commitment to the environment.

But the powerful coalition does not stop there. Although support from the chief executive will spur broad-scale organizational support, a core nucleus of champions must include participants from throughout the organization and beyond. The larger the organization, the larger the necessary coalition. For example, when the McDonald's–EDF waste reduction task force was established, the core staff included representatives of the operations, government relations, environmental affairs, and corporate communications departments as well as suppliers, and EDF itself became part of the guiding coalition for developing the task force's decisions.[19] When the Wellcraft Marine Corporation, a boat manufacturer in Sarasota, Florida, decided to switch from an acetone cleaning agent to a less volatile and toxic compound, the program committee consisted of representatives from the safety, chemical engineering, production engineering, and environmental management departments.[20]

Once the guiding coalition is developed, direct and open communication among its members is necessary in order to form a solid working base. Meeting and sharing assessments of the problems faced by the company and the opportunities they create can foster a minimum level of trust, communication, and commitment. To facilitate greater cohesion, many companies hold a series of retreats for the guiding management team to foster a solid sense of common identity and purpose among members.

Create a Vision

Even if all employees accept the need for change, it is important that they understand the goals of the initiative and their role in the process. The guiding coalition must develop a picture of the future that is relatively easy to communicate and that goes beyond the numbers and figures of a standard five-year plan. This vision generally emerges from a draft developed by one or two individuals and is fine-tuned over a period of months to fit a format that appeals to customers, stockholders, and employees. One component of this vision is a visible title for the initiative, such as the Xerox Corporation's Environmental Leadership Program or 3M's 3P (Pollution Prevention Pays) program. According to John Kotter, a rule of thumb is that "if you can't communicate the vision to someone in five minutes or less and get a reaction that signifies both understanding and interest, you are not yet done with this phase of the transformation process."[21] However, going beyond catchy slogans, the vision must also have a set of goals, methods, plans, directives, and timetables to support an overarching mission that is clearly communicated. For example, as of 1992, 40 percent of U.S. companies had included environmental responsibility in their corporate ethics statements.[22] However, it has been shown that written codes do not correlate with a decrease in the number of corporate violations of the law.[23]

Phase Three: Movement

Once the foundations have been laid for effectively unfreezing the organization, the actual movement, or implementation of the change plan, should be relatively easy. In fact, according to organizational and behavior professors Gregory Northcraft and Margaret Neale, "the ease of implementation should be a good gauge of how well the unfreezing process has broken down any pockets of resistance to the change."[24] Four steps constitute the movement phase.

Communicate the Vision

The transformation process will not be possible unless the majority of employees, hundreds or even thousands of people, are willing to help, often to the point of making short-term sacrifices. To gain this level of buy-in, executives who are part of the management team must communicate the vision of the initiative by articulating it clearly and often and integrating it into all aspects of the corporation's goals and objectives. This includes speeches, newsletters, training programs, plant and office signage—every means of reminding employees of the changes that are taking place around them. A communication tool often neglected by executives is communication of the vision by example. If employees hear executives say one thing and then see them do another, cynicism will inhibit their conformance to the program's objectives. Furthermore, this vision will be received as legitimate only if it is consistently and thoroughly applied. An organization that touts recycling of office paper, for example, should also have recycling bins for glass, aluminum, and plastic, should place the bins throughout the workplace, and should service them diligently.

Empower Others to Act

Once begun, the transformation process involves all employees. Results of research conducted at Cornell University showed that the companies most successful at implementing programs to reduce toxic emissions were those that formally involved employees in the pollution prevention activities. Successful pollution prevention initiatives are not necessarily focused on technology; rather, they are focused on the organization and are best built on a platform of internal responsibility and accountability.[25] In developing this accountability, poorly designed organizational components (such as organizational structure, reward system, hierarchy of power, and accessibility of necessary information) can inhibit the full utilization of all personnel and reduce the chances of successful transformation. Organizational inhibitors create drag that will slow the momentum of the transformation process, divert resources from it, and stifle creative and cooperative action. No organization can eliminate all obstacles, but to the extent possible, obstacles must be either circumvented or eliminated as they emerge. Most likely, the great majority of them will have been identified during the vision creation stage. Once the obstacles have been cleared, the process of change can build momentum that will carry it through to successful completion.

Plan for and Create Short-Term Wins

Nothing helps build momentum more than visible success. Short-term wins show the organization what goals it is striving to achieve and present clear examples that these goals are real. Short-term wins can encourage participating members to increase their support and may coax noncommittal employees to join the effort. Full transformational processes take time and require continued support and attention. The visible achievement of program milestones is the best way to keep people involved and show that the program is progressing as it should.

Consolidate Improvements and Produce Still More Change

The message of this stage is quite simple—do not declare victory too soon. While celebrating a series of short-term wins, managers may feel inclined to relax their effort and rest assured that they have cleared a major hurdle, confident that the road to come will be easier. This attitude can kill the momentum so hard fought for in the preceding stages. Instead, clear signs of performance improvement should be taken as an opportunity to refine original goals, integrate them deeper into the organization, and strive for further change that will firmly establish itself in the organizational culture. It must be kept in mind that the mobilization costs in initiating the change process are high. If the objectives achieved are not progressive enough to anticipate environmental demands and successfully capitalize on them, the opportunity to correct these shortcomings probably will not come again.

Phase Four: Refreezing

Once the desired changes have been fully implemented, refreezing, the process of institutionalizing the new changes, can begin. Part of this process includes communicating to employees how the new changes have helped the organization improve performance. This undertaking should be every bit as prominent as the publicity efforts that kicked off the initiative. Employees must be shown in a tangible way that they have achieved the program's objectives and what that achievement means for organizational success.

Institutionalize New Approaches

The refreezing process also involves incorporating the new changes into the formal rules and informal habits of the organization. The changes must be able to be supported and continued without the involvement and oversight of the guiding management team. In short, the artifacts that embody the organization's culture must reflect the organizational change effort in their entirety to ensure that the process of cultural change is perpetuated. To develop tangible structures to ensure that this occurs, managers can turn to the processes by which employees are rewarded for their job performance, initially hired, socialized into the corporation, assigned their job tasks, and positioned within the structure of the organization.

Reward Structures

First and foremost, how are the reward structures organized within the company? If a plant manager receives pay increases and positive promotion reviews for increasing yield and output, will environmental issues be considered relevant to his or her daily responsibilities? Not likely. As one process engineer related: "At [a major pharmaceutical company] we have three primary company ethics: one, worker health and safety; two, environmental protection; and three, process profit. But when it comes time for performance reviews, we skip the first two and go straight to the third."[26] Regardless of the extent of top-level speeches and corporate environmental policies, reward structures greatly influence the way individual managers perform their job tasks. Steven Kerr, a management specialist with General Electric, described a process called "rewarding A while hoping for B," commenting that "managers who complain about lack of motivation in their workers might do well to consider the possibility that the reward systems they have installed are paying off for behavior other than what they are seeking."[27] Beyond pay, a reward structure can include elements of job design, noncash awards, benefits, perquisites, and advancement up the career ladder.

Rewards must be aligned so that each department manager will be required to consider how best to integrate environmental and economic interests. This is a necessary step in finding the most efficient corporate responses to environmental demands. For example, only the operations department knows how best to tailor operations to balance environmental and economic goals. The same is true for research and development, accounting, and other departments within the firm. Furthermore, only when each of these departments has full responsibility for (and bears the full cost of) the consequences of its environmental practices, rather than relying on the environmental affairs department to solve them, will incentives be aligned for these departments to consider such change.

SELECTION

Once reward structures are established, the criteria by which new employees are selected from the field of candidates must reflect the type of people who will be receptive to the organization's new cultural and performance expectations. Finding that type of individual is a matter of fit. Do the candidate's attributes and inclinations fit with the organization's expectations and objectives? Getting the best individuals into the organization is critical to the organization's performance. Getting the wrong individuals for the company's newly forming environmental values will result in a value incongruence that can precipitate any of several negative outcomes: internal tension and poor performance, active resistance and attempts to subvert the established values, or high turnover rate.[28] Many companies have established specific human resources programs to both select and, as discussed next, socialize new employees into the organization's environmental culture. More important, many companies find that a positive reputation regarding environmentalism enhances their ability to both obtain and retain the highest-quality people.

SOCIALIZATION

Once a new employee is selected, the task of socializing him or her into the new culture of the organization becomes critical. There must be a formal training and awareness program to convey to new employees the organization's goals, norms, and preferred ways of doing things. No new employee will be a perfect fit with an organization; the socialization process provides a means for molding the new employee to fit the organization. Socialization can include several techniques, such as following a prescribed socialization program, conducting initial and ongoing training courses, making role models visible (even to the point of assigning a mentor), and delineating a carefully outlined career ladder that highlights the reward structures for moving along it.

ORGANIZATIONAL STRUCTURE

Finally, of course, the organization's structure must be configured in a way that facilitates the new reward systems and organizational objectives. This structure is composed of both the formal and informal systems of regulated decision flows. The formal structure establishes direct and formal authority, reporting requirements, and responsibilities. The informal structure describes the more fluid communication patterns and power relationships that exist. Even though the reward structures may promote a set of actions and initiatives that favor new environmental strategies, structural arrangements must be established that allow those strategies to be implemented. Very often, it is the organizational structure that creates the greatest obstacles to a successful process of organizational change.

Resistance to Change

Organizational change involves the unlearning of what has been ingrained over the organization's history, and this often invites resistance. Basic assumptions about organizational procedures and the realities of the external environment can become rigidly set and be difficult to reset. At times, this rigidity can be positive, allowing an organization to react rapidly to changes in the environment that fall within the range of issues previously encountered. But it can also operate as a pattern of thought and action that limits possibilities for action. The structural inertia this creates can take many forms. This section considers five: habitual routine, resource limitations, communication breakdowns, fear of the unknown, and threats to established power bases.

First, rigid patterns of thought and action can be perpetuated by *habitual routine.* Often, habit stems from an individual's realization that changing what has become established will involve some form of short-term cost. Even though established routines may be inefficient or inconsistent with long-term objectives, they can be familiar, comfortable, and reliably predictable. Habitual routines can take the form of taken-for-granted engineering or managerial practices. For example, the Robbins Company, a metal finisher and plater in Attleboro, Massachusetts, began its pollution minimization strategy by reducing its use of what has become an increasingly expensive raw material, water. Since the amount of waste produced is directly correlated with the amount of water used, both raw material and waste disposal costs were dramatically reduced when the company altered its plating operation to make it a closed-loop system, reducing emissions to zero. Savings to the company have been calculated to be $71,000 per year. Yet when the company's environmental manager, Paul Clark, first attempted to reduce water usage, he was told by plant personnel that it was impossible. So he resorted to gradually closing the water feed valves late at night. Little by little, water usage was reduced without plant personnel noticing.[29]

Resource limitations can restrict an organization's ability to overcome sunk costs in plants, equipment, and personnel. They can become psychological roadblocks that bias managers against certain actions or responses to demands for change. Short-term demands may deny the manager any opportunity to consider long-term gains, which, although they may be encouraging, are only potential. Short-term costs predominate, influencing the manager to overdiscount the future. An example can be seen in some companies' attitudes toward the EPA's Green Lights Program, a voluntary program that encourages businesses to install energy-efficient lighting. These lighting upgrades help prevent unnecessary pollution through more efficient use of electricity while saving the organization money on electric bills. Yet many companies resist performing an energy audit of their facilities and developing a new lighting installation program, despite an average 28 percent internal rate of return on investments in lighting upgrades by Green Lights partners.[30] In many cases, the companies have invested heavily in their lighting plans and have irrationally committed themselves to the system as installed.

Interdepartmental *communication breakdowns* can perpetuate environmentally inefficient routines. Again, the EPA's Green Lights Program provides an example. In the face of possible cost benefits, established reward and incentive systems in organizations often mask the opportunities available through change. Energy costs are often paid out of overhead, whereas installation and maintenance of lighting systems are billed to the physical plant. Because of departmental responsibilities and reward structures, often neither department will recognize or respond to the need for change. The administrative department responsible for overhead may be unaware of the technical aspects and financial opportunities of lighting upgrades. The physical plant would be required to commit time and resources to the program while receiving none of the financial and publicity rewards, which would accrue to the administration. Breakdowns such as these have created an opportunity for entrepreneurs to offer lighting retrofit services. These companies provide the audit and the installation and are paid a percentage of energy savings.[31]

Fear of the unknown can drive organizational inertia and a continued reliance on basic underlying assumptions. Both external and internal change can be upsetting for organizational constituents, particularly when the outcome or consequences of change cannot be predicted. In reality, outcomes and consequences can never be predicted. In one example, boat manufacturer Wellcraft Marine Corporation went from creating 18.5 percent of Florida's acetone emissions in 1989 to less than 1 percent in 1992 by replacing acetone with a less volatile, toxic, and flammable substitute called diacetone alcohol (DAA). By making this switch, the company has also saved $91,608 per year while operating at only 33 percent capacity. Yet the initiative's champion, Bill McDonald, found that workers resisted the switch to DAA because the new solvent required different procedures. To gain acceptance for it, he worked hard to "sell" the new solvents to the workforce.[32]

Finally, *threats to established power bases* can cause resistance to organizational change. Every organization has a power structure that can bias the perspectives of those who benefit from it. Alterations in the structure and in the roles of the organization's members may be competence enhancing for some and competence destroying for others. The environmental management department may resist the transfer of some of its responsibilities to, say, the process engineering department because the very act may minimize its own usefulness. Conversely, without a clear view of the overall costs and benefits, the process engineering department may resist the addition of these new responsibilities because it sees the profitability of its other operations diminished as pollution minimization increases. In the face of such perceived threats, the instinct for self-preservation may override concerns for environmental or economic objectives in managerial decision making. The result may be organizational confusion or battles for survival among rival departments.

In the end, organizational culture and structure can restrict the development of new ways of thinking about the environment and its relationship to economic competitiveness. Overcoming these restrictions is the task of the manager acting as a change agent. But is the manager limited in the extent to which he or she can accomplish this task? Some argue that resistance to environmental strategy may originate from sources more deeply ingrained than cultural norms and routines, in the biases of individual employees (see box 8.2).

Tracking Progress in Organizational Strategy

As managers attempt to integrate environmental protection into the economic goals of the corporation, how can they track their progress and measure their success against long-term objectives? Management consultant Christopher Hunt and professor of management Ellen Auster have identified five generic stages for characterizing the hierarchy of increasingly ingrained underlying environmental values.[33] As shown in table 8.1, these stages differ in terms of criteria that blend both organizational and strategic aspects of

Box 8.2. Do the Obstacles to Environmental Strategy Lie on the Organizational or Individual Level?

How much can a manager change the way his or her employees think about environmental protection and its relation to the economic competitiveness of the firm? Although organizational change can bring about a more balanced culture and a tighter fit between these two issues, there are strong biases in the way individuals think that may limit how far such transformations can go. Professor Tom Gladwin of the University of Michigan argues that the worldviews of people in the developed and affluent societies of the world are biased against acknowledgment of the ecological harm caused by their behavior.* He points to their lifestyles, which are maintained through the exhaustion and dispersion of natural capital along with their continued ignorance that this resource base is being depleted at an unsustainable rate. Why does this seemingly irrational behavior persist? Professor Max Bazerman of Northwestern University sees four cognitive biases that push people to pursue unsustainable behavior: (1) vividness, (2) overdiscounting the future, (3) egocentrism, and (4) the mythical fixed pie. In the following discussion, he and his co-authors, Claire Buisseret and Kimberly Wade-Benzoni, apply these biases to the issue of climate change.

> *Vividness.* One problem facing environmentalists is the fact that people value more vivid symbols of the environment. This explains why people place less value on biodiversity than on a specific elephant, or why hunger organizations are better able to solicit funds to sponsor one child than to contribute to the broader hunger issue. A term exists to describe what will raise money: "charismatic mega-fauna." These are animals that strike a chord with people, because of their cuteness, originality, or other appeal. The fact that these charming animals depend on diversity to survive is lost on the public.
>
> In the face of the climate change issue, people will be swayed on the necessity for action if there is unusually hot weather. To the extent that the summer is hot, global warming becomes more salient to the public, to corporate actors, and to the US negotiating team. One major challenge of harnessing enthusiasm for dealing with climate change is that the costs of "solving" climate change (i.e., raising gas prices, driving electric cars, meeting emissions standards, or walking to work) are vivid, while the benefits (i.e., improved air quality and stabilized carbon dioxide levels) are not. Like the national debt, people may agree that there is a problem, but that does not mean that they are willing to sacrifice to solve this non-vivid threat.
>
> *Inappropriately high discount rates.* Herman Daly is quoted as saying, "we should not treat the earth as if it were a business in liquidation." We generally believe that we ought to pass on to future inhabitants the resources and systems of the natural environment in as good a state as we inherited them. However, our ongoing decisions are inconsistent with the above belief. Many pollutants have already surpassed rates that are physically sustainable. For example, to take the issue of climate change, human activity contributes millions of tons of CO_2 into the atmosphere annually. Problems that are in the distance, such as the potential effects of global warming, are often given insufficient attention.
>
> This "discounting of the future" can be disadvantageous in terms of an individual's self-interest, and also from an intergener-

(continues)

Box 8.2. *Continued*

ational, global, or environmental perspective, yet research shows the use of extremely high discount rates. For example, even when they would actually make back the extra costs in less than a year, many homeowners skimp on the amount of insulation they put in their attics and walls and do not buy more expensive, energy-efficient appliances.

Confronting global warming will involve costs now in order to avoid much larger (but non-vivid) costs in the distant future. The advantages of addressing the problem are likely to benefit future generations more so than ourselves. Yet it is easier for us to spend resources that afford our children immediate benefits (such as providing them with cars, clothing, and toys) than to deny them these resources in order to deal with an enormous issue like global warming, an issue that is truly central to the interests of future generations. Providing immediate tangible benefits for our children allows us the illusion of caring about future generations. The unfortunate result of inappropriately discounting the value of future benefits is our failure as a society to act on global climate change.

Egocentrism. Negotiations over climate change and environmental issues in general are particularly vulnerable to "egocentrism." Egocentric interpretations of fairness are judgments that are biased in a manner favoring the individuals making the judgments. Egocentrism exists to the extent that subjects differentially interpret what is fair in ways that serve their own interests. Thus, if two people dividing a limited pool of resources are each asked to assess the percentage of the resources that they deserve, and the two percentages exceed 100 percent, the combined perceptions are egocentric.

In the allocation of environmental resources, most people attempt to obtain benefits for and avoid burdens to themselves. They also want to preserve the positive self-image of being concerned about issues of justice and having contributed their fair share to the common good. Thus, when thinking about responsibility for global warming, the developed world blames the developing world for destroying the rain forest, and the developing world blames the developed world for over-consumption. In another example, consumers blame corporations for pollution, without accepting that their consumption creates the demand the corporations are meeting. Egocentric interpretations of fairness create a potential obstacle to the resolution of environmental conflict by allowing for a convenient reconciliation of two apparently conflicting goals: Individuals can have what they want, doing what they want to do (seize a larger share of a limited desirable resource, or a smaller share of an undesirable burden), and believe that their actions are fair and in line with what they should do (i.e., practice self-restraint in the use of the resource, or take at least partial responsibility for the burden).

Mythical fixed pie. Discussions of environmental issues are often partisan, with analysts on one side arguing that environmental protection is costly, and on the other that such protection is essential. Full acceptance of either view results in the mythical fixed pie, the idea that there is a limited set of outcomes, possibilities, or actual resources. Negotiators most often fail to reach optimal outcomes because they do not look for integrative trade-offs that can enlarge the pool of resources to be distributed. Instead, they approach the negotiation with a fixed-pie assumption, which creates a competitive situation, hinders cooperation, and masks potential trade-offs or creative opportunities that will improve the overall quality of the agreement. Not that environmental conflicts often have simple win-win solutions, but there are often trade-offs that can enhance the attractiveness of the solutions for all sides. Furthermore, when both sides assume that the other side's gain is their loss, reactive devaluation is likely to accompany the mythical fixed pie. In reactive devaluation, negotiators believe that if a deal or proposal is acceptable to their opponent, then it must be bad for them.[†]

Does this argument pose a challenge for you as a manager in developing an organization that balances economic and environmental performance? Are the opportunities of environmental strategy bound by the norms and beliefs of the society at large? Or can you develop an organization that transcends these bounds and help your workers see opportunities that are not visible in other arenas? Your answer to this question should reveal insights about whether you see the role of manager as profit oriented, as social activism, or as both.

[*] T. Gladwin, W. Newburry, and E. Reiskin, "Why Is the Northern Elite Mind Biased against Community, the Environment, and a Sustainable Future?" in *Environment, Ethics, and Behavior: The Psychology of Environmental Valuation and Degradation,* ed. M. Bazerman, D. Messick, A. Tenbrunsel, and K. Wade-Benzoni (San Francisco: New Lexington Press, 1997), 234–274.

[†] M. Bazerman, C. Buisseret, and K. Wade-Benzoni, "The Role of Judgment in Global Climate Change," in *Global Climate Change: A Senior Level Dialogue at the Intersection of Economics, Strategy, Technology, Science, Politics, and International Negotiation,* ed. A. Hoffman (San Francisco: New Lexington Press, 1998), 79–83.

environmental strategy. In short, they represent evolving cultural foundations for the way an organization perceives and takes action on environmental issues.

At the first stage of corporate environmental strategy development, *beginners* deal with environmental issues either by ignoring them or by adding responsibility for them to existing positions, such as that of plant manager. There is no effort to determine what the company's environmental requirements are or what the repercussions of poor environmental management would be. *Firefighters* may have a few employees dedicated to environmental concerns or a small centralized staff that assists individual plants in responding to crises, but they can deal with only a few issues at a time. Environmental-

Table 8.1. Developmental Stages of Corporate Environmental Strategy

Criteria	Stage 1: Beginner	Stage 2: Firefighter	Stage 3: Concerned Citizen	Stage 4: Pragmatist	Stage 5: Proactivist
Degree to which program reduces environmental risk	No protection	Minimal protection	Moderate protection	Comprehensive protection	Maximum protection
Commitment of organization					
General mind-set of corporate managers	Environmental management is unnecessary	Environmental issues should be addressed only as necessary	Environmental management is a worthwhile function	Environmental management is an important business function	Environmental management is a priority item
Resource commitment	Minimal resource commitment	Budgets for problems as they occur	Consistent yet minimal budget	Generally sufficient funding	Open-ended funding
Support and involvement of top management	No involvement	Piecemeal involvement	Commitment in theory	Awareness and moderate involvement	Active involvement
Program design					
Performance objectives	None	Resolve problems as they occur	Satisfy corporate responsibility	Minimize negative environmental effects	Actively manage environmental matters
Integration with company	Not integrated	Involved with other departments on piecemeal basis	Minimal interaction with other departments	Moderate integration with other departments	Actively involved with other departments
Reporting to top management	No reporting	Exception reporting only	Generation of voluminous reports that are rarely read	Consistent and targeted reporting	Personal meetings with managers and board of directors
Reporting structures	None	Exception reporting only	Internal reporting only	Mostly internal with some external reporting	Formalized internal and external reporting mechanisms
Involvement with:					
Legal counsel	None	Moderate	Moderate	High	Daily
Public relations	None	Moderate	Moderate	High	Daily
Manufacturing/production	None	None	None	Moderate	Daily
Product design	None	None	None	Minimal	Daily

Source: C. Hunt and E. Auster, "Proactive Environmental Management: Avoiding the Toxic Trap," *Sloan Management Review*, winter 1990, 9. © 1990 Sloan Management Review Association. Used with permission.

ism remains of low concern to top management. *Concerned citizens* express a commitment to good environmental management but have not implemented a fully adequate environmental program. Dedicated environmental departments may be staffed with technically adequate environmental specialists, but they lack the influence or political power to effect organizational change. *Pragmatists* take the time to actively manage environmental issues with sufficient expertise, funding, and authority. They evaluate potential risks and decrease risks wherever possible, but their focus is primarily on policing and prevention. Finally, *proactivists* employ strong, motivated, high-profile individuals who take the concept of environmental strategy to the level of upper-management decision making. Diffusion of environmental responsibilities throughout the organization is facilitated by employee training and awareness programs, and environmental concerns are given high priority among departments and seen as strategically important.

Hunt and Auster stress that specific requirements for particular companies vary depending on context: type of industry, company size, type of environmental problems encountered, complexity of the organization, and range of constituents applying pressure. Thus, a program considered proactivist in one context may be only marginally adequate in another. The program must be tailored to the particular company's needs and external demands. One final matter of context that Hunt and Auster consider to be critical is time. They close their article by pointing out that environmental strategy "is not about the short term, it's about the long haul. If neglected, it can seriously jeopardize a company's balance sheets and public image for years."[34]

Conclusion

In the end, organizational change is a critical component of effective environmental strategy. Altering accepted beliefs within the organization in order to identify the linkages between economic growth and environmental protection will present various degrees of challenge among firms. For some, environmentalism is easily subsumed under traditionally accepted values that the company already holds to be important. For example, the Volvo Car Corporation was able to incorporate some environmental values fairly quickly because these values could be easily subsumed under the traditional corporate values of safety and corporate responsibility. Likewise, Procter & Gamble found it easy to instill some environmental values into its product development function when these values were presented as consumer demand. Such metaphorical connections make the adoption of environmental practices more palatable to those most affected and speed the process of cultural change within the organization. The challenge for every manager is to figure out how best to translate environmental issues into the concerns and language most salient for the firm and context being changed.

In the future, an increasing number of companies and industries will be challenged to create new cultural metaphors for the environmental challenges before them. For example, the oil industry faces an evolving environment that may require a fundamental cultural evolution for its individual firms. Speaking at a conference in Houston, Texas, in February 1999, Mike Bowlin, chairman and chief executive of the Atlantic Richfield Company (ARCO), the fifth largest U.S. oil and gas company, warned that "we've embarked on the beginning of the last days of the Age of Oil."[35] He predicted that there would be a healthy market for oil in the first decades of the twenty-first century but that demand for crude oil would eventually be surpassed by that for cleaner-burning fuels and renewable energy sources. "The challenge is not merely to survive today's low prices," he said, "but to plan for a future in which hydrocarbons are just one of a wide variety of fuels that will build the global economy of the 21st century."[36] This change will require more than simply an alteration of the products that oil companies sell. It will involve a cultural shift in terms of the fundamental objectives, tasks, and role that oil companies will play in the future economy. As Seth Dunn, research associate at Worldwatch Institute, observed, "Companies in the oil industry are beginning to realize that to survive in the long run they will need to become part of the energy business, and not purely the extractive business."[37]

Some companies will resist such changes and continue to press on with established beliefs and perspectives. Others will embrace the emerging future and react quickly, altering their organizations to create the most efficient and effective environmental strategy. Rather than responding to technology and performance standards dictated by the EPA, Walter Quanstrom, EH&S vice president for the Amoco Corporation (now BP Amoco), said that he envisions an organization fully prepared to take the lead on environmental strategy: "If you give this company a mark on the wall and tell them to go for it, I have no doubt as to their capability to achieve it." A former refinery manager agreed: "When we push for more flexible options, I'm taking a lot on faith. I have to believe that we have engineers who know our processes a lot better than some 25 year old [EPA] engineer in Cincinnati or at Research Triangle Park."[38] In explaining his company's plans to sell cleaner-burning fuels in 1999, John Browne, chief executive officer of BP Amoco, again looked to the organization: "I simply got tired of being on the defensive, and so did our staff. That's hardly the way to give people the sense that they are working for a great organization. It isn't the way to convince investors and customers that the business is in tune with the market."[39]

Further Reading

Bazerman, M., D. Messick, A. Tenbrunsel, and K. Wade-Benzoni, eds. *Environment, Ethics, and Behavior: The Psychology of Environmental Valuation and Degradation.* San Francisco: New Lexington Press, 1997.

Lovins, A., and H. Lovins. *Climate: Making Sense and Making Money.* Snowmass, Colo.: Rocky Mountain Institute, 1997.

Lovins, L., H. Lovins, and E. von Weizsacker. *Factor Four.* London: Earthscan Publications, 1998.

McKibben, B. "Not So Fast." *New York Times Magazine,* 23 July 1995, 24, 25.

Schmidheiny, S., and World Business Council for Sustainable Development. "Managing Change in Business" and "Managing Corporate Change." Chaps. 6 and 11 in *Changing Course: A Global Business Perspective on Development and the Environment,* 82–96, 185–204. Cambridge, Mass.: MIT Press, 1992.

Smart, B. "Engaging the Organization." Chap. 5 in *Beyond Compliance: A New Industry View of the Environment,* 97–120. Washington, D.C.: World Resources Institute, 1992.

Wade-Benzoni, K., and M. Bazerman, eds. "Barriers to Wiser Agreements between Environmental and Economic Concerns." *American Behavioral Scientist* 42, no. 8 (May 1999): 1254–1408.

Chapter 9

THE ORGANIZATION LIES WITHIN A
BROADER INSTITUTIONAL CONTEXT

Does the integration of economic growth and environmental protection take place solely within the culture and perspectives of the individual firm? If company managers can see strategy and organizational design in a new way, are the opportunities endless? Whereas the previous two chapters addressed the opportunities of environmental strategy, this chapter considers its larger context. Organizational managers do not exist in a vacuum, able to choose freely among an unlimited array of strategies for action. They are part of a broader institutional context that comprises economic, social, and political systems. Indeed, even as these institutions change to create opportunities for environmental strategy, they can also remain static and limit the range of those opportunities. Competitive environmental strategy must be decided within the confines of that range.

For example, as regulations become more diverse and flexible, they create opportunities for creative compliance strategies. But those opportunities are limited by the culture of the regulatory agency and the strict code of its statutes. As banks begin to redefine underwriting procedures to include assessments of corporate environmental considerations, they create opportunities for proactive firms by lowering their cost of capital. But the connection between the two is bounded by the extent of the awareness of these financial institutions and their appreciation for environmental performance. The list goes on. Although the institutions of consumers, investors, shareholders, and others described in chapters 2 through 6 create opportunities for environmental strategy, they can also create limitations. They are dual-edged swords. Just as the business context is altered by external pressures for environmentalism, the firm is constrained by those very same forces. Although firms have been changing dramatically since the early 1970s in their response to environmental pressures, in some ways they are outpacing the social change taking place around them. In many arenas, continued change will require alterations of the very institutions that have been driving the process. Many of these continue to support an underlying belief that economic growth and environmental protection are mutually exclusive.

Competitive environmental strategy must be developed with an appreciation of this institutional context. The bounds of these institutions are not fixed and rigid. Progressive corporations can and do alter them in ways that favor their strategic interests. The important point of this chapter is that institutions can both liberate and constrain organizational and strategic innovation regarding the environment, and it is important to understand the ways in which they do so. Where these institutions act as constraints, managers must consider ways to change them to match their own interests.

Institutions as Drivers and Constraints

This chapter discusses six institutional arenas that have created change for corporations and that must themselves undergo continued change if the mutual compatibility of economic growth and environmental protection is to be fully realized. Although other institutions can act as drivers and constraints, this discussion focuses on environmental standards, educational curricula, economic performance metrics, international regimes, economic infrastructure, and physical infrastructure.[1]

Environmental Standards

Government standards in the United States have produced impressive results for a cleaner environment since the early 1970s.[2] During the 1990s alone, air pollution from lead declined by 78 percent, carbon monoxide and sulfur dioxide levels declined by 37 percent, and particulate levels decreased by 37 percent. Yet the process by which these changes were achieved and the regulatory systems that drove that process are becoming out of date. In fact, the General Accounting Office (GAO) concluded in 1999 that

> although the current regulatory system for environmental protection has had its successes, it has proven to be costly and, at times, inflexible. . . . This framework, composed of largely prescriptive, medium-specific laws, imposes requirements that have led to, and tend to reinforce, many of the existing practices and behaviors that EPA is seeking to change . . . the agency faces several challenges, including helping its rank-and-file employees to understand and support changes to the current regulatory system and obtaining consensus among the agency's varied stakeholders on what these changes should be.[3]

Some observers are beginning to argue that environmental regulation may be the biggest challenge faced by environmentalists today. Although regulations can force behaviors that are easily monitored by oversight agencies, they perpetuate perceptions about the relationship between economics and the environment that may be contrary to the goals of both. They are based on underlying beliefs that support the view of economic and environmental interests as mutually exclusive. Four aspects of this regulatory culture are particularly important for understanding how this is so.

First, the regulatory structure is based on a perception of environmental issues as compartmentalized by medium—air, water, pesticides, radiation, solid waste, and so forth. Although obviously inappropriate as a framework for understanding the inherently transmedium nature of pollution, this conception is perpetuated by a formal organizational structure within the Environmental Protection Agency (EPA) that is an artifact of its early formation. Although many advisors to the agency's first administrator recommended an intermedium approach that would have regulated an industrial facility as a unit, considering the effects of its operations on the environment as a whole, political realities forced the creation of the new agency through consolidation of existing departments scattered throughout the federal government. These departments were based on medium-specific mandates, so the resultant agency was similarly structured. But this structure institutionalized a framework that inhibits creative environmental problem solving by focusing on compartmentalized solutions.

A second important aspect of the regulatory structure is its command-and-control format. In 1970, many believed that once the government set standards and began to enforce them, industry would fall in line and environmental problems would essentially disappear.[4] During its first sixty days, the EPA brought five times as many enforcement actions as all the agencies it inherited had brought during any similar period.[5] This focus on punishing polluters was justified on political grounds as necessary to establish credibility, but it also set up the adversarial relationship between industry and government that continues today—the third problematic aspect of the current regulatory structure. This adversarial relationship supports a belief that government regulators and industry decision makers cannot find solutions that offer mutual gain.

Finally, a fourth aspect of the original environmental regulatory structure that institutionalizes our beliefs about the relationship between economics and the environment is its focus on the technological-fix solution to environmental problems. Since the 1970s, regulations have been based on prescript, technology-based standards. The catchword for the early 1970s was *technology forcing*. It was thought that new federal rules would force industry to use new pollution-free technology, and as new plants replaced old ones, eventually the problem of pollution would disappear.[6] Today, that mind-set is manifested in regulations that prescribe best demonstrated available technology (BDAT) for specific environmental problems across disparate industries.

Over time, this (1) media-segmented, (2) command-and-control, (3) adversarial, and (4) technology-based approach to environmental regulation has come to be the standard approach for understanding the nature of environmental issues, regulatory solutions, and the "inherent" policy trade-offs among government, industry, and activist communities. Many, however, now view this paradigm as out of date and overly restrictive of corporate environmental initiatives beyond the need to ensure compliance.[7] In many ways, legal standards lock organizations into a focus on strict legal compliance rather than on attainment of internally consistent environmental goals or more subtle societal interests.[8] Decision makers may evaluate suboptimal choices (both economically and environmentally) that adhere to a standard more highly than optimal choices that violate the standard. Once standards are written, program managers in both government agencies and corporations become constrained by a compliance mind-set and bureaucratic procedures, which attenuate the search for creative solutions to complex environmental problems. A given rule structure dictates which pollutants and sources to control, to what extent, and with which technologies across a broad spectrum of disassociated industries. It often ignores the technological and logistic issues associated with overlapping regulatory programs as well as the multimedia and multi-objective effects of a particular rule or policy.[9] At times, standards can explicitly restrict environmentally optimal solutions.

For example, the permitting requirements under the Resource Conservation and Recovery Act (RCRA) often restrict hazardous waste recycling initiatives by imposing strict regulations on those wastes once they are created. Any company that creates hazardous wastes and then attempts to recycle or reuse them is required to obtain a "Part B" permit for treatment of a hazardous waste, an extremely expensive and time-consuming process.[10] In the eyes of many corporate managers, such as Thomas Zosel, manager of the Minnesota Mining and Manufacturing Company's 3P (Pollution Prevention Pays) program, "RCRA permits are so extensive and expensive to develop that many companies forego recycling to cut all the regulatory hassle required by RCRA."[11]

Standards-based systems can also change incentive systems for individuals and promote self-interested behavior that interferes with overarching societal interests. Suboptimal outcomes are the product of both unintentional and intentional actions on the part of the decision maker. Unintentional actions may result from individuals "just following the rules," creativity not being rewarded, a "use it or lose it" rationale, intrinsic motivation being replaced with extrinsic motivation, or a "no law against it" mentality. Intentional actions include attempts to "beat the system."[12]

For example, in 1995 the EPA listed *n*-methyl-2-pyrrolidone (NMP) as one of the chemicals for which industry must report emissions. NMP is a common replacement in the adhesives industry for chlorinated solvents. It is nonflammable, practically nonvolatile, and 80 to 90 percent recyclable. The listing was prompted by a study citing a potentially remote health effect. Many companies reverted to flammable and volatile (but nonreportable) solvents in order to avoid the reporting burden associated with use of NMP. The end result of the NMP listing was reversion to a less safe and potentially more environmentally harmful option.

Similarly, multiple government programs compete with environmental objectives. For example, the Internal Revenue Code often works at cross purposes with the objectives of the Endangered Species Act of 1973 (ESA). Currently, both estate and property taxes are calculated on the basis of the land's "highest and best use value," which usually means development. These taxes serve as an incentive for landowners to (1) develop their land, (2) harvest the land's resources to pay the taxes, or (3) sell off parcels of the land to pay the taxes, thereby breaking up biologically valuable properties. Some are pushing for estate tax reform that would allow heirs to defer or avoid applicable estate taxes on land in return for managing the land in ways that benefit endangered species.[13]

National policies regarding federal land management also create incentives for behavior that is contrary to the public interest in environmental protection. Forest products companies often acquire from governments the right to log national forests at prices far below reasonable market rates. The government pays for miles of logging roads in the 192 million acres of national forests and often does not enforce reforestation programs once the timber has been cleared. Through such subsidies, the USDA Forest Service is estimated to have lost more than $88 million in 1997.[14] This provides incentives for companies to cut forests that would not otherwise be economically harvested. Cattle-grazing policy on federal lands yields similarly dysfunctional behavior. Select cattle ranchers have been grazing herds for years on the 268 million acres of western rangeland operated by the Bureau of Land Management (BLM) and the Forest Service. The fees they pay, however, are as little as one-fourth of those paid by ranchers for grazing on private lands. This costs the federal government tens of millions of dollars in lost revenue each year, gives an unfair advantage to ranchers with federal grazing permits, and does not allow enough income to protect the land from overgrazing. The Natural Resources Defense Council estimates that 68 percent of western rangeland is in unsatisfactory condition and that more than half of the plants that once grew in those areas have disappeared.[15]

Solutions to these kinds of limiting structures have been proposed in several forms. Environmental regulations are being restructured to trigger corporate environmental action through generally accepted economic means, including introduction of surrogate or artificial prices such as unit taxes, effluent fees, or, more recently, market incentives to provide the needed signals to economize on the use of these resources.[16] But for the long term, changes in environmental policy should fundamentally reconfigure the role and objectives of both oversight agencies and the regulated community. Such reconfiguration could provide flexibility and autonomy for corporations to define which emission sources to control through site-specific compliance strategies that achieve broadly defined objectives.[17] Environmental policy could also focus on the secondary effects of regulatory programs, stimulating both direct and indirect pressures by changing core business networks, such as financial markets, international regimes, and consumer demands. Such programmatic changes could trigger new types of organizational response and eliminate competing institutional pressures from multiple constituencies.[18]

For example, since 1998, the Forest Service, under its director, Michael Dombeck, has taken a new tack, focusing on habitat, water, and soil conservation more than on resource extraction and revenue generation on federal lands. Dombeck has announced cutbacks in timber harvest, protection of watersheds, and restoration of wildlife habitat as the agency's new goals.[19] But this will not come to pass without significant cultural upheaval. To so dramatically change regulatory programs will require alterations in basic notions about the culture and role of government agencies. Changes in Forest Service policies have prompted fierce criticism not only from logging and mining interests but also from within the agency's own ranks.

Similarly, changes in environmental protection policy will create resistance from within the ranks of the EPA. Challenges to fundamental aspects of environmental policy will necessitate new types of relationships and shared responsibilities between the regulators and the regulated community that break down accepted notions of command-and-control, media-based, technology-forcing, adversarial regulation. These changes will not come easily. The GAO pointed out that "EPA has had difficulty in achieving 'buy-in' among the agency's rank and file, who have grown accustomed to prescriptive, medium-specific (air, land, or water) regulation during the agency's almost 30-year history. Both headquarters and regional EPA management have acknowledged that achieving full commitment to reinvention by the agency's rank and file is a challenge and that it will take time for changes to the organization's culture to filter down to EPA line staff."[20]

Educational Curricula

Academic institutions have made great strides in introducing environmental issues into their programs through creation of environmental majors and electives, integration of environmental topics into existing course curricula, and formation of joint degrees.[21] However, in many ways, academic programs continue to keep environmental and economic issues separate, thus perpetuating the notion that environmental protection and economic growth are incompatible.

For example, undergraduate chemical engineering education often overlooks waste considerations in the economic calculations of chemical plant design. Where these concerns are addressed, it is often only in a process design diagram with an arrow aiming off the page and labeled "To Waste." Students are systematically taught to ignore the costs associated with wastes and any opportunities to reduce wastes at the source. Business management education treats environmental concerns as an issue of "socially responsible business" and outside the rubric of core decision-making logic.[22] Finally, economic education treats environmental protection as a market externality,[23] the consequence of an absence of prices for certain scarce environmental resources, such as clean air and water.

Throughout each of the educational curricula just described, economic benefit and environmental responsibility are presented as separate and opposing outcomes. Such a framework minimizes the potential for innovative solutions. The underlying beliefs of educational institutions support the ideas that market and engineering objectives are inconsistent with environmental protection and that decision makers will not find it in their interest to incorporate environmentally sensible policies.

Historians and environmental management experts now argue that the contemporary ideologies of educational training (and of capitalism more broadly) rest on fundamental assumptions that perpetuate a disconnection between environmental and economic sustainability.[24] In the pursuit of economic progress, organizations and individuals are depicted as independent actors bartering in a market without social structure, where resource extraction and development are the right of the property owner to the exclusion of other stakeholder interests and unlimited progress is possible through exploitation of nature's infinite resources. Scholars in the environmental management community challenge theory and practice for supporting these assumptions by promoting an uncritical belief in (1) the necessity of increasing economic growth; (2) the perception of nature as a limitless sink; (3) the superiority of technological development for controlling natural systems; (4) the social and physical autonomy of the firm; and (5) the profit motive as a singular objective of the firm.[25] These aspects of educational curricula lie at the center of notions about the role of the business manager and the engineer in interacting with the environment and the function of academia in training them for that role.

To resolve this disconnection, universities have begun connecting educational programs and environmental issues in terms that complement existing curricula. For example, management schools are starting to incorporate environmental issues into the management curriculum by teaching them in the language of core business disciplines such as strategy, finance, marketing, accounting, and organizational behavior. But even though this strategy is helpful in the short run, it does not challenge the basic precepts of corporate objectives and responsibilities. In the long run, integration efforts must challenge the fundamental assumptions of the disciplines within educational curricula. The content of educational curricula in science, politics, and business, for instance, could be redefined such that humans are no longer accorded a status separate from nature. Nature itself would no longer be viewed as inert, infinitely divisible, and moved by external rather than internal forces. Business management (both education and practice) could be redefined in a way that treats the firm as socially and physically connected to the ecosystem and to other societies; the profit motive could be redefined as just one of many prime objectives of the firm; and economic growth could be redefined to include concerns for information intensiveness, community consciousness, and the experiential quality of economic activity rather than merely its material and energy intensiveness.[26]

Economic Performance Metrics

Corporations appreciate what they can measure, and all measurements and metrics have values and assumptions embedded within their definitions and formulas that determine what is important and what is unimportant. Often, these assumptions are unseen and unquestioned. What is considered "value" in net present value? Does the depletion of natural capital fit into the equation for return on equity? Economic and environmental value is embedded within the performance measures used throughout industry to judge economic performance, process criteria, and corporate health and success. Clearly, these can produce actions that deviate from long-term environmental objectives by supporting the belief that economic and environmental objectives are separate and distinct.

For example, gross domestic product (GDP) is the foremost economic indicator of national economic progress. It is a measure of all financial transactions involving products and services, but it does not acknowledge (or value) a distinction between those transactions that add to the well-being of a country and those that diminish it. Any productive activity in which money changes hands—including the sale of any natural resource, such as timber, ore, water, plants, or animals—will register as growth in GDP. This creates perverse economic signals that promote shortsighted economic activity at the expense of environmental objectives.[27] For example, GDP treats natural disasters as economic gain. Hurricane Andrew was a disaster for southern Florida, but contributions from recovery programs were reflected in GDP as a $15 billion boost to the economy. GDP increases with polluting activities and then again with pollution cleanup.[28] For example, throughout the twentieth century, economic activity and GDP increased through the low-cost and socially inappropriate disposal of hazardous wastes. Now, under the aegis of the Superfund program, it will cost an estimated $750 billion to clean them up, an amount that will again be added to GDP.[29] As a result, pollution becomes a double benefit for the economy, and the true relationship between economics and the environment becomes clouded.

GDP also treats the depletion of natural capital as income rather than as depreciation of a capital asset. The more a country depletes its natural capital base and, with it, its ability to produce income in the future, the more its GDP will go up. But if such extraction is occurring faster than the resource can be replenished, the net resource pool will be diminished for future generations, dooming them to a lower standard of living. In fact, as the resource pool declines, GDP calculations will reveal an optimistic scenario. Behind the mirage of present-day GDP growth is the hidden reality of an overutilized resource base and undermined financial security for future generations. In each of these examples, economic calculations encourage environmental degradation over environmental conservation.

Whereas GDP calculations distort corporate decision making through national economic signals, banking calculations alter strategic decision making more directly. Accepted financial objectives are often based on assumptions that undervalue environmental resources, discount the future, and uncritically favor economic objectives over environmental objectives.[30] For example, return on investment criteria must support the debt load expected by lending institutions and corporate investors. But financial markets have payback horizons that are not in sync with the long time horizons of ecological systems. For forest products companies, such economic pressures will lead them to diminish the natural capital asset base on which their long-term success depends by harvesting timber at rates that exceed maximum sustainable yield. The short-term economic interests of financial markets take precedence over long-term environmental cycles.

Not necessarily the most egregious but clearly the most criticized government policies for economic development can also perpetuate environmentally dysfunctional behavior. According to the Worldwatch Institute, governments spend more than $500 billion per year to subsidize deforestation, overfishing, and other environmentally destructive behavior. For example, subsidies for the global fishing fleet have helped produce enough boats, hooks, and nets to catch twice the available fish; the cost of protecting a job mining hard coal in Germany through subsidies was $72,800 in 1998, making it cheaper to shut down the mine and pay the miners not to work; in 1990, the government of Indonesia sold rain forest logging rights for nearly $2 billion less than they were worth, an amount equal to nearly 50 percent of what other countries gave the country in development aid and loans.[31]

Global government subsidies place the world's rapidly depleting fisheries at increased risk due to shortsighted economic priorities. Ninety percent of the world's fish catch is taken from coastal waters and is therefore under some form of government control.[32] But because governments have invested heavily in protecting domestic fishing industries, subsidies distort economic signals of decline. In 1994, it cost $92 billion worldwide to pull in $70 billion worth of fish.[33] The magnitude of this dysfunctional behavior worsens if the inefficiency and waste resulting from by-catch is included. The Food and Agriculture Organization of the United Nations estimates that 27 million tons of fish per year (about 33 percent of the total catch) are by-catch—fish discarded dead from fishing boats because they are too small, of the wrong species, or out of season.[34] In 1996, 15 percent of the yearly take from the Bering Strait off the Alaskan coast was by-catch. This amount of fish equaled 50 million meals, enough to treat everyone in the states of California and New York to a fish fry.[35]

Another area in which government subsidies have heavily distorted market signals and isolated them from environmental objectives is in price supports for gasoline. A 1998 report by the International Center for Technology Assessment (ICTA) determined that gasoline costs the U.S. economy $5.60 to $15.14 per gallon through such subsidies as industry tax breaks, costs associated with tailpipe emissions, and military protection of oil supplies.[36] In all, the group identified more than forty "externalities" totaling $558 million to $1.69 billion. Although environmental health and safety costs are the most difficult to quantify, the report's authors state that they are "the largest portion of the externalized price Americans pay for their gasoline."[37] The ICTA concluded that if the U.S. government ended all tax breaks and subsidies to the domestic oil industry and other production costs were factored into the final price of gasoline, consumers could pay as much as $15 per gallon.[38]

Overcoming these institutionalized biases will require a revamping of the economic formulas that measure economic activity and, more important, alteration of the supporting structures utilized by all constituents that use the formulas. Within corporations and between corporations and financial institutions, environmental issues could be framed as a business issue that complements the overall business strategy.[39] Traditional business terms such as *return on investment* and *net present value* could be adopted to sell the costs and benefits of environmental initiatives to business management and capital markets.[40] This would trigger support for the perception that environmental initiatives are consistent with economic objectives.

Alternatively, traditional metrics and the assumptions that underlie them could be challenged and restructured. Redefining Progress, a nonprofit organization based in San Francisco,[41] has been promoting a redefinition of GDP formulas, focusing on two widely recognized problems facing national accountants. The first and less difficult problem is that of measuring and accounting for resource depletion. The second and greater challenge is the quantification of pollution issues. More specifically, GDP must be altered in terms of how it measures the physical change in (or level of) environmental quality and how it values this change when there is no market price as a guide.[42] To challenge the underlying values of GDP calculations more directly, some suggest redefining the concept of growth or, more important, ending the assumption that anything called growth is automatically good. Rather than measuring the quantity of economic activity, new measurements could replace GDP to measure the quality of economic activity. It comes down to an issue of measuring not only how much money is being spent but also what it is being spent on that could stand as the measure of true progress.[43]

International Regimes

The institutionalized separation of environmental and economic interests may be the most pronounced in the arena of international regimes. International standards for global trade are very much in their infancy and are often established with a clear set of underlying assumptions that place economic growth and environmental protection in separate domains, with compatible solutions ruled out. Although several international trade agreements have environmental implications, the World Trade Organization (WTO) most clearly illustrates how institutions perpetuate the separation of environmental and economic interests. The WTO's central premise of nondiscrimination clearly places free trade over environmental protection. The 1991 dispute over dolphin-safe tuna and the 1998 dispute over turtle-safe shrimp exemplified this priority (see chapter 3). In both cases, the United States was found in violation of free-trade agreements due to their domestic environmental standards.

In an odd alliance, conservation groups and conservative Republicans pressed the Clinton administration to defy these decisions, arguing that the WTO was subverting domestic environmental policy.[44] Environmental NGOs challenged the underlying logic of the decisions as promoting economic trade at the expense of environmental protection. Conservative Republicans believed that the WTO's decisions challenged national sovereignty in developing domestic standards. Both groups feared that pressure from foreign countries (supported by domestically disadvantaged companies) would cause domestic environmental standards to be driven down to the lowest common denominator, creating environmental damage as well as an unfair trade position for domestic producers. Hard-won domestic environmental victories might be lost in the name of international trade equity. Underlying this possible outcome is the institution-alized notion that trade interests will rule out any attempt at balancing environmental objectives and commercial objectives.[45] International regimes can, however, be amended in such a way that environmental interests can be introduced as compatible with and supportive of preexisting goals of economic growth and increased world trade. In 1999, the director general of the WTO called for the creation of a World Environment Organization to parallel the WTO. Through a global institution comparable to the WTO, international regimes could be restructured in a way that supplants the imperative for global free trade with an imperative for economic and environmental sustainability of world communities.

Economic Infrastructure

Economic infrastructure in the form of market rules can perpetuate the disconnection between economic growth and environmental protection. Market incentive structures can also obscure opportunities to correct environmental destruction. For example, manufacturers produce television sets and videocassette recorders that remain in "standby" mode when not in use so that consumers can turn them on with remote-control devices, save preset stations, and encounter no warm-up delay. However, the manufacturers have no incentive to reduce the amount of power used in standby mode because they do not pay the energy bills. Consumers, likewise, have little incentive to be concerned because the incremental costs are so low. Yet in the aggregate, the United States uses about 1,000 megawatts annually to maintain this feature—about the output of one Chernobyl-sized power station.[46] Without properly aligned incentives, this energy waste will continue. In 1998, the EPA identified this issue as important and has sought the voluntary compliance of appliance and computer makers to decrease standby energy use.

Other market incentive structures among organizations yield similarly inefficient action. Architects and engineers are compensated on a percentage of the cost of the building or equipment specified at construction, not over its lifetime. They are actually penalized for eliminating equipment that may be costly at the beginning but cheaper over the long term. This has led the United States to misallocate about $1 trillion for air-conditioning equipment that would not have been necessary had buildings been designed to produce the same or better comfort at lower cost.[47] Landlords have no incentive to improve the energy efficiency of their apartments because renters pay the energy costs.[48] Manufacturers have no incentive to reduce packaging because consumers pay the price of its disposal. Finally, domestic standards for energy pricing allow regulated utilities to increase profits on the basis of increased energy use and, conversely, penalize them for reducing consumers' energy bills. As a result, shareholders and customers have opposite goals, with wastefully increased energy use as the end result.[49]

Market inefficiencies can also be seen in the ambiguity of private property rights.[50] Under the guise of economic freedom, a company has the legal right to exploit a natural resource toward whatever ends it sees fit, thereby maximizing its individual benefits. The negative consequences of such action may be distributed, however, and sent off-site to be borne by others. The full social costs are not included in the developer's economic calculations and remain external to development considerations. The rights of the individual end up being placed above the rights of the broader society. In effect, the developer defaults on responsible management of the societal commons in pursuit of private gains. For example, forced restriction on cod fishing in the Georges Bank off the New England coast in the mid 1990s was the direct result of individual, federally subsidized fishermen seeking individual gain at the cost of the entire fishing industry and society at large.[51] Similarly, a 1994 timber sale by the Bureau of Land Management (BLM) in southern Oregon allowed increased logging, which the National Marine Fisheries Service determined would adversely affect the nearby Umpqua River, which is the centerpiece of a $36 million sportfishing industry and the habitat of the threatened Umpqua cutthroat trout. Portions of the river are part of the National Wild and Scenic Rivers System, which supports rafting, sightseeing, and, most economically important, fishing.[52]

This confusion over property rights abounds in debates over natural resources. The rights of the waterfront landowner, the sportfisherman, and the municipal water department are imposed on when an upstream developer fills in a wetland habitat, causing increased flooding, loss of aquatic spawning grounds, and a reduction in the natural water-filtering capacity of the river ecosystem. The rights of the salmon fishery and the sportfisherman are imposed on when an upstream timber company clear-cuts a forest, creating erosion that chokes rivers. The rights of the taxpayer are imposed on when tax-supported federal flood insurance is provided to individuals living on floodplains, and they are imposed on further still when water quality declines as a result of those individuals exercising their right to maintain leaching septic systems on coastal properties. The rights of the hunter, birder, and hiker are imposed on when critical habitat is destroyed, upsetting the balance of the ecosystem and reducing the populations of particular animal or plant species. In each of these cases, there are tangible economic costs to individual economic interests and to the economy as a whole. In the forced extinction of unique species, there are intangible costs associated with the loss of value belonging to the whole of humankind.

Resolution of these kinds of issues will require an alteration in perceptions of the systemic aspects of the economy. This can be achieved by fostering more direct connections between customers and producers or by reframing property rights in broader terms than material possession. Just as scientists talk of systemic thinking and the interconnectedness of the ecosystem, these values could be projected to the social economy. Resource management could be reframed in terms of transboundary rights and the need to include the full societal costs in the equity of individual developers' decisions. The actions of one economic actor are not performed in a vacuum, separated from their effects on others. What is at issue here is who should be assigned the property right of a balanced ecosystem. Should the developer pay the price for its destruction? Or should society pay the price for its protection? The equitable solution should place the economic burden on the party who receives the economic benefit.

Physical Infrastructure

Just as economic infrastructure guides corporate action by establishing the context in which it takes place, so, too, does physical infrastructure. The buildings we inhabit, the transportation modes we utilize, and the exchange forums we engage in all create the context for our environmental and economic actions. For example, some large residential buildings have been constructed with only one trash chute, causing a physical limitation to recycling programs that require trash segregation. Allowing cars to turn right on a red signal can increase their average speed from eight to thirteen miles per hour, reducing emissions by as much as 20 percent. Rail routes in the United States have historically been built to carry people from the suburbs into the city, whereas much suburban traffic now moves from one suburb to another. Some institutions can be changed easily, some we must change despite difficulties, and some we cannot change without significant disruption.

Consider how you might build a sustainable Boston, New York, or San Francisco if you were to design it from scratch. Would it look as it looks today? Not likely. Many of our urban centers have been in place for hundreds of years and were not built in the most efficient terms as far as maximizing resource conservation. We cannot simply tear them down and start from scratch. But in some ways, we can make alterations that can bring us closer to becoming a resource-efficient society. For example, heat islands are found in many large U.S. cities. Urban areas are often as much as 5 degrees Fahrenheit warmer than surrounding suburbs. Only about 1 percent of this heat gain is due to heat loss from buildings and cars. A study by the Department of Energy (DOE) found that the majority of the heat emanates from dark horizontal surfaces.[53] This has significant economic costs in terms of energy use and medical costs. One-sixth of U.S. electricity consumption goes toward cooling buildings, at an annual cost of roughly $40 billion. Moreover, high temperatures convert nitrogen oxides and volatile organic compounds from cars and smokestacks into ground-level ozone, a main ingredient of smog. Ozone is estimated to be responsible for about $3 billion in health-related costs each year in the Los Angeles Basin alone.

But through the use of lighter colors for roofs and pavement and the planting of trees in urban areas, temperatures, energy use, and smog could all be reduced. The DOE estimates that such initiatives in Los Angeles could lower the average summer afternoon temperature by 5 degrees Fahrenheit, reducing the need for air-conditioning by 18 percent, for a savings of $175 million per year. This initiative would also reduce smog levels, for an additional savings of $360 million in smog-related expenses.

However, this kind of change will require an alteration of institutions on many levels. First, the roofing industry must be enticed to change material options for new construction and renovation. In the United States, buildings were constructed with white roofs through the 1960s. But as air-conditioning became more widespread, priorities shifted. The typical "white" shingle of today is coated with only one-sixth the white pigment used in the 1960s. Under the summer sun, these modern shingles are 20 degrees Fahrenheit hotter than their 1960s predecessors. Next, the asphalt paving industry must change its material aggregate mix. Asphalt pavement is about seven-eighths aggregate and one-eighth black asphalt. The DOE estimates that the use of white aggregate could triple the solar reflectivity of city streets, sidewalks, and parking lots. Unfortunately, although the technical specifications for the properties of aggregate cover thousands of pages, there are none for color. Local municipalities and utilities can also play a role in this kind of transformation, encouraging the planting of trees, which provide cooling shade and, through transpiration of water, cool the leaves and the surrounding air. A single, properly watered tree can lose forty gallons of water per day through evapotranspiration, offsetting the heat equivalent of one hundred hundred-watt lamps burning eight hours per day.[54] Forward-looking utility regulations can allow utilities to raise rates slightly by implementing energy conservation programs such as this. Bringing this kind of change to fruition would require coordination among all these institutional actors and about fifteen years to implement. But other institutional changes have yielded such systemic changes.

Consider recycling initiatives in the United States. How would you get them started if you were faced with a clean slate? Governments cannot simply mandate that paper, aluminum, or glass "will" be recycled. In the 1980s, municipalities in the Northeast established mandatory programs for the recycling of newspaper. Soon, the supply far outweighed the demand and falling costs in the marketplace undercut the incentive to recycle.[55] Efficient recycling can take place only when the necessary infrastructure is developed and integrated. The system must include economic signals and physical capacity. First, contractors must collect and sort municipal and industrial garbage. Second, manufacturers must invest millions of dollars to develop the processing capacity to recycle these materials. Third, a system needs to be developed to enable collectors and recyclers to find each other in order to exchange the raw materials. Fourth, a new market for recycled material must emerge. None of these steps can work without the others working in tandem. Supply without balance in capacity or demand is useless; forcing one side of the equation without giving attention to the others will invite failure.

It took many years for recycling efforts in the United States to be institutionalized into an efficient system. But around 1995, the pieces started to fall into place. The supply of recycled material was supported by curbside recycling programs and collection from large office buildings. Participation in curbside recycling grew from only

1,000 communities in 1988 to nearly 7,000 in 1995 and nearly 9,000 in 1996. From 1994 to 1995, wastepaper collection increased from 24 million tons to 39 million tons; collection of waste glass increased from 2.5 million tons to 3 million tons; and collection of waste plastic increased from 181,500 tons to 690,000 tons. Market signals supported this expansion as the price for a ton of waste office paper grew from $15 in 1993 to $85 in 1994, the price for a ton of waste newspaper increased from $30 in 1993 to $55 in 1994, that for a ton of corrugated cardboard increased from $35 in 1993 to $110 in 1994, and that for a ton of steel cans increased from $30 in 1992 to $110 in 1994.[56]

Driving these market shifts were other alterations in the economic and physical systems of recycling. In October 1995, the Chicago Board of Trade reduced transaction costs between buyers and sellers of waste materials by setting up an exchange for purchase and sale of waste glass, paper, aluminum, plastic, and other recyclable materials. To bolster demand for recycled paper, President Clinton signed an executive order mandating that government agencies purchase recycled material wherever possible. Most important, paper companies capitalized on the growing market for recycled paper by increasing plant capacity by 4 million tons from 1995 to 1996, compared with an increase of a mere 700,000 tons from 1993 to 1994. Overall, the industry invested $7.5 billion in capital expenditures from 1988 to 1995.

Some of the big winners in this system are the large waste haulers, such as Waste Management and Browning Ferris Industries (BFI) (acquired by Allied Waste Industries, Inc. in 1999), which effectively collect revenues on both ends of the resource stream: once to collect waste and again to sell the sorted material. Recycling revenues for BFI increased from $32 million in 1990 to $359 million in 1994 and $550 million in 1995. Although it rebated much of this revenue back to customers so as not to lose them, the company enjoyed operating income from recycling that totaled $23.2 million in the second quarter of 1995, compared with $1.3 million in the same quarter in 1994.[57] But this opportunity did not come without risks. The company is highly capitalized in collection. To mitigate that risk and insulate itself from market fluctuations, it established long-term contracts with the communities it serves and the mills it supplies.

As in any market system, recycling lends itself to fluctuations in price and materials and even competition from other environmental initiatives. For example, in 1996, Germany found itself in a "refuse crisis." To handle its growing need for waste disposal and recycling, the country had been investing in expensive waste-to-energy incinerators and lavish landfills since the early 1980s. But simultaneously, the country had been on a waste reduction campaign, cutting back on unnecessary packaging and requiring more recycling. As a result, from 1990 to 1993, household trash decreased by 50 percent while waste from all sources decreased by 16 percent. This left much of the waste management infrastructure without source material. To deal with the crisis, Germany was forced to import trash from as far away as Brazil to keep its system going. One paper factory was even forced to stop selling its waste to a Belgian cement company (which paid $162 per ton) and send it instead to the city waste disposal plant (at a cost of $324 per ton).[58]

Conclusion

Institutions create opportunities for environmental strategy as well as restraints on it. In addition to the challenge of identifying the opportunities that environmental issues present, a critical task for the corporate manager is to identify how those institutions similarly inhibit the capitalization of such opportunities. Although regulatory structures are changing such that more creative compliance strategies are becoming possible, historical and cultural artifacts remain within regulatory agencies that can pose a significant threat. For example, in 1993, the Amoco Corporation developed an alliance with the Environmental Protection Agency in the Yorktown project discussed in chapter 2, encountering both new opportunities and culturally based resistance. On the one hand, the company was breaking historical barriers of mistrust and suspicion between the industry and the agency and developing new inroads for giving input to regulatory initiatives. But on the other hand, such a redefinition of the relationship challenged the notions held by some within the agency about what that relationship would be. At one point in the project, the developing trust between the two organizations was shattered when a separate division of the EPA announced a nationwide crackdown to enforce lead laws. As part of that crackdown, the agency hit Amoco's Yorktown refinery with a $5.5 million fine. Virtually everyone at the oil company and a few people at the EPA thought that this was retribution for getting too cozy. Gordon Binder, chief of staff to William Reilly, administrator of the EPA at that time, identified the problem: "It raised a very real dilemma. When you are working with industry cooperatively, shouldn't you reward good behavior? At the same time, you've got your established procedures."[59]

Regulatory structures are but one type of institution that can inhibit environmental strategies. As pointed out in this chapter, there are others; and beyond those mentioned here, many more exist. After these obstacles are identified, the next task is to determine how to overcome them and how much energy and resources will be needed to do so. In fact, this is a dilemma faced continually by environmental NGOs as they undertake their task of changing the way society perceives environmental problems (see box 9.1). The next chapter presents two sectoral studies that consider this question more closely.

Box 9.1. How Do You Change Institutions?

The ultimate objective of any environmental NGO is broad societal change. Thus, in the end, it is institutional change that poses the greatest hurdles for future environmental solutions. Consider what will happen if automakers can successfully shift to alternative-fuel vehicles. The design that ultimately succeeds will carry with it a whole host of institutional issues. If electric vehicles prove to be the automobile of the future, what will happen to the gasoline filling stations that have become a fixture of the American landscape? Will they be replaced by electric filling stations or battery replacement stations? If so, will they be operated by oil companies or electric utilities? If fuel cells become the dominant design, what fuel will they use, and how will it be administered? In either case, what would such a shift mean for the thousands of automobile mechanics and repair stations around the country? Will the skills needed to maintain the new vehicles be com-

(*continues*)

Box 9.1. *Continued*

plementary to those needed for gasoline engines? Will mechanics be retrained for the new types of mechanical problems inherent in electric motors, or will they be replaced by newly educated repair specialists? Finally, a new industry of parts suppliers must be developed with the economies of scale required to bring the price of electric car parts down to a level that will make the entire automobile cost-effective. Even simple language will evolve in describing the driving experience. In an electric car, what does it mean to "step on the gas"?

Enormous institutional issues also accompany efforts to resolve the issue of global climate change. In 1997, the developed countries of the world agreed to reduce their emissions of greenhouse gases. As of 1999, the world's governments (including the U.S. government) had yet to ratify the treaty. But if it is ratified, the process of institutional change will have only just begun. New economic and physical infrastructure must be developed to resolve many issues. International institutions must be developed to measure national and global carbon emissions and disseminate the data. They must also find a means to verify those measurements, enforce national goals and timetables, and establish an international trading system that efficiently minimizes transaction costs. National institutions must be developed to apportion the country's goals among individual industries within the economy. Approaches to these issues will be extremely complex and will require change in every sector of the economy and society.*

If you were the director of an environmental NGO, how would you work to hasten the institutional changes needed to support automotive redesign or greenhouse gas controls? To what would you devote the limited resources at your disposal? In trying to promote social change, it can be difficult to tell which is the tail and which is the dog. Would you focus on the general public, driving social change from the grass roots by educating people about these complicated issues? Or would you focus on lobbying efforts and try to drive change from above through government mandate? Would you develop alliances with businesses and try to convince and coerce them to begin the change process? Or would you focus on the capital markets and try to drive corporate change through their most important resources? In which area can you gain the best results with the most efficient expenditure of effort? Is efficiency dependent on timing as well? Would you harbor your resources, implementing them in the wake of a major environmental disaster like the chemical release at Bhopal or the *Exxon Valdez* oil spill? The answers to these questions are critical for both those trying to promote change and those trying to respond to the change others produce. Both environmental activists and corporate decision makers can find themselves in either position.

---

* A. Hoffman, "The Long Road to Institutional Change," in *Global Climate Change: A Senior Level Dialogue at the Intersection of Economics, Strategy, Technology, Science, Politics, and International Negotiation*, ed. A. Hoffman (San Francisco: New Lexington Press, 1998), 215–218.

Further Reading

Capra, F. *The Turning Point: Science, Society, and the Rising Culture*. New York: Bantam Books, 1982.

Clayre, A., ed. *Nature and Industrialization*. London: Oxford University Press, 1977.

Cronon, W. *Changes in the Land: Indians, Colonists, and the Ecology of New England*. New York: Hill & Wang, 1983.

Evernden, N. *The Natural Alien: Humankind and Environment.* Toronto: University of Toronto Press, 1985.

———. *The Social Creation of Nature.* Baltimore: Johns Hopkins University Press, 1992.

Livingston, J. *Rogue Primate: An Exploration of Human Domestication.* Toronto: Key Porter Books, 1994.

Quinn, D. *Ishmael: An Adventure of the Mind and Spirit.* New York: Bantam Books, 1992.

Rowe, J., and M. Anielski. *The Genuine Progress Indicator.* San Francisco: Redefining Progress, 1999.

Part IV

COMPETITIVE ENVIRONMENTAL STRATEGY

Chapter 10

ENVIRONMENTAL STRATEGY IN
AN INSTITUTIONAL CONTEXT:
TWO SECTORAL STUDIES

As the previous chapter illustrated, competitive environmental strategy cannot be decided solely within the confines of the individual firm but often must be developed in concert with constituents outside the firm and within the business system. Environmental and business strategy must be linked with business relationships and networks. It involves a redefinition of those relationships as well as the perceptions of the materials and processes that are exchanged within them. In short, it redefines the business system. In dealing with this redefinition, the effective manager must acknowledge both (1) opportunities, the extent to which the changing business system drives environmental strategy, and (2) limitations, the extent to which environmental strategy must drive change within the business system to be successful. This chapter examines the redefinition of business systems through these two different perspectives.

The first perspective asks the question, *What is wood?* Through this example, we can see how institutions create opportunities for the forest products industry. Key constituents such as trade associations, suppliers, buyers, international regimes, and regulatory agencies have altered the basic conceptions of raw material, product, and process within the industry.

The second perspective asks the question, *What is a house?* Through this example, we can see how institutions form a constraint on environmental strategy. A small group of actors are trying to redefine the home construction industry in terms of environmental attributes. But to succeed, they must trigger changes within the business system that remains an obstacle to the achievement of their goal.

The two examples present a counterbalance between an industry in which business managers must respond to changes within the business system and an industry in which business managers must change the business system in order to achieve their objective. One represents the benefits of institutional context—opportunities for those who can see beyond limitations. The other represents the constraints of institutional context—limitations for those who can see opportunities. With these as examples, the reader can consider further applications of the principles discussed.

Institutions as Opportunity: Environmentalism and the Forest Products Industry

What is wood? Far from certain, the answer to this question is changing significantly. In 1600, forests covered about 1 billion acres, or approximately 46 percent, of the United States.[1] Until 1920, great areas of forest were cleared for agriculture, but that process has largely halted. As shown in figure 10.1, forest growth has continually exceeded harvest since the 1940s, and in 1991, growth exceeded harvest by 20 percent. In 1995, forests covered approximately 737 million acres, or about one-third of the country. Two-thirds of this forestland (490 million acres) was classified as timberland, capable of growing twenty cubic feet of commercial-quality wood per year.[2]

But environmental pressures are undeniably changing the industry. Traditional business interests such as suppliers, buyers, customers, trade associations, and others are driving environmental concerns deeper into the basic aspects of the operations and purpose of forest products companies. In the face of such evolving demands, environmental strategy has become an integral component of success in the industry's future. In the words of Carl Geist, vice president of the Weyerhaeuser Company's Pulp business, those companies that survive will shift their "paradigm from correcting environmental problems at the tail end of our operations—our effluent and air treatment systems—to eliminating them at the front end in the design of our projects and processes."[3] To make this shift, forest products companies must redefine some of the basic aspects of their business in response to environmental pressures from the external business system.

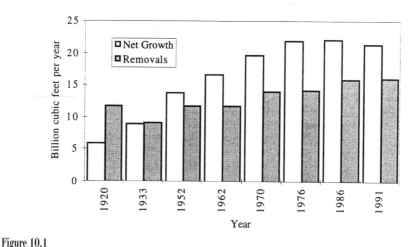

Figure 10.1

U.S. Timber Growth and Removals, 1920–1991

Source: D. Powell et al., *Forest Resources of the United States, 1992,* General Technical Report no. RM-234 (Washington, D.C.: U.S. Department of Agriculture, Forest Service, 1993), 16.

What Is the Forest Product Industry's Raw Material?

An important supplier of raw materials to the forest products industry is the government. Between 1980 and 1989, an average of 12.95 billion board feet of timber was produced annually in northern California and the Pacific Northwest. One-third of this came from federal lands. Overall, of the 490 million acres of timberland nationwide, federal, state, and local governments control 131 million, or about 27 percent. But economic and social demographics are affecting the availability of this supply. The traditional interests of logging, mining, and grazing in federal land-use policy are being supplanted by the needs and desires of an increasingly urban and environmentally minded nation. The general public is voicing concerns for a protected environment, and those concerns are being translated into shifts in timber supply from federal land (as well as private lands). A 1993 bill sponsored by the Clinton administration allowed only 1.1 billion board feet of lumber to be produced annually on federal lands. This amount is less than one-quarter of the 1980–1989 annual average. As shown in figure 10.2, sales of timber from national forests have been declining greatly since the late 1980s. A Forest Service study recently predicted that recreation will provide as much as 75 percent of the agency's revenue by the year 2000. (The Forest Service manages nearly 10 percent of the landmass of the United States.) Simultaneously, Forest Service proceeds from logging are expected to drop to as little as 3 percent.[4]

In the face of changes in the supply of raw materials, the forest products industry is evolving. Winners and losers are emerging on the basis of which companies can react strategically to shifting supplies. Many forest products companies have responded to these pressures by looking for new sources of raw material. One solution being explored is the use of managed tree farming as a way to increase yield and decrease harvest uncertainty. Presently, 30 percent of the country's timber harvest comes from old-growth

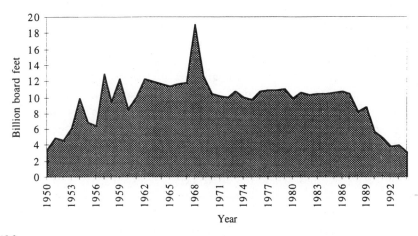

Figure 10.2

National Forest Timber Sales, 1950–1994

Source: American Forest and Paper Association, *U.S. Forests, 1995: Facts and Figures* (Washington, D.C.: American Forest and Paper Association, 1995), 10. © American Forest and Paper Association. All rights reserved. Used with permission.

forests, 10 percent from exotic plantations, 24 percent from other plantations, and 36 percent from second-growth, managed forests. But with alterations in cutting and planting techniques, more than 90 percent of the world's demand for pulp or construction material from forests could be satisfied with commodity-grade wood—wood that can be produced in managed high-yield, intensive forest plantations. The remaining 10 percent of demand, for specialty-grade wood, could be met by specialized tree plantations, such as teak plantations. It is estimated that overall, the area devoted to timber production under an intensive plantation model would be just 5 percent of the total forested area of the globe. This gain would be realized through technological innovations that have increased productivity and yields in intensively managed forests.

One such innovation is the selective breeding of particular tree species, either native or transplanted, that enjoy rapid growth rates.[5] For example, the southern pine has been a mainstay timber product in the southern United States, but it grows very slowly, at a rate of 12 cubic meters per hectare per year (cmhy).[6] It can take as long as ninety years for a southern yellow pine to reach maturity. Similarly, the eucalyptus grows at a rate of 11–12 cmhy. However, when this species is transplanted from its native Australia and New Zealand to South Africa, it grows at a much improved rate of 25 cmhy.[7] Even more impressive, gmelina trees planted in Costa Rica by the Stone Container Corporation grow at an astonishing rate of eighteen feet per year, allowing the company to harvest trees roughly sixty feet tall and eight inches in diameter on only a four-year cycle. Although Greenpeace has raised concerns about the ecological effects of such fast-growing trees on indigenous species, many other forest products companies are seeking similarly advantageous growing conditions. The Champion International Corporation and the Simpson Paper Company have bought or entered into partnerships with plantations in Chile to grow radiata pine, a species native to California, and with plantations in Argentina and Brazil to grow eucalyptus and southern yellow pine, such as loblolly pine. International Paper recently acquired a stake in New Zealand's Carter Holt Harvey Ltd. and in Copec, a company that owns more than a million acres in Chile. International Paper has been drawn to Chile by the fact that land costs half as much as in the United States and the trees grow much faster.[8]

Beyond plantation harvesting, some companies are looking for sources of wood other than raw trees for their material needs. The Goodwin Heart Pine Company,[9] for example, is able to deliver a quality of lumber that is extremely rare in today's markets by retrieving logs from riverbeds. In the 1700s and 1800s, vast tracts of southern lands were clear-cut to the riverbanks, where southern longleaf yellow pine and cypress logs were rafted downstream to nearby sawmills. Along the way, some of these large timbers sank or were buried in the mud, where they have been preserved from insects and rot ever since. Goodwin sends in divers and recovers these logs by hand, carefully kiln-dries them, and prepares them for sale. Because these trees take 200 to 500 years to mature, the wood the company offers is of unusual beauty, strength, and durability. The company guarantees 100 percent heart face (no knots) on every board and claims to be the only provider of twelve-inch-wide flooring planks. Scarcity of such large-sized, old-growth raw material helps to establish the market for these planks.

Other companies, such as The Joinery Company[10] and the G. R. Plume Company,[11] look not to riverbeds but to old buildings for their raw materials. The companies reclaim Douglas fir and pine timbers from buildings constructed at the turn of the twentieth century and then clean them, resaw them, and refinish them to create trusses, arches, columns, beams, and plank flooring. Again, these sources of raw material offer a quality that is extremely rare in the younger commercial forests that dominate present supplies.

Finally, research is exploring ways to make dimensional lumber (lumber used for framing, such as two-by-fours, two-by-sixes, etc.) not from trees but from cornstalks and other cellulose-containing material. Using agricultural and timber waste, researchers are developing a process whereby the materials are ground into a fine paste, mixed with stabilizing agents to bind them, and then extruded into any shape desired. Such a process would reduce the demands on forestland, reuse materials that are typically discarded or burned, and create a product that could conceivably be more uniform (no knots), straighter, and more stable than standard dimensional lumber. Agriboard Industries, for example, developed a process that used agricultural by-products to make structural insulated panel systems for exterior walls, roofs, and floors. It used residual fibers from wheat or other cereals to make a core material that was laminated between two skins of oriented strand board. With Agriboard cores instead of two-by-four wood studs, the panels used 65 percent less lumber than is used in conventional house construction. The National Association of Home Builders Research Foundation found that the load-bearing capacity of the panels was three to five times that required by the Uniform Building Code.[12] (In July 1999, Agriboard ceased operations due to a loss of funding.)

What Is the Process for Harvesting This Raw Material?

Forest products companies are under pressure from several fronts to alter their harvesting strategies and move increasingly toward sustainable forestry practices. These pressures are emerging from both inside and outside the industry. Inside, the industry's trade group, the American Forest and Paper Association, whose 200 corporate members own or control about 52 million acres of U.S. forestland, unveiled its Sustainable Forestry Initiative in 1995. This initiative requires members to practice and promote responsible forestry, and to protect certain lands, water quality, and wildlife habitat. This is not an easy set of standards to live with, and as many as 25 members either resigned or refused to sign the initiative and were asked to leave the trade group.

Outside the industry, buyers and consumers are applying pressure as well. For example, in 1997, The Home Depot announced that it would join Sears, Roebuck and Company, Orchard Supply Hardware, HomeBase, Inc., the Hechinger Company, and 900 other retail chains in boycotting wood or wood products that come from ancient redwood trees. Specifically, the company stated that it would not sell redwood from trees older than 300 years of age, and it informed a supplier, the Louisiana-Pacific Corporation, that it would accept only second- and third-growth redwood.[13]

To help appeal to consumers, several forestry certification programs are emerging. Although no universally accepted guidelines for sustainable forestry exist, the organizations operating the three largest programs—the Forest Stewardship Council,[14] Smart-Wood,[15] and Scientific Certification Systems (SCS)[16]—are working to decide how best to evaluate forest management. Although their approaches differ slightly, each uses similar criteria in labeling a forest operation as a "certified well-managed forest." They consider whether the timber resources are sustainable (produced through a sustained-yield harvest). They give equal weight to the entire forest ecosystem, which includes adequate wildlife habitat, watershed protection, and the economic and cultural effects of the operation on the local community.[17] SCS, for example, will spend as long as five months evaluating a forestry company and rate the company according to three categories: sustainability of timber resources, management of the forest ecosystem, and socioeconomic benefits. As of 1997, more than 22 million acres of forestland had been certified in twenty-four countries worldwide, representing just 1 percent of the total market. In the United States, the amount of certified forestland doubled in 1997, to 3.6 million acres.[18]

However, because these programs are relatively new, "green" wood is not yet available everywhere or for all business applications. Although certain organizations have agreed to use certified wood in certain projects (such as the Bank of America Corporation, Habitat for Humanity International, The Nature Company, the Turner Construction Company, and the San Francisco International Airport), it remains primarily a niche market for consumers, sold for either the same price or a small premium. Paul Fuge, owner of Plaza Hardware Inc. in Santa Fe, New Mexico, believes that "if price and quality are competitive and customers are given a choice, they'll usually buy green certified wood." He has watched sales of certified wood in his store rise from zero in 1993 to $600,000 in 1997.[19] A survey of wood products manufacturers conducted by Mater Engineering, Ltd. for the National Wildlife Federation showed that 21 percent of respondents would pay a premium for "green" lumber if they could pass the cost along to the customer. Paul Sampson, president of A. E. Sampson & Son, Inc., a sawmill in Warren, Maine, said he believes that "at a 5 percent premium, 30 percent of customers go certified, and at a 10 percent premium, it shrinks to 10 percent of customers."[20]

To help spur such market acceptance, a group of buyers, resellers, and secondary manufacturers of forest products formed the Forest Products Buyers Group[21] in partnership with environmental groups (such as the Natural Resources Defense Council, the Rainforest Alliance, the World Resources Institute, and the World Wildlife Fund) and others. (In 1997, the group emerged with the Good Wood Alliance to become the Certified Forest Products Council.) The group promotes sustainable forestry practices and provides leadership in buying independently certified forest products. Its goals are to strengthen and promote links between buyers and suppliers of independently certified wood products and to educate producers, buyers, and consumers about opportunities to promote responsible forest management practices through the sale and purchase of wood that is certified to be sustainably grown and harvested.

These programs are not without their problems, however. In 1997, The Home Depot stopped offering certified sustainable wood from the Collins Pine Company of Portland, Oregon, citing supply problems. The large retailer was frustrated because the amount of lumber that the relatively small company could provide did not meet its inventory needs. The retailer became increasingly impatient, keeping dual inventories and segregated streams of supply and distribution for certified and noncertified wood products.[22] But at times, customers voice their concerns in the face of such actions. In 1998, the Rainforest Action Network (RAN) placed The Home Depot on its list of environmentally incorrect places to shop because of the retailer's sales of wood products made from old-growth forests in Canada and the United States. The forest advocacy movement had been successful in convincing other firms to stop their use of old-growth products—including Mitsubishi Motor Sales of America, Inc. and Mitsubishi Electric USA; the Kimberly-Clark Corporation; the Minnesota Mining and Manufacturing Company (3M); Nike, Inc.; Levi Strauss & Company; and the Anderson Corporation—but the Home Depot campaign was the largest it had ever launched. The group planned newspaper advertisements, frequent pickets, and civil disobedience at selected stores around the United States.[23]

There is also growing concern that certified wood may run afoul of international trade agreements and the World Trade Organization (WTO). As discussed in chapter 3, WTO rules state that countries cannot discriminate against "like" products because of the way they are produced (as when the WTO ruled in 1998 that the United States could not ban the importation of shrimp caught in nets lacking turtle-excluding devices). Because a piece of wood from a well-managed forest looks no different from a piece of wood from any other forest, the two are the same in the eyes of trade law, and therefore import restrictions would be considered a form of trade barrier. Although certified wood remains a small part of the market and therefore negligible in terms of world trade, the concern looms. For example, when the New York City Council, the Los Angeles City Council, and the California State Assembly all considered bills to require government purchase of only certified wood, they were warned of possible trade violations.[24]

What Is the Industry's Product?

To respond to a growing shift in consumer and buyer demand, some companies have begun to look for new types of products. Some are simple; others are more sophisticated. On the simple side, Idaho Forest Industries has begun producing and marketing one-and-one-fourth-inch-thick studs. This smaller size consumes 17 percent less wood than a standard one-and-one-half-inch-thick stud. At present, builders can use the slimmed-down studs only for interior, non-weight-bearing walls. But according to the company's marketing vice president, Jim Scharnhorst, "the $1^{1}/_{4}$ inch studs are just as strong as $1^{1}/_{2}$ inch thick ones."[25] The company is trying to get the product listed as acceptable in the Uniform Building Code. Environmentally, this product will lower demands on forests. Economically, the smaller size makes better use of side-cut pieces, which normally go into making one-by-four-inch wood and wood chips. Finally, builders gain because they pay $40 less per thousand board feet than they would for standard two-by-four studs.

In another simple example, the Big City Forest Company is looking to used pallets as a source of valuable lumber. Pallets have a short life span, often being damaged after a single use. In the United States, several million pallets that carry goods into the country go to waste each year. In New York City alone, businesses spend $130 million per year to dispose of pallets, usually by chipping them for fuel or burial. An interesting twist is that pallets entering the United States with overseas shipments are often made from exotic woods—rosewood, cherry, oak, mahogany, and maple—that are cheaper where they originated. Big City Forest charges $0.75 for each pallet dropped at its door in New York City, an amount substantially less than the $5 each charged by carters. The company uses about 60 percent of the wood to make new pallets, with the best-quality planks set aside for more valuable products. For example, as chips, the wood is worth about $30 per ton. But as flooring, the wood is worth $1,200 per ton, and as furniture, about $6,000 per ton. The largest market the company sees is flooring: every year, 1.5 billion board feet of oak is wasted in pallets while 500 million board feet of lumber from newly cut oaks goes to floors.[26]

In a more sophisticated example, producing microlaminated beams is a way to use small pieces of lumber to make large-dimension "engineered wood." Such beams are of unusual uniformity and structural strength compared with solid wood beams. Trus Joist MacMillan,[27] for example, makes wooden I-beams for flooring joists in new home construction. These beams are made of an upper and lower member that is a microlaminated two-by-four with the center vertical member made of a type of chipboard, a glued plywood mesh of smaller chips of wood. These I-beams are straighter and more stable than standard dimensional lumber (such as two-by-tens and two-by-twelves). The company has recently begun to offer microlaminated two-by-fours that, again, are made from smaller pieces of wood rather than single trees.

Moving from composites of small pieces of wood to composites of wood and other products, the Trex Company[28] offers a composite called Trex Wood-Polymer lumber for use in decks, and the Mobil Chemical Company offers a competing product called Timbrex, manufactured with 50 percent sawdust from old wooden pallets and 50 percent postconsumer polyethylene recycled from grocery bags. These products are designed to resist damaging ultraviolet rays, moisture, and insects and will not rot, warp, split, or splinter. They are dyed throughout, thereby eliminating the need for chemical sealants, paints, or stains. The idea of using fillers (such as wood) in plastics has been around since the turn of the twentieth century, gaining more momentum in the 1970s with increases in the costs of oil and oil-based products such as plastics.[29]

One industry in which such composites have found wide application is the automobile manufacturing industry, where pressure for reduced automobile weight is being driven by demand for higher gas mileage. The industry needs lightweight, strong materials for components, and one source of such materials is composites of wood fiber filler (such as old newspapers) and polypropylene. Replacing standard plastic injection-molded components, these wood-plastic composites are stronger, lighter, cheaper, and more easily processed than straight plastic components. They are molded at lower temperatures, resulting in lower energy costs, and involve reduced cycle times.[30] It is estimated that the substitution of composites in one-half of currently used automotive plastics would reduce the weight of one year's production of cars and trucks by more than 630 million pounds and could save as much as $145 million per year in decreased material costs.

Who Are the Industry's Customers?

People value nature and are willing to pay to protect it and enjoy it. In Idaho, for example, the state commerce department estimated that tourism returned $1.4 billion to the state's economy in 1989—slightly more than the $1 billion generated by Idaho's livestock and mining industries combined.[31] Nationwide, the number of anglers increased by 11 percent from 1985 to 1991.[32] The nation's 50 million anglers drive an industry worth $69.4 billion per year and are responsible for creating millions of jobs.[33] The number of hunters increased by 3 percent over the same time period, with a corresponding 7 percent increase in expenditures, to $12 billion.[34] Texas draws more hunters than does any other state, generating $1 billion in income annually. Thirty-nine percent of this money accrues to private landowners, with the rest going to restaurants, motels, and equipment suppliers.[35] Moreover, the number of "nonconsumptive" participants (hikers, birders, etc.) increased by 10 percent over the 1985–1991 period.[36] Today, birding has become one of North America's fastest-growing hobbies, with enthusiasts spending $18 billion per year on travel and equipment.[37] Overall, Department of Commerce data reveal that more than 108 million Americans (nearly two in every five) participated in some form of wildlife-related activity in 1991.[38]

Perceiving an economic opportunity, some forest products companies have capitalized on these trends. International Paper, for example, instituted a fee-based recreation program in its commercial forests in Texas, Louisiana, and Arkansas. The program charges hunters for access and leases small tracts of land on which families can park their motor homes and enjoy the woods. After three years, the company's revenues from the program tripled, growing to 25 percent of its total profits from the area. The Deseret Land and Livestock Company in southern Texas pursued a similar strategy to augment income from its cattle ranch. By charging fees, the company now makes 60 percent of its income from hunters and nature lovers.[39]

Looking beyond individual consumers to pay for standing forest stock, industry representatives are beginning to view international carbon markets as a potential source of income. An economic and environmental opportunity may lie in the emerging structure for controlling greenhouse gas emissions and curbing global climate change. Several industry experts, such as W. Henson Moore of the American Forest and Paper Association, argue that U.S. forest products companies own a current standing inventory of 60 billion metric tons of sequestered carbon, an amount equal to roughly forty years of total U.S. emissions. Products developed from these forests (paper, furniture, lumber, etc.) store another 265 million tons of carbon per year.[40] If carbon-emitting activities are to be taxed, forestry executives want carbon-containing activities to be rewarded through economic means. Such rewards could help encourage developing countries to join in the global carbon control initiative. They would reduce pressures for deforestation and direct economic capital to forest protection.

Who Are the Industry's Competitors?

With a decreasing supply of lumber available from federal lands, the price of timber has increased. Figure 10.3 shows the growth in sawtimber stumpage prices for several tree species from national forests.

While stumpage prices have shown this rapid growth, steel prices have remained relatively stable. As a result, the economics of building a house with steel versus the eco-

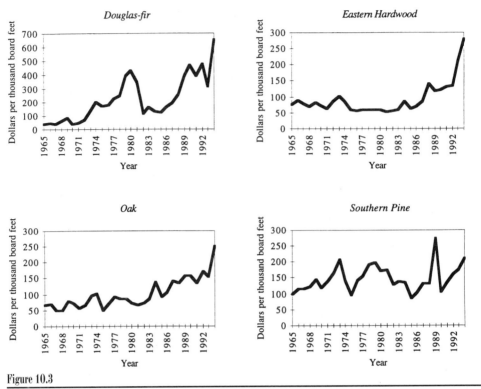

Figure 10.3

National Forest Sawtimber Stumpage Prices, 1965–1994

Source: J. Howard, *U.S. Timber Production, Trade, Consumption, and Price Statistics, 1965–1994,* General Technical Report no. FPL-GTR-98 (Madison, Wis.: U.S. Department of Agriculture, Forest Service, Forest Products Laboratory, 1997), 7.

nomics of using wood have become increasingly competitive since the mid-1990s. Attempting to capitalize on this economic opportunity, the steel industry has sponsored an advertising campaign touting the environmental benefits of steel and calling it the most recycled material in the world. One advertisement reads: "Framing an average size house with steel uses the equivalent of only six recycled cars. On the other hand, framing that same house with wood takes an acre of trees. . . . You've always trusted steel to protect you and your family. Now you can trust it to protect our environment."[41] With the environment as the new battleground, the forest products industry finds itself in direct competition with the steel industry.

Who Are the Industry's Allies?

Even on private lands, pressures are increasing for reduction of the volume of logs cut and change in the processes used in cutting them. Outraged by clear-cutting that has stripped woodlands bare, fouled streams, and destroyed wildlife habitats, legislatures in thirteen states have restricted logging practices on private lands.[42] In Maine, a public referendum to ban all clear-cutting was barely defeated in 1996. To gain assistance in preventing such restrictions on logging practices, many forest products companies are turning to alliances with former foes: environmental groups and the government. In 1997, for example, representatives of Crown Vantage Inc., a paper company based in Oakland, California, met with representatives from Boston's Appalachian Mountain Club and the federal government to develop an environmentally friendly logging plan for the company's 6,200 acres of forestland in New Hampshire. Formerly enemies in a conflict over the management of these forests, these new allies have developed a plan to limit cutting within 300 feet of rivers and streams and have instituted selective cutting programs in sensitive habitat. Crown Vantage estimates that its immediate yield in selected areas will drop to about $300 per acre.[43] But satisfying these important stakeholders will go a long way toward helping the company shape its business environment and maintain some of its operating freedom. With a similar objective in mind, Champion International instituted company-wide restrictions on logging within 330 feet of many woodland streams.

Although such changes at large companies are a step that pleases environmentalists, an equally important concern involves the practices of independent loggers, who supply, for example, as much as 85 percent of Crown Vantage's raw material. These independents are often one- or two-person operations with chain saws, a skidder to move logs, and a truck. Taking its environmental concerns to such suppliers, Crown Vantage is donating instructors and cash to a new logger-education program that aims to certify loggers by teaching safety and environmentally correct procedures. This will remain a tough sell, however, because many of these independents have been in business for decades and will resist change. As one logger said, "I've been in the woods since I was seven years old, operating with horses and motor skidder, so I already know what to do."[44] Despite such resistance, this example shows how environmental strategy is shifting from buyer to supplier.

Forest Products in Response to Institutional Change

Environmentalism can be seen to be redefining the business system of the forest products industry. New types of pressure from trade associations, buyers' groups, suppliers, major retailers, environmental NGOs, the government, international environmental organizations, the World Trade Organization, competing industries, the voting public, and hunters, birders, fishers, and hikers are all changing basic notions about the industry's raw materials, products, processes, competitors, and allies. This is far from an exhaustive list; the alterations within the industry could be extended to other aspects of business system redefinition as well. But on the whole, this example illustrates how environmentalism has already redefined many aspects of an industry's business system and penetrated many existing networks. The next example illustrates how those who wish to change the home construction industry to make it more environmentally friendly must change components of the business system in order to succeed.

Institutions as a Constraint: Environmentalism and the Home Construction Industry

What is a house?[45] Although traditional notions of shelter and comfort are not altered by environmentalism, several groups, such as the Department of Energy's Building America Program, the Center for Sustainable Building and Technology,[46] and the Green Development Services group of the Rocky Mountain Institute,[47] are attempting to change the way those things are achieved. Without compromising the amenities of a traditional home, the innovations these organizations are promoting work to integrate environmentally sound elements into both new and existing homes. To the home owner, many of these measures may go virtually unnoticed because quality would not be compromised. But unlike the situation in the forest products industry, which is being driven by emerging environmental concerns, adoption of environmentally sound elements in the home construction industry will require alterations in a business system that has yet to change. In this section, we first examine three categories of features of an environmentally sound home—energy use reduction, use of sustainable building materials, and water conservation—and then discuss the obstacles to their adoption that lie within the business system.

Energy Use Reduction

Because energy conservation also means reduced monthly utility bills, home owners are naturally more aware of the potential for reducing cost by conserving energy. One of the most efficient methods of reducing energy expenditures is the use of solar energy as a replacement for the conventional energy supplies of oil, gas, or electricity. Solar energy applications vary according to region. Complementing solar energy systems, other energy conservation opportunities include the use of shading and windbreaks, natural lighting, ventilation, energy-conserving windows, insulation, and energy-efficient appliances.

Solar Energy

Solar energy can be captured through either passive or active systems. Passive systems are designed to utilize solar radiation directly, whereas active solar technology uses a panel of silicon semiconductors to turn photons from the sun into electricity. At present, the installation cost for the latter systems, known as photovoltaic systems, is prohibitively high. Assuming no government subsidies, the cost of photovoltaics ranges from thirty to forty cents per kilowatt-hour (compared with four to five cents per kilowatt-hour for oil, gas, or coal) over the lifetime of the system. Photovoltaic systems become cost-effective only when competing against a high initial charge for extending power lines a great distance. Photovoltaic systems are also attractive in areas receiving a greater amount of sunlight because the payback period can be greatly reduced.

Passive solar systems use natural means and no mechanical energy to perform the heating function. Radiant energy from the sun is converted to heat, usually after transmission through window glazing. The heat is transferred throughout the house by natural means or is used directly in the building. There are two approaches to passive solar design. The simplest type of passive solar heating system is called "direct gain." Spaces are heated directly by sunlight passing through a relatively large surface, usually on the south side of the house. Components within the house such as carpets, furniture, walls, and other building elements then absorb the solar energy and convert it to heat, which radiates into the home. Direct gain passive solar design is effective at providing heat during daylight hours, but heat escapes from the building at night. To eliminate such heat loss, it is necessary to install insulation either within or behind the south-facing opening. The insulation can be a movable array of rigid insulation boards or a shade type of insulation that rolls up near the ceiling, depending on customer preference.

The second class of passive solar system is "indirect gain," in which solar radiation is converted to heat at an intermediate location and then released into the space by means of radiation, conduction, and convection processes. The most popular approach to this design is to install a water bag and solar pond along with movable insulation on the roof. In some cases, a greenhouse room with subterranean heat storage can be constructed on the south side of the house. The greenhouse is heated directly by sunlight and functions as a direct gain space. Heat can be stored in a deep gravel-bed floor and transferred into the house by means of conduction. The common wall that separates the greenhouse from the living unit performs heat storage as well as heat transfer. Movable insulation is required to prevent excessive heat loss from the greenhouse in the evening hours and during the winter months.

Shading and Windbreaks

Shading is the most effective method of reducing heat gain during summer, when the sun is positioned high in the sky, thus reducing the amount of energy needed to operate air-conditioning. Properly shaded houses have less need for costly air-conditioning during summer months yet allow sunlight to enter in the winter, when the sun is low in the sky. For example, shade trees can be planted on the south and west sides of the building to protect the end units of townhouses from solar radiation. The trees planted should be those that lose their leaves in winter, allowing the sunlight to enter, and then fill out again when summer arrives, providing the necessary shade. For houses subject to constant winter winds, energy saving can be further achieved through evergreen windbreaks, which can save as much as 10 percent of heating costs during winter. The location of windbreaks is the key to their effectiveness. Most cold winter winds come from the north or the west. Therefore, windbreaks should be located on these sides, extending to the east side where space permits. The south side should be left open for shade trees that allow the sun's radiation to enter during winter. Maximum wind reduction occurs at a distance four to six times the height of a windbreak tree. Rapidly growing species are best, those that reach one to one and one-half times the height of the house at maturity.

Natural Lighting

One important feature of energy conservation is reduced use of electricity in lighting the house. This can be achieved through the use of natural lighting. Passive solar systems and skylights are one method for accomplishing this task through the external shell of the home. Glass transoms and interior windows are a way to transmit the light internally. One creative option for accomplishing both simultaneously is the use of tubular skylight systems, which replace electric lighting during daytime and illuminate an area of as much as 400 square feet.[48] With tubular skylights, daylight passes through a clear acrylic dome on the roof or exterior wall and reflects down through a pipe with superreflective interior walls. Another translucent dome on the inside end of the pipe spreads light into the room more diffusely than does a conventional skylight. At an installation cost of approximately $200 per unit, tubular skylights can also be less expensive than conventional skylights, although the quality of the light may not be as good.

Ventilation

In a properly ventilated home, less energy is needed for heating and cooling. For one thing, natural ventilation is used during summer to allow prevailing winds to penetrate. The house should be designed so that it captures cross and upward ventilation. This ventilation allows fresh air to flow through and out of the house naturally, thus reducing the energy used for mechanical ventilation and reducing any contaminants from indoor air pollution. Mechanical ventilation systems are crucial for any house, but they are more important for a sustainable home, where air infiltration seals are so tight that only a small amount of fresh air can penetrate, increasing the risk of indoor air pollution. To solve this problem without wasting energy in heating and cooling, heat-recovery ventilation systems use the heated exhaust air from the house to heat the incoming cool, fresh air. This reduces the amount of energy used in heating. The system works reversibly during the summer, when it cools the incoming fresh air, thus reducing air-conditioning costs.

Windows

Windows are a key element of a passive solar heating system. In the average home, windows account for approximately 20 to 30 percent of heat loss. Therefore, window glazing and insulation are two of the most important components of an energy conservation program. The most energy-efficient windows are double glazed, with either air or an inert gas (such as argon) trapped between the two sealed panes. The trapped gas acts as an insulator. Although argon gas is better than air for this purpose, the window's energy efficiency is reduced over a twenty-year period as a result of gas escape. For further energy efficiency, windows can be layered with a low-emissivity metallic coating, which reflects most heat yet allows light to pass through. Windows that are more energy efficient are priced 10 percent higher than the high-quality version of standard double-glazed windows. To control costs, windows can be selected with various efficiencies on the basis of their intended application. On south-facing windows, normal double-paned glass could be used. To protect the house from the cold winds that come from the north and northeast, double-glazed windows insulated with argon gas and treated with a low-emissivity coating could be installed. On the west side of the house, which is usually subjected to strong sunlight in the afternoon, low-emissivity glass with heat mirrors could be installed. Heat mirrors reflect the sunlight, thus reducing heat radiation while allowing light to penetrate.

Insulation

Insulation of all walls, ceilings, attic spaces, and foundations is another crucial component of energy conservation. It isolates the house in terms of both temperature and sound. Insulation comes in many different forms, such as loose fill, rigid board, fiberglass blanket, and sprayed foam. Unfortunately, all types of insulation have both environmental limitations and benefits, balancing insulation value and toxic components.

For example, some of the highest-rated insulation emits small amounts of formaldehyde and volatile organic compounds, which are harmful or act as irritants to humans. The highest insulation rating (R-value) can be achieved through polyisocyanurate rigid board insulation (R-6.5 per inch). The standard insulation used by contractors is fiberglass batt insulation (R-3.2 per inch). Overall, a well-insulated home can realize energy savings of approximately 40 percent. For balancing cost, insulation value, and use of toxic compounds, rigid board made from synthetic foam blown with hydrochlorofluorocarbons (HCFCs), which are less ozone depleting than chlorofluorocarbons (CFCs), and cotton batt insulation, made from 75 percent recycled cotton fibers and 25 percent polyester, work best for lightweight interior walls. Looking to the future, Owens-Corning is experimenting with vacuum panels for ceilings that may rate as high as R-75 per inch.

Appliances

On average, the refrigerator accounts for one-third of the energy expended in a household. Recent, more energy-efficient refrigerator designs feature improved cabinet insulation, high-efficiency compressor and fans, and the use of HFC-134a instead of CFC-12 (Freon) as a refrigerant. These refrigerators, dubbed "superefficient" refrigerators, use 25 percent less electricity than the average ones. The operating cost of these refrigerators is less than $50 per year, compared with the industry average of $70 per year. The price, around $1,500, is comparable to the price of high-quality models that are not superefficient.

The oven in a sustainable home is a gas-fueled convection oven, and the furnace is a gas-fueled condensing or pulse furnace, which burns fuel more efficiently than other designs and minimizes heat loss through flue exhausts. Gas furnaces have been demonstrated to be as much as 70 percent more energy efficient than electric furnaces. The central air-conditioning system of a sustainable home runs (if one is installed at all) on HCFC-22, which is not as damaging to the ozone layer as are CFCs. Energy consumption in a sustainable home is further reduced by the use of compact fluorescent lamps, which can decrease lighting energy consumption by 40 percent.

Building Materials

On the whole, the sustainable home would be constructed from recycled building materials and would make use of nontoxic interior coatings and coverings, such as formaldehyde-free adhesives, coverings made from natural materials, and water-based, solvent-free paints. Materials would be manufactured with limited use of fossil fuels, would not pollute the air inside or outside the home, and at the end of the home's useful life, would be reusable or recyclable. Truly, there exists no such perfect material, but there are preferable building materials. These criteria can be applied to several types of material used in home construction.

Concrete

Conventional concrete is composed of three major components: aggregates (usually gravel, crushed stone, and sand), portland cement, and water. Portland cement is made from lime, silica, iron, and alumina (aluminum oxide). The manufacture of portland cement requires great inputs of energy and results in air pollution in the form of carbon dioxide emissions as well as an alkaline waste stream. There exist several variations on traditional concrete production methods, including incorporation of waste material (such as fly ash) into the aggregate, cogeneration of energy during the production process, and substitution of non–portland cement ingredients in the cementitious portion of the concrete. Some of these variations, such as substitution of blast furnace slag for a portion of the portland cement, can enhance the structural properties of the concrete while keeping slag and fly ash out of landfills.

Recycled Steel

Framing accounts for as much as 70 percent of the approximately 11,000 board feet of lumber used to build a typical house. Some sustainable homes use steel studs with a high proportion of recycled steel in their framing. Steel is one of the most recyclable materials on earth, it reduces demand on forest resources, and in many ways it is superior to wood. It is resistant to termites, rot, and ultraviolet light and hence requires no sealers or preservatives. Steel studs do not warp, bend, bow, absorb moisture, check, or crack, and they are noncombustible. They are stronger than wood, able to withstand 50,000 pounds per square inch of pressure, compared with 36,000 pounds per square inch for a conventional two-by-four. Steel is lighter than wood, and given its greater strength, fewer studs, joists, and rafters are required in standard home construction, thereby lowering transportation and handling costs. Finally, steel is priced comparably to wood, so few incremental costs are incurred by the home owner.

Roofing

There are many alternatives to standard cedar or asphalt shingles. While they may not have precisely the same charm and look as these materials, they are made from recycled or recyclable materials that can minimize the demand on forests and fossil fuel–based sources. These include "fiber-cement composite shingles; shakes made from small diameter and fast-growing species, or fiber reclaimed from wood waste; organic asphalt shingles made with a base of recycled 'mixed' waste paper; and roof shingles made from recycled plastic resins (which are recyclable too). If these are not appealing or right for the particular situation, then other types of roofing should be considered, such as clay tiles, fiber-cement composite slates, and recycled metal roof decking."[49] The James Hardie Building Products Inc. produces a fiber-cement roofing shingle in which much of the wood fiber comes from sawmill wastes. These products carry a 30-year warranty,[50] whereas most asphalt shingles come with a 10- to 15-year warranty. Classic Products makes a competing roofing material made from recycled aluminum that is capable of sustaining hurricane force winds and carries a lifetime warranty.[51]

Sealants

Caulks and sealants have many uses, including conserving energy in the home and consequently reducing the environmental pollution resulting from energy production. The average home has more than 200 square inches of cracks and gaps, which are believed to be the cause of 30 to 50 percent of total household heat loss. However, many of the chemicals used in manufacturing sealants are potentially toxic. Few are made of natural ingredients or ingredients low in volatile organic compounds (VOCs). Those considered safe for indoor use are products made with oleoresins, acrylic latex, polyurethane, silicone, and polysulfide. There is no significant price differential for these products.

Wallboard

Materials used in conventional wallboard are mainly composed of gypsum and paper. These materials cause concern because of pollutants emitted by the paper-milling industry, energy consumed during manufacturing, and questions regarding waste disposal and indoor air quality. Studies have shown that gypsum wallboard is a significant source of VOCs, including formaldehyde. Several wallboards on the market made from recycled materials, including gypsum, newsprint, and wood fiber, do not emit formaldehyde or other health-threatening pollutants. Gypsum is created as a by-product of fossil-fuel combustion and other industrial processes. Louisiana-Pacific's FiberBond fiber-reinforced gypsum board is made from gypsum, perlite, and recycled newspapers and telephone directories. This gypsum costs the same as other wallboards but does not threaten indoor air quality.

Flooring

Carpets, which are often made with phenolic resins and toxic adhesives, are a major source of indoor air pollution. One alternative to these materials is natural wool fibers, undyed and untreated, with a natural rubber latex backing. Wool carpeting is made from renewable resources, does not emit potentially toxic fumes, consumes less water during production, and generates less toxic wastewater. Wool carpeting is also extremely durable and long lasting.

The standard material for kitchen floors is vinyl; however, linoleum is a more attractive substitute, being made from natural powdered cork, linseed oil (made from flaxseed), wood resin, and wood flour pressed onto a backing of burlap. Unlike vinyl, linoleum is not made with fossil fuels and does not emit VOCs and toxins, either during manufacturing or after installation. Linoleum is produced from self-generating materials, is biodegradable, and is in many ways superior to vinyl. It is extremely durable and long lasting. But because vinyl flooring is cheaper (by roughly $2 per square foot), linoleum is no longer produced in the United States and must be imported from Europe. One downside of linoleum is that it requires more energy to produce than vinyl flooring.

Ceramic Tile

Sustainable ceramic tile applications rely on materials made from recycled glass. Terra-Green Technologies, for example, produces tiles that contain at least 55 percent recycled postindustrial and postconsumer glass. The manufacturing method employs no toxic substances and does not generate toxic waste. Heat generated in the firing process is recaptured for use in other manufacturing processes, which minimizes energy consumption. The ceramic waste materials that are by-products of the production process are themselves recovered and recycled. There is a price premium for these tiles of roughly $1.50 per square foot over the $3.50 per square foot for conventional tile.

Paint

Paint is used on almost every surface in the home and is the major cause of indoor air pollution. Paints are generally made of heavy metals for pigment, with either petroleum-based materials or water as the carrier. In the sustainable home, the preferred paint products are those containing no VOCs. However, these products come at a high premium, averaging approximately $24.95 per gallon versus $16.50 per gallon for a contractor's standard grade. However, these VOC-free paints are more durable, providing premium quality as well as environmental performance.

Wood Trim

Wood for the sustainable home, when possible, is purchased from companies certified by Scientific Certification Systems, SmartWood, or the Forest Stewardship Council, to be certain that both tropical and domestic woods have been harvested with minimal damage to forest ecosystems. But overall, a minimum of solid wood is used in a sustainable home. Instead, wood substitutes are sought, such as wood laminates and recycled plastic-wood composites, such as Timbrex and Trex Wood-Polymer lumber. Such products can be used in window trim, decks, columns, railings, landscape pavers, and boxes and fencing. Alternative forms of hardboard siding are also available, such as a siding product manufactured by the Abitibi-Price Corporation that contains 85 percent recovered wood fiber and roundwood, materials that were formerly wasted by-products of sawmills. For example, roundwood unsuitable for dimensional lumber because it is too small, knotty, or uneven is used by hardboard mills. Branches and treetops are also manufactured into hardboard, as are wood chips salvaged from land that has been cleared for roads and developments and sawdust from furniture manufacturers, mill shops, and other sawmills. Finally, exterior doors can be manufactured with waste material from lumber mills and sawmills. These doors are often more durable than solid-core doors and can be as much as 50 percent cheaper (approximately $30, compared with $75 for a solid-core door).

Water Conservation

Decreased water consumption leads to lower water and sewer expenses as well as decreased energy expenditures for heating water. Although these concerns vary by region, water usage is becoming an important consideration in some areas where the water table has been significantly drawn down. Water use can be minimized through the use of low-flow fixtures and appliances, composting toilets, gray-water reuse systems, and drinking-water filtration systems.

Fixtures

Low-flow shower heads, low-flush toilets, and faucet aerators have become the industry standard in new home construction, often driven by federal requirements for flow rates. Low-flush toilets use 1.6 gallons per flush, a federally mandated criterion. Faucets should be fitted with aerators, which reduce water-heating energy consumption by controlling flow rate. Bathroom faucets should have aerators that deliver one-half to one gallon of water per minute; kitchen faucets should have a flow rate of two to four gallons per minute.

Composting Toilets

Composting toilet systems were once found only in the dwellings of dedicated environmentalists and in backcountry cottages, but modern, efficient systems have received the approval of the National Sanitation Foundation and may be attractively incorporated into any home. For a family of four, the composting chamber needs to be emptied only twice per year; the resultant compost is inoffensive and safe and may be used as a soil conditioner. These systems are available in waterless and ultra-low-flow (one pint per flush) models and incorporate temperature-controlled heating elements and variable-speed fans for efficient oxygen transfer and optimal temperature control in the composting chamber. Power for the heating element and fans can be provided via electric or battery systems; for the battery systems, appropriately sized photovoltaic panels can be included for recharging. Liquid is removed from the system by evaporation or, in the low-flow models, through a filter system and an external drainage gallery. Cost considerations may make composting toilet systems prohibitive in urban areas. The systems are most attractive for homes being constructed in areas not serviced by municipal sewage systems. In these instances, the alternative cost of building a septic system and field make the composting toilet a prudent economic option.[52]

Gray-Water Systems

Gray water, the used water from showers, sinks, and appliances, may be collected separately from black water (sewage) and used for lawn irrigation, car washing, and other appropriate outdoor water uses as well as toilet flushing, dramatically decreasing a household's overall water usage by means of internal recycling. A gray-water system requires separate drainage pipes, filter, and storage tank. The water savings that can be realized with a gray-water system depend greatly on the amount of outdoor water use, which is largely a function of climate.

Appliances

Overall, efficient appliances and efficient lighting can lead to a potential reduction in energy demand of 50 to 75 percent. Water and energy use are greatly affected by the home owner's choice of dishwasher, clothes washer, and clothes dryer. For example, heating of water for an automatic dishwasher can represent about 80 percent of the energy required to run the appliance. The average dishwasher requires a temperature of 140 degrees Fahrenheit for optimum cleaning, but such a high setting results in excessive standby heat loss. Dishwashers can be built or set to run at a water temperature of 120 degrees Fahrenheit with a choice of shorter cycles. Further, good insulation can both reduce energy use and result in a very quiet wash. For household laundry, horizontal-axis, front-loading washers use far less water (and hence energy) than do competing models. The front-loading design allows more thorough drainage by means of spinning, thus reducing the energy required for operation of the dryer. ASKO, a Swedish appliance manufacturer, offers ultra-efficient dishwashers, clothes washers, and clothes dryers that have been ranked most efficient by both the American Council for an Energy-Efficient Economy and *Consumer Reports* magazine.[53] ASKO's dishwasher uses only 4.6 gallons of water per load, and its clothes washer uses only 14 gallons. The payback time for the dishwasher is less than three years.

Certain minor modifications and features in a house's water-heating system can also yield greater energy efficiency. These include installation of a timer, to turn the heater down at night and up in the morning, and insulation of water heaters and water pipes. These additions will result in lower standby heat loss.

Home Construction as a Driver of Institutional Change

To many, these types of environmental amenities might seem to be a great idea and an attractive business opportunity. Yet the obstacles to gaining their acceptance are not strictly technological, strategic, or organizational. They are primarily institutional. A builder cannot simply decide unilaterally to offer sustainable homes and expect to yield rapid profits from this untapped market segment. Key constituents of the business system must be persuaded to endorse rather than resist their adoption.

First, *building inspectors* are often resistant to many of the innovations integral to an environmentally sound home. They may be unfamiliar with these deviations from normal building practice and are, therefore, hesitant to approve them. Or in many cases the source of their resistance can be found in the building codes themselves. Many regional building codes, for example, do not allow the installation of composting toilet systems or gray-water systems. These systems simply have not developed enough of a track record to have been brought to the attention of codifiers as reliable alternatives.

Second, *architects* and *landscape designers* are also often unfamiliar with the principles of environmentally sound architecture and therefore do not integrate these principles into new home designs. They may not know of the materials and equipment that exist, and more important, they may not understand the interactions among different systems. For example, gray-water installations must be designed with an appreciation for the types of plants that will be used in landscaping. Care must be taken to ensure safe operation with regard to water quality and increased salt and nutrient load on lawns.[54] Similarly, passive solar systems must be designed with an appreciation for associated features related to ventilation, shade trees, and windbreaks.

Third, *builders* and *subcontractors* may be unfamiliar with new equipment and require special training, which adds to the uncertainty and cost of the system. For example, past problems associated with ultra-low-flow toilets have been due to inappropriate dimensions of pipes installed by plumbers. With such uncertainties, many builders may resist installing equipment in fear of unpredictable warranty service. Many regions have only a handful of builders who understand environmentally sound building techniques and are willing to offer them to the public.

Fourth, *suppliers* of equipment are often difficult to locate and may lack the economies of scale needed to offer competitive pricing. Prices for "green" equipment will remain high as long as sales do not meet the economy-of-scale production levels that will bring them down. But as earth friendly homes become more common and the technologies for environmentally friendly materials and appliances improve, costs should drop below the average 5 percent premium that green features generally add to the cost of a new home today.[55]

Fifth, *retail outlets* and *wholesale outlets* are a critical component of the business system of new home construction. Retail outlets play a major role in ensuring that start-up manufacturers of green products can maintain the feedback, high-visibility marketing, and cash flow necessary to stay in business and lower manufacturing costs.

Sixth, *banks* are often unwilling to provide financing for certain environmentally sound technologies, fearing that they are unproven or believing that they are unnecessary. For example, lenders generally will not provide financing for photovoltaic systems if more traditional (and more certain) grid-connected power is available.

Finally, *home buyers* may resist buying products and services that lack a track record or that appeal to a sense of values that they do not share. First, of course, is the question of whether home owners will pay a premium for an environmentally sound home. As in all environmentally friendly products, such a willingness to pay is difficult to measure. In a nationwide survey conducted by *Professional Builder and Remodeler* magazine, 31 percent of respondents said that they were willing to pay $1,000 to $1,999 more for an environmentally healthy home. This balances with the estimated average of 25 percent "true-blue greens" and "greenback greens" in the general population, as measured by S. C. Johnson & Son, Inc. and Roper Starch Worldwide, Inc., who will allow environmental considerations to alter their buying decisions (see chapter 5).[56]

A major problem in home buying, however, is a tendency to overdiscount the future. Although many elements of an environmentally sound home (such as composting toilet systems and insulation) may have a short payback horizon, they may still fail to gain market acceptance. In today's world, the average home owner may not remain in the same location long enough to realize the savings and therefore will not invest in them. Even in the case of appliances, which are portable and for which the payback period can be less than five years, home owners are often unwilling to make the initial investment. Further, those who buy homes as investment properties may not see a benefit in energy-saving attributes because it is the renter of the property who will pay the energy and heating bills.

Overcoming Obstacles

Some organizations are working to eliminate these obstacles. For example, to improve the track record of environmentally sound homes and provide information and education about them, the Center for Sustainable Building and Technology has instituted a national public education program by retrofitting a series of demonstration homes in each of the Environmental Protection Agency's ten regions. The first Sustainable Housing Demonstration Project was completed in 1999 in Cambridge, Massachusetts.[57] The retrofitted house has a 50 to 75 percent reduction in energy use, a 50 percent reduction in water consumption, and a 75 percent reduction in household waste as a result of composting and recycling. The home is now open to builders, architects, designers, building inspectors, and others as a showcase for the potential of environmentally sound design and construction. Similarly, the Remanufacturing Industries Council International sponsors the American Green Dream House contest, annually giving away a "green" home to a contest entrant who pledges to recycle and use recycled products.[58]

To provide incentives for builders to construct and market environmentally sound homes, the Home Builders Association of Metro Denver and the Home Builders Association of Kitsap County (near Seattle, Washington)[56] have launched builder-initiated rating systems to reward environmentally responsible design and construction. The programs award points for eighty-five environmentally friendly measures in eight categories—adherence to "green" codes and regulations; appropriate site treatment; reduction, reuse, and recycling of materials; use of resource-efficient products; maximization of energy efficiency; promotion of good air quality and health; proper hazardous waste management; and environmentally responsible operation and maintenance.[57] The point total determines the home's rating as either one, two, or three stars. A three-star rating is difficult to achieve and usually involves some form of price increase, but one- and two-star ratings generally have no effect on price. Suppliers, subcontractors, and real estate agents can also take part in the program as "participating partners." All involved can expect to gain a marketing advantage for building or selling an environmentally friendly new home or remodeling project.

One drastic way to gain buy-in from home owners is to convince people to alter their beliefs about lifestyle. For example, an ecologically sound cohousing development was opened in Cambridge, Massachusetts, creating a collective that shares environmentally friendly amenities. Although this involved an alteration in lifestyle that many people may be unwilling to make, the collective professes to have cost 15 percent less than conventional housing and to use 60 percent less energy.[59] The development houses eighty-five residents who own their own units (such as studios for $85,000 and four-bedroom townhouses for $300,000) but share communal areas for dining, cooking, doing laundry, reading, and meeting. In this way, the community has no duplication of resources (such as having eighty-five washing machines) and promotes a more communal lifestyle. Further, the complex was built on a brownfield site; it is heated and cooled by a ground-source heat pump, which extracts water from the ground; and recycled materials were used in the building process.

In the end, the definition of what is a house is in flux. Activists, architects, builders, and suppliers are trying to change the way homes are designed, constructed, and bought by developing a new set of institutions to deliver this product to the consumer. It is too soon to say whether their efforts will succeed. But their efforts cannot be ignored or written off as separate and inconsequential for the home-building industry. This market may emerge as an important subset of the overall housing market, or it may represent industry-wide shifts through changes in building codes and industry standards. Forward-looking business managers will monitor the progress of this movement for future business opportunities.

Conclusion

Seeing the opportunities in environmental issues requires managers to see products and processes in a new perspective as redefined by the environmental issues. This chapter offered just two examples of such a shift in thinking, but endless scenarios are possible (see box 10.1). The key is to identify the source of environmental pressures within a particular industry and then deduce their effects on taken-for-granted business processes. Further, however, competitive environmental strategy is not simply an alteration of mind-set. It involves more than looking beyond that which is taken for granted and per-

Box 10.1. What Is an Oil Leak?

What is an oil leak? It used to be that an oil leak was an accepted aspect of any oil storage system. The oil stain in the driveway was an inevitable fixture of every suburban home. The joke with riders of Harley-Davidson motorcycles riders was, "How do you know when your Harley needs oil? When it stops leaking." This acceptance of leaks carried over into industrial processes as well. Many of the oldest oil refineries in the United States have several feet of raw product floating on top of the groundwater that lies beneath the facility. In many cases, workers who venture into an excavated pit in such facilities must breathe bottled air. But more recently, conceptions of what is an oil leak have started to shift. This shift has been brought about by consideration of some of the broader institutional perspectives of spilled oil.

For example, Carl Reller of the Alaska Health Project considered the definition of an oil leak from several perspectives and came up with some interesting answers.[*] First, he estimated that more than 100 million gallons of lubricating and hydraulic oil are lost each year in the United States as a result of leakage alone. To put this number in perspective, that is about equal to the Trans-Alaska Pipeline dumping its entire contents on the ground for two days. More important, he pointed out that an oil leak is more than an environmental hazard and a loss of raw materials. It is wasted money. Reller developed a list of what a leak costs in dollars, based on the number of seconds it takes for a drop to drip (see table 10.1). Although he considered only the cost of the oil and the cleanup, other stakeholders may assign other costs to such leaks. For example, insurance companies may view leaking flanges as a sign of poor operational management and higher liability risk. Further, leaks may create an unsafe environment for workers, both increasing liability and lowering worker morale. Banks may also view leaks as operational mismanagement and allow this connection to temper their loan procedures, altering the company's cost of capital. Prevention involves instituting a program for inspecting and tightening pipe seals, joints, and flanges.

In a related way, engineering managers may reconsider the definition of some basic industrial processes in the face of environmental protection. For example, in 1993 the Amoco Pipeline Company, faced with increasing controls under the Clean Air Act Amendments of 1990, began to reconsider the definition of a pipeline. Originally designed as a system to transport oil across the country in the quickest manner possible,

Table 10.1. An Oil Leak as Dollars and Cents

Rate	Gallons per Year[a]	Dollars per Year Lost[b]	Tons of Contaminated Soils[c]	Solid Disposal Cost[d]
drop/10 seconds	40	$240	150	$12,000
drop/5 seconds	80	$480	300	$24,000
drop/second	410	$2,460	1,500	$120,000
3 drops/second	1,200	$7,200	4,500	$360,000
stream that breaks into drips	8,600	$51,600	32,000	$2,560,000

[a] Drops approximately 11/64 inch diameter
[b] Replacement lubricating oil at $1.50/quart
[c] Average 1000 ppm total petroleum hydrocarbons
[d] Based on excavating soil in Anchorage is acceptable for recycling into asphalt. Actual cost could be 2 to 7 times greater if the soil has too much silt/clay or contains other toxic wastes such as chlorinated solvents of PCBs.

Source: Alaska Department of Environmental Conservation

(continues)

Box 10.1. *Continued*

the pipeline system is now being reconsidered in terms of the environmental and liability risks it poses. The system, as designed, encompasses 12,000 miles of pipeline throughout the Midwest and the southern United States. The pipeline contains roughly 1,500 pumps, 20,000 valves, 50,000 flanges, and 1,400 sampling points as well as 562 tanks that store 37 million barrels of oil. The entire system moves about 550 million barrels of oil per year, with an estimated evaporative loss of 50,000 barrels per year. This amounts to only 0.009 percent of the entire throughput but has a value of approximately $900,000 (at $18 per barrel).

Through careful analysis, it was found that only 0.4 percent of these losses came from pipe flanges. The rest came from the system's 562 active storage tanks. In considering how to cut back on those emissions and comply with the requirements of the Clean Air Act Amendments, the company explored several options. First, all the non-white tanks could be painted white. Because darker tanks get hotter in the sun, the lighter color would cut down on emissions by 10 percent, to 45,000 barrels per year. Second, the company could retrofit all fixed-roof tanks with floating roofs. Floating roofs minimize the air space above the standing oil and thereby reduce evaporation. This change could reduce emissions by another 90 percent, to 4,800 barrels per year. Although the costs are quite high on an absolute basis, the potential costs of millions of dollars for permits and emissions charges imposed by the Clean Air Act Amendments altered the economics of the calculation and drove such technical improvements in the pipeline system. Looking even deeper, this analysis drove the company to reconsider the need for many of the tanks in the system. Many of the tanks had been built when redundancy may have optimized engineering efficiency, but that redundancy now creates tremendous inefficiencies and environmental implications. Further, some of these redundant tanks were built at the turn of the twentieth century and may pose serious liability risks. In the end, the company discovered that 24 percent of emissions came from the ten worst tanks. Because these represented only 1.7 percent of pipeline capacity, eliminating them from the system was an extremely cost-effective solution.

* C. Reller, "Waste Minimization Tip: Dollars Down the Drain by Leaks and Drips," *DEC Pollution Prevention Bulletin* 1, no. 1 (March–April 1991): 1.

ceiving the opportunities that lie just within reach. Strategic opportunity must be grounded in the drivers that create it. At times, companies may not be able to take advantage of a shift in environmental technology unless they can force others to follow. For example, in 1991, the Atlantic Richfield Company (ARCO) developed a new gasoline formulation called EC-X that was expected to reduce some automobile emissions by as much as 50 percent. However, the formulation also would have cost as much as sixteen cents more per gallon.[60] The company's announcement of the breakthrough was accompanied by an announcement that it had no plans to introduce the product at the pump. Instead, the announcement appears to have been meant as a signal to the California Air Resources Board that the technology exists. By making the announcement, ARCO was able to influence the board to set more stringent standards that all companies would have to comply with but that ARCO was already prepared to meet.

Finding opportunities in environmental strategy involves reading, understanding, and influencing the sources of institutional change within the business system. With the proper cues and the vision to see how the business environment is changing and how environmental protection is finding a more prominent place in it, one can find new opportunities. But with that vision, one should also be cognizant of the limitations that are simultaneously created, and with that cognition comes a realization of what is possible given the existing context and what further possibilities can be revealed if the firm can trigger change within that context. The important lesson is that environmental strategy involves an alteration of the firm's strategy, its organizational design, and its external environment. All three are interrelated. As such, in this final chapter on the importance of strategically monitoring and managing the external environment, this book has come full circle. Environmental strategy is driven by demands that emerge from within the business system and that are embodied within the organizational structure and strategy of the firm. Similarly, a self-directed strategy may emerge from within the organizational structure of the firm, but its success will often require an alteration of the business system of which it is a part. The next and final chapter will sum up the concept of environmental strategy, consider its full scope within the context of the issue of global climate change, and discuss how this relates to the energy issue of sustainable development.

Further Reading

Demkin, J., ed., American Institute of Architects. *Environmental Resource Guide*. New York: John Wiley & Sons, 1996.

Environmental Building News (monthly newsletter on environmentally responsible design and construction). R.R. 1, Box 161, Brattleboro, VT 05301; (802) 257-7300. Internet: http://www.ebuild.com.

Lopez Barnett, D., and W. Browning. *A Primer on Sustainable Building*. Snowmass, Colo.: Rocky Mountain Institute, 1993.

Marinelli, J., and P. Bierman-Lytle. *Your Natural Home: The Complete Sourcebook and Design Manual for Creating a Healthy, Beautiful, and Environmentally Sensitive House*. New York: Little, Brown and Company, 1995.

Pearson, D., ed. *The Natural House Catalog: Everything You Need to Create an Environmentally Friendly Home*. New York: Simon & Schuster, Fireside, 1996.

Chapter 11

ENVIRONMENTAL STRATEGY AND SUSTAINABLE DEVELOPMENT

Analyzing the environmental movement, Anthony Downs (now at the Brookings Institution) saw "a systematic cycle of heightened public interest and then increasing boredom with major issues," which moved through five stages: (1) after receiving initial concerned attention, (2) the issue would enjoy growing widespread enthusiasm, but (3) the true costs of significant progress would then become apparent, and in response, (4) public interest would decline such that (5) it would be replaced by another issue in the public eye.[1] He identified environmentalism to be in the fourth stage, moving into the fifth, and predicted that the intensity of public environmental interest was about to inexorably decline.[2] His article was written in 1972.

Given the short memory span of the American public, Downs's argument is internally logical. Yet obviously, history has proven his prognosis wrong. The important question is why. The answer lies in the evolution of the meaning of environmentalism. Through the introduction of new constituents and new conceptions, environmentalism has been continually redefined. What Downs called ecology in 1972 has evolved successively into environmental management, waste minimization, pollution prevention, product stewardship, eco-efficiency, environmental strategy, and sustainable development. These evolving conceptions of corporate environmentalism are the product of new perspectives on environmental problems and an expanding constituency defining both how to view these problems and what the appropriate solutions should be. What environmental protection means today is far different from what it meant twenty, ten, or even five years ago, and, more importantly, it is far different than what it will mean tomorrow.

In fact, today environmental protection has evolved to such a point that the business manager need not even believe in the validity of environmental issues to take them seriously as a business concern. Environmental and economic interests are merging. The two realms are no longer separate: What matters for corporate decision makers is that key business constituents such as insurance companies, investors, banks, buyers, suppliers, customers, and others possess concern for the environment and translate it through core business channels. Environmental protection is becoming less and less an environmental issue and more an issue of risk management, capital acquisition, and consumer demand, among others. As such, it is becoming a composite of core organizational functions, no longer distinct from the central objectives of the firm. In each case, the firm already has a structure and a language with which to conceptualize the issue and formulate a response. By realizing this fit, firms can begin to see environmental issues as something internally manageable rather than externally directed. The company must make the cultural shift from environmental management to environmental strategy by diffusing environmental responsibilities throughout the organization.

The model in figure 11.1 is not static. The merger of environmental protection and economic growth continues. New concerns and new awareness are driving environmental concerns deeper into core business networks and therefore deeper into the core objectives of the firm. Just as we may now look back with amazement at the practices of past generations ("the solution to pollution is dilution," ocean dumping of radioactive wastes, inundation of neighborhoods with DDT), future generations may look back with similar amazement at the practices we take for granted today. It is fair to say that there may never be a static definition of a "green" company. There will be only notions of how companies are changing in response to an evolving economic, social, and political environment. Thus, corporate managers will want to consider both how far this intersection process has gone and what shape it may take in the future.

Some propose that the intersection process is nearly complete and that corporate environmentalism is moving on to other issues. One article notes that "the year 1998 is somewhat of a watershed for environmental management. With several years' implementation under their belts, leading companies have more or less mastered the art of environmental auditing and internalized the logic of continuous improvement. Few now question the rationale of sound environmental performance or the consensus that a robust environmental management system (EMS) is a proxy for good management."[3]

Is this an accurate depiction of the present state of environmental strategy? Have the circles in figure 11.1 intersected to their fullest extent, creating a critical mass for corporate change? This may be the state of affairs within some leading firms, but the intersection process will not be complete until all relevant components of the business network occupy this overlapping space. Although some companies may, for example, view a robust environmental management system (EMS) as a proxy for good management, the important question is whether insurance companies, mutual fund managers, individual

Environmental Strategy

Economic Growth

Environmental Protection

Figure 11.1

The Intersection of Business and Environmental Interests: *Environmental Strategy*

investors, and bankers make this connection. The entire institutional system, not just individual companies, must integrate environmental protection into its driving objectives.

Although it would be premature to suggest that the merger between environmental and business interests has run its course, its trajectory is clear and cannot be stopped. Competitive environmental strategy involves identifying that trajectory and staying ahead of the change it creates. Decision makers must consider the future form of environmental demands and attempt to drive them in ways that will fit with their own objectives. At a 1998 conference at Northwestern University, several senior executives identified some important points about this task:

> *Steven Percy, chairman and chief executive officer, BP America, Inc.:* "We believe that there is nothing that is really proprietary about environmental strategy. Knowledge moves pretty fast and it's about being ahead of the curve, but also understanding that the curve is going to keep beating you so you have to keep running pretty fast. By collaborating, sharing ideas, you are actually moving that much faster. You are at the leading edge and you are benefiting from that."

> *G. Mustafa Mohataren, chief economist, General Motors Corporation:* "To some extent, I agree with you that there is not that much proprietary technology. But, don't sell short the amount of competition that goes on. To some extent, you collaborate as an insurance policy. There are a number of technologies out there. We don't know which technology at the end of the day will prevail. So if we identify a competitor as being advanced in a particular technology while we are much more advanced in a different technology, it pays both of us to share what we've accomplished because neither one knows which technology is going to succeed in the end. I wouldn't be sitting here if I knew the answer as to which technology would prevail in the end."

> *John Creighton, retired chief executive officer and president, Weyerhaeuser Company:* "I can see a great deal of sharing in the basic processes and that you try and differentiate yourself as you get closer to your customer. But, we are part of an industry. We are going to be regulated, not as a company, but as an industry. I think it makes a lot of sense if we've got something in our basic process to bring the rest of the industry along, we share it. If it's patentable, we'll patent it and get royalties. I think that because the industry is looked at as a whole, there is a lot of advantage in sharing and pulling the industry forward with us."

> *Amory Lovins, director of research and vice president, Rocky Mountain Institute:* "I think Steve [Percy] is right, and I would go further. What's critical in the efficiency revolution is not the technology, it's the design mentality. The winners will be like those that Edwin Land talked about when he said, 'People who seem to have had a new idea have often simply stopped having an old idea.' They will be the ones with the most integrative designs and the ones that are most open to collaboration with a wide range of other stakeholders that they may not have previously talked to."[4]

In the end, environmental strategy requires the firm to stay ahead of a constantly moving curve by collaborating and sharing ideas with environmental nongovernmental organizations (NGOs), the government, capital markets, and others so that new possibilities not easily visible through the perspectives of the single organization can become clear. To the extent that individual gain is limited by the reputation of the industry, it also involves working with industry competitors. And it is about both having new ideas and letting go of old ones.

The chief executive officer of E. I. du Pont de Nemours and Company, John Krol, sees environmental protection as "the major business opportunity" at the end of the millennium.[5] But to see this opportunity, the manager must first let go of the old idea of environmental protection and economic growth as mutually exclusive. Shifting from environmental management to environmental strategy involves both the emergence of a new idea and the breakdown of an old one. Companies such as S. C. Johnson & Son, Inc., the Minnesota Mining and Manufacturing Company (3M), the Dow Chemical Company, the Weyerhaeuser Company, and Interface, Inc. have begun to make this shift. Gilbert Hedstrom, managing director for the environmental consulting practice of Arthur D. Little, Inc., said: "Environmental considerations for these companies have become a fundamental part of their business strategy. . . . They're saying 'Don't just green your company—commercialize environmentalism.'"[6] As an illustration of how things can be seen in a new way, we can analyze both the opportunities in a present-day environmental issue—climate change—and the opportunities in an issue that lurks on the horizon—sustainable development.

The Business Strategy of Global Climate Change

What is global climate change? It seems a straightforward question. At its most basic level, it is a *scientific* issue. The earth's atmosphere creates a natural greenhouse effect that, like a greenhouse constructed for plants, traps the sun's heat and keeps it warmer inside. (Strictly speaking, the mechanism of a greenhouse building is different because its elevated temperature is more a result of the glass structure's trapping of warm air than a result of reflecting heat. Nevertheless, the analogy is helpful.) Visible light passes through the atmosphere, striking the earth's surface and heating it. This surface heat radiates back up as infrared light. Naturally occurring "greenhouse gases" absorb part of the infrared light in the lower atmosphere, keeping the earth warmer. But human activities are increasing the concentrations of greenhouse gases—most notably carbon dioxide (CO_2) but also methane (CH_4), nitrous oxide (N_2O), and tropospheric (near-surface) ozone (O_3). Atmospheric CO_2 levels began to increase in the nineteenth century with the industrial revolution and are expected to double preindustrial levels by the year 2065. Such increases are expected to alter the global climate. Commonly predicted effects include drier weather in midcontinental areas (including the U.S. Midwest), sea-level rise, more violent storms, and northward migration of vector-borne tropical diseases and climate-sensitive species.[7] Although most climatologists consider these effects plausible, they cannot predict with certainty whether they will occur or the full extent to which they can be attributed directly to human activities.

Despite this uncertainty, the Intergovernmental Panel on Climate Change—the scientific research organization created by the United Nations to study climate change—concluded in 1995 that "the balance of evidence suggests a discernible human influence on the global climate and that climate is expected to continue to change over the next century."[8] Although there were dissenting views, the report was supported by more than two thousand scientists in more than one hundred countries. With this pronouncement, climate change became an *international policy* issue.

In December 1997, representatives from the developed countries of the world met in Kyoto, Japan, to discuss reductions in greenhouse gas emissions. After two weeks of deliberation, 140 countries agreed to reduce their emissions of heat-trapping gases by an average of 5.2 percent below 1990 levels between 2008 and 2012. With this treaty (the Kyoto Protocol, see chapter 3), the issue of climate change became one of *domestic policy* and therefore one of *corporate strategy.*

Any attempt to limit emissions of greenhouse gases will have a direct effect on the price of energy. Any change in the price of energy will have a direct effect on the cost structure of virtually every sector of the economy. Some economic models predict a cost to gross domestic product of nearly 2 percent, an amount roughly equal to the $150 billion per year presently spent on all environmental regulatory programs in the United States. But other models using more optimistic assumptions predict that the gross domestic product could rise by an equal amount. A report by the World Resources Institute noted that 80 percent of the variance in these economic models is caused by seven key assumptions, as shown in figure 11.2.

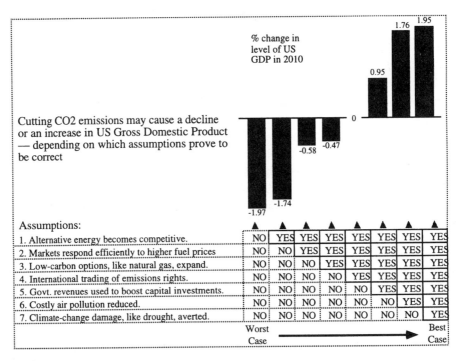

Assumptions:	Worst Case							Best Case
1. Alternative energy becomes competitive.	NO	YES	YES	YES	YES	YES	YES	YES
2. Markets respond efficiently to higher fuel prices	NO	NO	YES	YES	YES	YES	YES	YES
3. Low-carbon options, like natural gas, expand.	NO	NO	NO	YES	YES	YES	YES	YES
4. International trading of emissions rights.	NO	NO	NO	NO	YES	YES	YES	YES
5. Govt. revenues used to boost capital investments.	NO	NO	NO	NO	NO	YES	YES	YES
6. Costly air pollution reduced.	NO	NO	NO	NO	NO	NO	YES	YES
7. Climate-change damage, like drought, averted.	NO	NO	NO	NO	NO	NO	NO	YES

Figure 11.2

How Climate Change Controls May Affect the Economy

Source: D. Stipp, "The Cost of Cooling It," *Fortune,* 8 December 1997, 129. © 1997 Time Inc. All rights reserved. Reprinted with permission.

Some of these assumptions depend on corporate action, such as the development of competitive forms of alternative energy and the expanded use of low-carbon fuels such as natural gas. Others depend on policy makers and the ultimate form of the final treaty, such as the development of international trading in emissions rights (much like the tradable permit program discussed in chapter 2) and the use of government tax breaks to stimulate investments in low-emission technologies. Finally, some assumptions depend on consumers, such as whether the economy will respond efficiently to higher energy prices and whether people will drive less or lower their thermostats if the cost of energy goes up. In each case, the issue is less environmental and more related to key business constituents.

For the corporation, the strategy of climate change involves making decisions under conditions of uncertainty. This uncertainty takes several forms, and their inclusion in the final negotiated treaty is critical if companies are to respond strategically. First, climate change can be thought of as an issue of *capital asset management.* Corporations invest more than $700 billion per year in new plants and equipment and evaluate the profitability of those investments on the basis of an expected useful life span. Premature retirement of that capital stock is a recipe for economic disaster. Forcing technologies to become obsolete before their time threatens corporate viability in terms of both manufacturing and technology development. Instead, competitive climate change strategy involves the transition to cleaner technologies at a pace that is economically and technologically appropriate. Rather than precise timetables for climate controls to be mandated, users and developers of technology need extended time horizons to plan for, develop, and perfect substitutes. The treaty proposed in Kyoto allows a four-year time horizon (2008–2012) for meeting emission reduction goals. Is this time period adequate? Many are now pushing for even greater flexibility by granting credit for early reductions between now and 2008.[9]

Second, climate change can be thought of as a matter of *market economics.* Companies make capital investments wherever the expected return is greatest. Competitive climate change strategy involves making investments wherever the most emissions reductions can be achieved at the lowest economic cost. If it costs $100 per ton to eliminate carbon emissions in the United States and $5 per ton to eliminate carbon emissions in China, competitive U.S. companies will seek to make the Chinese investment and receive domestic credit. Termed joint implementation, this promotes technology transfer to the developing world while ensuring domestic companies an economic return on such transfers. For example, power generation in the developing world is expected to increase by 45 percent from 1993 to 2008. These countries may choose to build plants with the cheapest technology in terms of both capital outlays and fuel source. But joint implementation in the final negotiated climate agreement will shift market economics of power equipment to encourage the transfer of more energy efficient, low polluting, and higher costing technology to overseas projects.

Third, climate change can be thought of as an issue of *global competitiveness.* The treaty proposed in Kyoto does not push for the early entry of developing countries. This exclusion was based on the ideas that (1) developed countries are the number one emitters of carbon and therefore should cut back first and (2) on an aggregate basis, developed countries have put more carbon into the atmosphere over the past fifty years than anyone else (have "fouled the nest") and therefore should take concerted action and assume leadership in responding. Although this argument may make sense on an emotional level, it makes little sense on either an economic or an environmental level. Economically, if the developing world is left out of the solution, industries in the United States, western Europe, and the rest of the developed world will be put at a distinct economic disadvantage. If world energy cost structures are altered, many industries may be forced to compete with companies in countries where the same environmental standards do not exist and therefore the cost of energy is lower. Environmentally, countries in the developing world (particularly China, Brazil, and India) are expanding their power generation base at such a pace that they will be the dominant carbon emitters early in the twenty-first century. As such, they must be included in the solution. If they are not, any efforts by the developed world will be eclipsed and become futile. Environmentally and economically, omission of the developing world would limit opportunities for competitive climate change strategy.

Finally, climate change strategy is an issue of *managing institutional change* by engaging the government, the press, and the public. Corporate executives cannot blindly resist the rising tide of this issue but must instead become an integral and constructive component of the change taking place. Unfortunately, large segments of the industrial community have chosen not to do so. The Global Climate Coalition, an organization that represents electric utilities and automobile, mining, and coal companies on the issue of climate change, has argued that the Kyoto Protocol would bind the United States "to economic and regulatory obligations that could have serious impacts on American industry and its job holders for the next 40 years."[10] A report funded by the American Petroleum Institute concludes that controls on climate change will mean that "jobs will disappear and lifestyles will be pinched as our industrial infrastructure shrinks" and predicts that gasoline prices will increase by "50 cents to $1.50 per gallon."[11] The Western Fuels Association, Inc. (WFA), a cooperative of consumer-owned electric utilities operating coal-fired power plants in the Rocky Mountain, Great Plains, and southwestern states and Louisiana, has argued that controls on greenhouse gas emissions "would boost the cost of production, lead to increased imports, slash employment and domestic output, and in some cases eliminate all U.S. production."[12] Further, the WFA has argued that increasing levels of atmospheric carbon dioxide would actually be good for the country (and the world) because they would promote increased plant growth.[13]

Ultimately, it is questionable what is to be gained from this kind of confrontational positioning and sensationally pessimistic appeals. First, such positioning makes industry into the perfect villain for the public press. In his book *The Heat Is On*, Ross Gelbspan charges that the oil and coal industries are engaged in a "deliberate campaign . . . to confuse the public about global warming and the disruptive weather patterns that mark its initial stages"[14] and that "in tandem with the Organization of Petroleum Exporting Countries (OPEC) . . . [they are attempting] to frustrate diplomatic attempts to address the crisis meaningfully."[15] Second, industry's pessimistic appeals damage its credibility in the overall environmental arena. This is familiar terrain. From claims that "the personal auto will be put out of financial reach of many Americans by politically inspired auto [emission] standards"[16] in the early 1970s (it was not) to predictions that the Clean Air Act Amendments of 1990 would cost electric utilities $4 billion to $5 billion per year[17] (they did not), industry has repeatedly predicted economic disaster as a result of environmental protection. As editorialist Bob Herbert pointed out in a 1997 *New York Times* editorial, "The problem with the industry groups is that they lack credibility. They *always* claim that taking steps to improve air quality will lead to economic catastrophe."[18]

Predictions of economic disaster from climate change controls fly in the face of more credible predictions to the contrary. In February 1997, more than two thousand economists (including eight Nobel laureates) endorsed a report concluding that "global climate change carries with it significant environmental, economic, social and geopolitical risks" and stating that "preventive steps are justified," but "economic studies have found that there are many potential policies to reduce greenhouse-gas emissions for which the total benefits outweigh the total costs. For the United States in particular, sound economic analysis shows that there are policy options that would slow climate change without harming American living standards, and these measures may in fact improve U.S. productivity in the longer run."[19]

In the end, as particular companies continue to contradict the trajectory of social thought and institutional change, they become excluded from the ongoing political debate. The momentum for controls to prevent climate change has begun and will continue, with or without industry participation. While industry groups such as the Global Climate Coalition and the Western Fuels Association are attempting to portray the costs of climate change control as too high to justify the action, companies such as the British Petroleum Company (now BP Amoco) are shaping the future of their business environment by engaging the debate in a more constructive fashion.

BP Amoco, the first company to publicly acknowledge the need to mitigate climate change, has set a strategic path for responding to the issue. In the words of the company's chief executive officer, John Browne, "we must now focus on what can and what should be done, not because we can be certain climate change is happening, but because the possibility can't be ignored. If we are all to take responsibility for the future of our planet, then it falls to us to begin to take precautionary action now."[20] The company has embarked on an aggressive strategy to be the market leader for solar power in a post–climate change treaty world. To get in on the ground floor of what it expects to be a huge market, BP Amoco has spent $160 million in developing solar energy and enjoys 10 percent of the world's solar market. Further, the synergies in solar energy technology in the recently merged British Petroleum Company and Amoco Corporation will have tremendous strategic implications. Some expect that solar power will meet 5 percent of the world's energy needs by 2020 and 50 percent by 2050; in response to this forecast, the company has set a target of $1 billion in solar energy revenues in the first decade of the twenty-first century.[21]

BP Amoco has also made a commitment to conduct research and development to improve environmental technologies and develop its own internal emissions trading system in conjunction with the Environmental Defense Fund. Browne stated, "The more we thought about this, the more we found that we could improve our environmental performance . . . and actually get higher financial returns."[22] For its efforts, the company has been winning accolades from government agencies and environmental NGOs. In the Sydney 2000 Olympic Games in Australia, the company will be on prominent display; it is building a completely solar-powered Olympic village.[23]

But more than gaining accolades from government and environmentalists and preparing for the future business environment, BP Amoco is engaging important stakeholders and helping to shape that future business environment. The company is now engaged in direct policy discussions with governments in Europe, the United States, and developing countries as well as key environmental NGOs. BP Amoco now enjoys direct input on the critical business issues in the final implementation of the Kyoto Protocol as it continues to evolve. But the company's influence on the environment does not stop there. By quitting the Global Climate Coalition, BP Amoco put pressure on other companies to defect from the lobbying group while enjoying first-mover advantages for its actions. The Royal Dutch/Shell Group of Companies, for example, has been working to keep up, quitting the Global Climate Coalition and making a $500 million commitment to solar energy and other renewable energy sources.

In the end, to deal strategically with the potential for controls on greenhouse gas emissions, companies must break down old ideas about environmental issues and replace them with new ideas that acknowledge their complementarity with strategic issues. A climate change treaty represents not a regulatory response to an environmental issue but a market transition triggered by an environmental issue. Simply put, it amounts to the establishment of a new worldwide market in pollution, pollution credits, money, and emission abatement technology. In such transitions, there will be losers and winners: those with an interest in resisting and trying to delay such a market transformation and those who will capitalize on it.

As market expectations shift and technological development advances, companies must anticipate the change and decide what strategic tack they should take. To meet this challenge, they must consider what form climate change pressures will take on the basis of who is applying them. Will governments negotiate a treaty that allows them adequate flexibility to respond strategically? Will consumers respond by buying low-emission products? Will insurance companies cut back on investments in and underwriting of carbon-intensive industries? Will competitors take advantage of first-mover opportunities by adopting programs for early emissions reductions? All of these questions will determine what kind of strategy the firm must take. The question in the minds of strategic decision makers should not be whether climate change is happening but rather what form a final treaty will take, what the resultant business environment will look like, and thus what costs or opportunities it might create and how each of these issues can be influenced to favor one's own strategic interests.

The Emerging Strategic Issue of Sustainable Development

Climate change presents new challenges to the traditional format for responding to environmental issues. It represents at its core the globalization of environmental problems and the need for an internationally coordinated response. The evolution of the meaning of environmental issues continues; on the horizon, another form of environmental issue

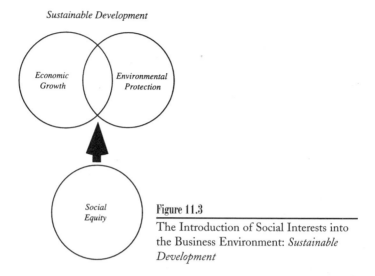

Sustainable Development

Economic Growth

Environmental Protection

Social Equity

Figure 11.3

The Introduction of Social Interests into the Business Environment: *Sustainable Development*

is becoming visible. The issue of environmental strategy is slowly being eclipsed by the issue of sustainable development. As shown in figure 11.3, the dual concerns of economic growth and environmental protection are now being expanded into a triad that includes social equity, with a focus on problems such as human rights abuses, child labor, oppressive work conditions, unfair labor practices, and irresponsible investment decisions.

The issue of sustainable development has many proponents. John Elkington, chairman of SustainAbility, a sustainable development consulting firm, argues that the business environment is evolving such that corporations will increasingly need to attend to the "triple bottom line" of sustainability—economic prosperity, environmental quality, and social justice—in their strategic planning processes.[24] Professor Stuart Hart of the University of North Carolina adds that "today many companies have accepted their responsibility to do no harm to the environment. Products and production processes are becoming cleaner; and where such change is under way, the environment is on the mend. . . . But the distance we've traveled will seem small when, in 30 years, we look back at the 1990s. Beyond greening lies an enormous challenge and an enormous opportunity. The challenge is to develop a *sustainable global economy:* an economy that the planet is capable of supporting indefinitely."[25] Nancy Bennett, program officer for the Division of Technology, Industry and Economics of the United Nations Environment Programme (UNEP), concurs: "Environmental management (EM) has come and is certainly not about to go, but the next big challenge is about integrating social issues into traditional EM tools."[26]

But has the issue of social equity entered the sphere of the business system? Does it intersect with the issue of economic growth in the same way that environmental protection does? Or does it remain separate and distinct? The concept at present remains vague and ambiguous. But as the world's markets become more global and corporations become more multinational in nature, critics of the social implications of that process are beginning to emerge. Some, such as George Soros, head of Soros Fund Management,[27] and Dani Rodrik, professor of international political economy at Harvard,[28] point out that without a political, social, moral, and ethical infrastructure for a global society, the global economy will be based on rules determined by economic success. In other words, wealth will determine who has power and what forms of interaction will take place between institutions in the global economy. It will determine what is right, what is wrong, who is legitimate, who is not. Soros argues that monetary and transactional markets do not provide an adequate basis for social cohesion. Yet they have replaced politics as the form of interaction between international economies. More directly, politics has failed as a medium for harmonizing global interaction. One of the great defects of the global capitalist system, he argues, is that it has allowed the market mechanism and the profit motive to penetrate into fields of activity where they do not properly belong. Non-market interests remain unexpressed, overlooked, and uncared for. Soros worries that there is a vacuum where there should be rules and norms being established to take care of collective interests. His concern is that markets acknowledge individual interests only as demonstrated through the self-interested pocketbook. He fears that in the end, we may have global mob rule based on the enforced supremacy of market values over all political and social values, and in the process, the developing countries will become further marginalized—they will have less and less wealth, but with technology, they will see more and more of what they are missing.[29]

In the wake of these concerns and others (such as recent concerns about child labor and human rights abuses in developing countries), corporations have begun to acknowledge a social justice aspect of their operations. But much as in the industrial environmentalism of the 1960s described in chapter 1, corporations have begun to identify sustainability on their own terms. They have developed task forces, established vice president positions, and joined government studies (such as the President's Council on Sustainable Development) to address the agenda and business implications of sustainability. The term, although still vaguely defined, has entered the lexicon of modern business.

Corporate executives can now be heard making proclamations about their perspective on sustainable development. Edgar S. Woolard Jr., while chairman of DuPont, wrote, "Industry, as society's producer, has a special role to play in creating sustainable development, and some of us in the industrial community are working on ways to make sustainability a characteristic of industrial programs."[30] Frank Popoff, chairman of the board of directors of the Dow Chemical Company, wrote, "If we view sustainable development as an opportunity for growth and not as prohibitive, industry can shape a new social and ethical framework for assessing our relationship with our environment and each other."[31] And in the Ford Motor Company's 1998 Annual Report, chairman of the board William C. Ford Jr. wrote, "A good company delivers excellent products and services, a great one delivers excellent products and services and strives to make the world a better place. Great companies understand that to fully meet the expectations of consumers, they must address the concerns of society. That is the only way to ensure sustainable development and growth. It also is the best way to richly reward shareholders."[32]

Is there more to these kinds of statements than just rhetoric? Several companies have taken an aggressive stance on establishing sustainability strategies and thereby influencing the norms within the business environment. In 1998, Nike, Inc. announced sweeping improvements in worldwide operations for its half million workers in 350 countries. The company set a minimum worker age of eighteen and established a timetable for instituting U.S. air quality standards at all its facilities. The company also created a new Corporate Responsibility Division with seventy-five employees and helped negotiate an agreement between labor rights groups and the apparel industry to allow independent groups to monitor factories for fair labor practices.

The Royal Dutch/Shell group has also taken an aggressive lead on sustainability, in large part to counter the damaging effects of its experiences with the execution of Ken Saro-Wiwa and eight Ogoni Indians in Nigeria. The company is working to develop a new management system with performance metrics to address its financial, environmental, and social performance in an integrated and quantifiable manner. In 1998, Shell published its first sustainability report, with the bold title "Profits and Principles: Does There Have to Be a Choice?" The report is a self-proclaimed description of how the company's operations in 125 countries are "striving to live up to our responsibilities—financial, social and environmental."[33] It includes an analysis of how the company is living up to its Statement of General Business Principles; an invitation for shareholders to report back with their perspectives on the company's performance; a message from the chairman; a contribution from a noted environmentalist; and the results of an auditor's report, verifying the assertions made in the report.

But the question remains as to the imperative of the sustainability agenda. Is the business environment changing? Will the actions of companies such as Nike and Shell set new standards that other companies will have to follow? Some companies have begun to develop sustainability reports, incorporating their social and ethical auditing into a new form of social report, much like the currently used annual environmental report.[34] British Telecommunications PLC, for example, has published a sustainability report that explores the social and ethical responsibilities of a multinational telecommunications company.

But progress is slow. The World Business Council for Sustainable Development (WBCSD) notes that the Nike and Shell examples are not the norm. Although there are 34,000 multinational companies worldwide, a 1998 WBCSD report noted that the "same few names come up again and again" when corporate social responsibility issues are discussed and that "there is a tremendous job to be done in bringing the 'silent majority' into the debate."[35] The group is actively trying to build these issues into board-level strategic thinking and encourage multinationals to build a clear management structure for dealing with social equity issues in worldwide operations.

In actual deed, companies remain unclear regarding a future direction for sustainable development and rely on environmental strategy as a guidepost for near-term strategies. According to Robin Bidwell, chairman of ERM international, a member of the WBCSD, "the environment is one of the key drivers" of the sustainable development agenda: "Eco-efficiency is a key element in future business strategy as it provides a framework for businesses to look at how the longer term pressures will affect their market positioning and costs of doing business."[36] Eco-efficiency constitutes a major portion of Nike's sustainability strategy, with the company pledged to make all products recyclable and review all chemicals in its products, beginning with a phaseout of polyvinyl chloride (PVC), a toxic chemical.[37]

To resolve the ambiguity inherent in the issue of sustainability, international environmental organizations, governing bodies, and academia have been developing new ideas that involve more complexity than corporate social reporting has thus far been able to capture.[38] To a large extent, these constituents argue that sustainable development represents a significant departure from notions that are presently being constructed. The evolutionary concept of sustainability as defined by industry, they argue, allows companies to embrace sustainability "without commitment."[39] It becomes merely a tool, a mechanism, a set of actions, or a selective set of strategies driven by the existing norms of corporate practice.[40] Instead, they argue, sustainable development should challenge existing beliefs about the corporation's environmental and social responsibilities. In this way, it also challenges the underlying assumptions of the market economy.[41]

The United Nations Commission on Sustainable Development has proposed a set of 134 indicators for use in measuring sustainability that, if institutionalized, may act as a guide for a market transition in the future. Among them are income inequality; population growth rate; difference between male and female school enrollment rates; per capita consumption of fossil fuels for transportation; ratio of average house price to average income; living space (floor area) per person; environmentally adjusted net domestic product; energy consumption; intensity of materials use; percentage of population with adequate excreta disposal facilities; share of renewable energy resources consumed; annual withdrawals of groundwater and surface water; ratio of debt service to export earnings; maximum sustainable yield for fisheries; changes in land use; percentage of arable land irrigated; energy use in agriculture; emissions of greenhouse gases; waste recycling and reuse; and access to information.[42]

Such notions appear heretical when compared with the traditional measures and objectives of economic growth and business strategy. Yet some business constituents are attempting to forge links between the two today. In the United Kingdom, for example, more than $3.2 million was invested in ethical investment funds in 1998. This represented a 50 percent increase over 1997 investments and a 400 percent increase over investments of the previous five years. Two large insurance companies also entered the market for ethically screened funds: the Sun Life Assurance Company and the Standard Life Assurance Company, the largest European insurance company.[43] On the whole, however, linkages between social equity and economic growth have yet to form in the core networks of the firm.

Not until insurance companies, competitors, banks, governments, and investors let social equity influence their decision-making procedures and demand the same from corporations will it move beyond an issue of "social responsibility" and become an issue of competitive strategy. At present, the issue of social equity remains separate and distinct from core business interests, as depicted in figure 11.3. It remains a new and emergent area, originating from business signals that lie outside the realm of standard business decision making. As stated in a 1998 WBCSD discussion paper: "The key to the urgency of the response is the degree to which the issue is seen as a threat to, or an opportunity for, the business. The closer the issue is to the company's direct commercial interest, the more likely it is to be acted upon."[44] This urgency will emerge as key constituents begin to adopt sustainability criteria in their decision making.

This is a likely future as our awareness of global social equity issues evolves, just as it continues to do for issues of environmental protection. It is likely that eventually, social equity will merge with economic growth and environmental protection and be brought into the same realm as the three spheres begin to intersect. In the face of this trajectory, some companies will fall back on traditional routines and attempt to delay or ignore its arrival. This, however, is a shortsighted approach. Other companies will take part in influencing the final form of sustainability and prepare long-term strategies to deal with the market transition it creates.

In the final analysis, long-term strategy boils down to decision making under conditions of uncertainty. A component of that strategy should include executives working to minimize the uncertainty by engaging key constituents who will be influential in forming the notion of sustainability that ultimately emerges. The constituents who will be prominent in that debate should determine who the strategic company should engage. Will it be certain environmental NGOs? International governments? Insurance companies? The future form of the business strategy of sustainable development lies in the business constituency that draws it into the realm of business interests. Clearly, the actions of some forward-looking firms can hasten its arrival.

But the important point is that sustainability could eventually represent a market transition. It is unlikely to be permanently relegated to the realm of social responsibility. If it emerges in the realm of corporate strategy, it could alter core market dynamics, change the rules of the marketplace, and thus change the role and objective of the firm in the way it competes within that market. Therefore, just as environmental issues have entered the realm of business and must be considered as business issues, sustainable development looms on the horizon and appears to be following a similar path. The business manager will face many questions: When will sustainable development emerge as a key business issue? Am I aware of the proper cues as to when this may be happening? Can I influence them in a way that fits with my business objectives? What strategy will I employ when I detect the emerging form of this issue? And how will I time my strategic efforts so as to gain maximum advantage when it does emerge?

Conclusion

Fundamentally, engaging in competitive environmental strategy involves merely responding to a changing business environment. Corporate decision makers who fail to do so are irresponsibly ignoring important market indicators, environmental protection today, and sustainable development tomorrow. A report by Arthur D. Little, Inc. notes that companies that can gain first-mover advantage by anticipating or driving the market transition caused by sustainability will enjoy a business environment more aligned with their core business strategies. With that advantage will come strategic flexibility and the ability to capitalize on opportunities that emerge through shifts in customer needs and the demands of other business constituents for sustainable products and services.[45]

But more than mere business opportunities, environmental strategy and sustainable development represent alterations to market norms such that corporations can become a solution to important social issues. As the most powerful force in the world today, corporations must perform this role if we are to achieve a sustainable future. Many social issues today are simply too complex for solutions to be found through any one organizational entity, such as government. They involve an increasingly complex interplay of social, political, scientific, technological, and economic considerations. Finding solutions will require an equally complex interplay and exchange among activists, politicians, scientists, engineers, academics, and business managers. Ultimately, however, the locus of the response must be in the business environment. As multinational corporations grow in their influence on global systems, exercising what historian Paul Kennedy describes as "more global reach than global responsibility,"[46] their input and their power must be brought to bear on global issues. The integration of environmental protection and social equity into baseline concerns for economic growth are needed and natural progressions in bringing market institutions in line with social needs.

Further Reading

Downs, A. "Up and Down with Ecology: The 'Issue-Attention' Cycle." *Public Interest* 28 (1972): 38–50.

Elkington, J. *Cannibals with Forks: The Triple Bottom Line of Twenty-First Century Business.* Oxford, England: Capstone Publishing, 1998.

Hart, S. "Beyond Greening: Strategies for a Sustainable World." *Harvard Business Review,* January–February 1997, 66–76.

Hoffman, A., ed. *Global Climate Change: A Senior Level Dialogue at the Intersection of Economics, Strategy, Technology, Science, Politics, and International Negotiation.* San Francisco: New Lexington Press, 1998.

Rodrik, D. *Has Globalization Gone Too Far?* Washington, D.C.: Institute for International Economics, 1997.

Soros, G. *The Crisis of Global Capitalism: Open Society Endangered.* New York: Public Affairs Information Service, 1998.

Appendix A

U . S . E n v i r o n m e n t a l   L a w s

The following is a list of major federal environmental laws in the United States. These laws, and others enacted by states, have various requirements and are enforced by various agencies. This list was developed from a U.S. government document and is therefore part of the public domain.[1]

Clean Air Act of 1970 (CAA)

42 U.S.C. §§ 7401 et seq. (1970)

The Clean Air Act of 1970 (CAA) is a comprehensive federal law that regulates airborne emissions from area, stationary, and mobile sources. This law authorizes the Environmental Protection Agency (EPA) to establish national ambient air quality standards (NAAQS) to protect public health and the environment. The goal of the act was for NAAQS to be set and achieved in every state by 1975. This setting of maximum pollutant standards was coupled with a directive for individual states to develop state implementation plans (SIPs) applicable to appropriate industrial sources of pollution.

The act was amended in 1977 primarily to set new goals (dates) for achieving attainment of NAAQS because many areas of the country had failed to meet the deadlines. The Clean Air Act Amendments of 1990 were intended in large part to meet unaddressed or insufficiently addressed problems such as acid rain, ground-level ozone emissions, stratospheric ozone depletion, and airborne toxins.

Clean Water Act (CWA)

33 U.S.C. §§ 121 et seq. (1977)

The Clean Water Act (CWA) is a 1977 amendment to the Federal Water Pollution Control Act of 1972, which set out the basic structure regulating discharges of pollutants into waters of the United States. This law gave the EPA authority to set effluent standards on an industry-by-industry basis (technology based) and continued the requirements to set water quality standards for all contaminants in surface waters. The CWA makes it unlawful for any person to discharge any pollutant from a point source into navigable waters unless a permit is obtained from the National Pollutant Discharge Elimination System (NPDES) Permitting Program. The 1977 amendments focused on toxic substances, authorized citizen suit provisions, and funded sewage treatment plants (publicly owned treatment works, or POTWs) under the Construction Grants Program.

The CWA authorizes the EPA to delegate many permitting, administrative, and enforcement aspects of the law to state governments. In states with the authority to implement CWA programs, the EPA retains oversight responsibilities.

Comprehensive Environmental Response, Compensation, and Liability Act (CERCLA or Superfund)

42 U.S.C. §§ 9601 et seq. (1980)

The Comprehensive Environmental Response, Compensation, and Liability Act (CERCLA, pronounced *serk*-la) provides a federal Superfund to clean up uncontrolled or abandoned hazardous waste sites as well as accidents, spills, and other emergency releases of pollutants and contaminants into the environment. Through the act, the EPA was given power to seek out parties responsible for releases and ensure their cooperation in the cleanup. The EPA cleans up "orphan" sites when potentially responsible parties (PRPs) cannot be identified or located or when they fail to act. Through various enforcement tools, the EPA obtains private-party cleanup through orders, consent decrees, and other small-party settlements. The EPA also recovers costs from financially viable individuals and companies once a response action has been completed.

The EPA is authorized to implement the act in all fifty states and U.S. territories. Superfund site identification, monitoring, and response activities in states are coordinated through state environmental protection or waste management agencies.

Emergency Planning and Community Right-to-Know Act of 1986 (EPCRA)

42 U.S.C. §§ 11011 et seq. (1986)

Also known as Title III of the Superfund Amendments and Reauthorization Act of 1986 (SARA), the Emergency Planning and Community Right-to-Know Act of 1986 (EPCRA) was enacted by Congress as the national legislation on community safety. This law was designed to help communities safeguard public health and safety and protect the environment from chemical hazards.

To implement EPCRA, Congress required each state to appoint a State Emergency Response Commission (SERC). The SERCs were required to divide their states into Emergency Planning Districts and to name a Local Emergency Planning Committee (LEPC) for each district. Board representation by firefighters, health officials, government officials, media representatives, community groups, personnel of industrial facilities, and emergency managers ensures that all necessary elements of the planning process are represented.

Endangered Species Act of 1973

7 U.S.C. § 136; 16 U.S.C. §§ 460 et seq. (1973)

The Endangered Species Act of 1973 provides a program for the conservation of threatened and endangered plants and animals and their habitats. The U.S. Fish and Wildlife Service (FWS) of the Department of the Interior maintains the lists of endangered species (as of 1995, these numbered 632, of which 326 were plants) and threatened species (190, of which 78 were plants). Categories include birds, insects, fish, reptiles, mammals, crustaceans, flowers, grasses, and trees. Anyone can petition the FWS to list a species or to prevent some activity, such as logging, mining, or dam building, that might endanger a species. The law prohibits any action, administrative or real, that results in a "taking" of a listed species or adversely affects habitat. Likewise, importation, exportation, and interstate and foreign commerce of listed species are all prohibited.

The EPA's decision to register a pesticide is based in part on the risk of it adversely affecting endangered species as well as on its environmental fate (how the pesticide will affect habitat). Under the Federal Insecticide, Fungicide, and Rodenticide Act (see the entry that follows), the EPA can issue emergency suspensions of certain pesticides to halt or restrict their use if an endangered species will be adversely affected by them. Under a new program, the EPA, the FWS, and the U.S. Department of Agriculture are distributing hundreds of county bulletins that include habitat maps, pesticide use limitations, and other actions required to protect listed species.

In addition, government agencies are enforcing regulations under various treaties, including the Convention on International Trade in Endangered Species of Wild Fauna and Flora (CITES). The United States and seventy other countries have established procedures to regulate the importation and exportation of imperiled species and their habitat. The U.S. Fish and Wildlife Service works with the U.S. Customs Service to stop the illegal trade of such species, including black rhinoceroses, African elephants, tropical birds and fish, orchids, and various corals.

Federal Insecticide, Fungicide, and Rodenticide Act (FIFRA)

7 U.S.C. §§ 135 et seq. (1972)

The primary focus of the Federal Insecticide, Fungicide, and Rodenticide Act (FIFRA) was to provide federal control of pesticide distribution, sale, and use. The EPA was given authority under FIFRA not only to study the consequences of pesticide use but also to require users (farmers, utility companies, and others) to register when purchasing pesticides. Under later amendments to the law, users also must take exams for certification as applicators of pesticides. All pesticides used in the United States must be registered (licensed) by the EPA. Registration ensures that pesticides will be properly labeled and that if used in accordance with specifications, they will not cause unreasonable harm to the environment.

(Federal) Freedom of Information Act (FOIA)

5 U.S.C. §§ 552 (1966)

The Freedom of Information Act (FOIA) provides specifically that "any person" can request government information. Citizens who make requests are not required to identify themselves or explain why they want the information they have requested. The position of Congress in passing the FOIA was that the workings of government are "for and by the people" and that the benefits of government information should be made available to everyone.

All branches of the federal government must adhere to the provisions of the FOIA, with certain restrictions for work in progress (early drafts), documents related to the enforcement of confidential information, classified documents, and national security information.

National Environmental Policy Act of 1969 (NEPA)

42 U.S.C. §§ 4321 et seq. (1969)

The National Environmental Policy Act of 1969 (NEPA) was one of the first laws to establish the broad national framework for environmental protection. NEPA's basic policy is to ensure that all branches of government give proper consideration to the environment prior to undertaking any major federal action that significantly affects the environment. NEPA requirements are invoked when construction of airports, buildings, military complexes, and highways, purchases of parkland, and other such federal activities are proposed. Environmental assessments (EAs) and environmental impact statements (EISs), which are assessments of the likelihood of adverse effects from alternative courses of action, are required from all federal agencies and are the most visible NEPA requirements.

Occupational Safety and Health Act of 1970

29 U.S.C. §§ 61 et seq. (1970)

Congress passed the Occupational Safety and Health Act of 1970 to ensure worker and workplace safety. The goal was to ensure that employers provide their workers with a place of employment free from recognized hazards to safety and health, such as exposure to toxic chemicals, excessive noise, mechanical dangers, heat or cold stress, and unsanitary conditions. In order to establish standards for workplace health and safety, the act also created the National Institute for Occupational Safety and Health (NIOSH) as the research institution for the Occupational Safety and Health Administration (OSHA). OSHA is a division of the U.S. Department of Labor, which oversees administration of the act and enforces federal standards in all fifty states.

Oil Pollution Act of 1990 (OPA)

33 U.S.C. §§ 2702–2761

The Oil Pollution Act of 1990 (OPA) streamlined and strengthened the EPA's ability to prevent and respond to catastrophic oil spills. Under the act, a trust fund financed by a tax on oil is made available to clean up spills when the responsible party is incapable or unwilling to do so. The OPA requires oil storage facilities and vessels to submit to the federal government response plans detailing how they will respond to large discharges. The EPA has published regulations for aboveground storage facilities; the United States Coast Guard has done so for oil tankers. The OPA also requires the development of area contingency plans to prepare and plan for oil spill response on a regional scale.

Pollution Prevention Act of 1990

42 U.S.C. §§ 13101 and 13102; §§ 6602 et seq. (1990)

The Pollution Prevention Act of 1990 focused industry, government, and public attention on reducing pollution through cost-effective changes in production, operation, and raw materials use. Opportunities for source reduction are often not realized because existing regulations, and the industrial resources required for compliance, focus on treatment and disposal. Pollution prevention is fundamentally different from and more desirable than waste management or pollution control. It also includes practices that increase efficiency in the use of energy, water, and other natural resources and protect the country's resource base through conservation. Practices include recycling, source reduction, and sustainable agriculture.

Resource Conservation and Recovery Act (RCRA)

42 U.S.C. §§ 321 et seq. (1976)

The 1976 Resource Conservation and Recovery Act (RCRA, pronounced *rick*-rah) gave the EPA authority to control hazardous waste "from cradle to grave." This includes the generation, transportation, treatment, storage, and disposal of hazardous waste. RCRA also set forth a framework for the management of nonhazardous solid waste.

The 1986 amendment to RCRA enabled the EPA to address environmental problems that could result from storage of petroleum and other hazardous substances in underground tanks. RCRA focuses only on active and future facilities and does not address abandoned or historical sites (see the entry for the Comprehensive Environmental Response, Compensation, and Liability Act, or CERCLA).

RCRA was amended by the federal Hazardous and Solid Waste Amendments of 1984 (HSWA, pronounced *hiss*-wa), which required the phasing out of land disposal of hazardous waste. Some other mandates of this strict law include increased enforcement authority for the EPA, more stringent standards for hazardous waste management, and a comprehensive underground storage tank program.

Safe Drinking Water Act (SDWA)

43 U.S.C. §§ 300f et seq. (1974)

The Safe Drinking Water Act (SDWA) was established to protect the quality of drinking water in the United States. This law focuses on all waters actually or potentially designated for drinking use, whether from aboveground or underground sources. The act authorized the EPA to establish safe standards for purity and required all owners and operators of public water systems to comply with primary (health-related) standards. State governments, which assume this power from the EPA, also encourage the attainment of secondary (nuisance-related) standards.

Superfund Amendments and Reauthorization Act of 1986 (SARA)

42 U.S.C. §§ 9601 et seq. (1986)

The Superfund Amendments and Reauthorization Act of 1986 (SARA) reauthorized CERCLA to continue cleanup activities around the United States. Several site-specific amendments, definitions, clarifications, and technical requirements were added to the legislation, including additional enforcement authorities.

Title III of SARA also authorized the Emergency Planning and Community Right-to-Know Act of 1986 (EPCRA).

Toxic Substances Control Act (TSCA)

15 U.S.C. §§ 2601 et seq. (1976)

The Toxic Substances Control Act (TSCA) was enacted in 1986 by Congress to test, regulate, and screen all chemicals produced in or imported into the United States. Many thousands of chemicals and compounds with unknown toxic or dangerous characteristics are developed each year. To prevent tragic consequences, TSCA requires that any chemical destined to reach the consumer marketplace be tested for toxicity prior to commercial manufacture.

Existing chemicals that pose health or environmental hazards are tracked and reported under TSCA. Procedures are also authorized for corrective action under TSCA in cases of cleanup of contamination by toxic materials. TSCA supplements other federal statutes, including the Clean Air Act and the Toxics Release Inventory under EPCRA.

Appendix B

Environmental Information Resources

Journals and Magazines

ENVIRONMENTAL BUSINESS

Corporate Environmental Strategy

Pollution Prevention Review

Tomorrow: Global Environment Business

Total Quality Environmental Management

ENVIRONMENTAL POLICY AND LAW

Amicus Journal

Ecology Law Quarterly

Environmental Affairs

Environmental Forum

EPA Journal

ENVIRONMENTAL SOCIOLOGY

Business and Society Review

Rural Sociology

Society and Natural Resources

GENERAL ENVIRONMENT

Audubon

Ecologist

E Magazine

Environment

Sierra

ENVIRONMENTAL SCIENCE AND TECHNOLOGY

Environmental Manager

Environmental Progress

Environmental Science and Technology

Journal of Environmental Engineering

Journal of Industrial Ecology

Internet-Based Resources[1]

ECONET

Internet: http://www.igc.org/igc/gateway/enindex.html
EcoNet is part of the Institute for Global Communications, a collection of on-line networks dedicated to linking activists to information and to one another. The site provides archives of environmental data and links to information found elsewhere on the Internet. For more information, send a blank e-mail message to econet-info@igc.apc.org.

ELECTRONIC GREEN JOURNAL

Internet: http://egj.lib.uidaho.edu/index.html
A professionally refereed publication devoted to international environmental topics, the *Electronic Green Journal* is especially helpful to librarians seeking to increase their own knowledge about environmental issues. To subscribe, send an e-mail message to major-domo@uidaho.edu with the message SUBSCRIBE egj [your e-mail address].

ENVIROLINK

Internet: http://envirolink.org/
EnviroLink is a clearinghouse of environmental information on the Internet. It archives fact sheets, activist alerts, and press releases and also offers a directory of environmental products, forums for activists, and links to environmental information elsewhere on the

Internet. This user-friendly site groups materials under broad topics such as forest issues, global warming, and indigenous rights.

ENVIROENE

Internet: http://es.epa.gov/
Enviroene is a joint program of the EPA, the Department of Energy, and the Department of Defense. It provides a single source of information and databases about pollution prevention compliance, assurance, and enforcement. It is especially useful for small businesses.

EPA CONCERNED CITIZENS

Internet: http://www.epa.gov/epahome/Citizen.html
The EPA's Concerned Citizens Web site offers a series of fact sheets, brochures, and papers on topics such as safety, pollution prevention, recycling, and conservation in the home, garden, and workplace; protecting children from toxins, sun, lead, and other potential environmental health threats; transportation; community involvement; global environmental issues; and environmental emergencies.

EPA ENVIRO-NEWSBRIEF

Internet: http://www.epa.gov/natlibra/hqirc/enb.htm
Produced by the EPA's Headquarters Information Resources Center, Enviro-NewsBrief provides a summary of the news that affects the EPA, especially appointments to the EPA and other environment-related appointments; the Council on Environmental Quality; changes to the Office of Management and Budget's process of regulatory review; regulatory reform; "reinventing government"; environmental legislation, especially reauthorization of key legislation; federal employee issues; and interagency work on environmental issues. To subscribe, send an e-mail message to listserver@unixmail. rtpnc.epa.gov with the following message: SUBSCRIBE environb-1 [firstname lastname]. For more information, contact the EPA's Headquarters Information Resources Center at (202) 260-5922 or send an e-mail message to library-hq@epa-mail.epa.gov.

EPA ONLINE LIBRARY SYSTEM

Internet: http://www.epa.gov/natlibra/ols.htm
The Internet library of the Environmental Protection Agency (EPA) offers the digital holdings of regional EPA libraries and state environmental and health libraries. In addition to a national catalog of citations with abstracts for selected titles, the system features searchable databases on subjects such as hazardous waste and environmental financing. Access EPA, a source for EPA documents (see General Environment Information Sources), is also available through this system.

LYCOS SEARCH ENGINE

Internet: http://www.lycos.com/

The Lycos search engine is useful if browsing the previously listed sites does not produce the needed information. This Internet tool allows you to search millions of Internet files by keyword in a matter of seconds by typing simple phrases such as *energy data* or *toxic materials*. If Lycos finds relevant files, you can connect directly to them.

NATIONAL LIBRARY FOR THE ENVIRONMENT (NLE)

Internet: http://www.cnie.org

The National Library for the Environment (NLE) is a project of the Committee for the National Institute for the Environment (CNIE), a nonprofit organization dedicated to improving the scientific basis for making decisions on environmental issues through a nonregulatory federal scientific agency known as the National Institute for the Environment (NIE). The NLE contains three sections: Congressional Research Service Reports, CES Briefing Books, and Reference Resources.

NATIONAL RESPONSE CENTER (NRC)

Internet: http://www.nrc.uscg.mil/ (**National Response Center**)
http://www.epa.gov/ERNS/ (**Emergency Response Notification System**)

The National Response Center (NRC), the federal government's national communications center, is staffed twenty-four hours a day by U.S. Coast Guard officers and marine science technicians. The NRC receives all reports of releases involving hazardous substances and oil as required by federal notification laws and maintains the reports in a national database called the Emergency Response Notification System.

RACHEL'S ENVIRONMENT AND HEALTH WEEKLY

Internet: http://www.rachel.org/bulletin/index.cfm?St=1

Rachel's Environment and Health Weekly is published by the Environmental Research Foundation. To subscribe, send an e-mail message to listserv@rachel.org with the words SUBSCRIBE rachel-weekly [your name] in the body of the message.

RIGHT-TO-KNOW NETWORK (RTK NET)

Internet: http://www.rtk.net/

The Right-to-Know Network (RTK NET) provides free on-line access to more than 100 gigabytes of quantitative databases and numerous text files and conferences about the environment, housing, and sustainable development.

TOMORROW MAGAZINE

Internet: http://www.tomorrow-web.com
This Web site provides past issues of *Tomorrow* magazine, up-to-the-minute news about issues dealing with the environment and business, and links to corporate environmental Web pages and other related information.

WWW VIRTUAL LIBRARY—ENVIRONMENT

Internet: http://earthsystems.org/Environment.shtml
The WWW Virtual Library—Environment provides links to scientific environmental information in addition to the full text of many environmental magazines and technical reports. Look here for academic discussions of climate change, alternative fuels, and other important issues.

Environmental/Business Career Newsletters

ENVIRONMENTAL CAREER OPPORTUNITIES
P.O. Box 560
Stanardsville, VA 22973
(301) 320-2002

GALLON ENVIRONMENT LETTER/GREEN JOBS AVAILABLE REPORT (CANADIAN)
Canadian Institute for Business and the Environment
Institut Canadien du Commerce et de l'Environnement
506 Victoria Avenue, Montreal, Quebec H3Y 2R5
(514) 369-0230
E-mail: cibe@web.net

Environmental/Business Career Organizations

ENVIRONMENTAL CAREERS ORGANIZATION
179 South Street
Boston, MA 02111
(617) 426-4375
Internet: http://www.eco.org

The Environmental Careers Organization (ECO) is a national, nonprofit, educational organization. ECO's mission is to protect and enhance the environment through the development of professionals, the promotion of careers, and the impression of individual action. This is accomplished through internships, career advice, career products, and research and consulting.

ENVIRONMENTAL PROJECT RESOURCES, LLC
>   (860) 628-4126
>   Fax: (800) 683-8221
>   E-mail: info@epr-environmental.com
>   Internet: http://www.epr-environmental.com

Environmental Project Resources (EPR) is a free Web-based company and full-time environment, health, and safety (EH&S) employment service. EPR, based in Southington, Connecticut, provides temporary and contract EH&S specialists to corporations, consultants, and the legal community worldwide. EPR has a worldwide presence, with associates located in the United States, Australia, China, India, Ireland, England, France, Holland, Ukraine, Germany, Italy, Brazil, and Canada. In addition to providing temporary EH&S specialists, EPR also provides a means by which employers can post their full-time job openings on the EPR Web site. Other features of EPR's online service include: (1) an organized list of links to EH&S resources on the Internet; (2) access to the Web sites and environmental reports of some of the world's leading corporations; (3) a software page where EH&S professionals can find solutions to their program and data management needs; and (4) a news and regulatory update page that provides links to the best EH&S news sources on the web.

NET IMPACT: NEW LEADERS FOR BETTER BUSINESS
>   609 Mission Street
>   3rd Floor
>   San Francisco, CA 94105
>   (415) 778-8366
>   Internet: http://www.srb.org

Net Impact is a network of emerging business leaders committed to using the power of business to create a better world. Originally founded as Students for Responsible Business in 1993, Net Impact has developed from an idea shared by 17 business students into a mission-driven network of 1,500 new leaders for better business. Through the central office and 50 local chapters, they provide a portfolio of programs to help members broaden their business education, refine their leadership skills, and pursue their professional goals, while they build their network.

Environmental/Business Career Books

Bennett, S. *Ecopreneuring*. New York: John Wiley & Sons, 1991.

Berle, G. *The Green Entrepreneur: Business Opportunities That Can Save the Earth and Make You Money*. New York: Liberty Hall Press, 1991.

Cohn, S. *Green at Work: Finding a Business Career That Works for the Environment*. Rev. ed. Washington, D.C.: Island Press, 1995.

Environmental Careers Organization. *The Complete Guide to Environmental Careers in the Twenty-First Century*. Washington D.C.: Island Press, 1998.

General Environmental Information Sources

AGENCY FOR TOXIC SUBSTANCES AND DISEASE REGISTRY (ATSDR), DEPARTMENT OF
HEALTH AND HUMAN SERVICES

> 1600 Clifton Road (MS-E60)
> Atlanta, GA 30333
> (404) 639-0500, (404) 639-0501
> E-mail: mcg@atsdhs1.em.cdc.gov
> Internet: http://atsdr1.atsdr.cdc.gov:8080/

Part of the federal Department of Health and Human Services, the Agency for Toxic
Substances and Disease Registry (ATSDR) is charged with providing the public with
technical information about the health effects associated with hazardous waste sites,
including those designated as Superfund sites. The ATSDR manages the Hazardous
Substance Release and Health Effects Database (HazDat), an on-line database containing information about releases of hazardous substances. The agency also offers a database called ToxFAQs (Frequently Asked Questions about Contaminants Found at Hazardous Waste Sites) containing a series of fact sheets on toxic substances commonly
found at hazardous waste sites.

CENTER FOR CIVIC NETWORKING

> National Programs Office
> P.O. Box 5352
> Washington, DC 20009
> (202) 362-3831
> E-mail: rciville@civicnet.org
> Internet: http://civic.net/ccn.html

The Center for Civic Networking promotes the application of telecommunications and
information technology to strengthen community and economic development, citizen
participation, and revitalization of civic institutions.

CENTER FOR ENVIRONMENTAL HEALTH STUDIES, JOHN SNOW, INC.

> 44 Farnsworth Street
> Boston, MA 02210-1214
> (617) 482-9485
> Internet: http://www.jsi.com/99web/environmental/index.htm

The John Snow, Inc. Center for Environmental Health Studies provides expert assistance to community and labor groups, advocates, and government agencies concerning
the health effects of exposure to hazardous chemicals. The center collaborates with the
EPA to conduct outreach and training for librarians.

CENTER FOR HEALTH, ENVIRONMENT AND JUSTICE

P.O. Box 6806
Falls Church, VA 22040
(703) 237-2249
E-mail: cchw@essential.org
Internet: http://www.essential.org/cchw/

The Center for Health, Environment and Justice, formerly the Citizens Clearinghouse for Hazardous Waste, is an environmental justice center that supports and builds community-based organizations working to establish recycling centers and prevent construction of hazardous waste landfills and chemical plants.

ENVIRONMENTAL HEALTH CLEARINGHOUSE

100 Capitola Drive
Durham, NC 27713
(919) 361-0570
Internet: http://infoventures.com/e-hlth/

The Environmental Health Clearinghouse is a clearinghouse of information about environmental health issues created through a collaboration between the National Institute of Environmental Health Sciences (NIEHS) and Information Ventures, Inc. It provides information about NIEHS research activities and refers the public to appropriate information centers, government agencies, and private organizations.

ENVIRONMENTAL JUSTICE RESOURCE CENTER, CLARK ATLANTA UNIVERSITY

223 James P. Brawley Drive, SW
Atlanta, GA 30314
(404) 880-6911
E-mail: ejrc@cau.edu
Internet: http://www.ejrc.cau.edu/

The Clark Atlanta University Environmental Justice Resource Center is an environmental justice center that supports organizing efforts throughout the southeastern United States. The center helps develop partnerships between universities and community groups.

ENVIRONMENTAL PROTECTION AGENCY

Public Information Center
401 M Street, NW
Washington, DC 20460
(800) 490-9198
Internet: http://www.epa.gov/

EPA documents are available to the public free of charge through Access EPA, a publication of the EPA's Online Library System, which catalogs EPA documents up to 1994 and provides information about how to order them. (See the entry under Internet-Based Resources.)

ENVIRONMENTAL RESEARCH FOUNDATION
> P.O. Box 5036
> Annapolis, MD 21403
> E-mail: erf@rachel.org
> Internet: http://www.rachel.org/home_eng.htm

The Environmental Research Foundation provides news, technical assistance, and information about environmental issues and hazards, particularly as they pertain to environmental justice. The foundation publishes *Rachel's Environment and Health Weekly*, available on-line (see the entry under Internet-Based Resources).

ENVIRONMENT AND RESOURCE MANAGEMENT DIVISION, SPECIAL LIBRARIES ASSOCIATION
> 1700 18th Street, NW
> Washington, DC 20009-2508
> (202) 234-4700
> Internet: http://www.wco.com/~rteeter/ermd/ermd.html

The Environment and Resource Management Division of the Special Libraries Association is concerned with increasing knowledge and communication among librarians about sources of environmental and public health information. A newsletter provides librarians with up-to-date information about development of environmental collections.

INFORM, INC.
> 120 Wall Street
> New York, NY 10005-4001
> (212) 361-2400
> Internet: http://www.informinc.org/

INFORM, Inc. examines business and municipal practices that affect the environment and public health, assesses changes business and government are making to improve their performance, identifies new business strategies and technologies contributing to an environmentally sustainable economy, and provides members with community right-to-know publications and information.

NATIONAL CENTER FOR ENVIRONMENTAL HEALTH (NCEH), CENTERS FOR DISEASE
CONTROL AND PREVENTION, DEPARTMENT OF HEALTH AND HUMAN SERVICES

Publications and Activities Department
4770 Buford Highway, NE
Atlanta, GA 30341-3724
(770) 488-7030
E-mail: ncehinfo@cdc.gov
Internet: http://www.cdc.gov/nceh/ncehhome.htm

The National Center for Environmental Health (NCEH) is a federal agency within the
Centers for Disease Control and Prevention of the Department of Health and Human
Services. The NCEH directs research programs to investigate and prevent adverse health
effects of exposure to environmental hazards.

NATIONAL LEAD INFORMATION CENTER

National University Continuing Education Association/Regional
Lead Training Centers Project
1 DuPont Circle, Suite 615
Washington, DC 20036
(800) 424-5323
Internet: http://www.epa.gov/lead/nlic.htm

A project of the EPA, the National Lead Information Center maintains a hot line and
provides educational resources about lead hazards.

OMB WATCH

1742 Connecticut Avenue, NW
Washington, DC 20009
(202) 234-8494
E-mail: ombwatch@ombwatch.org
Internet: http://www.ombwatch.org/ombwatch.html

A consumer advocacy group, OMB Watch maintains the Right-to-Know Network
(RTK NET), through which citizens can gain access to the Toxics Release Inventory.

TASK FORCE ON THE ENVIRONMENT, SOCIAL RESPONSIBILITIES ROUND TABLE,
AMERICAN LIBRARY ASSOCIATION

50 East Huron Street
Chicago, IL 60611
(800) 545-2433
Internet: http://www.ala.org/alaorg/rtables/srrt/tfoe/

The Task Force on the Environment is one of the issues-oriented task forces making up the American Library Association's Social Responsibilities Round Table. A professional caucus concerned with environmentally sound practices within libraries, the task force also seeks to enhance awareness of environmental issues.

Notes

Preface

1. J. Finlay, R. Bunch, and B. Neubert, *Grey Pinstripes with Green Ties: MBA Programs Where the Environment Matters* (Washington, D.C.: World Resources Institute, 1998), 7.
2. A. Hoffman, "Environmental Education in Business School," *Environment* 41, no. 1 (1999): 4–5.
3. C. Fishman, "I Want to Pioneer the Company of the Next Industrial Revolution," *Fast Company*, April–May 1998, 136–142.
4. J. Browne, "Climate Change: The New Agenda," in *Global Climate Change: A Senior Level Dialogue at the Intersection of Economics, Strategy, Technology, Science, Politics, and International Negotiation*, ed. A. Hoffman (San Francisco: New Lexington Press, 1998): 53–62.
5. L. Ember, "Strategies for Reducing Pollution at the Source Are Gaining Ground," *Chemical and Engineering News* (8 July 1991): 12.
6. B. Wagner, "The Greening of the Engineer," *U.S. News and World Report*, 21 March 1994, 90–91.
7. Times Mirror Magazines, Inc., *The Environmental Two Step: Looking Forward, Moving Backward* (New York: Times Mirror Magazines, 1995), iv.

Chapter 1: From Environmental Management to Environmental Strategy

1. E. Pendleton, *A Survey of the Environmental Construction Market*, Working Paper no. CCRE 92-39 (Cambridge: Massachusetts Institute of Technology, Department of Civil and Environmental Engineering, 1992).
2. A. Kumar Naj, "Industrial Switch: Some Firms Reduce Pollution with Clean Manufacturing," *Wall Street Journal*, 24 December 1990, A1.
3. "DuPont to Spend Big to Cut Plant Pollution," *Engineering News Record* (5 August 1991): 22.
4. C. Arnst et al., "When Green Begets Green," *Business Week*, 10 November 1997, 98–106.
5. C. Karrass, *The Negotiating Game: How to Get What You Want* (New York: Harper & Row, Publishers, Thomas Y. Crowell, 1970); H. Cohen, *You Can Negotiate Anything* (Secaucus, N.J.: Lyle Stuart, 1980).

6. R. Fisher and W. Ury, *Getting to Yes* (New York: Penguin Books, 1981).

7. K. Palmer, W. Oates, and P. Portney, "Tightening Environmental Standards: The Benefit–Cost or the No-Cost Paradigm?" *Journal of Economic Perspectives* 9, no. 4 (1995): 121.

8. N. Walley and B. Whitehead, "It's Not Easy Being Green," *Harvard Business Review,* May–June 1994, 46–51.

9. J. Ausubel and H. Sladovich, *Technology and Environment* (Washington, D.C.: National Academy of Engineering, 1989).

10. Walley and Whitehead, "It's Not Easy Being Green," 46–47.

11. M. Porter and C. van der Linde, "Green and Competitive: Ending the Stalemate," *Harvard Business Review,* September–October 1995, 125.

12. M. Porter and C. van der Linde, "Toward a New Conception of the Environment–Competitiveness Relationship," *Journal of Economic Perspectives* 9, no. 4 (1995): 105.

13. A. Gore, *Earth in the Balance* (Boston: Houghton Mifflin Company, 1992), 342.

14. Porter and van der Linde, "Green and Competitive," 127.

15. M. McSorley, "EPA, Company Happy with Freon Gone," *Manchester Union Leader,* 22 March 1993, 4.

16. A. Hoffman, M. Bazerman, and S. Yaffee, "Balancing Business Interests and Endangered Species Protection," *Sloan Management Review* 39, no. 1 (1997): 59–73.

17. T. Egan, "Oregon, Foiling Forecasters, Thrives as It Protects Owls," *New York Times,* 11 October 1994, 1.

18. T. M. Power, "Economics and the Environment," *Greenline* 30 (4 January 1996): 1.

19. A. Lovins, "Energy Efficiency: The 'No Regrets Policy' and Market Failures," in *Global Climate Change: A Senior-Level Dialogue at the Intersection of Economics, Strategy, Technology, Science, Politics, and International Negotiation,* ed. A. Hoffman (San Francisco: New Lexington Press), 194–196.

20. M. Neale and M. Bazerman, *Cognition and Rationality in Negotiation* (New York: Free Press, 1991); M. Bazerman, *Judgment in Managerial Decision Making,* 4th ed. (New York: John Wiley & Sons, 1998).

21. B. Hampton, *The Great American Wolf* (New York: Henry Holt & Company, 1997).

22. Times Mirror Magazines, Inc., *The Environmental Two Step: Looking Forward, Moving Backward* (New York: Times Mirror Magazines, 1995), iv.

23. M. Cropper and W. Oates, "Environmental Economics: A Survey," *Journal of Economic Literature* 30 (1992): 675–740.

24. Environmental Protection Agency, *Enforcement Accomplishments Report, FY 1991,* Report no. 300-R92-008 (Washington, D.C.: U.S. Government Printing Office, 1992).

25. F. Buttel, "Environmentalism: Origins, Processes, and Implications for Rural Social Change," *Rural Sociology* 57, no. 1 (1992): 14.

26. C. Morrison, *Managing Environmental Affairs: Corporate Practices in the U.S., Canada, and Europe* (New York: Conference Board, 1991), 18. Founded in 1916, the Conference Board provides a variety of forums and professionally managed research programs to identify and report objectively on key areas of changing management concern, opportunity, and action. The Conference Board, 845 Third Avenue, New York, NY 10022-6601; telephone (212) 759-0900, fax (212) 980-7014.

27. A. Hoffman, *From Heresy to Dogma: An Institutional History of Corporate Environmentalism* (San Francisco: New Lexington Press, 1997).

28. A. Hoffman and J. Ehrenfeld, "Corporate Environmentalism, Sustainability, and Management Studies," in *Environmental Strategies for Industry: The Future of Corporate Practice,* ed. N. Roome (Washington, D.C.: Island Press, 1998), 55–73.

29. M. Hannan and J. Freeman, "The Population Ecology of Organizations," *American Journal of Sociology* 82 (1977): 929–964.

30. Hoffman and Ehrenfeld, "Corporate Environmentalism."

31. A. Hoffman, ed., *Global Climate Change: A Senior Level Dialogue at the Intersection of Economics, Strategy, Technology, Science, Politics, and International Negotiation* (San Francisco: New Lexington Press, 1998), 32.

32. F. Popoff, "Pollution Prevention: No Longer a Pipe Dream," *Business Week*, 30 December 1991, 90.

33. T. Lefferre, "The Decade of the Environment," *Chemtech* (May 1990): 262.

34. E. Woolard, "An Industry Approach to Sustainable Development," *Issues in Science and Technology* (spring 1992): 29–33.

35. R. Kennedy, "Achieving Environmental Excellence: Ten Tools for CEOs," *Prism* (published by Arthur D. Little, Inc., Cambridge, Mass.) (third quarter 1991): 79.

36. L. Lund, *Corporate Organization for Environmental Policy-Making* (New York: Conference Board, 1974), 2.

37. Morrison, *Managing Environmental Affairs.*

38. Hoffman, *From Heresy to Dogma.*

39. I. Schwartz, "More of Management Moves into the Environment Picture," *Chemical Week* 112, no. 7 (14 February 1973): 59.

40. Lund, *Corporate Organization.*

41. Schwartz, "More of Management," 61.

42. D. Sarokin et al., *Cutting Chemical Wastes: What Twenty-Nine Organic Chemical Plants Are Doing to Reduce Hazardous Wastes* (New York: INFORM, 1985), 32.

43. A recent poll showed that "the number of [college] freshmen who say it's important to take personal steps to clean up the environment . . . continued a decline that began after 1992, when the survey found record levels of interest." R. Sanchez, "College Freshmen Have the Blahs: Survey Indicates Academic, Civic Apathy Reach Record Levels," *Washington Post*, 12 January 1998, A1.

44. A. Downs, "Up and Down with Ecology: The 'Issue-Attention' Cycle," *Public Interest* 28 (1972): 38–50.

45. A. Hoffman, "Teaching Old Dogs New Tricks: Creating Incentives for Industry to Adopt Pollution Prevention," *Pollution Prevention Review* 3, no. 1 (1992): 1–11.

46. J. Nash et al., "Polaroid's Environmental Accounting and Reporting System," *Total Quality Environmental Management* (autumn 1992): 3–15.

47. W. Miller, "The IW Survey: Encouraging Findings," *Industry Week* 247, no. 2 (1998): 62.

48. Hoffman, *From Heresy to Dogma*, 148.

49. C. Walsh, "Automakers Ask EPA to Cut Sulfur in Gas," *Wall Street Journal*, 21 June 1999, B13G.

50. Sierra Club Legal Defense Fund, *The Endangered Species Act Works: Success Stories* (Washington, D.C.: Sierra Club Legal Defense Fund, 1995).

51. Ibid.

52. General Accounting Office, *Endangered Species Act: Information on Species Protection on Nonfederal Lands*, CRED-95-16 (Washington, D.C.: General Accounting Office, 1994).

53. H. El Nasser, "Sprawl Fight Creates Odd Alliances," *USA Today*, 15 February 1999, 3A.

54. Raytheon Electronic Systems, 180 Hartwell Road, Bedford, MA 01730.

55. J. Cushman, "GM Agrees to Cadillac Recall in Federal Pollution Complaint," *New York Times*, 1 December 1999, A1, A12.

56. "Rubber Reborn: 1996 Discover Awards," *Discover*, July 1996, 88.

57. D. Byrom, *Biomaterials: Novel Materials from Biological Sources* (New York: Stockton Press, 1991).

58. N. Myers, *The Sinking Ark* (Elmsford, N.Y.: Pergamon Press, 1979), 71.

59. National Wildlife Federation, *Nature's Pharmacy: Human Life Depends on the Rich Diversity of Life* (Washington, D.C.: National Wildlife Federation, 1994).

60. G. Kolata, "The Aura of a Miracle Fades from a Cancer Drug," *New York Times*, 7 November 1993, A1.

61. N. Myers, *A Wealth of Wild Species* (Boulder, Colo.: Westview Press, 1983), 90.

62. B. Wagner, "Nature's Tropical Medical Chest," *U.S. News and World Report*, 1 November 1993, 77; E. Pennisi, "Pharming Frogs," *Science News* 142 (1992): 40–42.

63. M. Grever, *Drug Discovery and Development from Natural Sources: The National Cancer Institute Experience*, Subcommittee on Environment and Natural Resources, Committee on Merchant Marine and Fisheries, U.S. House of Representatives, Washington, D.C., 9 November 1993.

64. Endangered Species Coalition, *The Endangered Species Act Protects Us* (Washington, D.C.: Endangered Species Coalition, 1995).

65. T. Eisner and E. Beiring, "Biotic Exploration Fund: Protecting Biodiversity through Chemical Prospecting," *BioScience* 44, no. 2 (1994): 95–98.

66. "Watts in the Dump: 1996 Discover Awards," *Discover*, July 1996, 87.

67. J. Fialka, "Once a Pollutant, 'Scrubber Sludge' Finds a Market," *Wall Street Journal*, 5 October 1998, B1.

68. A. Hoffman, "The Environmental Transformation of American Industry: An Institutional Account of Organizational Evolution in the Chemical and Petroleum Industries" (Ph.D. diss., Massachusetts Institute of Technology, Sloan School of Management, 1995), 262.

Part II: Drivers of Environmental Protection in a Changing Business Context

1. World Business Council for Sustainable Development (WBCSD), *Exploring Sustainable Development: WBCSD Global Scenario* (London: WBCSD, 1997).

2. World Resources Institute, *World Resources, 1994–1995* (New York: Oxford University Press, 1994).

3. B. Crossette, "Kofi Annan's Astonishing Facts," *New York Times*, 27 September 1998, 4–16; B. Crossette, "Most Consuming More and the Rich Much More," *New York Times*, 13 September 1998, A3.

4. World Resources Institute, *World Resources, 1994–1995*, 214.

5. Ibid.

6. R. Engelman and P. LeRoy, *Conserving Land: Population and Sustainable Food Production* (Washington, D.C.: Population Action International, 1995).

7. U.S. Department of Agriculture, *Summary Report, 1992: National Resources Inventory* (Washington, D.C.: Natural Resources Conservation Service, 1995).

8. World Resources Institute, *World Resources, 1994–1995*.

9. Population Action International, *Why Population Matters* (Washington, D.C.: Population Action International, 1996), 29.

10. E. O. Wilson, *The Diversity of Life* (Cambridge, Mass.: Harvard University Press, 1992).

11. W. Reid, "How Many Species Will There Be?" in S. Kawano, J. H. Connell, and T. Hidaka, eds., *Evolution and Coadaptation in Biotic Communities* (Tokyo: University of Tokyo Press, 1988), 17.

12. C. Nickerson, "Stripping the Sea's Life," *Boston Globe,* 17 April 1994, 1, 24, 25.
13. World Resources Institute, *World Resources, 1994–1995,* 214.
14. Ibid., 33.
15. R. Russell, "UN Paints Grim Global Picture," *Boston Globe,* 22 September 1999, A5.
16. World Resources Institute, *World Resources, 1994–1998.*
17. Environmental Protection Agency, *1990 Toxics Release Inventory,* Report no. 700-S-92-002 (Washington, D.C.: Environmental Protection Agency, 1992).
18. World Resources Institute, *World Resources, 1994–1995,* 214.
19. Office of Science and Technology Policy, *Climate Change: State of Knowledge* (Washington, D.C.: Executive Office of the President, 1997).
20. Ibid.
21. Intergovernmental Panel on Climate Change, *Climate Change: The IPCC Scientific Assessment* (Cambridge, England: Cambridge University Press, 1990).

Chapter 2: Regulatory Drivers

1. Report Center at the University of Connecticut, Public Opinion Online, *NBC News/Wall Street Journal Poll,* telephone survey between January 14 and 17 1995.
2. Environmental Protection Agency, *U.S. EPA Oral History Interview No. 1: William D. Ruckelshaus* (Washington, D.C.: U.S. Government Printing Office, 1993).
3. Ibid.
4. M. Landy, M. Roberts, and S. Thomas, *The Environmental Protection Agency: Asking the Wrong Questions* (New York: Oxford University Press, 1990).
5. S. Novick, "The Twenty-Year Evolution of Pollution Law: A Look Back," *Environmental Forum* (January 1986): 12–18.
6. P. Myers, "The Road We've Traveled," *EPA Journal* 16, no. 5 (1990): 57–60.
7. Ibid.
8. A. Hoffman, "An Uneasy Rebirth at Love Canal," *Environment* 37, no. 2 (1995): 4–9, 25–31.
9. R. Dunlap, "Trends in Public Opinion toward Environmental Issues: 1965–1990," *Society and Natural Resources* 4 (1991): 285–312.
10. C. Bukro, "EPA Making Polluters Pay—in Prison," *Chicago Tribune,* 19 July 1993, 1, 4.
11. Environmental Protection Agency, *Enforcement Accomplishments Report, FY 1991,* Report no. 300-R92-008 (Washington, D.C.: U.S. Government Printing Office, 1992).
12. Environmental Protection Agency, *Enforcement and Compliance Assurance Accomplishments Report.*
13. General Accounting Office, *Major Management Challenges and Program Risks: Environmental Protection Agency,* Report no. GAO/OCG-99-17 (Washington, D.C.: U.S. Government Printing Office, 1999), 17.
14. T. Lefferre, "The Decade of the Environment," *Chemtech* (May 1990): 262.
15. Internet: http://www.epa.gov/oeca/sfi.
16. J. Fialka, "EPA Puts Records about Polluters on the Internet," *Wall Street Journal,* 4 May 1998, A8.
17. "EPA, Citing Terrorism, to Keep Some Plant Hazard Data Offline," *SEJournal* (November 1998): 1, 10.
18. "Senate Passes Bill to Limit Access to Hazardous Chemical Accident Scenarios," *Daily Environment Reports* (June 25, 1999): A1–2.
19. Environmental Protection Agency, *EPA Green Lights Program Snapshot for January 1997* (Washington, D.C.: Environmental Protection Agency, 1997).

20. A. Hoffman, "The Many Faces of Environmental Stewardship," *Chemical Week* 157, no. 1 (1995): 65.

21. R. Hahn and R. Stavins, "Incentive-Based Environmental Regulation: A New Era from an Old Idea," *Ecology Law Quarterly* 18, no. 1 (1991): 1–42.

22. "Japan Government Prepares Recycling Bill for Waste Appliances," *Earth Vision News Reports,* 29 December 1997, 1.

23. C. Frankel and W. Coddington, "Environmental Marketing," chap. 15 in *Environmental Strategies Handbook,* ed. R. Kolluru (New York: McGraw-Hill, 1994): 643–677.

24. B. Mohl, "Wasted Effort?" *Boston Globe Magazine,* 16 November 1997, 23, 24, 31–38.

25. A. Hoffman, ed., *Global Climate Change: A Senior Level Dialogue at the Intersection of Economics, Strategy, Technology, Science, Politics, and International Negotiation* (San Francisco: New Lexington Press, 1998).

26. To find out more about purchasing sulfur dioxide permits, call the Acid Rain Hotline at (202) 564-9620 or The Clean Air Conservancy at (800) 2BUYAIR or (216) 523-1111.

27. M. Sandel, "It's Immoral to Buy the Right to Pollute," editorial, *New York Times,* 15 December 1997, A19.

28. M. Santoli, "Cantor Fitzgerald Seeks to Become Hub of Environmental Brokerage Market," *Wall Street Journal,* 12 September 1994, A11D.

29. P. Kraul, "This Commodity's Smokin'," *Los Angeles Times,* 30 April 1997, D2.

30. J. Bailey, "Utilities Overcomply with Clean Air Act, Are Stockpiling Pollution Allowances," *Wall Street Journal,* 15 November 1995, A8.

31. J. Bradley, "Buying High, Selling Low," *E Magazine,* July–August 1996, 14–15.

32. "Acid Rain Allowance Generates $32 Million in Sales; Prices Up Dramatically," *Daily Environment Report,* 27 March 1997, AA-1.

33. M. Golden, "Credits to Emit Sulfur Dioxide Fetch Record $53 Million at Annual EPA Sale," *Wall Street Journal,* 29 March 1999, B7C.

34. P. Kilborn, "East's Coal Towns Wither in the Name of Clean Air," *New York Times,* 15 February 1996, A1, A10.

35. A. Hoffman, *From Heresy to Dogma: An Institutional History of Corporate Environmentalism* (San Francisco: New Lexington Press, 1997), 189.

36. R. Stegemeier, *Straight Talk: The Future of Energy in the Global Economy* (Los Angeles: Unocal Corporation, 1995).

37. Greenwire, "Put It in Reverse," *Tomorrow* 7, no. 1 (1998): 38.

38. P. Nieuwenhuis, "End of the Road: Legislation is Making Carmakers Think Hard about Recycler and Producer Responsibility," *Tomorrow* 9, no. 5 (1999): 16.

39. A. Hoffman, M. Bazerman, and S. Yaffee, "Balancing Business Interests and Endangered Species Protection," *Sloan Management Review* 39, no. 1 (1997): 59–73.

40. Hoffman, *From Heresy to Dogma,* 189.

41. General Accounting Office, *Major Management Challenges and Program Risks,* 22–23.

42. The Global Environmental Management Initiative (GEMI) is a nonprofit organization of leading companies dedicated to fostering environmental, health, and safety excellence worldwide. Internet: http://www.gemi.org.

43. Global Environmental Management Initiative (GEMI), *Environmental Improvement through Business Incentives* (Washington, D.C.: GEMI, 1999).

Chapter 3: International Drivers

1. The classic reference is David Ricardo's *Principles of Political Economy and Taxation,* first published in 1817.

2. The structure of this section was based largely on Bhagwati, J. "The Case for Free Trade." *Scientific American,* November 1993, 42–49; and Daly, H. "The Perils of Free Trade." *Scientific American,* November 1992, 50–57.

3. J. Bhagwati, "The Case for Free Trade," *Scientific American,* November 1993, 43.

4. H. Daly, "The Perils of Free Trade." *Scientific American,* November 1992, 52.

5. M. Porter, "America's Green Strategy," *Scientific American,* April 1991, 168.

6. G. Grossman and A. Krueger, "Environmental Impacts of a North American Free Trade Agreement," in *The Mexico–U.S. Free Trade Agreement,* ed. P. Garber (Cambridge, Mass.: MIT Press, 1993).

7. Bhagwati, "Case for Free Trade," 44.

8. Ibid., 46.

9. The structure of the next two sections was based largely on Ferrantino, M., *A Brief Description of International Institutional Linkages in Trade and the Environment,* Working Paper no. 94-11-A (Washington, D.C.: United States International Trade Commission, Office of Economics, 1994); and F. Reinhardt and E. Prewitt, *Environment and International Trade,* Case Studies no. 794018 (Boston: Harvard Business School Press, 1994).

10. M. Ferrantino, *A Brief Description of International Institutional Linkages in Trade and the Environment,* Working Paper no. 94-11-A (Washington, D.C.: United States International Trade Commission, Office of Economics, 1994), 1.

11. "GATTery v. Greenery," *Economist,* 30 May 1992, 12.

12. J. Cushman, "Trade Group Strikes Blow at U.S. Environmental Law," *New York Times,* 7 April 1998, D1.

13. Ferrantino, *International Institutional Linkages,* 3.

14. Ibid., 8.

15. Ibid., 6.

16. "GATTery v. Greenery," 13.

17. F. Reinhardt and E. Prewitt, *Environment and International Trade,* Case Studies, no. 794018 (Boston: Harvard Business School Press, 1994), 11.

18. J. Maxwell and S. Weiner, "Green Consciousness or Dollar Diplomacy? The British Response to the Threat of Ozone Depletion," *International Environmental Affairs* (winter 1993): 19–41.

19. J. Cushman, "U.S. Prosecutors in Six Cities File Charges of Smuggling Refrigeration Gas," *New York Times,* 10 January 1997, 12.

20. "Going Abroad," *Economist,* 29 May 1993, 17.

21. "Hazardous Waste Exports Banned under New Accord," *Chemical Marketing Reporter,* 2 October 1995, 29; "Ban on Waste Exports outside OECD Pushed through Basel Treaty Meeting," *International Environment Reporter,* 4 October 1995.

22. Reinhardt and Prewitt, *Environment and International Trade,* 11.

23. P. Lewis, "World Forestry Talks End in Division on Whether to Curb Logging," *New York Times,* 22 February 1997, 7.

24. Ferrantino, *International Institutional Linkages,* 9.

25. Intergovernmental Panel on Climate Change, *Climate Change, 1995: IPCC Second Assessment Synthesis of Scientific-Technical Information Relevant to Interpreting Article 2 of the UN Framework Convention on Climate Change* (Cambridge, England: Cambridge University Press, 1996).

26. A. Hoffman, ed., *Global Climate Change: A Senior Level Dialogue at the Intersection of Economics, Strategy, Technology, Science, Politics, and International Negotiation* (San Francisco: New Lexington Press, 1998), 25.

27. *Introduction to the GEF* (Washington, D.C.: Global Environment Facility, GEF Secretariat).

28. Internet: http://www.iso14000.com/.

29. C. Frankel, "In Search of ISO 14001," *Tomorrow* 8, no. 2 (1998): 24–25.
30. Ibid.
31. B. Birchard, "Green Management Lurches Ahead," *Tomorrow* 9, no. 1 (1999): 32–33.
32. Reuters, "Eight Countries Agree to Fight Environmental Crime," *New York Times*, 6 April 1998, A4.
33. C. Nickerson, "Canadian Fishermen End Blockade of an Alaskan Ferry," *Boston Globe*, 23 July 1997, A18.
34. L. Goering, "Pollution Test Case Pits Ecuadorians against U.S. Firm," *Chicago Tribune*, 25 June 1996, 1, 14.
35. "Texaco and Ecuador," editorial, *New York Times*, 19 February 1999, A22.
36. J. Friedland, "Oil Companies Strive to Turn a New Leaf to Save Rain Forest," *Wall Street Journal*, 17 July 1997, A1, A8.
37. Ibid., A1.
38. Ibid., A8.
39. "Shell Cancels Gas Project: Company Rocks Peru Economy with Plan to Pull Out of Camisea Fields," *CNN Financial Network*, 16 July 1998, 1. Internet: http://cnnfn.com/hot-stories/companies/9807/16/peru/#TOP.
40. Mobil Corporation, "People Form the Bridge," *New York Times*, 13 May 1999, A31.

Chapter 4: Resource Drivers

1. R. Costanza et al., "The Value of the World's Ecosystem Services and Natural Capital," *Nature* 387 (May 1997): 253–260.
2. W. Stevens, "How Much Is Nature Worth? For You, $33 Trillion," *New York Times*, 20 May 1997, B7, B9.
3. A. Revkin, "New York Begins Spending to Save City's Reservoirs," *New York Times*, 22 January 1997, A1.
4. J. Jablonski and L. Pasquini, *Prosper through Environmental Leadership: Succeeding in Tough Times* (Albuquerque, N.M.: Technical Management Consortium, 1994).
5. B. Smart, *Beyond Compliance: A New Industry View of the Environment* (Washington, D.C.: World Resources Institute, 1992), 174.
6. A. Goodman, "Chain Reaction: You're Not There until Your Suppliers Are There," *Tomorrow* 8, no. 4 (1998): 26–28.
7. E. von Hippel, *The Sources of Innovation* (New York: Oxford University Press, 1988).
8. Ibid., 4.
9. J. Maxwell et al., "Preventing Waste beyond the Company Walls: P&G's Response to the Need for Environmental Quality," *Pollution Prevention Review* 3, no. 3 (summer 1993): 317–333.
10. S. Mehegan, "Green on Green," *Brandweek*, 20 May 1996, 43–50.
11. Smart, *Beyond Compliance*, 170.
12. "Insurance Liability for Pollution Claims," *TechLaw Update* (third quarter 1990): 4.
13. P. Shrivastava, "Long-Term Recovery from the Bhopal Crisis," in *The Long Road to Recovery: Community Responses to Industrial Disaster*, ed. J. Mitchell (New York: United Nations University Press, 1996), 121–147.
14. Ibid.
15. A. Hoffman, *From Heresy to Dogma: An Institutional History of Corporate Environmentalism* (San Francisco: New Lexington Press, 1997).
16. General Accounting Office, *Hazardous Waste: The Cost and Availability of Pollution Insurance* (Washington, D.C.: U.S. Government Printing Office, 1988), 3.

17. A. Hoffman, *The Hazardous Waste Remediation Market: Innovative Technological Development, and the Market Entry of the Construction Industry*, CCRE Working Paper no. 92-1 (Cambridge: Massachusetts Institute of Technology, Department of Civil and Environmental Engineering, 1992).

18. S. Schmidheiny, F. Zorraquin, and World Business Council for Sustainable Development, *Financing Change: The Financial Community, Eco-Efficiency, and Sustainable Development* (Cambridge, Mass.: MIT Press, 1996), 118.

19. C. Frankel, "Putting a Premium on the Environment," *Tomorrow* 6, no. 3 (1996): 18.

20. Ibid.

21. Ibid.

22. Schmidheiny, *Financing Change*.

23. C. Brauner, *Global Warming: Element of Risk* (Zurich: Swiss Re, 1994), 5.

24. J. Leggett, ed., *Climate Change and the Financial Sector: The Emerging Threat—the Solar Solution* (Munich: Gerling Akademie Verlag, 1996).

25. E. Mills, "Energy Efficiency Can Cut Losses," *Reinsurance* (March 1997): 24.

26. A. Streeter, J. Garman, and H. Yanulis, "Weathering More Storms," *Tomorrow* 9, no. 1 (1999): 42.

27. SunLight Power International, "Swiss Reinsurance Company Pledges $2.75 million to SunLight Power International, European Insurance Companies Back Solar to Mitigate Global Warming," press release, 11 July 1997.

28. A. Hoffman, *The Hazardous Waste Remediation Market*.

29. P. Marcotte, "Real Property," *ABA Journal* (1 November 1987): 69.

30. European Bank for Reconstruction and Development (EBRD), *The Basic Documents of the European Bank for Reconstruction and Development* (London: EBRD, 1991).

31. Schmidheiny, *Financing Change*, 100.

32. A. Monroe, "The Looming Ecowar: Environmentalists' New Tactics Threaten to Take a Toll on Wall Street Financings," *Investment Dealers' Digest*, 24 May 1999, 20–25.

33. C. Frankel, "The Americas Want In," *Tomorrow* 6, no. 3 (1996): 18.

34. Interfaith Center on Corporate Responsibility (ICCR), *Corporate Examiner* (New York: ICCR, 1989–1994).

35. This type of pressure was used successfully on at least two other occasions. In 1977, the Sullivan Principles used investor resolutions to convince companies to discontinue operations and cut ties (such as licensing and franchise agreements) with South Africa. Similarly, the McBride Principles coerced companies through investor resolutions to endorse a nondiscrimination code aimed at creating equal opportunity for Catholics in Northern Ireland.

36. A. Hoffman, "A Strategic Response to Investor Activism," *Sloan Management Review* 37, no. 2 (1996): 51–64.

37. P. Waldman, "A Rainforest Tribe Brings Its Eco-Battle to Corporate America: U'wa Chiefs and U.S. Activists Stage a Week of Protest over Occidental Oil Plan," *Wall Street Journal*, 7 June 1999, A1.

38. Monroe, "The Looming Ecowar," 20.

39. Ibid.

40. L. Tantillo, "Wall Street Likes What It Sees," *Chemical Week* (11 October 1989): 25–26.

41. B. Stutz, "Cleaning Up," *Atlantic*, October 1989, 48.

42. Office of Science and Technology Policy, *Technology for a Sustainable Future*, Report no. 386-802/00037 (Washington, D.C.: U.S. Government Printing Office, 1994), 70.

43. L. Descano and B. Gentry, "How to Communicate Environmental Performance to the Capital Markets," *CMA News* (April 1998): 33–37.

44. Internet: http://www.icfkaiser.com.

45. S. Feldman, P. Soyka, and P. Ameer, *Does Improving a Firm's Environmental Management System and Environmental Performance Result in a Higher Stock Price?* (Fairfax, Va.: ICF Kaiser International, 1996).
46. C. Frankel, "If You're So Rich, Why Ain't Ya Smart?" *Tomorrow* 8, no. 5 (1998): 50–51.
47. R. House, "Eco Funds Inch Forward," *Tomorrow* 6, no. 3 (1996): 14–16.
48. M. Wright, "God, Mammon, and the Market," *Tomorrow* 6, no. 3 (1996): 10–11.
49. House, "Eco Funds Inch Forward."
50. C. Deutsch, "For Wall Street, Increasing Evidence That Green Begets Green," *New York Times,* 19 July 1998, 7.
51. Ibid.
52. S. Bailey and S. Syre, "Do-Good Investing Fund Does Well, Beats S&P Again," *Boston Globe,* 5 March 1998, C1.
53. Deutsch, "For Wall Street, Increasing Evidence."
54. Ibid.
55. "Counting on the Environment," *Business Ethics* (January–February 1998): 10.
56. A. White and D. Zinkl, "Raising Standardization," *Environmental Forum* (January–February 1998): 28–37.
57. Aspen Institute, *Uncovering Value: Integrating Environmental and Financial Performance* (Queenstown, Md.: Aspen Institute Publications Office, 1998), 3.
58. E. Nieves, "Lumber Company Approves U.S. Deal to Save Redwoods," *New York Times,* 3 March 1999, A1, A12.

Chapter 5: Market Drivers

1. A. Streeter, J. Garman, and H. Yanulis, "Solar Service Stations," *Tomorrow* 9, no. 3 (1999): 34.
2. A. Streeter, J. Garman, and H. Yanulis, "Send It Again, Sam," *Tomorrow* 8, no. 4 (1998): 37.
3. Greenwire, "PET Underwear," *Tomorrow* 7, no. 5 (1997): 34.
4. R. Dunlap, "Trends in Public Opinion toward Environmental Issues: 1965–1990," *Society and Natural Resources* 4 (1991): 285–312.
5. Times Mirror Magazines, Inc., *The Environmental Two Step: Looking Forward, Moving Backward* (New York: Times Mirror Magazines, 1995), 16.
6. F. Krupp, "Win/Win on the Environmental Front," *EPA Journal* 16, no. 5 (1990): 30–31.
7. Times Mirror, *Environmental Two Step.*
8. S. C. Johnson/Roper (1993) *The Environment: Public Attitudes and Individual Behavior, North America: Canada, Mexico, United States,* 35. Commissioned by S. C. Johnson (a leading multinational company with operations in nearly 60 countries worldwide) and conducted by Roper Starch © 1993. All rights reserved. Used with permission.
9. Ibid., 30.
10. Ibid., 31.
11. Ibid.
12. Ibid.
13. Ibid.
14. Ibid., 35.
15. C. Frankel and W. Coddington, "Environmental Marketing," chapter 15 in *Environmental Strategies Handbook,* ed. R. Kolluru (New York: McGraw-Hill, 1994), 643–677.
16. Times Mirror, *Environmental Two Step,* 26.
17. Ibid.

18. Ibid.

19. Ibid.

20. M. Burros, "A New Goal beyond Organic: Clean Food," *New York Times,* 7 February 1996, B1, B5.

21. A. Bradbury, "Alive and Sticking," *Tomorrow* 8, no. 6 (1998): 20–22.

22. Contact: Arthur Weissman, president. Telephone: (202) 872-6400; e-mail: aweissman@greenseal.org; Internet: http://www.greenseal.org.

23. Contact: Sharon Bryan, European Commission. Telephone: +32-2-295-7755; e-mail: ecolabel@dg11.cec.be; Internet: http://europa.eu.int/ecolabel.

24. Contact: Helena Andersson. Telephone: 46 (0)31-711 64 50; e-mail: gbg@snf.se; Internet: http://www.snf.se/hmv/hmveng/ecolabelling.htm.

25. Contact: Ning Yu, director, Environment and Development Foundation. Telephone: +886-35-916221; e-mail: ningyu@edf.org.tw; Internet: http://www.greenmark.itri.org.tw/eng/english.htm.

26. Contact: Heather Bailey. Telephone: +263-4-302-886; e-mail: e2000@samara.co.zw.

27. Contact: Kevin Gallagher, TerraChoice Environmental Services Inc. Telephone: (800) 478-0399 x 222; e-mail: jpaterson@terrachoice.ca; Internet: http://www.environmental-choice.com.

28. Contact: Sang Young Lee. Telephone: +82-2-597-0124; e-mail: ecomark@chollian.net.

29. Contact: Takao Kawamoto. Telephone: +81-3-3508-2651; Internet: http://www.eic.or.jp/jea (in Japanese), http://www.jeas.or.jp/english/index.html (in English).

30. Contact: Harald Neitzel, Federal Environment Agency. Telephone: +49-30-8903-3703; e-mail: harald.neitzel@uba.de; Internet: http://www.blauer-engel.de (in German), http://www.blauer-engel.de/Englisch/index.htm (in English).

31. Contact: Marje Russ. Telephone: +64-9-525-6655; e-mail: mruss@ianz.govt.nz; Internet: http://www.ianz.govt.nz.

32. Contact: Bjorn-Erik Lonn. Telephone: +47-2236-0710; Internet: http://www.ecolabel.no (in Norwegian), http://www.ecolabel.no/ecolabel/english/index.html (in English).

33. Contact: Andre Mascini. Telephone: +31-70-358-6300; e-mail: milieukeur@milieukeur.nl; Internet: http://www.milieukeur.nl (in German), http://www.milieukeur.nl/english/ (in English).

34. J. Gerstenzang, "Survey Bolsters Global Warming Fight," *Los Angeles Times,* 21 November 1997, A4.

35. "Patagonia Is First Company to Buy 100% Wind for California Operations," *Wind Energy Weekly* 17, no. 805 (1998): 1–2.

36. J. Robbins, "Sheep Ranchers Use Llamas to Foster Ecologically Friendly Wool Market," *New York Times,* 15 December 1997, A12.

37. The report is available on the Internet at http://www.neetf.org and can be obtained by contacting the National Environmental Education & Training Foundation, 1701 H Street, NW, Suite 900, Washington, DC 20006-3915; (202) 833-2933.

38. National Environmental Education & Training Foundation, "Environmental Myths Impede Future Progress," *NEETF Update* (winter 1999): 1.

39. A. Hoffman, *From Heresy to Dogma: An Institutional History of Corporate Environmentalism* (San Francisco: New Lexington Press, 1997), 77.

40. Ibid., 189.

41. K. Bradsher, "U.S. Auto Makers Showing Interest in Fuel Efficiency," *New York Times,* 5 January 1998, A1, A12.

42. B. Bahree, C. Cooper, and S. Liesman, "Bigger Oil: BP to Acquire Amoco in Huge Deal Spurred by Low Energy Prices," *Wall Street Journal,* 12 August 1998, A1.

43. L. Kay and M. Wright, "May I Green Your Room Now?" *Tomorrow* 7, no. 4 (1997): 16–18.

44. Ibid.

45. Cambridge Reports/Research International, *Corporate EQ Scores 1992: Americans Rate Corporate Environmental Performance* (Cambridge, Mass.: Cambridge Reports/Research International, 1992).

46. K. Dickerson, "In Defense of Our Industry's Reputation—Is Anyone Interested?" (presentation at the 1997 Montreux Energy Conference, Aspen, Colo., 24–27 September 1997).

47. A. Hoffman, "The Many Faces of Environmental Stewardship," *Chemical Week* 157, no. 1 (1995): 63–65.

48. Ibid., 63.

49. C. McCoy, "Two Big Firms to Vie to Build a Better Fridge," *Wall Street Journal,* 8 December 1992, B1.

50. J. Holusha, "Whirlpool Takes Top Prize in Redesigning Refrigerator," *New York Times,* 30 June 1993, D4.

51. G. McKinney, "Environmental Technology for Competitiveness: A Call for a Cooperative Pollution Prevention Initiative" (speech given at the National Technology Initiative Conference, Massachusetts Institute of Technology, Cambridge, Mass., 12 February 1992).

52. C. Solomon, "Hard Times for Advisors on Cleanups," *Wall Street Journal,* 11 February 1998, NE1.

53. International Technology Corp. (IT) (approximate annual gross revenues of $400 million) acquired OH Materials Corp. (approximate annual gross revenues of $600 million). Tetra Tech (approximate gross revenues of $58 million) acquired Halliburton/Brown & Root's environmental business (NUS Corp.) (gross annual revenues of $80 million). The management of ATC Corp. acquired control of ATC ($180 million gross revenues). URS Corp. (gross annual revenues $400 million) acquired Woodward Clyde (approximate gross revenues of $340 million). And, an investor group acquired a 10 percent interest in ICF Kaiser (approximate gross revenues of $1 billion).

54. Environmental Financial Consulting Group, *Quarterly Overview Letter, January 1998* (New York: Environmental Financial Consulting Group, 1998).

Chapter 6: Social Drivers

1. V. Hodgkinson, M. Wietzman, J. Abrahams, E. Critchfield, and D. Stevenson, eds. *Non-Profit Almanac* (San Francisco: Jossey-Bass Publishers, 1993).

2. Gale Research Inc., *Ward's Business Directory of U.S. Private and Public Companies, 1994* (Detroit: Gale Research, 1994).

3. Neil Evernden wrote: "The term 'environmentalist' was not chosen by the individuals so described. It was seized upon by members of the popular press as a means of labeling a newly prominent segment of society. . . . In fact, the act of labeling a group may constitute an effective means of suppression, even if the label seems neutral or objective. For in giving this particular name, not only have the labelers forced an artificial association on a very diverse group of individuals, but they have also given a terse public statement of what 'those people' are presumed to want. Environmentalists want environment—obviously. But this may be entirely wrong, a possibility that few environmentalists have contemplated even though many have lamented the term itself. For in the very real sense there can only be environment in a society that holds certain assumptions, and there can only be an environmental crisis in a society that believes in environment." N. Evernden, *The Natural Alien: Humankind and Environment* (Toronto: University of Toronto Press, 1985), 125.

4. T. Wikle, "Geographical Patterns of Membership in U.S. Environmental Organizations," *Professional Geographer* 47, no. 1 (1995): 41–48.
5. Gale Research Inc., *The Encyclopedia of Associations* (Detroit: Gale Research, 1993).
6. C. McCoy, "Two U.S. Members of Mitsubishi Group and Environmental Activists Reach Pact," *Wall Street Journal*, 11 February 1998, A8.
7. A. Goodman and A. Streeter, "Companies of the Year," *Tomorrow* 9, no. 1 (1999): 14–16.
8. L. Orti, *Environmental Alliances: Critical Factors for Success* (New York: Conference Board, 1995).
9. The Alliance for Environmental Innovation, 6 North Market Building, Faneuil Hall Marketplace, Boston, MA 02109.
10. Orti, *Environmental Alliances*, 9.
11. Ibid.
12. Internet: http://www.scorecard.org/.
13. A. Goodman, "Campaigning for Greener Greenbacks," *Tomorrow* 9, no. 1 (1999): 53.
14. M. Wald, "Hybrid Bus Is Environmentally Friendly," *New York Times*, 8 February 1999, A16.
15. A. Hoffman, "An Uneasy Rebirth at Love Canal," *Environment* 37, no. 2 (1995): 4–9, 25–31.
16. M. Dowie, *Losing Ground: American Environmentalism at the Close of the Twentieth Century* (Cambridge, Mass.: MIT Press, 1995), 207.
17. *Responsible Care Progress Report, 1994–95* (Arlington, Va.: Chemical Manufacturers Association, 1995).
18. D. Protess et al., "The Impact of Investigative Reporting on Public Opinion and Policy-Making: Targeting Toxic Waste," *Public Opinion Quarterly* 51, no. 2 (1987): 166–185.
19. A. Hoffman, "Who Loves Love Canal?" *Tomorrow* 3, no. 3 (1993): 58–64.
20. J. Graves, "Who Scores Best on the Environment?" *Fortune*, 26 July 1993, 114–121.
21. R. Lindzen, "Global Warming: The Origins and Nature of Alleged Scientific Consensus," *Regulation* 15, no. 2 (1992): 87–98.
22. C. Deutsch, "Recycling Advocates Don't Take Less News Coverage Lightly," *New York Times*, 17 February 1997, 31.
23. Ibid.
24. Ibid.
25. Ibid.
26. A. Hoffman, *From Heresy to Dogma: An Institutional History of Corporate Environmentalism*, (San Francisco: New Lexington Press, 1997).
27. Environmental Protection Agency, *Supporting Background Document for Proposed Response Action Contractor Indemnification Guidelines* (McLean, Va.: PRC Environmental Management, 1989), 4–82.
28. Ibid., 22.
29. Ibid., 25.
30. A. Dembner, "Movement Is Strong on Campus," *Boston Globe*, 12 November 1994, 28.
31. J. Makower, "Business Schools Get in Line," *Tomorrow* 3, no. 3 (1993): 50–53; K. Mangan, "The Greening of the MBA," *Chronicle of Higher Education*, 2 November 1994, A19–A20; A. Pham, "Business Schools See Green," *Boston Globe*, 28 June 1994, 35; B. Wagner, "The Greening of the Engineer," *U.S. News and World Report*, 21 March 1994, 90–91; S. Friedman, "Teaching the Beat: Rising Interest in E-Journalism Reflected in Academic Option," *SEJournal* 6, no. 1 (1996): 1, 7.
32. Wagner, "Greening of the Engineer."
33. Mangan, "The Greening of the MBA," 1994.

34. J. Finlay, R. Bunch, and B. Neubert, *Grey Pinstripes with Green Ties: MBA Programs Where the Environment Matters* (Washington, D.C.: World Resources Institute, 1998).

35. Dembner, "Movement Is Strong on Campus."

36. J. Cushman, "Critics Rise Up against Environmental Education," *New York Times*, 22 April 1997, A8.

37. Ibid.

38. National Science and Technology Council, *Technology for a Sustainable Future: A Framework for Action* (Washington, D.C.: Office of Science and Technology Policy, 1994), 100.

39. Cushman, "Critics Rise Up."

40. A. Leopold, *A Sand County Almanac, and Sketches Here and There* (New York: Oxford University Press, 1949), 210.

41. J. Passmore, *Man's Responsibility for Nature: Ecological Problems and Western Traditions* (New York: Charles Scribner's Sons, 1974), 6.

42. L. White, "The Historical Roots of Our Ecological Crisis," *Science* 155 (10 March 1967): 1203–1207.

43. A. Hoffman and J. Ehrenfeld, "Corporate Environmentalism, Sustainability, and Management Studies," in *Sustainability Strategies for Industry: The Future of Corporate Practice*, ed. N. Roome (Washington, D.C.: Island Press, 1998), 55–73.

44. G. Hardin, "The Tragedy of the Commons: The Population Problem Has no Technical Solution; It Requires a Fundamental Extension of Morality," *Science* 162 (13 December 1968): 1244.

45. Associated Press, "Presbyterians Ratify Teaching on Sex, Ecology," *Boston Globe*, 9 June 1991, 4.

46. K. Woodward and R. Nordland, "New Rules for an Old Faith," *Newsweek*, 30 November 1992, 71.

47. *Catechism of the Catholic Church* (Liguori, Mo.: Liguori Publications, 1994), 580.

48. L. Stammer, "Harming the Environment Is Sinful, Prelate Says," *Los Angeles Times*, 9 November 1997, 1A.

49. Ibid.

50. His Holiness Tenzin Gyatso, the Fourteenth Dalai Lama of Tibet, "A Tibetan Buddhist Perspective on Spirit in Nature," in *Spirit and Nature: Why the Environment Is a Religious Issue*, ed. S. Rockefeller and J. Elder (Boston: Beacon Press, 1992), 109–124.

51. A. Shenandoah, "A Tradition of Thanksgiving," in Rockefeller and Elder, *Spirit and Nature*, 19.

52. S. Kloehn, "Evangelicals See Beasts as Blessed by Their Creator," *Chicago Tribune*, 10 February 1997, A1, A16.

53. P. Steinfels, "Evangelical Group Defends Endangered-Species Laws as a Modern Noah's Ark," *New York Times*, 31 January 1996, C19.

54. "Mainstream," *Greenline* 15 (11 December 1995): 1.

55. "Green Cross," *Greenline* 48 (31 January 1996): 1.

56. J. Cushman, "Religious Groups Mount a Campaign to Support Pact on Global Warming," *New York Times*, 15 August 1998, A10.

57. Ibid.

58. Internet: http://www.powersavers.com/commonwealthnews/21press.htm.

59. In the fall of 1990, a four-day symposium titled "Spirit and Nature: Religion, Ethics, and Environmental Crisis" was held at Middlebury College in Middlebury, Vermont. It included speakers representing the Buddhist, Christian, Islamic, Jewish, Native American, and liberal democratic traditions. The proceedings were published in a book, S. Rockefeller and J. Elder, eds., *Spirit and Nature: Why the Environment Is a Religious Issue* (Boston: Beacon Press, 1992), and a docu-

mentary videotape titled *Moyers/Spirit and Nature.* Copies of the videotape may be obtained from Spirit and Nature, P.O. Box 2284, South Burlington, VT 05407; (800) 336-1917.

60. C. Morrison, *Managing Environmental Affairs: Corporate Practices in the U.S., Canada, and Europe* (New York: Conference Board, 1991), 18.

61. C. Fishman, "I Want to Pioneer the Company of the Next Industrial Revolution," *Fast Company* (April–May 1998), 138.

62. J. Magretta, "Growth through Global Sustainability: An Interview with Monsanto's CEO, Robert B. Shapiro," *Harvard Business Review,* January–February 1997, 78–88.

63. J. Browne, "Climate Change: The New Agenda," in *Global Climate Change: A Senior Level Dialogue at the Intersection of Economics, Strategy, Technology, Science, Politics, and International Negotiation,* ed. A. Hoffman (San Francisco: New Lexington Press, 1998), 53–62.

64. From online discussion on Tuesday, June 24, 1997 at 2:01 EDT.

Part III: New "Rules of the Game"

1. M. Friedman, "The Social Responsibility of Business Is to Increase Its Profits," *New York Times Magazine,* 13 September 1970, 126.

2. W. Meckling and M. Jensen, "Reflections on the Corporation as a Social Invention," *Midland Corporate Finance Journal* (fall 1983): 4.

Chapter 7: Altering Strategic Objectives

1. Aspen Institute, *Uncovering Value: Integrating Environmental and Financial Performance* (Queenstown, Md.: Aspen Institute Publications Office, 1998), 7.

2. Global Environmental Management Initiative (GEMI), *Environment: Value to Business* (Washington, D.C.: GEMI, 1999), 2–11. © 1999 by GEMI. All rights reserved. Reprinted with permission.

3. W. Stevens, "Expectations Aside, Water Use in U.S. Is Showing Decline," *New York Times,* 11 November 1998, A16.

4. J. Holusha, "Pulp Mills Turn Over a New Leaf: Some Companies See Green as Just Good Business," *New York Times,* 9 March 1996, 21, 23.

5. Ibid.

6. Ibid.

7. A. Goodman, "The Negative Power of Emissions," *Tomorrow* 5, no. 7 (1997): 50.

8. Ibid.

9. R. Cavanagh and Natural Resources Defense Council, "Global Energy, Emissions, and Regulatory Outlook" (presentation at the Fourth Aspen Energy and Environment Roundtable, Aspen, Colo., 25 September 1997); see also D. Hawkins and E. Svenson, *Benchmarking Air Emissions of Electric Utility Generators in the U.S.* (Washington, D.C.: Natural Resources Defense Council, 1998).

10. "New Paints, Greater Efficiency Cut TRI Releases by Automakers," *Daily Environment Report,* 12 March 1999, 3–4.

11. Ibid.

12. M. Krebs, "New Ford Division to Focus on Recycling of Auto Parts," *New York Times,* 27 April 1999, C6.

13. Ibid.

14. K. Henry, "Auto Recycling Plant Divides, Conquers," *Baltimore Sun,* 3 June 1999, D1.

15. W. Abernathy and J. Utterback, "Patterns of Industrial Innovation," *Technology Review* (June–July 1978): 40–47.

16. D. Sahal, "Technological Guideposts and Innovation Avenues," *Research Policy* (April 1985): 61–82.
17. R. Blumenstein, "Electric Car Drives Factory Innovations," *Wall Street Journal*, 27 February 1997, B1.
18. M. Krebs, "Planting the Seeds for a Crop of Lean, Green Machines," *New York Times*, March 15, 1998, Section 12, p. 1.
19. K. Bradsher, "U.S. Auto Makers Showing Interest in Fuel Efficiency," *New York Times*, 5 January 1998, A1.
20. J. Ball, "GM, Toyota to Announce Pact to Develop 'Alternative-Fuel Vehicles' through 2004," *Wall Street Journal*, 19 April 1999, A6.
21. Arthur D. Little, Inc., "The U.S. Department of Energy and Arthur D. Little Unveil First-Ever On-Board Gasoline Powered 'Fuel Cell' for the Automobile," press release, 1997.
22. K. Naughton, "Detroit's Impossible Dream," *Business Week*, 12 March 1998, 66.
23. "Magazine's Crystal Ball Sees 'Smog-Alert' Maps and Pollution-Eating Cars," *Environment Writer*, December 1996, 5. Or contact the World Future Society, 7910 Woodmont Ave., Suite 450, Bethesda, MD 02814; (301) 656-8274.
24. A. Streeter, J. Garman, and H. Yanulis, "New Volvo Burns Smog, Too," *Tomorrow* 8, no. 4 (1998), 32.
25. C. Frankel and K. Loughran, "Good News, Bad News for EV's," *Tomorrow* 6, no. 6 (1996): 33.
26. A. Streeter, J. Garman, H. Yanulis, and K. Loughran, "Chinese under Cover," *Tomorrow* 8, no. 5 (1998): 33.
27. R. Rosenberg, "A High-Tech Charge into Scooters," *Boston Globe*, 24 December 1997, D1, D4.
28. J. Bailey, "1001 Uses for Millions of Old Tires," *Chicago Tribune*, 19 November 1995, 1, 6.
29. Yellow Cab Shoe Company, 88 Hatch Street, Suite 303, New Bedford, MA 02745. Internet: http://www.yellowcabshoes.com.
30. Cycloid Company, 301 Commerce Park Drive, Cranberry Township, PA 16066. Internet: http://www.cycloid.com.
31. National Science and Technology Council, *Technology for a Sustainable Future: A Framework for Action* (Washington, D.C.: Office of Science and Technology Policy, 1994), 42–43.
32. Ibid., 3.
33. Ibid.
34. Information was provided by Environmental Business International Inc., San Diego, Calif.
35. National Science and Technology Council, *Technology for a Sustainable Future*, 40.
36. Information was provided by Environmental Business International Inc., San Diego, Calif.
37. G. McKinney, "Environmental Technology for Competitiveness: A Call for a Cooperative Pollution Prevention Initiative" (speech given at the National Technology Initiative Conference, Massachusetts Institute of Technology, Cambridge, Mass., 12 February 1992).
38. Monsanto Company, *Annual Report* (St. Louis, Mo.: Monsanto Company, 1996), 8.
39. Ibid.
40. P. Kennedy, *Preparing for the Twenty-First Century* (New York: Random House, 1993), 22.
41. Population Action International, *Why Population Matters* (Washington, D.C.: Population Action International, 1996).
42. T. Malthus, *Principles of Population* (1817; reprint, 5th ed., Homewood, Ill.: Richard D. Irwin, 1963); T. Malthus, *On Population: Three Essays by Thomas Malthus, Julian Huxley, and Frederick Osborn* (1830; reprint, New York: New American Library, Mentor Books, 1960).
43. D. King, "It's Clean, It's Green, and It'll Feed the World," *Tomorrow* 2, no. 7 (1997): 10–12.

44. L. Grant, "Monsanto's Bet: There's Gold in Going Green," *Fortune,* 14 April 1997, 116–118.
45. R. Weiss, "Corn Seed Producers Move to Avert Pesticide Resistance," *Washington Post,* 9 January 1999, A4.
46. V. Klinkenborg, "Biotechnology and the Future of Agriculture," *New York Times,* 8 December 1997, A21.
47. Ibid.
48. S. Kilman and H. Cooper, "Monsanto Falls Flat Trying to Sell Bioengineered Food," *Wall Street Journal,* 11 May 1999, A1.
49. Bill McDonough, dean of the University of Virginia School of Architecture. J. Magretta, "Growth through Global Sustainability: An Interview with Monsanto's CEO, Robert B. Shapiro," *Harvard Business Review,* January–February 1997, 83.
50. F. Capra and G. Pauli, eds., *Steering Business toward Sustainability* (New York: United Nations University Press, 1995), 4.
51. A. Lovins, L. H. Lovins, and P. Hawken, "A Road Map for Natural Capitalism," *Harvard Business Review,* May–June 1999, 145–158.
52. C. Arnst et al., "When Green Begets Green," *Business Week,* 10 November 1997, 102.
53. J. Powell, "Carpet Recycling Obstacles," *Resource Recycling* (April 1997): 42.
54. "Industry Forest Excels in First SCS Evaluation," *Wood Technology* 120, no. 3 (1993), 12.
55. S. Landis, "Supply and Demand for Certified Wood," *Understory,* (Fall/Winter 1997): 1.
56. P. Kennedy, *Preparing for the Twenty-First Century* (New York: Random House, 1993), 96.
57. H. Jonas, "Technology and Responsibility: Reflections on the New Tasks of Ethics," *Social Research* 40 (1973): 31–54.
58. Ibid., 40.
59. S. J. Gould, cited in W. Calvin, "The Emergence of Intelligence," *Scientific American* 271, no. 4 (1994): 107.
60. C. S. Lewis, *The Abolition of Man* (New York: Macmillan Company, 1953), 44.

Chapter 8: Strategy Originates within the Organization

1. M. Bazerman and A. Hoffman, "Sources of Environmentally Destructive Behavior: Individual, Organizational, and Institutional Perspectives," *Research in Organizational Behavior* 21 (1999): 39–79.
2. For studies of the connection between culture and technology development, see M. Smith and L. Marx, *Does Technology Drive History?* (Cambridge, Mass.: MIT Press, 1994); R. Thomas, *What Machines Can't Do: Politics and Technology in the Industrial Enterprise* (Berkeley: University of California Press, 1994); S. Barley, "Technology as an Occasion for Structuring," *Administrative Science Quarterly* 31 (1986): 78–108; P. David, "Clio and the Economics of QWERTY," *Economic History* 75 (1985): 227–332; and N. Rosenberg, *Inside the Black Box* (Cambridge, England: Cambridge University Press, 1982).
3. J. Jubeir, "Educating Environmental Managers for Tomorrow," *EPA Journal* 21, no. 2 (1995): 31–33.
4. A. Hoffman, *From Heresy to Dogma: An Institutional History of Corporate Environmentalism* (San Francisco: New Lexington Press, 1997).
5. "Ignoring the Environment Can Be a Waste of Money," *Treasury Manager's Report* 4, no. 3 (2 February 1996): 1.
6. A. Lovins and H. Lovins, *Climate: Making Sense and Making Money* (Snowmass, Colo.: Rocky Mountain Institute, 1997).
7. M. Brown and M. Levine, eds., *Scenarios of U.S. Carbon Reductions: Potential Impacts of Energy*

Technologies by 2010 and Beyond, Interlaboratory Working Group on Energy-Efficient and Low-Carbon Technologies Report no. LBNL-40533 (Washington, D.C.: Department of Energy, Office of Energy Efficiency and Renewable Energy, 1997).

8. A. Hoffman, *The Hazardous Waste Remediation Market: Innovative Technological Development and the Market Entry of the Construction Industry,* CCRE Working Paper no. 92-1 (Cambridge: Massachusetts Institute of Technology, Department of Civil and Environmental Engineering, 1992).

9. L. Greer and C. Van Loben Sels, "When Pollution Prevention Meets the Bottom Line: Cost Savings Are Not Always Enough to Convince Industry to Adopt Prevention Actions," *Environmental Science and Technology* (September 1997): 418A–422A.

10. R. Shelton and J. Shopley, "Hitting the Green Wall," *Perspectives* (Cambridge, Mass.: Arthur D. Little, 1995).

11. Ibid.

12. J. Kotter, "Why Transformation Efforts Fail," *Harvard Business Review,* March–April 1995, 59.

13. K. Lewin, "Group Decision and Social Charge," in *Readings in Social Psychology,* ed. T. M. Newcomb and E. L. Hartley (New York: Holt, Rinehart & Winston, 1947).

14. Kotter, "Why Transformation Efforts Fail."

15. J. Katzenbach et al., *Real Change Leaders* (New York: Random House, 1995).

16. Ibid., 8.

17. Hoffman, *From Heresy to Dogma.*

18. Kotter, "Why Transformation Efforts Fail."

19. S. Livesey, *McDonald's and the Environment,* Case Studies, no. 9-391-108 (Boston: Harvard Business School Press, 1990).

20. M. Melody, "Boatmaker Finds Solvent Substitute, Cuts Emission, Costs," *Hazmat World* (February 1992): 36–39.

21. Kotter, "Why Transformation Efforts Fail," 63.

22. R. Berenbeim, *Corporate Ethics Practices* (New York: Conference Board, 1992).

23. Ibid.

24. G. Northcraft and M. Neale, *Organizational Behavior: A Management Challenge,* 2nd ed. (Fort Worth: Dryden Press, 1994), 609.

25. J. Bunge, E. Cohen-Rosenthal, and A. Ruiz-Quintanilla, *Employee Participation in Pollution Prevention: Preliminary Analysis of the Toxics Release Inventory* (Ithaca, N.Y.: Cornell University, Center for Advanced Human Resource Studies, 1995).

26. Interview with the author, December 1992.

27. S. Kerr, "On the Folly of Rewarding A while Hoping for B," *Academy of Management Executive* 9, no. 1 (1995): 13.

28. A. Hoffman, "The Importance of Fit between Individual Values and Organizational Culture in the Greening of Industry," *Business Strategy and the Environment* 2, no. 4 (1993): 10–18.

29. M. Berube, *From Pollution Control to Zero Discharge: Overcoming the Obstacles* (Cambridge: Massachusetts Institute of Technology, Center for Technology, Policy, and Industrial Development, 1991).

30. Environmental Protection Agency, *EPA Green Lights Program Snapshot for January 1997* (Washington, D.C.: Environmental Protection Agency, 1997).

31. A. Lehmbeck, "New Energy Systems Will Net Savings for Eastpointe," *Eastsider* (East Detroit, Mich.), 26 December 1996.

32. Melody, "Boatmaker Finds Solvent Substitute."

33. C. Hunt and E. Auster, "Proactive Environmental Management: Avoiding the Toxic Trap," *Sloan Management Review* (winter 1990): 7–18.

34. Ibid., 18.

35. "ARCO Chief Warns of Shift from Oil to Other Energy," *Wall Street Journal*, 10 February 1999, B5.

36. Ibid.

37. D. Johansen, "Digging Upwards: Sucking Things out of the Ground Used to Be Simple and Brutal. Now, Top Companies Are Developing a Butterfly-Wing Touch," *Tomorrow* 8, no. 4 (1998): 10–11.

38. Hoffman, *From Heresy to Dogma*, 189.

39. M. Hamilton, "BP Amoco to Offer Cleaner Fuels in Cities Choked by Pollution," *Washington Post*, 25 January 1999, A9.

Chapter 9: The Organization Lies within a Broader Institutional Context

1. M. Bazerman and A. Hoffman, "Sources of Environmentally Destructive Behavior: Individual, Organizational, and Institutional Perspectives," *Research in Organizational Behavior* 21 (1999): 39–79; A. Hoffman and M. Ventresca, "The Institutional Framing of Policy Debates: Economics versus the Environment," *American Behavioral Scientist* 42, no. 8 (1999): 1369–1393.

2. G. Easterbrook, *A Moment on the Earth* (New York: Viking Press, 1995).

3. General Accounting Office, *Major Management Challenges and Program Risks: Environmental Protection Agency*, Report no. GAO/OCG-99-17 (Washington, D.C.: U.S. Government Printing Office, 1999), 9.

4. Environmental Protection Agency, *U.S. EPA Oral History Interview No. 1: William D. Ruckelshaus* (Washington, D.C.: U.S. Government Printing Office, 1993).

5. M. Landy, M. Roberts, and S. Thomas, *The Environmental Protection Agency: Asking the Wrong Questions* (New York: Oxford University Press, 1990).

6. S. Novick, "The Twenty Year Evolution of Pollution Law: A Look Back," *Environmental Forum* (January 1986): 12–18.

7. R. Schmitt, "The AMOCO/EPA Yorktown Experience and Regulating the Right Thing," *Natural Resources and Environment* (summer 1994): 11–13, 51.

8. A. Tenbrunsel et al., "The Dysfunctional Effects of Standards on Environmental Attitudes and Choices," in *Environment, Ethics, and Behavior: The Psychology of Environmental Valuation and Degradation*, ed. M. Bazerman et al. (San Francisco: New Lexington Press, 1997).

9. B. Raffle and D. Mitchell, *Effective Environmental Strategies: Opportunities for Innovation and Flexibility under Federal Environmental Law* (Chicago: Amoco Corporation, 1993).

10. R. Byers, "Regulatory Barriers to Pollution Prevention," *Journal of the Air and Waste Management Association* 41, no. 4 (1991): 418–422.

11. L. Ember, "Strategies for Reducing Pollution at the Source Are Gaining Ground," *Chemical and Engineering News* (8 July 1991): 12.

12. Tenbrunsel et al., "Dysfunctional Effects of Standards."

13. A. Hoffman, M. Bazerman, and S. Yaffee, "Balancing Business Interests and Endangered Species Protection," *Sloan Management Review* 39, no. 1 (1997): 59–73.

14. Associated Press, "Logging in National Forests Cost U.S. $88M Last Year, Congress Told," *Boston Globe*, 11 June 1998, A16.

15. P. Davis, "East Meets West in Latest Fight over Grazing Fee Increase," *Congressional Quarterly* (22 June 1991): 1656–1658.

16. R. Hahn and R. Stavins, "Incentive-Based Environmental Regulation: A New Era from an Old Idea," *Ecology Law Quarterly* 18, no. 1 (1991): 1–42.

17. R. Schmitt, "The AMOCO/EPA Yorktown Experience."

18. A. Hoffman, *From Heresy to Dogma: An Institutional History of Corporate Environmentalism* (San Francisco: New Lexington Press, 1997).

19. "The Forest Service's New Deal," editorial, *New York Times*, 16 February 1999, A18.

20. General Accounting Office, *Major Management Challenges*, 24.

21. J. Jubeir, "Educating Environmental Managers for Tomorrow," *EPA Journal* 21, no. 2 (1995): 31–33.

22. A. Hoffman, "Environmental Education in Business School," *Environment* 41, no. 1 (1999): 4–5.

23. M. Cropper and W. Oates, "Environmental Economics: A Survey," *Journal of Economic Literature* 30 (1992): 675–740.

24. C. Merchant, *The Death of Nature: Women, Ecology, and the Scientific Revolution* (New York: Harper & Row, Publishers, 1980); T. Gladwin, T. Freeman, and J. Kennelly, "Ending Our Denial and Destruction of Nature: Toward Biophysical Sustainable Management Theory," unpublished manuscript (New York: New York University, Stern School of Business, 1994).

25. F. Capra, *The Turning Point: Science, Society, and the Rising Culture* (New York: Bantam Books, 1982); H. Daly and J. Cobb, *For the Common Good* (Boston: Beacon Press, 1994); H. Daly, *Steady-State Economics*, 2d ed. (Washington, D.C.: Island Press, 1991); T. Gladwin, J. Kennelly, and T. Krause, "Shifting Paradigms for Sustainable Development: Implications for Management Theory and Research," *Academy of Management Review* 20, no. 4 (1995): 874–907.

26. Daly, *Steady-State Economics;* Daly and Cobb, *For the Common Good.*

27. Redefining Progress, *What's Wrong with GDP* (San Francisco: Redefining Progress, 1996).

28. Ibid.

29. M. Russell, E. Colglazier, and B. Tonn, "The U.S. Hazardous Waste Legacy," *Environment* (July–August 1992): 12–15, 34–39.

30. S. Schmidheiny, F. Zorraquin, and World Business Council for Sustainable Development, *Financing Change: The Financial Community, Eco-Efficiency, and Sustainable Development* (Cambridge, Mass.: MIT Press, 1996).

31. J. Perry, "Subsidies Gone Wrong," *Tomorrow* 7, no. 2 (1997): 36.

32. C. Nickerson, "Stripping the Sea's Life," *Boston Globe*, 17 April 1994, 1, 24, 25.

33. Ibid.

34. M. Sissenwine, "The Current Status of America's Fisheries," in *Summary Report: Can America Save Its Fisheries? A Sea Grant National Issues Forum*, ed. N. Blanton, K. Hart, and S. Wittman (College Park, Md.: National Oceanic and Atmospheric Administration, National Sea Grant College Program, 11 September 1995), 3–6.

35. "Pollock Overboard," *Economist*, 6 January 1996, 21.

36. International Center for Technology Assessment, *The Real Price of Gasoline, Report No. 3: An Analysis of the Hidden External Costs Consumers Pay to Fuel Their Automobiles* (Washington, D.C.: International Center for Technology Assessment, 1998).

37. "Estimate Puts True Cost of Gasoline at between $5.60 and $15.14 per Gallon," *Daily Environment Report*, 18 November 1998, A3.

38. A. Streeter, J. Garman, and H. Yanulis, "It Would Be Pain at the Pump," *Tomorrow* 9, no. 1 (1999): 43.

39. Global Environmental Management Initiative (GEMI), *Environment: Value to Business* (Washington, D.C.: GEMI, 1999).

40. R. Shelton and J. Shopley, "Hitting the Green Wall," *Perspectives* (Cambridge, Mass.: Arthur D. Little, 1995).

41. Redefining Progress, One Kearny Street, 4th Floor, San Francisco, CA 94108; (415) 781-1191.

42. G. Atkinson, "Greening the National Accounts," *Environment* 37, no. 5 (1995): 25–28.

43. J. Rowe and J. Silverstein, "The GDP Myth: Why 'Growth' Isn't Always a Good Thing," *Washington Monthly* (March 1999): 17–21.

44. J. Cushman, "Trade Group Strikes Blow at U.S. Environmental Law," *New York Times,* 7 April 1998, D1.

45. M. Ferrantino, *A Brief Description of International Institutional Linkages in Trade and the Environment,* Working Paper no. 94-11-A (Washington, D.C.: United States International Trade Commission, Office of Economics, 1994).

46. A. Lovins and H. Lovins, *Climate: Making Sense and Making Money* (Snowmass, Colo.: Rocky Mountain Institute, 1997).

47. D. Houghton et al., *The State of the Art: Space Cooling and Air Handling* (Snowmass, Colo.: Rocky Mountain Institute, 1992).

48. A. Lovins, "Stabilizing the Climate Is Not Costly, but Profitable," in *Global Climate Change: A Senior-Level Debate at the Intersection of Economics, Strategy, Technology, Science, Politics, and International Negotiation,* ed. A. Hoffman (San Francisco: New Lexington Press, 1998), 143–147.

49. Lovins and Lovins, *Climate.*

50. A. Hoffman, M. Bazerman, and S. Yaffee, "Balancing Business Interests and Endangered Species Protection," *Sloan Management Review* 39, no. 1 (1997): 59–73.

51. C. Nickerson, "Stripping the Sea's Life," *Boston Globe,* 17 April 1994, 1, 24, 25.

52. T. Egan, "Recriminations as Northwest Loggers Return," *New York Times,* 5 December 1995, 1, A13.

53. A. Rosenfeld et al., "Painting the Town White—and Green," *Technology Review* (February–March 1997): 52–59.

54. Ibid.

55. T. Tietenberg, *Environmental and Natural Resource Economics* (New York: HarperCollins Publishing Company, 1992), 191.

56. J. Holisha, "Recycled Material Is Finding a New and Lucrative Market," *New York Times,* 8 October 1994, A1.

57. J. Holisha, "Browning Ferris Profits Two Ways: Collecting and Recycling It," *New York Times,* 27 June 1995, D8.

58. S. Sullivan, "Germany Garbage Gap Alert: There's Not Enough Trash to Go Round," *Newsweek,* 28 October 1996, 17.

59. C. Solomon, "Clearing the Air: What Really Pollutes?" *Wall Street Journal,* 29 March 1993, 1.

Chapter 10: Environmental Strategy in an Institutional Context: Two Sectoral Studies

1. An area is classified as forestland by the American Forest and Paper Association if it is at least one acre in size and contains about 10 percent tree cover.

2. American Forest and Paper Association (AF&PA), *U.S. Forests, 1995: Facts and Figures* (Washington, D.C.: AF&PA, 1995).

3. C. Geist, "The Pulp and Paper Industry: Who Will Survive?" (speech delivered at the Fourth International Market Pulp Conference, Charleston, S.C., 9 June 1997).

4. J. Hughes, "King of the Hill," *Ski,* January 1998, 21–22.

5. R. Sedjo and D. Botkin, "Using Forest Plantations to Spare Natural Forests," *Environment* 39, no. 10 (1997): 15–20, 30.

6. T. Coile and F. Schumaker, *Soil-Site Relations, Stand Structure, and Yields of Slash and Loblolly Pine Plantations in the Southern United States* (Durham, N.C.: T. S. Coile, 1964). (A hectare equals approximately 2.47 acres.)

7. M. Bazett, *Industrial Wood, Study No. 3: Shell/World Wildlife Fund Tree Plantation Review* (Panda House, Weyside Park, Godalming, Surrey, England: World Wide Fund for Nature, 1993).

8. P. Berman and P. Speigel, "Viva St. Spotted Owl!" *Fortune,* 12 February 1996, 44–45.

9. Goodwin Heart Pine Company, Route 2, P.O. Box 119-AA, Micanopy, FL 32667; (800) 336-3118.

10. The Joinery Company, Department FH, P.O. Box 518, Tarboro, NC 27886; (800) 726-7463.

11. G. R. Plume Company, 1301 Meador Avenue, Suites B-11 and B-12, Bellingham, WA 98226; (360) 676-5658.

12. G. Faulkner, "Building with Grain," *In Business* (January–February 1997): 14.

13. J. Kay, "Home Depot Says No to Old-Growth Redwood," *San Francisco Examiner,* 8 May 1997, D1.

14. Forest Stewardship Council, (802) 244-6247. Internet: http://www.fscus.org.

15. SmartWood, (802) 434-5491. Internet: http://www.smartwood.org.

16. Scientific Certification Systems, (510) 832-1415. Internet: http://www.scs1.com.

17. S. Polson, "Cutting with Conscience," *E Magazine,* May–June 1996, 42–43.

18. D. Dulken, "Forest Certification: Separating Good Boards from Bad," *SEJournal* (summer 1998): 16.

19. N. Ulman, "Going Green: A Maine Forest Firm Prospers by Earning Eco-Friendly Label," *Wall Street Journal,* 26 November 1997, A1, A8.

20. Ibid.

21. The Certified Forest Products Council (CFPC) is an independent, not-for-profit, voluntary business initiative that was established in fall 1997 through the merger of the Forest Products Buyers Group and the Good Wood Alliance. The CFPC promotes the specification and purchase of certified forest products within the business community. Certified Forest Products Council, One Wall Street Tower, 20 Exchange Place, Floor 32, New York, NY 10005; (888) 981-5858. E-mail: http://www.certifiedwood.org.

22. S. Landis, "Supply and Demand for Certified Wood," *Understory* (fall–winter 1997): 1.

23. M. Hornblower, "Next Stop, Home Depot," *Time,* 19 October 1998, 70.

24. M. Holloway, "Will It Be 'Timber!' for Green Logs?" *Business Week,* 19 October 1998, 81, 83.

25. R. Schwolsky, "Stud Lite from the Spud State," *Builder* (December 1995): 108.

26. A. Revkin, "Taking Lowly Pallets and Finding Treasure," *New York Times,* 5 March 1997, A13.

27. Trus Joist MacMillan, 200 East Mallard Drive, Boise, ID 83706; (800) 338-0515.

28. Trex Company: (200) BUY-TREX.

29. B. English, J. Youngquist, and R. Rowell, *Alternative Uses for Waste Paper in Wood-Based Composite Products* (Madison, Wis.: Forest Products Research Laboratory, 1995).

30. D. Vesey, *Application Opportunities of Filled and Reinforced Plastics in the Automotive Industry* (Detroit: Chrysler Corporation, 1995).

31. P. Davis, "Cry for Preservation, Recreation Changing Public Land Policy," *Congressional Quarterly* (3 August 1991): 2145–2151.

32. Department of Commerce, *National Survey of Fishing, Hunting, and Wildlife-Associated Recreation* (Washington, D.C.: U.S. Government Printing Office, 1991).

33. R. Boyle, "President Clinton Signs Order for Fishing Area Restoration," *Outdoor Life* 196, no. 4 (1995): 10.

34. Department of Commerce, *National Survey.*

35. S. Pendleton, "Birds Get a Break in Texas with Land Conversion Law," *Christian Science Monitor,* 15 November 1995, 8.
36. Department of Commerce, *National Survey.*
37. Pendleton, "Birds Get a Break."
38. Department of Commerce, *National Survey.*
39. J. Hood, "How Green Was My Balance Sheet," *Policy Review,* no. 74 (fall 1995): 80.
40. H. Moore, "The Unique Role of the U.S. Forest Products Industry in Mitigating Climate Change," in *Global Climate Change: A Senior Level Debate at the Intersection of Economics, Strategy, Technology, Science, Politics, and International Negotiation,* ed. A. Hoffman (San Francisco: New Lexington Press, 1998), 102–108.
41. Internet: http://www.thenewsteel.org.
42. N. Ulman, "Timber Industry Turns to Former Opponents to Clean Up Its Act," *Wall Street Journal,* 12 March 1997, A1, A6.
43. Ibid.
44. Ibid.
45. I would like to thank Virginia Breclaw, Sonali Desai, Liza Ngamtrakulpanit, Katherine Schmits, Douglas Stilwell, and Sally Torbik for their assistance in collecting material used in this section.
46. Diane Cotman, executive director, Center for Sustainable Building and Technology, 221 Concord Avenue, Cambridge, MA 02138; (617) 868-7788.
47. William Browning, director, Green Development Services Group, Rocky Mountain Institute, 1739 Snowmass Creek Road, Snowmass, CO 81654-9199; (970) 339-0473.
48. Three manufacturers of tubular skylights are:
    • Huvco LLC, 3426 Distillery Road, Ijamsville, MD 21745; 800-832-6116 (http:www.huvco.com)
    • Sunstar, 21602 North 2nd Ave., Suite 4, Phoenix, AZ 85027; 800-SUN-SOON (http:www.sunstarskylights.com)
    • The Sun Pipe Co., Inc., P.O. Box 2223, Northbrook, IL 60065; 800-844-4786 (http:www.sunpipe.com).
49. Pearson, D. *The Natural Home Catalog: Everything You Need to Create an Environmentally Friendly Home* (New York: Fireside Books, 1996), 32.
50. James Hardie Building Products Inc., 10901 Elm Ave., Fontana, CA 92335; (909) 356-6300. Internet: http://www.jameshardie.com/buildingproducts.htm.
51. Classic Products, 8510 Industry Park Drive, P.O. Box 701, Piqua, OH 45356; (513) 773-9840. Internet: http://www.oldhousejournal.com/rdir/04160.asp.
52. B. Burdge, "Methane, Compost, and Anaerobic Digestion," *Countryside and Small Stock Journal* 70, no. 1 (January 1995): 39.
53. "Dishwashers," *Consumer Reports* 60, no. 8 (August 1995): 533; "Dishwashers Update," *Consumer Reports* 60, no. 10 (October 1995): 669; "Washing Machines," *Consumer Reports* 60, no. 2 (February 1995): 96.
54. J. Rose et al., "Microbial Quality and Persistence of Enteric Pathogens in Graywater from Various Sources," *Water Research* 25, no. 1 (1991): 37–42.
55. N. Holt, "How 'Green' Is Your Household?" *Wall Street Journal,* 22 May 1998, W8.
56. S. C. Johnson/Roper, *The Environment: Public Attitudes and Individual Behavior, North America: Canada, Mexico, United States.* Commissioned by S. C. Johnson & Son, Inc. (Racine, Wis.: S. C. Johnson & Son, 1993).
57. Center for Sustainable Building and Technology, 136 Appleton Street, Cambridge, MA 02138.

58. For more information, contact America Recycles Day Contest, c/o Remanufacturing Industries Council International, P.O. Box 10807, Chantilly, VA 20153-0807.

59. Home Builders Association of Kitsap County, 5251 Auto Center Way, Bremerton, WA 98312; (800) 200-5778.

60. M. Walker, "Program Wants Home Builders at One with the Earth," *Bremerton Sun*, 6 February 1997, D1, D2.

61. P. Brown, "Honk If You Like Ecological Housing," *New York Times*, 16 April 1998, F1.

62. P. Elmer-DeWitt, "Gee, Your Car Smells Terrific," *Time*, 22 July 1991, 48.

Chapter 11: Environmental Strategy and Sustainable Development

1. A. Downs, "Up and Down with Ecology: The 'Issue-Attention' Cycle," *Public Interest* 28 (1972): 38–50.

2. Ibid.

3. A. Spencer-Cooke, "Bigger, Broader, Better," *Tomorrow* 8, no. 6 (1998): 10–11.

4. "A Senior Level Dialogue on Climate Change: Science, Policy, and Strategy" (conference held at J. L. Kellogg Graduate School of Management, Northwestern University, Evanston, Ill., 2 November 1998). Internet: http://www.kellogg.nwu.edu/confer/climate/index.html (section 3, lines 82–86).

5. C. Arnst et al., "When Green Begets Green," *Business Week*, 10 November 1997, 98–106.

6. Ibid., 99.

7. Intergovernmental Panel on Climate Change, *Climate Change: The IPCC Scientific Assessment* (Cambridge, England: Cambridge University Press, 1990); D. Abrahamson, "Climate Change and Energy Supply: A Comparison of Solar and Nuclear Options," in *Energy and Environment*, ed. J. Byrne and D. Rich (New Brunswick, N.J.: Transaction Publishers, 1992), 115–140; R. Peters and T. Lovejoy, eds., *Global Warming and Biological Diversity* (New Haven, Conn.: Yale University Press, 1992).

8. Intergovernmental Panel on Climate Change, *Climate Change, 1995: IPCC Second Assessment Synthesis of Scientific-Technical Information Relevant to Interpreting Article 2 of the UN Framework Convention on Climate Change*, (Cambridge, England: Cambridge University Press, 1996).

9. "Chafee Pushes Early Action Credits: Industry Representatives Show Support," *Daily Environment Report*, 3 December 1998, AA-1.

10. F. Palmer, "Fossil Fuels or the Rio Treaty: Competing Visions for the Future" (speech given at COALTRANS 96, Madrid, Spain, 21 October 1996).

11. Mobil Corporation, "Stop, Look, and Listen before We Leap," *New York Times*, 6 March 1997, A19.

12. T. Moore, "Global Warming: Uncertain Science; Certain Disaster," *World Climate Report* 2, no. 18 (1997): 2.

13. J. Fialka, "Global-Warming Debate Gets No Consensus in Industry," *Wall Street Journal*, 16 April 1998, A24.

14. R. Gelbspan, *The Heat Is On: The High Stakes Battle over Earth's Threatened Climate* (Reading, Mass.: Addison-Wesley Publishing Company, 1997), jacket copy.

15. Ibid., 8.

16. "Bad Auto-Emission Controls Being Forced on Motorists," *Oil and Gas Journal* (11 September 1972): 45.

17. J. Bailey, "Utilities Overcomply with Clean Air Act, Are Stockpiling Pollution Allowances," *Wall Street Journal*, 15 November 1995, A6.

18. B. Herbert, "Bad Air Day," *New York Times,* 10 February 1997, A18.

19. Redefining Progress, *Economists' Statement on Climate Change* (San Francisco: Redefining Progress, 1997).

20. J. Browne, "Climate Change: The New Agenda," in *Global Climate Change: A Senior Level Dialogue at the Intersection of Economics, Strategy, Technology, Science, Politics, and International Negotiation,* ed. A. Hoffman (San Francisco: New Lexington Press, 1998), 53–62.

21. D. Johansen, "Digging Upwards: Sucking Things out of the Ground Used to Be Simple and Brutal. Now, Top Companies Are Developing a Butterfly-Wing Touch," *Tomorrow* 8, no. 4 (1998): 10–11.

22. Arnst et al., "When Green Begets Green."

23. Ibid.

24. J. Elkington, *Cannibals with Forks: The Triple Bottom Line of Twenty-First Century Business* (Oxford, England: Capstone Publishing, 1998).

25. S. Hart, "Beyond Greening: Strategies for a Sustainable World," *Harvard Business Review,* January–February 1997, 67.

26. Spencer-Cooke, "Bigger, Broader, Better," 10.

27. G. Soros, *The Crisis of Global Capitalism: Open Society Endangered* (New York: Public Affairs Information Service, 1998).

28. D. Rodrik, *Has Globalization Gone Too Far?* (Washington, D.C.: Institute for International Economics, 1997).

29. Soros, *The Crisis of Global Capitalism.*

30. E. Woolard, "An Industry Approach to Sustainable Development," *Issues in Science and Technology* (spring 1992): 29.

31. S. Schmidheiny and World Business Council for Sustainable Development, *Changing Course: A Global Business Perspective on Development and the Environment* (Cambridge, Mass.: MIT Press, 1992), 87.

32. William C. Ford Jr., "Ford in the 21st Century," *1998 Annual Report* (Dearborn, Mich.: Ford Motor Co., 1998), 2.

33. R. Knight, *Profits and Principles: Does There Have to Be a Choice?* (London: Shell International Ltd., 1998), 2.

34. J. Elkington and F. Van Dijk, "And Now, Social Reporting," *Tomorrow* 9, no. 1 (1999): 56–59.

35. "Gaining Momentum," *Tomorrow* 8, no. 6 (1998): 41.

36. "The Business Way Forward," *Tomorrow* 8, no. 6 (1998): 42.

37. A. Goodman and A. Streeter, "Companies of the Year," *Tomorrow* 9, no. 1 (1999): 14–16.

38. P. D. Jennings and P. Zandbergen, "Ecologically Sustainable Organizations: An Institutional Approach," *Academy of Management Review* 20, no. 4 (1995): 1015–1052; S. Hart, "A Natural Resource Based View of the Firm," *Academy of Management Review* 20, no. 4 (1995): 986–1014.

39. M. Jacobs, *The Green Economy: Environment, Sustainable Development, and the Politics of the Future* (Vancouver, B.C.: University of British Columbia Press, 1993), 59.

40. M. Colby, *The Evolution of Paradigms of Environmental Management in Development,* SPR Planning Paper no. 1 (Washington, D.C.: World Bank, Strategic Planning and Review Department, Strategic Planning Division, 1989).

41. T. Gladwin, J. Kennelly, and T. Krause, "Shifting Paradigms for Sustainable Development: Implications for Management Theory and Research," *Academy of Management Review* 20, no. 4 (1995): 874–907; H. Daly and J. Cobb, *For the Common Good* (Boston: Beacon Press, 1994); H. Daly, *Steady-State Economics,* 2d ed. (Washington, D.C.: Island Press, 1991).

42. A. Farrell and M. Hart, "What Does Sustainability Really Mean? The Search for Useful Indicators," *Environment* 40, no. 9 (November 1998): 4–9, 26–31.

43. A. Streeter, J. Garman, and H. Yanulis, "Making Dough Do Good," *Tomorrow* 8, no. 6 (1998): 35.
44. "Pragmatism Is the Driving Force," *Tomorrow* 8, no. 6 (1998): 43.
45. G. Hedstrom, S. Poltorzycki, and P. Stroh, "Sustainable Development: The Next Generation of Business Opportunity," *Prism* (fourth quarter 1998): 5–19.
46. P. Kennedy, *Preparing for the Twenty-First Century* (New York: Random House, 1993), 47.

Appendix A: U.S. Environmental Laws

1. Environmental Protection Agency, *Guide to Environmental Issues* (Washington, D.C.: U.S. Government Printing Office, 1995), 72–77.

Appendix B: Environmental Information Resources

1. *The Environmentalist's Guide to the Public Library,* updated ed. (New York, NY: Libraries for the Future, 1997), 24–26. © Libraries for the Future. All rights reserved. Used with permission. A good source for keeping up with new government sites is *The Internet Connection: Your Guide to Government Resources* (Bernan Press, query@bernan.com).

About the Author

ANDREW J. HOFFMAN is assistant professor of organizational behavior at the Boston University School of Management. He is the author of more than thirty research articles and has published two books about corporate environmental issues: *From Heresy to Dogma* (1997) and *Global Climate Change* (1998). He is a member of the editorial board of Organizations and Environment, a member of the advisory board of the Kellogg Environmental Research Center, and a member of the Academy of Management and the Society of Environmental Journalists. He was awarded the Klegerman Award for Environmental Excellence at the Massachusetts Institute of Technology in 1995 and the Environmental Council Post Doctoral Fellowship at Northwestern University from 1995 to 1997, during which period he served on the organizational behavior faculty at Northwestern's J. L. Kellogg Graduate School of Management. Before entering academics, he worked for the Environmental Protection Agency; Metcalf & Eddy, Inc.; the Amoco Oil Corporation; and T & T Construction and Design Inc. He earned his doctorate (1995) and his master's degree (1991) from the Massachusetts Institute of Technology and his bachelor's degree (1983) from the University of Massachusetts at Amherst.

Index

Abitibi-Price Corporation, 220
Academia as social driver, 118–19, 188–89
Accounting policies, corporate, 166–67
Advertising Standards Authority, 105
Agriboard Industries, 207
Air-conditioning, 194–95, 215
Air pollution, 145–46
Alliance for Environmental Innovation, 79,
  110
Altering strategic objectives, 131–59
  biotechnology, 151–55
  competitive strategy, 131–36
    capital investment, 134–35
    market growth, 135–36
    operational efficiency, 133–34
    regulatory compliance, 132–33
    risk management, 134
    strategic direction, 136
  conclusion, 157–58
  shifting from a product to a service focus,
    155–56
  technological strategy, *see* Technological
    dimensions of corporate
    environmentalism
American Automobile Manufacturers
  Association (AAMA), 100
American Council for an Energy-Efficient
  Economy, 221
American Forest and Paper Association
  (AF&PA), 99, 207
American Green Dream House, 223
American Petroleum Institute (API), 101, 234

American Plastics Council, 97
American Textile Manufacturers Institute
  (ATMI), 98–99
Amoco Corporation, 48, 85, 94, 170, 182,
  197, 225–26, 235–36
Anderson, Ray, 124, 156
Anderson Corporation, 209
Appalachian Mountain Club, 213
Appliances:
  energy use reduction and, 217
  water conservation and, 221–22
Arctic National Wildlife Refuge (ANWR),
  125
Arthur D. Little, Inc., 166
ASKO, 221
Aspen Institute, 79, 81–82
Asphalt paving industry, 195
Assessment technologies, 148
Atlantic Richfield Company (ARCO), 226
Audi, 96
Auster, Ellen, 176, 181
Automated Credit Exchange (ACE), 47
Automobile industry:
  air pollution from, 91–92, 145–46, 226
  competition in, 19–20
  composite components for, 210
  fuel economy in, 93, 143–45
  gasoline and, 91–92
  institutional change and, 197–98
  product recalls in, 21
  recycling in, 49, 140–42
Avoidance technologies, 147–48